WINNERS
and
LOSERS

WINNERS
and
LOSERS

Battles, Retreats, Gains,
Losses, and Ruins
from the Vietnam War

GLORIA EMERSON

W. W. NORTON & COMPANY
New York • London

First published as a Norton paperback 1992, reissued 2014

For information about permission to reproduce selections from this book,
write to Permissions, W. W. Norton & Company, Inc.,
500 Fifth Avenue, New York, NY 10110

For information about special discounts for bulk purchases, please contact
W. W. Norton Special Sales at specialsales@wwnorton.com or 800-233-4830

Manufacturing by Courier Westford
Book design by Brooke Koven
Production manager: Louise Parsamo

Library of Congress Cataloging-in-Publication Data

Emerson, Gloria.
Winners and losers : battles, retreats, gains, losses, and ruins
from the Vietnam War / Gloria Emerson.
pages cm
Originally published: New York : Random House, 1976.
Includes bibliographical references and index.
ISBN 978-0-393-34933-7 (pbk.)
1. Vietnam War, 1961–1975—United States. 2. Vietnam War,
1961–1975—Influence. 3. United States—History—1945– I. Title.
DS558.2.E46 2014
959.704'3—dc23

2014011583

W. W. Norton & Company, Inc.
500 Fifth Avenue, New York, N.Y. 10110
www.wwnorton.com

W. W. Norton & Company Ltd.
Castle House, 75/76 Wells Street, London W1T 3QT

1 2 3 4 5 6 7 8 9 0

For Craig R. Whitney

CONTENTS

PREFACE

GLORIA

She was six feet tall and lean. She had once worked as a model, and someone in Vietnam had given her the name "Long Lady." When I first met her on a street in Saigon in the fall of 1971, I noticed that only she showed no sign of the crushing heat: her safari jacket was crisp, and her dark hair shining. But then apparently she always looked perfectly turned out, even after spending a night on some awful fire base. Like many tall women of her generation, she was slightly awkward. Bending down to listen to the smaller Vietnamese, she reminded me of a Great Blue Heron looking into a pond. Otherwise she had no patience. In a café with colleagues she would light a cigarette, announce some new drama, wave her long arms, and fidget if you bored her. Many were terrified of her. You never knew whether she would tell you a funny story or denounce you for some outrage, such as failing to collect sweaters for the legless Vietnamese the Quakers cared for in Quang Ngai province. By then she had been, as they said, "in country" for almost two years as a correspondent for the *New York Times*, and in Saigon she was a famous figure.

The previous year she had written a story that infuriated—and shamed—the Army brass, perhaps more than any other. She had found two enlisted men in the 1st Air Cavalry Division who had been ordered to write a citation for a Silver Star to be awarded to a brigadier general before he moved on to a new post, but given no information about any brave or gallant action on the part of the general, they had made it all up—and as it turned out, they and others had done this many times before. Once she had actually stopped a military operation. Discovering that a unit of South Vietnamese troops with American advisors were forcing villagers at gunpoint to clear land mines by hand and causing many civilian casualties, she went to the base near the Cambodian border. Finding the American head of the advisory team, a captain, taking a nap, she had kicked his bunk as hard as she could and said, "Tell me everything you know right now, and I'll go easy on you." According to a witness, the captain replied apologetically like a school kid to his teacher. Her story brought the practice of using civilians to a halt.[1]

Gloria was skilled at drawing people out. She'd know the name of your four-year-old nephew, and if you weren't careful, she'd find out the problems you had with your exes. But no one in the press corps knew much about Gloria's past. Few even knew how old she was. Occasionally in passing she would mention an ex-husband or her lack of a college education, but when asked directly about her past, she would always deflect the question with a joke or a change of subject. She does the same here. *Winners and Losers* is a very personal book, but she hardly ever speaks of herself. Indeed, you have to search to find the word "I."

Buried deep in the book is the fact that Gloria first went to Vietnam in 1956. She describes the Saigon of the period as "a soft, plump, clean place of greens and yellows." Twenty pages later we learn that she went "by chance," wanting to "imitate a grandmother who went from Titusville, Pennsylvania, to China" and

---

1. Ronald Moreau, "A Letter from Ronald Moreau in Islamabad," *Newsweek*, Tuesday, 28 September, 2004, http://gloriaemerson.com/memories_gloria.html (accessed 14 January, 2014).

because of a "charming young man" she had met in New York. She tells us nothing else about her family or her early life. Fortunately, Joyce Hoffman in *On Their Own*, a book about women journalists in Vietnam, did the research. According to Hoffman, one of Gloria's ancestors was Ralph Waldo Emerson, and her great-grandfather was Byron D. Benson, one of the country's first oil magnates. (The grandmother who went to China was a leader in the women's suffrage movement.) Her father, William B. Emerson, the heir to a considerable fortune, married an Irish chorus girl, and Gloria, born in 1929, was their only child. Brought up on the Upper East Side in Manhattan, Gloria could look forward to expensive schools and glamorous parties, but at some point in her youth, her father lost most of his money and both parents descended into alcoholism. She went to public schools and never to college, presumably because her parents couldn't afford it. Her life became a struggle. Her mother died of liver disease in 1951, and desperately in need of a job, Gloria went to work at *Promenade*, a give-away magazine distributed in New York hotels. Three years later she married and joined the staff of the flagship Hearst paper in New York. Her husband, about whom we know little, committed suicide sometime later. At the *Journal-American*—a paper that specialized in celebrities, lurid crimes, and right-wing editorials— she was relegated to the women's page, where she wrote about shoes, handbags, and dresses under a series of pseudonyms.

The "charming young man" Gloria met in 1956 was John (Demi) Gates Jr., whom she describes as "an original and romantic man of a certain impeccable eastern background, which meant St. Paul's School, Harvard, debutante parties and the New York Social Register"—in other words, the kind of man she had been brought up to marry. A lieutenant in the U.S. Marine Corps, working for the CIA, he went to Saigon, and not long afterward Gloria followed with a one-way ticket and just a few dollars in her pocket. She went hoping to learn how to be a journalist and to write for magazines, but the American public had small interest in Vietnam at the time. Through Gates she found a job with Operation Brotherhood, a public health project manned by Filipinos and financed by the CIA. Her romance with Gates was tumultuous, but she traveled with the OB medical teams and fell in love with Vietnam. In *Winners and Losers* she describes the period mainly by quoting Gerald Hickey, an anthropologist and a great storyteller who educated journalists about Vietnam for two decades.

Back in the United States, Gloria landed a job with the *New York Times*, joining the staff of a section known as Food, Fashions, Family, and Furnishings. Nan Robertson, Charlotte Curtis, and others on the staff were fine journalists and talented writers, but in the 1950s the women's page was ghetto-walled off from the rest of the paper. Thrilled to be at the *Times*, Gloria worked ferociously hard and developed imaginative ways of describing fashion trends. Before long, however, she, like many of the others, wanted to join the wider world of journalism. In the early sixties she left the paper and went to Brussels with a new husband. The second marriage broke up within a few months, and she returned to the *Times*, once again to cover fashion but this time in Paris.

The bureaus in London and Paris were the most coveted posts on the paper, but in 1966 Gloria began urging the editors to send her to Vietnam. A few other newspapers—such as the *New York Herald Tribune*—had women correspondents in Vietnam, but the *Times* would not send a woman to cover the war—and perhaps particularly one versed in the ups and downs of hemlines in the Dior collections. In 1968 she covered the student rebellion in Paris, and in response to her pleas for release from the fashion beat, her editors sent her to Central Africa, where she reported on the famine in Biafra, and to Northern Ireland, where she wrote of the street fighting in Belfast. For four years she watched the flow of young male reporters coming through Paris or London on their way to Vietnam. It made her furious, for she had done all the reading and had made acquaintance with many Vietnamese in Paris. Her appeals became increasingly urgent, and in 1970 her editors finally relented and sent their first woman to Vietnam.

The Saigon that Gloria returned to was hardly recognizable to her: the trees had been cut down for the military traffic; the central boulevard, Nguyen Hue, was lined with squalid bars; and the street in front of the *Times* bureau was swarming with ragged street boys, many of them deformed. After five years of war, the American troops were slowly pulling out, but casualties remained high. The most experienced officers and NCOs had already done their tours of duty; the ranks were filled with draftees, and discipline was lax. On the rear bases soldiers openly smoked dope; some wore peace symbols on their helmets; and a few rebelled against their officers. In his memoir Colin Powell writes that it took ten years after the war to rebuild the Army into a fighting force. According to high officials, the country was "pacified," but what this meant was that millions of Vietnamese had been forced to leave their villages and move into refugee camps. President Nixon had announced that the war would be won by "Vietnamization"—or building up the ARVN (Army of the Republic of Vietnam) to take the place of the American troops. But, as Gloria writes, the ARVN was a "lost army." The soldiers had been told of the evils of Communism, but few knew what they were fighting for. The Saigon government was seen as a puppet of the Americans, and by 1970 the corruption, always endemic, had become overwhelming: soldiers didn't get their pay, and everyone saw the huge villas built by officers in Saigon. As one foreign service officer later told me, the density of the corruption was just about all that held the officer corps and the government together. Relations between the American brass and the press sank to a new low. The military briefers in Saigon continued to give "progress reports" on the numbers of enemy dead and "structures" destroyed. Their smug detachment from the reality of the war infuriated Gloria. After one briefing that particularly enraged her, she decided to make them as uncomfortable as possible. With the help of a young reporter she snuck into the briefing room at night and wrote, in three-foot-high letters, "Father, forgive them, for they know not what they do."[2]

Gloria sympathized with the "grunts" of both armies. In her *Times* stories she wrote movingly about the American GIs and the Vietnamese enlisted men caught up in a war that was not of their choosing. Often, too, she wrote about the Vietnamese villagers suffering from what she saw as the heedless and cruel means the American military used to prosecute the war. She wanted to save every one of them, and she gave generously, bringing wheelchairs from Hong Kong and collecting clothing from friends in the United States. Occasionally, to the dismay of her colleagues, she invited the street urchins to come in and take a shower in the bureau. Gloria, though, was no sentimentalist, and her colleagues admired her fearlessness and her ability to find stories that others missed. She bought $3 vials of heroin from a dozen places on the highway outside of Saigon to show how easy it was to procure drugs. She wrote the first press account of the underground prison cells, known as "the tiger cages," on Con Son Island. And during the disastrous ARVN incursion into Laos, she interviewed doctors and wounded soldiers under fire.

Gloria was a great interviewer. She could talk to GIs like a mother and to officers like their commander—or she could act the crazy lady who could embarrass you terribly if you didn't tell her what she wanted to know. (Her interview with Dr. Wesley Fishel in this book is a great example of interview-as-torture.) She understood that many people don't speak logically, but that non

---

2. Tom Fox, comments at Gloria Emerson's memorial service, http://gloriaem erson.com/memorial_gloria.html (accessed 14 January 2014).

sequiturs and self-contradictions are often a kind of poetry that reveals an emotion or a truth that people won't admit to directly. Her beloved translator, Nguyen Ngoc Luong, was an equally sensitive interviewer, and unlike any other interpreter I remember, he translated not just the sense of what people said but also the rich imagery of colloquial Vietnamese. I sometimes wonder whether Luong's translations didn't inspire some of Gloria's own locutions. In this book she describes a wealthy community near Houston, Texas, where "big low houses" on a lake "sit apart from each other in a rich, solemn stillness." She likens American journalists in Vietnam to "a great flock of gulls skimming over the corpses and the offal of the war, plunging into it and coming back up again."

When Gloria returned to the United States after two years in Vietnam, she couldn't get over how ignorant many Americans remained about a war that had taken the lives of more than 50,000 of the nation's young men. The indifference appalled her, and she found herself incapable of moving on to another subject in the way that most of her colleagues did. Luong wrote to her, "You are the only one who cannot overcome your Vietnam experience. There is an acute lack of forgetfulness in you of Vietnam." *Winners and Losers* is the result of that "acute lack"—and of her freedom from the straitjacket of the *Times* style in the 1970s.

Frances FitzGerald
New York, New York
January 2014

VIETNAM WAR CASUALTIES

U.S. military deaths: 57,690
South Vietnamese military deaths   223,748
Civilians killed in the war: 300,000 *(estimate)*
Total battle deaths in North Vietnam 666,000 *(not confirmed)*

FOREWORD

It is ten years now since the Vietnamese soldiers who fought our own Army walked into Saigon, uncertain of the city's streets, meeting no opposition at all, and who, on that last day of April, nearly stopped the American heart.

In our country Vietnam is not the name of a small nation with its own rivers and mountains, its little vegetable gardens with lettuce and peppers, its splendid beaches and rice fields, its children learning arithmetic, and the old men who love the roses they grow. There were orchards once, cattle once, birds once, and flowers whose names I did not know.

Now Vietnam is our word, meaning an American failure, a shorthand for a disaster, a tragedy of good intentions, a well-meaning misuse of American power, a noble cause ruined by a loss of will and no home front, a war of crime, a loathsome jungle where our army of children fought an army of fanatics.

It is a war whose origins and purpose were never understood although many Americans were old enough to remember the events that turned our attention to Vietnam and justified, in the minds of many men, the madness that was to follow. There was, as there is now, the fear that the Communists were seeking to control the world, and proof was at hand: the Greek civil war, 1947–1949, with the U.S. helping defeat the Communist guerrillas; the *loss* of *our* China when Mao Tse Tung prevailed in 1949;

the Korean war, beginning in 1950, which led President Harry S. Truman to order U.S. forces into battle without a declaration of war by Congress and against the advice of the Joint Chiefs of Staff. And, always, the domination of Eastern Europe by the Soviet Union in the postwar years, which became our septic wound that never healed and defied recovery. But none of these events are the reason for our war in Vietnam, only a possible explanation for the mentality in Washington that, early on, made the disaster so alluring. In a study by the Congressional Research Service, Library of Congress, for the Committee on Foreign Relations of the U.S. Senate, the report states: "The U.S. decision to become involved in the war in Indochina was made on April 24, 1950, when on the recommendation of the National Security Council, the President approved NSC 64, 'The Position of the U.S. with Respect to Indochina.' There is no indication that Truman or any of his associates consulted with any Member of Congress in making this first and fundamental commitment." The NSC 64 memorandum said: "It is important to United States security interests that all practicable measures be taken to avoid further communist expansion in Southeast Asia." NSC 64, the study says, was based on the domino theory, "which has been frequently and erroneously attributed to the Eisenhower administration." And NSC 64 said: "The neighboring countries of Thailand and Burma could be expected to fall under Communist domination if Indochina were controlled by a Communist-dominated government. The balance of Southeast Asia would then be in grave hazard."

France began war in Vietnam on November 26, 1944, to keep hold of its colony, while the forces led by Ho Chi Minh wanted total independence. On May 6, 1950, the Library of Congress study reveals, the new U.S. chargé in Saigon cabled Washington that Indochina was comparable to Greece; it, too, was a "neuralgic focus" for the Communists and if it fell "most of colored races of the world would in time fall to Communists' sickle. . . ." At

home the accusations of Senator Joseph McCarthy that Communist agents infested our government and military and that the
Truman administration was soft on Communism created panic,
a profound distress and shame, too, that such a man could create
so much disorder while possessing so little proof of what he was
charging.

These were the great magnets pulling us to Vietnam.

Many Americans still say, "Well, we shouldn't have gone in but
once we were there we should have tried to win it." It is as if these
civilians cannot grasp how ferociously we tried to have our own
way, how the U.S. military bombed and burned and defoliated
the south and had howitzers, year in and year out, fire at mountains where no human moved as if the mountains must be hum-
bled too. Some men, who were combatants, say their hands were
tied because they could not open up in certain areas in the south,
forgetting or never comprehending that it was our intention to
"win the hearts and minds" of the Vietnamese people and that it
would not do to kill all of them. The phrase was inspired by the
French in their own desperate and doomed struggle; we paid no
attention to what they could have taught us.

The times are unsettling, that small country still haunts and
jolts us, but our President cannot grasp the bare outlines of its
history. *President Reagan sidestepped a question today that sought
reassurance that the United States would not secretly become more
deeply involved in El Salvador's civil war, but in rejecting a reporter's
suggested analogy to Vietnam, Mr. Reagan seemed confused about
Vietnamese history.* In a story from Washington, D.C., about a
Presidential press conference in February 1982, Charles Mohr of
The New York Times, one of the best reporters to have covered
the war, listed and corrected the mistakes made by the nation's
Commander-in-Chief. Among them was Mr. Reagan's impression that North and South Vietnam, before colonization, were
two separate countries. They were not. The Geneva Accords in

1954, the year that French rule ended after the defeat at Dien-bienphu, provided for a temporary partition at the 17th parallel and called for national elections in 1956. President Reagan said at his press conference that Ho Chi Minh refused to participate, but it was not the Communist leader but rather the government of Ngo Dinh Diem in the south and his American sponsors who refused. The United States had not signed the accords but agreed not to undermine what was set forth. It was not President John F. Kennedy who sent in U.S. combat troops to South Vietnam, as Mr. Reagan said, but President Lyndon Johnson in March 1965.

This is how it is going.

Winners and Losers is not a history of the war or an analysis of its origins or U.S. policies. It is only the account of a woman who first went to Vietnam two years after the French lost all of it and the American "advisors" and CIA men were moving in. Fifteen years later she was sent back to Vietnam as a correspondent for *The New York Times* when the war was at its oldest. This is only a book by an American who witnessed the war for two years and came home with memories to harm the strongest heart, needing to love her country again and to listen to its people as she had never listened before.

In the last decade many veterans of Vietnam have spoken, some have even written their own books, giving a new, most dreadful, meaning to the old military term At Great Cost. After seeing the Vietnam memorial in Washington, D.C., which gives every name of the 58,022 Americans who died because of the undeclared war, one man told me space should have been left for the men who have begun to die from their exposure to Agent Orange. This is the herbicide containing the most deadly toxin, called dioxin. Our troops did not know they were being sentenced when they were sent on any of different missions to spray it: Crop Mission (used for fixed wing and helicopter), Defoliation (fixed wing only), Enemy Ground Supply Rt. (helicopter only), Friendly Line of Communication (helicopter only), Perimeter of Military Installation (helicopter only), Enemy Cache Site (helicopter only) and Waterway/Landing Zone (helicopter only). Areas were sprayed to deny crops or cover to the enemy or to kill growths and weeds around our own installations. So U.S. troops absorbed Agent Orange through the skin or in water they drank or when it reached their food. Now the Vietnamese and the Americans have this grief to share: children born in both countries with major birth defects.

In Binh Dinh, a province never pacified, 38,700 gallons were sprayed in 1966, 157,104 gallons in 1967 and 141,153 in 1969, according to the figures compiled by a man whose own health has been impaired by Agent Orange. He is George Ewalt, Jr., one of the plaintiffs in the veterans' lawsuit against the seven chemical companies that manufactured dioxin and settled, out of court, for the sum of $180 million to be divided among the veterans and their families.

An obsessive archivist of the records of Agent Orange sprayings and an infantryman who was on the M-60, Ewalt thinks the men sent to fight in Vietnam were the poor boys unable to seek draft deferments, who could not imagine what was waiting for them.

"Beautify America," Mr. Ewalt often says, "Clean up the street corners by drafting the kids who hang out there." In his Philadelphia neighborhood almost all were sucked into it.

It was this war that showed we are not a people made of a better clay, more decent and humane than those in countries many Americans think of as inferior to our own, not a people set apart. There were atrocities, photographs and films gave proof. And some veterans, possessed of a startling courage, gathered in Detroit in 1971 to testify how the United States was waging war in Indochina, and of what they had done. Their testimony was published in a book called *The Winter Soldier Investigation: An Inquiry into American War Crimes*, by the Beacon Press in Boston. It is something of a convenience now, when the war is being considered in a more forgiving light, that this small book is almost impossible to find.

Some men have a need to speak to stay sane but more keep their silence. What they might tell you are not war stories with the usual triumphant clang, only communiqués. A former lance corporal in the 9th Marines, George Swiers, remembers Marines pursuing a North Vietnamese Army unit in the Dong Ha Valley in Quang Tri province and then, in what he calls a "reverse ambush," being cornered. Pinned down, the water went, the ammunition went, the radio was out. When, at last, the men and their own dead were pulled out, Swiers was sent to the Cua Viet Marine Base where a Corporal Mendes cut his hair. He was handed a mirror and held it up to his face. "I had never seen that person," Swiers says. "I had no idea who that was."

Many Americans, sickened or puzzled or bored by the war, wishing to repudiate or forget it, did not notice or stayed apart from the returning veterans. They were seen as contaminated men or simply not seen at all. Cheated on their educational benefits or too suspicious to take advantage, needing jobs when no jobs were there or, despite qualifications, only getting the lowest-paying and meanest work, their problems ignored by the Veterans Administration, their lives were not pretty. Some of them are lost to us now and do not believe otherwise. Help has come, in certain ways, but not enough or too late. This is not to deny that a number of veterans did come home and learn how to release themselves from the war, or silently choke on it bit by bit.

Almost nothing is heard of the ordeal of the men who defied the draft and risked disgrace because they denounced the war that needed them. Last December in the Halfmoon Cafe on Madison Avenue in Albany, New York, the Vietnam Reconciliation Committee had its first informal meeting. Men who often tended to be adversaries spoke to each other: veterans of Vietnam and war resisters. YOU WERE NEVER MY ENEMY, said a sign in big blue letters above a map of Southeast Asia. Steve Trimm, who fled to Canada to escape a prison term for resisting the draft, now working in a hospital with psychiatric patients, stood to have his photograph taken with a high-school friend who won the Bronze Star for valor, a Silver Star, and a Purple Heart, beneath the sign. The man was Swiers. "He was the first person I knew to speak out against the war," Swiers said, adding he wished that he had listened to him. "I'm hoping that if people can see that the veteran, *of all people*, can finally accept me, maybe others would be more willing to," said Trimm, who spent five and a half years in Canada. It is seventeen years now since both men went inside the war, almost half their lives.

Villains are needed to explain the defeat. In the libel suit of General William C. Westmoreland against CBS, which aired a documentary Westmoreland believed made the claim that the general deceived President Johnson and the Joint Chiefs of Staff about the size and composition of enemy forces, Westmoreland told the jury that his troops never thought, and told him so, that they were "getting a fair shake from the media." That enlisted men in the field unburdened themselves to their commander of all U.S. troops is a revelation indeed; few generals ever know what their troops are thinking although they often pretend otherwise. Westmoreland did not make clear how infantrymen or the crews on tanks, how cooks or clerk-typists or artillerymen on fire support bases, knew what was being reported on American television networks or in American newspapers since all they saw was the Army newspaper, *Stars and Stripes*, and an Armed Forces television station. During the same trial a lieutenant general, who in 1974 and 1975 directed the intelligence arm of the Joint Chiefs of Staff, told the jury that South Vietnam would have prevailed if the United States had not cut military aid to the Saigon government in 1974 and if the press had not contributed to "defeat."

But the army of the Republic of South Vietnam, which the

Americans paid and equipped and monitored and advised, was once thought of as an army without a country and its ranks did not often love their large allies. The huge American press corps was not suspicious enough of the fraudulent body counts, the cover-ups, the deceitful official reports and the inflated pronouncements of the military. It was the generals and the colonels who dishonored themselves, not the journalists. The best of the journalists knew immense sorrow. "It seems the saddest story possible, with one more sad chapter following another," David Halberstam wrote in *The Best and the Brightest*. "Like almost everyone else I know who has been involved in Vietnam, I am haunted by the fact that somehow I was not better, that somehow it was all able to happen."

Here is the question to ask; the question posed by the father of a soldier killed at Fire Support Base Tomahawk: If we had done it, if we had won, what is it we would have won?

Among us are people trying to finish off the war at last in a decent and intelligent way. Delegations of veterans, including those who did the fighting, have returned to Vietnam, members of Vietnam Veterans of America, the largest and most coherent of a score of veterans' organizations. There are crucial issues to be discussed, its president, Robert Muller, has often said, and the two governments do not talk to each other. But the former commander-in-chief of the Veterans of Foreign Wars, Clifford Olson, Jr., thought this horrifying and so tried to block the granting of a federal charter by Congress to V.V.A. "It's despicable," wrote George Ewalt, Jr., to Olson in a letter of protest. That the reasons for returning were to exchange information on the effects of Agent Orange on Americans and Vietnamese and their afflicted children, to raise the question of the missing U.S. servicemen and to expedite the immigration of children of American fathers in Vietnam, appears not to have impressed the V.F.W. commander. That it would never be an easy trip, requiring each man to confront himself and the friends who died there, was of little consideration. Sometimes there is valor long after a war that is more startling in its way than what is done in battle. But the veterans themselves do not agree and have divided and regrouped.

There was one person in Vietnam, a Vietnamese called Luong, who helped me cover the war, both of us so new at it and going in so much deeper than we knew. For eight years I have been waiting for a letter from him, heard rumors that he was in bad shape, even under surveillance because he had worked for an American newspaper. I know how stubborn and proud you are, my last note said, but now have pity for your old friend and send word. The answer came in February 1984. It is only the voice of one Vietnamese, an exceptional man, not at all a typical letter but surely one that reveals something about the grace and courage and resiliency of his people. In the letter he calls the correspondents he knew his "relatives" and tells us not to worry. His four daughters were doing well in school, above average. The family made things to be sold in bookshops, and he is teaching.

"During the past few years I have always found one job or the other," Luong wrote. "Even too many at that. Of course they were the kind of jobs that one has to think up oneself in order to live and enjoy life. Every odd job my family and I work on together means food and must also mean fun, certainly."

Material difficulties are enormous, he said, but the family always had a simple way of living, so only the basic needs concerned them. A brother, a former officer, had been released after four years in a reeducation camp and had been unemployed for a very long time.

"The most terrible thing that can happen to a person, I think, is not to have any self-confidence. I still have plenty. I am still in good health, full of enthusiasm for work whether mental or manual, 18 hours a day. I still have books to read and friends to spend time with. . . . Thus I am not afraid of life's difficulties. You mentioned my pride and stubbornness. That was true in the old days and still is now, whether for good or bad, for advantage or disadvantage."

He avoided seeing foreigners in Ho Chi Minh City. "What's more I don't want to bother with letter writing and exchanges. There are a million troublesome things that go with it. I must resign myself to being rude and heartless to my friends," he wrote.

"You and my relatives want to file papers for me to go but I must decline your good intentions with thanks. My family has happiness, according to my way, right here in Vietnam."

His Vietnam is not now the Vietnam we once thought we knew so well. The old days of working with Americans was so far in the past he could not be held by them and was asking that I let him go. Always a kind man, he did not end the letter without sending a few words that might help me be more peaceful.

"Goodness, I wonder how I can tell you in words all that I want to say. . . . There have been so many changes lately, but love will always be strong."

January 1985
New York, New York

WINNERS
and
LOSERS

I

ENDINGS: ONE KIND OR ANOTHER

At first I could not understand such advice, did not even remember it for a very long time. The Vietnamese—his name does not matter—was a Communist, a southerner, who would only say of his own life that he came from Nha Trang. His English was not good, yet he understood Americans rather well: the war with them was then eleven years old. This was March 1972: I had come to Paris from Saigon, needing to believe I was finished with Vietnam at last because I had left it. He and I spoke in the white stucco villa in Verrières-le-Buisson that was headquarters for the delegation of the Provisional Revolutionary Government to the Paris peace talks. It was not unusual for an American to be in that large, dimmed room, with its vase of gladioli, its serious furniture, the pictures of Ho Chi Minh that made his eyes seem more quiet than in the photographs I had seen in books by Frenchmen about their Indochina, their war. Many Americans had been to Verrières-le-Buisson before me; some had even been invited to walk in the garden and had seen the little artificial lake with its swans.

But it could not have been so startling for them. Until that day I had never spoken to a Vietnamese who had chosen this side and was safe enough to tell me so. He and I did not even have to lower our voices. In Saigon a North Vietnamese infantryman, captured in the south and then freed, had sat in my room at the Hotel

Continental—room 53—describing the months his company had walked down the Ho Chi Minh trail. Viet Cong, the Americans called them all, VC, or Charlie when they were fighting them. On the field radios they called the enemy Victor Charlie, or just Charlie. Now Charlie is the name of a perfume by Revlon, but no one seems to mind or even notice, any more than they object to a perfume called Ambush.

One woman prisoner was twenty-five, living in a cement room with barbed wire as its ceiling, confined with six other Vietnamese. She did not want an orange and refused a cigarette. But she told me who she was, that her husband was an intelligence cadre, that her child was four months old, that she did not need a calendar to know how many days she had been there, and then the guards discovered I was crouching in that room where it was forbidden to be and drove me out. That was in a village called Cao Lanh in Kien Phuong province: it is important to remember, to spell the names correctly, to know the provinces, before we are persuaded that none of it happened, that none of us were in such places.

Somewhere in 1971, in a village called Duc Duc, there was a captured nurse handcuffed to a girl of sixteen. It was the nurse I thought of for too long: even now I can remember something about her face and the color of the jacket she wore—it was not black but a greenish shade. There were handcuffs pulling the nurse and the girl together: they were made by Smith and Wesson. Her husband had been a soldier with the National Liberation Front, she had moved with him and his unit, the nurse said. There had been hardships, she had lacked medical supplies. Cocoanut milk had once been used in transfusions because there was no blood, the nurse said. Her voice was matter-of-fact. She did not expect pity. The nurse acted as if now she was afraid of nothing. When the Saigon government troops stared at her, she turned her back on them, so the girl handcuffed to her had to shift too.

The soldiers did not like what the nurse called them, but they did nothing, standing there in a little schoolboy frieze, arms on each other's shoulders.

So often did I remember the nurse, so much later in places that had nothing to do with Duc Duc, that some Americans in the antiwar movement became impatient. Once I even mentioned her in a restaurant on Mott Street, wondering if she had endured. I was advised not to be foolish, to stop being morbid, I must realize that others had taken her place, the friends said, as if that was the point, as if it was the space she left that haunted me.

Their wrists were so thin it made me wonder if handcuffs came in sizes, if they were held by handcuffs made for children. When the nurse and the girl had to board the helicopter they suddenly held hands so tightly that even the government soldiers knew then of their terror. The prisoners could not help themselves from staring at the land that began to rush from them as the helicopter lifted. All of them, even the farmers who had kept their faces locked, stared down with mouths and eyes that told you in that instant they saw what they were losing.

All I want to explain is that in the years I was there when the Americans were fighting in Vietnam, you could not interview the Viet Cong, you did not travel with their soldiers at night, or watch them set up ambushes. You did not have tea and long talks with their cadres or leaders. They did not permit it, did not want reporters with them. All you usually saw were their wounded, their prisoners, their dead. This is what made it so peculiar on that March day in Verrières-le-Buisson, to be with that Vietnamese in his dark suit and dark shoes, speaking such excellent French, who knew the beaches of Nha Trang and the color of the air at six o'clock and how the lobster tasted. But we did not speak of such things: he did not permit himself to be sentimental with a stranger. We spoke of the war, of his people, of my own. He knew, as did everyone, that there were Americans who so loathed what

their government and their soldiers, their pilots and their diplomats, had done and were still doing, they honored the flag of his
government more than their own. He knew there were Americans who wanted to work in rice fields, who would live in bunkers
or care for the dying, who needed to offer themselves up, but his
advice had nothing to do with any of that.

"They must love their country," the Vietnamese said. "Love
your country as we love ours. If you do not, you cannot change
it." Afterward I stood outside the villa, outside the gate, looking
at the flag that flew from the balcony on the second floor. I had
never seen that blue-and-red flag, with its gold star, look so huge
and so new, only when it was stained, crumpled, folded, old. The
flag was always a good souvenir for Americans in Vietnam. Some
GIs—they were riflemen—preferred the hats, the belt buckles,
the sandals, the shell pouches or even the diaries of North Vietnamese soldiers, which they could not read. But a Viet Cong flag
was not bad at all. Yet no man was the same. Years later, when
there was no such name as War Zone C, I came to know an
ex-medic who has a photograph of a tiny Vietnamese child, a girl
in pajamas, holding two very large paper flowers. The medic kept
the photograph for himself after a firefight when his platoon had
searched the bodies of the men they had killed. The photograph
of the little girl stays in the same Bible he carried with him in the
war, as if by putting the child between its pages he protects her
from any harm, any more losses. That day in Verrières-le-Buisson,
I stood so still, staring so long at a flag being pushed by wind, that
a French policeman found it odd and suggested I move on.

GETTING BACK WAS not good. In New York a pleasant woman
asked me what I had worn to officers' dances; the question did not
make me smile. There were none; in any case, I would never have
gone. Others asked me how I had dressed, what I had eaten, what

war I would cover next, if I had seen anyone killed. "You will never, never regret the experience," a lady said as we both waited to have our hair cut in a place on 62nd Street. "It's a once-in-a-lifetime chance." No one meant to be cruel. I did not want people to tell me over and over to have a nice day, to take care, to have a nice day. It was all I heard. There were awards: I took them. The Penney-Missouri Magazine Award was for "Expanding Opportunities," as if no war need now shut out a clever, self-confident woman who did not mind a little mess, a little blood.

I went out on my own to collect evidence of what the war had done, as someone might go for the first time into a huge forest to collect leaves and branches, moss and soil, to take back and study. Some people said that because of Vietnam nothing would ever be the same, but others said this was not true. The war is boring, they said, it is much like having rheumatism, which will not kill you or quite go away. You learn to live with it. Once, driving in Texas, stopping by the Old and Lost River, I remembered what the Vietnamese in Paris had said: Love your country.

Turn the corner, people said to me in a kindly fashion. Forget the war. But I could not stop writing about it. Each time one more piece was published, there was always mail from men I did not know at all and did not ever meet.

"If you have reached the stage where you can write about it, you are almost home free," a man named David Preston wrote, marking the letter November 13, 10 A.M. "I began to see what had really been done to us all when I casually mentioned the bottle of Vicks we used to kill the stench of the dead on the airplanes, by rubbing it on our nostrils. It wasn't the reaction of the listeners so much as it was their matter-of-fact tone of voice that made the impact . . . You have finally realized what we almost all come to realize: you can chase people through all the words of all the languages, as Yossarian attempted, but you'll never make them understand. Never. So you give up trying."

Still another veteran, Jim Kairies, wrote this on lined yellow paper: on a cold night, a rainy one, he had worn his field jacket into a pleasant neighborhood bar. Sewn on his jacket were the Combat Infantryman's Badge, the patches of the 82d Airborne and 9th Division, jump wings, the rank of lieutenant. A man of his own age moved next to him at the bar, looked at him and asked: "Ever do any skydiving?" Kairies said no. A minute later the man asked him: "Sell your jacket?"

"You know the feeling when someone asks you if you brought back any souvenirs or 'What do you think of Vietnam?' or why do you have to use the word 'fuck' so much . . ." the letter said. "I was a line infantry officer trying to keep men eight years younger than myself in one piece while 'accomplishing the mission,' and I didn't have all the answers, and I was scared all the way, but I'm not ashamed."

The second summer back I saw a man with an open silky shirt wearing an eighteen-karat-gold dog tag from Cartier that cost one hundred and seventy-five dollars. Business has been very good. You can order a much cheaper one in sterling silver from the TWA Flight Shop. It is $23.95.

There were people who were exasperated and puzzled by my indifference to the women's liberation movement, which I had first known and admired in England when I lived there. I knew the immense value of the movement but I could not bear the posters SAVE OUR SISTERS IN DANANG or the women who would not join the antiwar movement because they felt it did not sufficiently stress rape as a crime, although, of course, it did. I could not rejoice when women I knew went back to school to be lawyers or doctors, when in 1973 I knew eleven Vietnam veterans, without college degrees, who were out of work. There were an estimated 36,000 Vietnam veterans unemployed in the New York area that year.

My own memories were too persistent and their bad endings made me deaf. Perhaps the interest in the women's movement, the early excitement over its huge importance, ended that night in Saigon in 1971 when Germaine Greer was there on a brief visit. One evening there were half a dozen of us in the same room. She was witty, wonderfully bright, very talkative. She looked nice. Her manners were charming and she made the men in the room light up. What really provoked her, she said, was seeing a group of Vietnamese women filling sandbags near Long Binh, the biggest U.S. Army base in Vietnam, the ugliest of places. What she resented was a sign in English, near the Vietnamese women, that said Men at Work.

It is true that I had trouble with officers in Vietnam, but none of it is important now. Sometimes they cared about where I would go to the bathroom and I did not. What is worth remembering is a mountain boy from North Carolina, whose name will not come back, telling me what he thought of "lifers." The enlisted men called the career officers "lifers," and later, in the last years of the war, they sometimes called them the "beggars." The boy was in a mortar crew; he was saying that he thought lifers didn't really like women or want them around much. And then he said something startling and wise: "We are their women. They've got us."

He meant the enlisted men and he was right. I had always known how women were leashed, confined, made so small and uncertain. But in Vietnam, among the most helpless and humiliated were the soldiers themselves.

During the war I was equal at last, and often it was too much to bear. But the truth is there were times when I was turned back, sent away, by Americans who did not want me with them on the line. Perhaps they saw I was clumsy or untrained, perhaps they thought I might bring them bad luck. I met soldiers, so much younger than myself, who felt that one dead white woman was more bothersome than ten dead men—and who needed more trouble? It did not happen often. I would protest and be very firm. But one time I was grateful to lose, and this is why.

In May 1970 I flew on medical evacuation missions with a twenty-year-old warrant officer named Conrad Graf. He was the pilot of the helicopter and you called him Mr. Graf. The aircraft was called a "dust-off"—helicopters raised a gale of dirt, grass, pebbles and leaves—and there were no gunners aboard. It was an ordinary thing for a reporter to do, riding choppers collecting the wrecked. One American, named John, was picked up for a head wound and lay on the floor, not dead or not alive. The medic could not stop the bleeding. There were never doors on the helicopters, so the wind moved his hair where the blood did not make it stick. It all becomes normal, the other correspondents, men, would say. In time you'll see. They lied.

Mr. Graf had to get in and out of small clearings in the jungle very fast. The light beating of that helicopter never seemed to stop: it barely touched the ground. The pilot could not help turning around, just once, to see the new wounded and the new dead. "I have to see their faces, I don't know why," Mr. Graf said.

Just before 8 P.M. the dust-off made a landing in a small clearing in a jungle northwest of Memot, in Cambodia. A light rain wet the faces and the bare chests of the Americans who ran toward us carrying two bamboo litters, pushing hard through the prop-wash to give us those bodies. It was almost dark. They had trouble getting the soldiers inside the plane in such a rush. Mr. Graf looked back several times in a worried way.

"Shit, man, shit, get the legs in," a GI yelled. It was true that the feet of the wounded hung over the stretchers. There was something wrong with those legs, too, the flesh and the cloth in strips and clots.

The wounded were aged nineteen and twenty-one. I did not want to know their names written on those big white tags the medics in the field always filled out. The men had tripped one of their own antipersonnel mines, a Claymore. The medic gave the nineteen-year-old morphine. Only once when he raised his hands and opened them, as though trying to clutch something only he could see, did the boy appear alive. The older soldier could not seem to shut his eyes. He was cold. I wanted to hold his hand, but once before I had done this, the GI had died, his fingers curled .with mine, and I had not wanted to let go, thinking the life would pass from me to him, until someone yanked my arm and parted us at last.

That night we flew to the 45th Surgical Hospital at the base camp of the 1st Brigade, 25th Infantry Division, at Tay Ninh. It seemed important to try to stay with the nineteen-year-old with the bloody, bent legs.

We stood outside the little room where they laid him, looking through a window, as a nurse and an orderly began to prepare him for surgery. They worked very fast, but something went wrong. The boy tried to rise up and push them away, making a noise I had never heard from a man: it was a long and hoarse shriek. He fought to get away from them, but there was no escape. Nguyen Ngoc Luong—the interpreter and my friend—said softly: "Do not go in there, you can do nothing." I held his arm, Luong held mine. We could not believe any of it.

That night they took off both legs above the knees. I had wanted, more than anything, to gain time for the boy, to make sure other doctors saw him and all were convinced the legs could not be mended. That is how much I knew—there are no second opinions. Later I found the Army doctor who had done it. He was drinking a Coca-Cola in the little bar for officers near the hospital. I said the nineteen-year-old had been in shock, but I was not brave enough to ask if perhaps a mistake had been made, why they had not waited.

"He wasn't in shock, he was just frightened to death," the doctor said. I did not know the difference then.

Mr. Graf, his co-pilot and the medic were on call from 8 A.M. to 11 P.M. They went out four or five times more, but I could not go with them. Mr. Graf said no, they were going into hot LZs. This meant they expected to take enemy fire in the landing zones. I did not argue with Mr. Graf, who had other things on his mind. Luong went, the photographer went, I stayed behind.

LONG AFTER TAY NINH, when I was living in Massachusetts, Luong wrote me a letter that put into words what the trouble was, what I had refused to admit. He said that whenever there was time, he and the reporters, the ones I knew and others who came after, would talk about me: "All have this remark about you: you are the only one who cannot overcome your Vietnam experience. There is an acute lack of forgetfulness in you about Vietnam, we think."

Each winter, walking the streets of different American cities, I used to look at the younger men in surplus Army jackets, some with the patches on them I knew so well: the Americal, the Big Red One, the Screaming Eagle, Tropic Lightning. For a long time I could not bear those field jackets, always suspecting they had been taken off the American corpses in Vietnam, sanitized, pressed and sold as surplus. The real surplus was the men who had first worn them and were wasted.

Different places did not much help me think of other things, or did different kinds of talk. Once during a weekend in Kingfield, Maine, where he has a house and land, the writer Richard Goodwin took me on a walk and pointed out an old, slanting tree. The tree was in danger; it was ill or something was putting it in peril. The little story did not interest me very much.

"You would care if the tree was in Vietnam," he said.

It was a veteran who helped the most. It was the ex-medic named David who kept the photograph of the Vietnamese child in his Bible. "Grow plants," he said, giving me some. His father thought he might consider prison, but he became a conscientious objector and went off as an infantry medic. He never carried a weapon. Once, for Christmas, he gave me a book he had read in Vietnam. It was *The Most of S.J. Perelman*. Inside he wrote: "This book, a Merck Manual, Isaiah II, and a few Ace bandages are all you really need." It used to upset him when he saw the advertisements used by the Army to increase recruitment. YOU DON'T GET TO BE INFANTRY SIMPLY BY CHOOSING IT, one of them said.

Many peculiar things were written about Vietnam veterans, as if all of the 2,300,000 men who were there during a twelve-year war came rushing back all at once. There were magazines I read, looking at winter coats and needing to care about such things again. In an article called "How to Treat a Viet Vet," *Glamour* warned its readers: "If you avoid arguments because he's been trained to killing and to anger, and you are afraid of his releasing them on you—another common problem—you've got to talk about it. Chances are he has been afraid about this, too." The article did not say that men served only one year in Vietnam, that probably only one in twenty saw combat, that others typed or cooked, made charts or bar graphs, trained dogs or answered telephones, were clerk-typists and mechanics, did laundry or maintained aircraft. They did not do the killing, they only made it possible.

It is almost never suggested in these glossy little pieces that the war was wrong, only that the men returning from it have something wrong with them which must be tolerated.

In giving advice on how to talk to Vietnam veterans, Barbara Walters, the television commentator, wrote: "Keep the discussion generalized. Ask him what life is like in the cities of Vietnam, as opposed to the rural areas. Ask if his attitude changed while he was away. Ask him about the commuter aspect of the war, that men were delivered to the battle every morning and returned to the base at night—was that easier on the nerves than sustained fighting, or worse? Ask, if the medical side of the war interests you, about the quickness of aid for the wounded ... Ask about the heat, the dampness, the housing."

Ask none of it. Soldiers in the field rarely saw any Vietnamese cities. They were even off-limits to Americans nearby on big bases. Men who went into battle were not flown back that night; the infantry often stayed out for weeks. The aid to the wounded was very fast if the weather was all right and there was no enemy fire. Men were kept alive with horrendous injuries, although many did not know why they were exposed to such wounds. The housing was an air mattress on the ground, just the ground, a tent, a barrack. It was hot, it was damp. Sometimes infantrymen did not wear underpants because they rotted from the water and the heat and caused infections.

On television the Vietnam veteran is always a psychopath who hallucinates and thinks he is in a firefight. The police and SWAT teams are gentle and patient. Not wanting to hurt the veteran, who is armed and shouting again to his platoon, they wait it out and capture him with great cleverness. The veteran is led off. He will receive the best medical treatment. There are wonderful psychiatrists waiting to help. Some lies are hilarious. I wanted to write this to Luong, but it would have been too hard to explain. I wanted to tell him that I could not forget Vietnam because I lived in the United States. But instead I wrote him in 1974 that there were potholes in the streets of New York as deep as the ones in Saigon, that many dogs defecated in the streets, so we were not the obsessively hygienic people the Vietnamese thought, that the telephones did not work as well as I remembered, that the mail was very slow, that many people dreaded any sickness because it cost too much to get well, that it was not wise to walk alone at night, and that the President of the United States and some of his closest advisors had committed criminal acts.

THE FIRST SUMMER, during a day on Fire Island, a woman whose house I visited during the McGovern campaign complained to me about the television coverage of the Vietnam war, which she thought was confusing. She could not tell the difference between old movies about World War II and the combat footage, the real film, from Vietnam. Her name was Cynthia Bernardi. When I called her up more than a year later, still puzzled what she meant, Mrs. Bernardi was very nice about it, for I had been brusque that day.

"They looked alike," she said. "The Second World War was very impressive to a child; it was also a kind of entertainment, and they painted Vietnam in the same style. It took some of the teeth out of it. It put Vietnam under the same moral umbrella as World War II."

Errol Flynn was fighting in Burma late the other night on television. The men in his company keep the sleeves of their uniforms rolled down although they are supposed to be perishing from the heat. There are no leeches. There are no sores on the back of their necks from the heat and filth. Their feet are often wet but do not crack and bleed. The soldiers look clean; their faces are too filled out. The movie has nothing to do with Vietnam, but I pay strict attention. Everything is different: the shape of helmets and the helmet covers, the uniforms, rifles, boots, language, jokes, faces. There are no helicopters. On the field radio the actors say "able" and "baker" not "alpha" and "bravo." All I learn is that even then soldiers used flares which light up the landscape at night like a strange and silvery sun so you can see who is out there to kill or to burn.

At the Brooklyn Museum that first summer there was an exhibition of sixty-eight photographs, black-and-white and color, called "Vietnam: A Photographic Essay of the Undeclared War in Southeast Asia." The pictures were the work of nine dead men; six of them were under thirty. Some of the photographers were still described as missing because their bodies had not been recovered. Most of the photographs were of American troops, but there was Kyiochi Sawada's picture of the Vietnamese prisoner being dragged by ropes around his ankles from the back of an armored personnel carrier. There was Larry Burrows' picture of a Vietnamese woman, tears coming from her mouth and eyes, mourning a lumpy bundle wrapped in plastic, a bundle smaller than she. The tied-up thing was her husband. The photographs were separated; each man's work was shown under his name. They covered wall after wall. I asked a young museum guard, standing in the center of sixty-eight photographs, surrounded by faces, what he thought.

"I don't know, I haven't seen them yet," the guard said, who had been there for five hours.

The exhibition went on tour throughout New York State for two years. In Schenectady, a number of seniors in a parochial school for boys, Bishop Gibbons High School, were taken to see it. Thirty-two of them wrote short essays about it in Father Snapp's English class. Everyone knew what he felt even if he could not spell words. The pictures of wounded children disturbed them; so did a photograph of a man falling out of a helicopter. They wrote about the way people's faces looked, and how GIs tried to help each other. A few essays mentioned the photograph of a Vietnamese being interrogated as he hung by his ankles from a tree.

One student, Joe Fox, wrote: "I myself don't think I could go to war after seeing this exhibition, not because of fear for myself but because I might kill or mame somebody like myself and I don't think anyone should have the power to do that." I wanted to write the boy called Joe Fox that the choice of killing or maiming might not be his to make, that once in the Army the soldier who would not fire or who wanted to be kind was considered a danger to his own people and to himself.

Still another, Tom Prindle, wrote this: "When I saw those pictures I realley was not surprised or shocked. After seeing so many of Vietnam pictures, scenes such as this are second nature to me ... The hundreds of Vietnamese with their hands atop their heads and the V.C. prisoner being dragged behind an armored car showed me the overpowering strength of my country and that war is a matter of fear. The dead V.C. sprawled around the flag gave me a sense of pride while the V.C. strung up by his heels disgusted me . . . It made me think as to was it really worth it? All in all I was not shocked or angered, since I expected these pictures to be what they were. I would have gotten just as much out of a WWII re-run movie. The only thing I really felt was pity."

Once, before I quit, the newspaper sent me to Social Circle, Georgia, to write a story on a contest of livestock auctioneers. I understood nothing and did not take notes on the cattle or the men who sold them. The little town made the contest into an excuse for a three-day celebration. I remember buying two cakes of Rosebud, a homemade sassafras soap, and watching Lester Maddox, a former governor of Georgia, ride a one-wheel bicycle backward in the parade down Main Street. I talked to some black men on a street corner as the parade went by. One wore the canvas and leather boots, another his Army shirt with the sleeves cut off. I wanted to stay with them. In Vietnam, Luong liked the black soldiers because they were not timid about themselves. He liked to see the black soldiers dapping. It was an elaborate ritual, a way for men to dance together, lightly and swiftly touching each other: palms, knuckles, wrists, arms, shoulders and chests. It ended in a loose hug. Twenty blacks—each man dapping with another man, then the next and the next—could slow down the war. No one could rush them or command them to cut it out. The Army was anxious to avoid trouble, to pacify the black troops as the racial disturbances increased.

There was so much Luong and I did not know when we started out, not even how much we were allowed to eat in the little mess hall run by the Americans in Hue. Among so much food, so much salad, there were piles of shined red apples and trays of hot cross buns. We were not certain that I might take two buns or that

Luong could put an apple in his pocket and eat one there. The apples astonished him. They were so costly in local markets that only invalids were given them. It was allowed; take all that you can eat, a black sergeant told him, smiling. Luong asked me if it was true that the blacks came from poorer places in America and did not have such rich lives. Yes, yes. He did not quite believe it.

"How is it then that they are always the biggest?" Luong asked.

In Social Circle the black men are suspicious and uneasy if I hang around them. I had picked up the habit, so used to armies, of talking to anyone, but back home it makes Americans uneasy, for they do not know what you have in mind.

One of them, Daniel, says he wants to go back to Vietnam, back to Marble Mountain. "I left something there."

"A girl?"

But he shakes his head: it is more important than that. He did not wish to tell me.

ON SUNDAY, WHICH was May 11, 1975, fat balloons bounced over Central Park. They were yellow and orange and white, with the words on them: *The War Is Over!* The more the balloons wiggled, the more they moved, the nicer it was. A thin man without a shirt, his beard the color of mustard, said he had not been persuaded the war was over until he saw the balloons and so many people in the park. It made the nails inside his head go away, the thin man said. It was an ending at last, the war in Vietnam and in Cambodia was finished, not only finished but over. There was a party; sixty thousand people came. They were young. But at some point during the day, perhaps when Joan Baez was singing, or when Peter Yarrow had begun the chorus of "If You Take My Hand, My Son," and we sang too, everyone was the same age for a little while. People sat on the hard ground in Sheep Meadow, a large area in Central Park where there are deep, bald patches in the grass. "Come celebrate the victory of the peace and of the people" the handbills for The War Is Over rally said. "Theater, music, dancing, street theater, political booths and very few speeches . . ." The celebration was organized in just ten days by a coalition of antiwar groups, by people who had held on, pushing together as they had so often done in the past. There were some of them on the platform in the park that day who could remember more than ten years of it: the marches, the protests, the moratoriums, the rallies, the bus rides to Washington, the mailings and the petitions and raising money, the draft-card burnings, the teach-ins, the speeches, the trials, the lying down on marble floors and on pavements, eyes shut, pretending to be the dead of Vietnam. The memories of it were all in music; the singing went on for hours. The performers were patient, waiting their turn. People who never waited, waited.

Phil Ochs sang, Pete Seeger sang, Barbara Dane sang, Odetta sang and people whose names and music I did not know. The speeches, as promised, were short. No one was allowed to ramble. A woman from Bronxville remembered her son who was killed in Quang Tri seven years ago. The war was not finished, the handsome lady from Bronxville said, not finished. There were half a million Americans either in exile, facing charges or with undesirable discharges because they had opposed the war. Representative Bella S. Abzug, Democrat from New York City, said that if the government could open its treasury to Vietnamese refugees, it could welcome back "our own young people." Actors spoke, a deserter from the Special Forces, a spokesman for the American Indian Movement. But it was the music that drenched the day, the songs like "Carry It On" and "This Land Is Your Land" that the crowd wanted, needed to hear. Later there were comments, worried ones, that the people in Sheep Meadow had seemed glazed, too dreamy, unpolitical. It was suggested that they had only come because of the fine weather and the music and not even in numbers larger than the crowds drawn by the free concerts of the New York Philharmonic.

In an article which said the antiwar movement had lost, since its understanding was primarily moral and not sufficiently political, an American writer, a very bright and good writer, referred to Thucydides, Book V, the Melian Dialogue. No one I know had read it. She thought the War Is Over rally had "the wanness of a class reunion." But some of the people who were there, who sat on the hard ground for six hours and were glad of it, felt they were rejoicing because of an American defeat that had been too long in coming. They were in need of a celebration. They wanted to hear "Weave Me the Sunshine," as I wanted to hear it, with its wonderfully childish lines "shine on me, shine on me again." The music—the silly, lovely, thumping, chilling music—was the history that day of people who did not have any other history; it was a record of how they had responded in the days when those like Father Daniel Berrigan told them "No to their no, Yes to all else" and perhaps a million people knew exactly what he had meant.

A girl with a baby—there were lots of babies—said she supposed no other country had ever had people who celebrated their own defeat. Once she had read that in the last few years another Vietnamese soldier died every eight minutes and that if you kept thinking of that you could go off the wall. But still, it was a hard day to holler, the girl with the baby said. She had gone to Hunter College, she had been tear-gassed at a demonstration, it had made her sinuses act up for months, she could not take it again.

Some of the songs were songs you heard over and over in Vietnam, where the soldiers did not want their music taken from them, so they carried cassette players everywhere. I was glad to miss Paul Simon singing "Bridge Over Troubled Waters." Even in delicatessens I do not easily hear it.

A young man came up to me, said he wanted to talk and had never been able to reach me on the telephone. I didn't bother to explain I don't answer the phone. He introduced himself. The young man said we had met in Vietnam when he was an information officer for the Americal Division. He was a lieutenant in Chu Lai. I never cared much for information officers, whose job was to see that reporters wrote what the Army hoped they would and to escort correspondents who might find out too much. It was a good job, as jobs went in Vietnam. He said how much he wanted my help in getting back to South Vietnam for a visit, and he went on talking for a few minutes before he noticed I was furious.

I said: "Why do you want to go back?"

"I just want to see it again."

I said: "Why? What reason would you give the new government in Saigon, why would they want someone like you, an officer from the Americal, in their country again?"

"I can't explain it, I just want to go. I want to see it again. There's a place I want to see . . ."

"They will only let Americans come back who have been in the antiwar movement, and maybe not even many of them. The Vietnamese don't want us back, we have no right to expect that."

He said: "There are people there . . . there is a hootch maid I'd like to see again."

A hootch maid was a Vietnamese woman who was paid by the soldiers to clean their rooms or barracks, do their laundry, shine their boots and provide whatever else she was willing to give. A colonel once told me that employing maids helped the economy of Vietnam. Maybe his words reminded me of that ugly conversation with the colonel. At any rate, he did not understand why I was getting so nasty, why he was provoking me so.

"What's her name?"

"I don't know her name."

The war had bothered him a lot, the last four years had been very hard, the veteran said in a low voice, in a final polite plea. I said lots of people in the park that day had had a hard time and left him.

Other men have had other reasons for wanting to go back; to

have been in a war does not mean you understand the memories of it. In 1972, in Cambridge, Massachusetts, on a winter afternoon in one of the coffee places in Harvard Square, a veteran who was a graduate student and a novelist was saying he would like to go back to Quang Ngai province. He was a nice man; there were few enough veterans at Harvard, his first novel was very fine. I tried to listen, but the story was such an old one by then, the ending was never easy to take. He had asked a village girl—she wore earrings, he remembered that, perhaps they were gold—if there were any VC around, was it okay for the platoon to go down the road. No VC. The girl was sure. The platoon moved on. But she deceived them. There were mines. Some of the Americans were wounded. The veteran wanted to go back and find the girl.

"I wouldn't hurt her, or do anything," the man said. "I just want to talk to her, to find out why she did it." The reasons seemed clear but the man could not understand them. Maybe he knows more now, but that day in Cambridge, it was already five years since he spoke to the girl with the earrings in Quang Ngai who had wanted the platoon to be blown apart.

After so many endings, the real end was very sharp and clear in the early hours of April 30, 1975, when Communist troops entered Saigon, in tanks, in trucks and then the infantry in Indian file, in damp and muddy uniforms and sandals made of rubber tires. By the evening of April 30 the city was calm.

Sometimes it is surprising how far you can be hurled back again: I have a last letter from Saigon and on the top of it is typed "Ho Chi Minh City, 23 May 1975." It was written by Nguyen Ngoc Luong, the longest letter he had ever sent. Luong liked to say his written English was "baby talk" long after he knew it was not really true. Some of his expressions—the American slang words—came from the "Dear Abby" column, which he liked to read in *Stars and Stripes* when there were long waits in the airports at Cantho, Danang, Phu Bai, Cam Ranh, at Hotel Three and the 8th Aerial Port in Saigon. I gave him a camera, and he became good at taking pictures, although his footwork was not perfect. He longed for the heavy dark necklaces of cameras and lenses that hung from the necks, from the arms of the war photographers who were everywhere and often moved like dancers, very fast, even the fat ones.

It was hard in the beginning for both of us when he came to work with me for *The New York Times*, it was so new for him, the asking of so many questions, the taking of notes, the details, the things we saw. Once he was working in my hotel room at the Continental, but stopped because the room was too large, so much space disturbed him. He was not good at all, the brilliance failed and the energy went, when we had to interview politicians or generals, anyone of rank or wealth.

In his letters he liked the abbreviations and language the reporters used for cables, in which capital letters could not be used.

Dear Gloria,

This is another baby-talk memo from NNL. Everything is all right with me and my whole family, at least for the moment. I received a letter from you well before the liberation of Saigon but I could not write you immediately because of evacuation of most of Viet staff so I had to be "political reporter," photographer and messenger at the same time. Mal Browne, Fox Butterfield and I had the most exciting days before VN history turned to a new page. Then all of a sudden Mal and Fox left, while Fox and I were getting out of office planning to go and see fighting right on the edge of Saigon. They left by noon 29 May in such a rush that Fox did not remember to pay his hotel bill! (I later paid his bill with money left over in office.) Next morning Big Minh announced surrender and NLF troops moved swiftly into Saigon. I moved around taking pictures as usual, with some fear and much more excitement. That afternoon I asked aypee to radio seven specials for NYT, but unfortunately all

*communication with outer world was cut that evening. So
no pix. Too bad. George Esper offered to buy my pix, and
I refused on the ground that I was still with NYT, and my
pix—good or bad—are for NYT. And I thought of those pix
in a very sentimental way: a message to the paper, to friends
like you, iver, craig, joe and barbara treaster, the markhams,
the shiplers, Fox and Mal, etc. . . . those I have worked with,
liked and loved, and I don't think that I would see again.
The message was that I am still alive and work as if nothing happens. The message is that I'm really a SOB who is
too proud to leave his country and throws himself into the
arms of foreigners, at their mercy. No, not that. I cannot
lower myself to the same level of nguyen van thieu, nguyen
cao ky, bao dai, etc. . . . Whatever will happen to me, to my
family, I chose to stay in my country with the simple peasants, simple cyclo drivers whom I have had the real respect.*

He wrote that he had, on the second day, decided to work for
the Associated Press:

*It is a way to save myself from the emptiness and nervousness
that all Saigonese have experienced up to this very day. An
unknown future, sloganized policies, everything is possible.
That is the dark side of life. I have kept myself busy by working
between 12 to 16 hours a day including what is called Sunday,
working to exhaustion, to have no time to think of that dark
side of life. And I kept telling me about the good things: witnessing the great moment of VN history, expecting the reunifi-
cation of the country, no more killing, no more foreign advisors
of all kinds, and later with stabilization and reorganization
each and every person may, for the first time in his life, to feel
really be himself, to feel really useful . . . I hate, as you already
know, those Vietnamese who do not share the sufferings of*

the majority of the people in the past two or three decades. I
have suffered in many ways, shattered in many ways, so I am
proud and I look down on many people especially the so-called
leaders, big and small, of the so-called Republic of Vietnam.

Forgive me about the above outburst! I will get back to
factual report. I have kept the bureau open with all the rest
of the Viet staff until May 9th when the office was sealed off.
I kept it open because of these reasons: (1) why not? (2) with
more than 100 foreign journalists in Saigon after Big Minh's
surrender and PRG takeover, there is a possibility that NYT
men might find a way to get here again (3) the rest of Viet
staff in office were so shaky and nervous that any kind of
command, of leadership was to them a kind of tranquilizer.

During the 1–9 May period I kept contact with NYT
bureau by calling every now and then from AP office.
But finally I could not do anything but let the new rul-
ers seal off the bureau. I had done my best . . .

Dear Gloria. Mai and I are expecting another child in three
or two months—at the same time of Craig's first child. I hope
that situation is still good then to send you a pix of the child (Mai
and my mother pray day and night that it would be a boy . . .)

Peter Arnett is scheduled to get out of VN tomorrow with
this letter and all the pix for NYT. I can't write letters to all
friends. Please send them my regards. Keep up the hope that
we may see each other again, somehow, sometime, in Vietnam.

There is no hope. I do not want to go back.

THERE WERE EIGHT to ten men who wanted to help build that
big platform for the party in Central Park. They began work early
on Saturday and finished it all by the next day, when, just before
noon, Pete Seeger, then Joan Baez, started the singing. One of the

men was Albert Lee Reynolds, a thirty-nine-year-old civil engineer from Elk City, Oklahoma, who worked at the World Trade Center. He carried boards, nailed them and built stalls for the little bright banners that ringed the field. The platform did him good: he liked working on something plain and strong in honor of such a day.

"I'm glad I hammered those nails down real good," he said. "I knew there would be a lot of people up there with bare feet." His wife, Linda, came down from 87th Street with their four-year-old daughter, Laurie, and one-year-old son, who wore a little white hat but began to turn pink from the sun on his shoulders and arms. Albert Lee Reynolds held the baby—whom he had wanted for so long, whom he had called Patrick Albert years before the birth—and raised him high, as if a baby could see and remember so much.

He is tall, with hair that was once redder, a quiet and quick man with light-blue eyes, sometimes humble, always polite. People meeting him for the first time, seeing that face and hearing Oklahoma in his voice still, do not expect him to feel what he does. He seems so mild and still shy. That Sunday, showing a friend how much the baby had grown, he said, "They'll never get this child, I'll never let them have this one." He had made such a vow so many times before, the friend only nodded, smiled, praised the chunky baby in the white hat.

He always speaks like this: it means he will not let the Army take the child if another Vietnam by any name should come. No Patton will ever lead him. For more than five years the name of General George S. Patton III had a curious effect on this man. He sees Patton as a symbol of something so fearful and so cruel that for a long while he could barely control his surprise and sorrow and fury that there were such men, and they were ours.

"I hate Patton," he said and wrote, over and over. "He loves war, he kills joyously. He is a slaughterer of children. Whether you believe as the Bible says that God created earth in seven days or you believe that man has slowly tried to pull himself out of the muck and ooze doesn't matter. We all aspire to being better. Patton runs contrary to that human, that decent instinct."

It began in New York years ago, in a place called the Cedar Bar, with an ugly story, no uglier than many I know, but startling for someone who worried that people with bare feet might hurt themselves on a platform with nails. A veteran who fought with the 11th Armored Cavalry Regiment commanded by Patton, then a colonel, told how he and others had taken revenge on dead enemy soldiers. It pleased Patton, the veteran said; the colonel liked his troops to show they were not little girls.

After that night in the bar, hearing so much over the beers, after he had read more about the war and heard still more stories from veterans: Albert Lee Reynolds wept often, was a trial to his wife, who rarely complained, went to meetings, wrote letters, gave away more money than he could afford, drank too much and invited veterans and deserters to sleep on the blue velvet couch in the small living room which opened out into a bed. The sofa, he called it. Some were men on the run.

Patton became the enemy: also the name for those in the military who called for war and needed the battle, eyes and mouths fierce with pleasure when they plunged into it, wanting the breaking and the bleeding and the moans, dragging with them into the darkness soldiers who were only boys and could not run away to hide from such cruel and powerful new fathers. This is how he saw it, still does.

A strange struggle began between the mild-mannered engineer and the Patton who would not go away, the Patton who had served two tours in Vietnam, won there a Distinguished Service Cross in 1968, a Bronze Star in 1969 and moved easily up the chain of command. Mr. Reynolds wanted to give back life, to help those who had been damaged by the war or who were still lost inside it. He wanted to undo what he felt men like Patton had done to them. Sometimes, when he felt a victory, he would write "Patton o—Reynolds 2."

He deeply admired the courage of Dr. Gordon Livingston, a West Point graduate and formerly a major in the Army Medical Corps, who served his third tour in Vietnam in 1968 with the 11th Armored Cavalry Regiment operating near Bien Hoa. During an Easter Sunday change-of-command ceremony for Patton, the doctor passed out a poem to some two hundred people:

> God, our heavenly Father, hear our prayer. We acknowledge our shortcomings and ask thy help in being better soldiers for thee. Grant us, O Lord, those things we need to do thy work more effectively. Give us this day a gun that will burn ten thousand rounds a second, a napalm which will burn a week. Help us to bring death and destruction wherever we go, for we do it in thy name and therefore it is meet and just . . . Forget not the least of thy children as they hide from us in the jungles; bring them under our merciful hand that we may end their suffering. In all things, O God, assist us, for we do our noble work in the knowledge that only with thy help can we avoid the catastrophe of peace which threatens us ever. All of which we ask in the name of thy son, George Patton. Amen.

In August 1973 Albert Lee Reynolds spent his vacation in Gainesville, Florida, helping out in the press office—such as it was— during the trial of seven antiwar veterans and a supporter accused by the U.S. government of plotting an assault by automatic weapons, crossbow and slingshot on the Republican National Convention in Miami Beach, 1972. Each morning the defendants had to pass through an electronic metal detector. He was there when three of them triggered it, and were ordered to take off their belts and shoes. The detectors had been set off by shrapnel still deep inside their bodies. None of the marshals looked embarrassed.

The U.S. District Court judge was often made impatient or furious by the defendants. He denied a request that the court observe sixty seconds of silent prayer and meditation to mark the end of U.S. bombing in Cambodia, saying it was inappropriate and utterly out of order. The veterans did it anyway.

When the Gainesville Eight trial ended in a victory for them, Mr. Reynolds gave a party and put up signs in his living room. One of them said *Patton 0—Mahoney 10*. It was in honor of Peter Paul Mahoney, a former seminarian who did not become a priest but a first lieutenant in Vietnam. During the trial the government called as witnesses their paid informers. One of them had been Peter Paul Mahoney's best friend. He tried to be charitable toward the informers. "I think his life ended at the close of his testimony," he said of one such man who lied. The party pleased him very much. He still has that sign.

The letters of Mr. Reynolds were very emotional, yet the younger people to whom he wrote, who would never have used his language, understood and did not mind. In a typical letter to Dee Knight, a draft evader in Toronto who was co-editor of AMEX, the magazine of exiled war resisters in Canada, he said: "The next time you meet one of our exiled friends who is depressed, who is tired—maybe one that just got in from Sweden—remind him that he has changed history. Remind him that Genghis Khan or Attila the Hun or Colonel Patton III . . . lost a bit when he was born."

There were hundreds and hundreds of such letters; for eight years he was unable to stop writing them. They spring from Albert Lee Reynolds like unending leaks in a pipe that looks fine but whose cracks grow deeper with each new wetness. He began in 1969, when he had been living in Bangkok for two years and was often sent to Vietnam by the firm Lyon Associates, who employed him as an engineer. He did structural designs for bridges of timber, of steel or concrete needed by the U.S. military, and sometimes for buildings for their bases. He thought Senator Fred Harris of Oklahoma would know what a man like him should do. "Please let me know if I can help in your antiwar program," he wrote from Bangkok on October 25, 1969. "I have approximately one month's vacation time coming." Senator Harris wrote him thank you but that his office did not have "any organized effort in this regard but was urging the Administration to move more rapidly in disengaging America from this tragic war." Mr. Reynolds knew nothing about the antiwar movement, the days of rage, the red elasticized armbands sold in college towns, the Presidio Twenty-Seven, the Chicago Seven, the Boston Five, the Harrisburg Seven, the Camden Twenty-Eight—none of it.

In 1965 he had been in Somalia for two years, then there were months in Beirut and Okinawa before Bangkok and Vietnam. For a long time he refused to believe that men and women in Congress do not open their mail, that others read and answer it for them. He kept writing. He went on hoping that some men in Washington who understood his background—because it was also theirs—would end the war and punish the men who prolonged it. In 1973, believing that the men in the White House must go, he wrote to another Oklahoman, The Honorable Carl Albert, Speaker of the House:

> They have abused us, Mr. Albert. They have abused the trust we gave them. You know this, as I do. Even though we come from opposite sides of Oklahoma—you from Flowery Mound and Bug Tussle, I from Elk City and Quarila and Anadarko and Chickasha and Eldorado—we both have the ingrained Oklahoma common sense of the farmers around Elk City to know when we're being abused or cheated or

hustled. I would watch the farmers around Elk City, when I was a boy, talk to the oil company lease hunters, when the oil field came in, and the farmers would usually pick up when the lease hunters tried to cheat them, and the lease hunters couldn't tell that the farmers were so perceptive because the farmers wore overalls then—one brand name I remember was "Osh-Kosh"—but the farmers had a sixth sense, Oklahoma version, which would tell them when they were being hustled.

His own father was born in 1907, at the time Oklahoma became the forty-sixth state, and named Okla in the excitement of that year. He married a schoolteacher named Laura. They moved to Elk City when their first son, Albert Lee, was ready for sixth grade. His mother, Laura, taught first grade in Elk City for thirty years and misses it now; all the years of being with children make her voice and face seem babylike. In Elk City High School no boy did better: he was president of the Student Council, drum major for the high school band, a member of the Honor Society, president of Teen Town—an organization for the healthy and suitable entertainment for the young—and valedictorian of the class of 1954. The Rotary Club voted him the best citizen of the year. There were no bad jolts for him, although sometimes the members of his family went down, never knowing why. There was his grandfather, Albert Reynolds, a homesteader who worked 160 acres, retiring with enough money in a savings account to keep him for a long time. But he lived another thirty years. The money went and the old man was fearful of being sent to the county farm, where the poorest and the weakest ended up. It was bad luck, too, that his father, Okla, was a cotton broker for a large Oklahoma firm who fired him when he was fifty-five and still had a mortgage to pay and could not make it farming a little cotton and some wheat on his own land.

Albert Lee Reynolds went to Oklahoma State University. He belonged to Pi Kappa Alpha and at the end of his senior year in 1959 the fraternity chose him as Outstanding Graduating Senior. There was an "Al Reynolds Day"—his parents came from Elk City for the dinner and to see him given a plaque. He went to graduate school at Yale for a master's degree in engineering; no one in Elk City had ever done that. It is a small, flat town in the western part of the state, a place with no surprises at all, with houses and refrigerators and backyards that you find everywhere. Older people can still tell you about the great punishing dust storms and droughts, and how more than forty-five years ago the poorest tenant farmers used old Highway 66 on their journey to California. When I was in Elk City, a teacher told me how children of the desperate would come to her school to ask for food. The principal told the teachers to give nothing to the children, so of course the woman obeyed him. She said so.

In 1970 and 1971 he thought he showed the classical signs of a man who was mentally ill, who had been driven to it by a war which everyone at home ignored. It did no good to say that his own father, Okla, would have understood the evil of the war, for Okla was dying during the months he and Linda were home in Oklahoma, and could not even hear about it. He could not be kind to John and Pauline Hassler, his wife's parents, who lived in Nichols Hills, a fancy suburb of Oklahoma City. There was the time when John Hassler said to a friend that the invasion of Cambodia by the Americans and South Vietnamese was probably a good thing and was mystified by his son-in-law's behavior. When in June 1970 Albert Lee and Linda Reynolds went to New York to live, his letters to the Hasslers were so harsh that Pauline Hassler began to intercept the mail he sent to her husband.

"I even wrote them a letter saying they were a witch and a warlock dancing on the graves of nineteen-year-olds," Mr. Reynolds said. "I thought they didn't understand the death and horror of it and I had to make them understand. Linda used to say 'Why have you singled them out for all this?'" But he could not tell her the reason, could never give her a good one. One time he even turned on Linda, whom he loves. It was a summer night in 1970. Leaving his office at the World Trade Center, he saw a group of men in wheelchairs at the foot of Dey Street. They were paraplegics, injured in Vietnam, trying to collect signatures for more extensive and better medical facilities for men like themselves with spinal-cord injuries. They had come from the V.A. Hospital on Kingsbridge Road in the Bronx. There were not many names on the petition, people were in a hurry to get home. When he came back that night to Linda, he was in the same state she had seen so many times in Bangkok when he had just come back from Saigon. He told her about the paraplegics. Linda was calm; she does not know how to be otherwise. That night he did not want her to be calm; he wanted her to cry out or rage too. He said she had no feelings about the death and horror of that war. He went at her, she cried out, he hit her again, she had no idea how to defend herself or push him back. He must have been crying and yelling all the time. He never forgave himself for that night—for years he kept confiding that he had broken her little finger—but it made him understand why men in Vietnam sometimes went "awry" when they came home, he said.

During the years in Southeast Asia, when he would feel himself lurching and falling back into the hole in his life, the hole he called Vietnam, the Bible would steady him or get him through the moments that were so hard. In Elk City his family always went to the First Baptist Church. For years Albert Lee Reynolds went to Sunday School at 9:45, a church service at 11 A.M. Then there was Training Union—an evening service for the young— before the last church service at 8 P.M. This was the reason he knew and loved the New Testament and could not help himself, so many years later, from quoting it to younger people in the antiwar movement. It did not matter if they happened to be Marxists or atheists or nihilists or were interested in Zen.

In March 1973 he volunteered to speak of his own experiences in Vietnam at the New York City Commission on Human Rights Hearings on the problems of Vietnam-era veterans. He put on his button, which said "I Support Vietnam Veterans Against the War." He told them what he had seen in Vietnam, what he had seen in the spinal-cord-injury ward at the Bronx V.A. hospital, where he had tried to be a volunteer but could not stand it. None of it was new; there were others who knew much more. His final words were: "What's done is done. We can't bring back the dead. We cannot repair those severed spinal cords. But we can, and must, help these veterans who are here today literally pouring out their souls trying to tell us what it's like. We must help them. Maybe that's the way to ask God's forgiveness. May God have mercy on our souls."

The way he talked, so different from others, startled some people and made a few men and women wipe their eyes, sigh and wipe again. But there were also those whom he made a little impatient. They thought he saw Vietnam as an aberration, that he had not learned the lessons of the war at all, or did not understand the reasons for it, and that he never spoke of the millions of victims who were Vietnamese. But he did not know any Vietnamese, he only saw them or exchanged a few words. There was a Vietnamese draftsman in his office and the whores who hung around hotels. He heard talk among Americans of how villagers were tortured; it was called the "Bell Telephone Hour." All that he knew he told. He never pretended to know more. It was always his belief then that if he kept on speaking about the carnage, other Americans would awaken and not let it happen again.

When the fiftieth-anniversary meeting of the American Orthopsychiatric Association met in New York at the Hotel Americana, he was one of the panelists in a round table called "The Vietnam

War: Consciousness and Conscience." There were many other workshops on the same day; not more than twenty people came to the Georgian Room.

He began: "I was a young man when we—my wife and I—set out to explore the world . . . the first overseas job was in Africa—that was the beginning—in and out of airports, strange ports in countries I had read about as a boy in geography class in Oklahoma. My wife was twenty-two and I was twenty-nine when it all began. When it was over, five years later, my wife was twenty-seven and I was an old man." Then it came out, as it had come out hundreds of times before: "In those days they were being slaughtered like animals—in droves—fresh from the high school study halls and the after-school football practice and from working on their old cars. Those were the days of Hamburger Hill. I wonder—I always will—what the real motivation was for the officers who made them run up Hamburger Hill to die. Was their motivation a mistaken belief that they were helping America? Or were they thinking about their next promotion and their combat proficiency report and their career records back in the Pentagon?"

His voice was not even as he went on. People were silent, as if he were pulling them into a place they had not been and did not want to go.

"Even animals—even animals—protect their young," Mr. Reynolds said.

The war electrocuted him. His office sent him out on a job to the Tan Son Nhut airport, where the military ran a mortuary for Americans. The bodies of the soldiers lay out of doors on concrete slabs. All was taken from them: fatigues and boots, socks and underwear, letters, pictures, dog tags, watches, love beads, peace signs on necklaces. The bodies were then hosed down—and it is this which he saw and remembered. He made the mistake of looking at faces, although in some cases the faces were gone. On another day in Vietnam he was being driven from Tan Son Nhut to downtown Saigon by a business associate, a heavy-soils engineer. Traffic was backed up because of ambulances crossing from the landing pads for medical evacuation helicopters bringing in the casualties from the field. The ambulances took them to the receiving area in back of 3d Field Hospital. It was not a great distance. The Americans were honking because the ambulances were holding them up, although they knew the ambulances must not stop. It was the honking that day—the way the heavy-soils engineer tapped his fingers on the wheel—that made him cave in, that finished the eager and hopeful man from Elk City, that made him something he could not even describe. He knew the receiving area at 3d Field Hospital because he had once gone there to get an ambulance for GIs injured in a jeep accident.

He speaks of it over and over again: how the soldiers lay so still on the canvas litters, their faces small, some blue, some too white; how their fatigues and boots were strained and mud-caked. He spoke of it so many times that his friends in New York, those who knew nothing and those who knew much more, grew accustomed to hearing it. They grew quite used to his letters that kept coming at them, always the same: the honking, the hosing, 3d Field. Sometimes he went to the 3d Field as a volunteer and the Red Cross ladies there asked him to push the magazine cart through the wards because it was a little too heavy for them. He remembers seeing a boy in a bed who wore a high school ring from Poteau, another small town in Oklahoma. It is always his habit to read class rings although he does not wear his own. The boy from Poteau had a terribly swollen face. They did not talk. In the wards, he knew the soldiers were people from his own life, his own class, people like his grandfather, Albert, and Okla, who were so easily made victims and did not know why.

"I was struggling desperately to avoid being sucked into that dark whirlpool of death and destruction and sickness, but it was no use," Mr. Reynolds said in the Georgian Room. "I went down—

America went down—we all went together." His eyes were very bright, but he was not weeping the way he used to during the nights in 1968, when there was fighting in Saigon, when he heard the war at night and prayed that God would stop it. Sometimes, when not even the gin-and-tonics would do it, he tried to put himself to sleep in Saigon by thinking again of Okla on his light-grey Ford tractor, going from one end of the field to the fence row and back again, always proud of such straight furrows. His life in America became strangely discolored and urgent.

He went to Fort Carson to testify for the accused in the court-martial of Private Richard Bucklin, who had gone to Sweden, then to Canada, before he came home to give himself up. The deserter had slept on the sofa of the Reynolds apartment in New York. He was charged with two separate violations of being AWOL. Before the trial Mr. Reynolds brooded too much about what he might say to make it clear, very clear, that Richard Bucklin was a decent and moral man, but on the witness stand his chance never came. He wanted the jury—officers and enlisted men—to see the courage of the accused man, but nothing of the sort happened. The defendant was sentenced to twelve months. Mr. Reynolds, who knew nothing of prisons, visited him at the United States Disciplinary Barracks, Fort Leavenworth, Kansas. The visit set him back quite a bit: the prisoners reminded him of the GIs in Vietnam. Many had been. Later that year he drove to Allenwood Federal Prison Camp to see a Presbyterian minister serving six months for burning down a small ROTC building in Hawaii. He bought a secondhand flute for seventy-five dollars to give to Nancy, the wife of the Reverend Robert A. Warner, because she had lost a silver flute she once owned and loved. It was left behind when the Warners, who lived underground for two years, made a sudden escape with their first child, a baby boy named Sunshine, from armed FBI agents looking for them.

Mr. Reynolds joined demonstrations, usually small and orderly ones. He always looked out of place; you had the feeling, as one girl put it, that he washed his face and hands before he went out to join them. In April 1973 he marched in the "Home With Honor" parade with a VVAW group; the youngest was three and the oldest of them was sixty-seven. They shouted, "No Honor Here, No Honor There." The parade, which had tens of thousands of marchers going up Broadway, lasted four hours; Army, Navy, Air Force and Coast Guard officers headed it. Among the marchers were an estimated one thousand Vietnam veterans still on active duty. The Vietnam Veterans Against the War group—which had fewer than two hundred people—carried huge banners asking for improved veterans benefits and unconditional amnesty. At the reviewing stand at 72nd Street and Central Park West, they knelt down on both knees. They chanted, "You can't turn your back on the truth, you can't turn your back on the truth . . ." The officers in the reviewing stand rose and turned their backs on the kneeling men and women, leaving only one man in uniform, a Medal of Honor winner, looking at them because no one had turned his wheelchair.

There were many people who waved miniature American flags; WABC donated twenty-five thousand of them. The weather made it a bright, sugary day; the large sidewalk crowds seemed cheerful and frisky. There were string bands, drum and bugle corps, fifes, bagpipes. He remembered how one man had kept shouting "Honor America, honor America" as they passed. That April day made him realize, he said, what it was to live in a country that had gone insane. Many people made a thumbs-down sign or shook their fists at the VVAW group; others, leaning over the sawhorses, spit at them, then spit again. Three antiwar veterans and a spectator were arrested at 62nd Street in a fight with a patrolman and a police captain. It was the only untoward incident of the day, the police said later.

He did not know how to make things better. In New York, for

five years, he held to the idea of eventually giving all the money back that he had made with Lyon Associates in 1968 and 1969. His total salary was $39,374.83; it was tax-free.

"It's dirty, filthy, bloody money," he told me. "Vietnam is full of bridges that I designed. I was one of the lower-paid civilians. It was a very profitable war—except for the soul or whatever it is that hurts so much now. All the time. All the time."

The giving-back began in 1970 when he went to the office of Vietnam Veterans Against the War to give them fifty dollars. Later, when VVAW accepted him, was sure he could not be an informer for the FBI, he went to them quite often and was most useful in helping to write letters on their behalf. It was the only place where he found his balance. He did not tell Linda that he wished he could rid himself of the $39,000. Most of the money was gone, but he did give away at least five thousand, mostly to veterans who were out of work, or those who needed a "little cushion," as he put it. They were the people he wanted to be with, not the men of his own age who had done well since he knew them at Oklahoma State and at Yale.

When a deserter was staying with them, his wife Linda worried that the FBI would burst in to capture the man and that their daughter Laurie would be taken away from them on the grounds they were unfit parents. He loved Linda for fearing for the child but it was not his fear.

"I don't see the FBI coming in the door," he said. "This may sound very naïve, but I'm very American. You know the song 'America'? And the words 'Thine alabaster cities shine'? Well, I've helped build those alabaster cities. Just because I think we were so horribly wrong in Vietnam doesn't mean I'm saying that I'm un-American." The alabaster cities are the two twin towers, each a hundred and ten stories high, the white spines of the World Trade Center in New York, which was largely financed by tax-exempt bonds issued by the Port Authority of New York City and New

Jersey. It cost $900,000,000 to build; one year it was reported that losses were running at $10,000,000. He thought the two towers were very beautiful; his New York firm did the structural designs.

One of the ways he tried to cure himself of Vietnam, aside from writing the letters, was to clip four or five newspapers a day and magazines. He kept the clippings in boxes in the bedroom—which annoyed Linda, for his files spilled everywhere—or sent them to people in the antiwar movement. The important passages he marked in red, filling them in with yellow so you could instantly see what had enraged him. *The slaughtering murderous bastard misses flying his helicopter* he wrote on an interview in a magazine with General William Westmoreland, who had commanded U.S. forces in Vietnam. When asked how the war affected the country, the general said he did not feel it was very great. "Nothing happened in Vietnam that hadn't happened in other wars," the general said. "But there was all this emphasis on the irregularities that occurred in Vietnam." *Irregularities!* Albert Lee Reynolds wrote on the margin. *The murderous slaughtering bastard.* When Secretary of Defense James Schlesinger said that the impact of losing part of Southeast Asia to Communists was "very slight weight indeed," he wrote, with his red pen, "*Then why why why were we there?*" He hated the Secretary of the Army, who wrote: "Is Army service an interruption in a young man or woman's life? Hardly. A golden opportunity is more nearly the truth." *Liar Murderer* he wrote. He hated President Ford for saying at the seventy-fifth annual convention of the Veterans of Foreign Wars in Chicago that "all wars are the glory and agony of the young." *No glory at 3d Field, no glory at mortuary, only death there* he wrote. The trouble was that he expected these men to repent.

"I want them to say they are sorry," he said. "They could do it again." It was a very long time before he realized no one was going to say such a thing.

When he was twenty, Albert Lee Reynolds went to Mexico and

visited the Basilica in Guadeloupe. Nearly twenty years later he can still see the penitents crawling on their knees over the paving stones, across a plaza, up the steps of the church, up the aisle, lurching slowly to the Shrine of Our Lady of Guadeloupe.

"America should be doing penance," he said, "She won't, of course, with her arrogance and her ignorance and her Cadillacs and bombers, but America should be crawling over those rough stones on her Red, White and Blue knees to do penance. We have abused and maimed and slaughtered our young. Look what we have done to Alton."

Then it was always Alton. He had been a corpsman, 2d Battalion, 9th Marines. In May of 1966, in an ambush south of Danang, he was hit twice in the leg with automatic-weapons fire. There was nothing unusual about this story except that when, at last, Alton was safe and out of there it all went wrong:

In Key West, at the naval hospital, I was in traction for six weeks with a splint on my leg. The flesh was draining constantly and they couldn't put a cast on the shattered bones because of this draining. They put four nails in my tibia with a bar and then I had a strap at the base of my heel which held up all the weight of my leg. I remember, even though I was getting morphine and Demerol every two hours, that I could feel the pressure from the strap and I kept complaining about it, but nothing was done, and when they took me down, the strap had cut through my Achilles tendon—severed it completely and destroyed my post-tibial nerve. They didn't tell me about that at the time. I thought my condition—the foot—was due to my gunshot wound in my leg, but it wasn't. It was due to the strap cutting through the Achilles tendon. I learned this from a private doctor in Miami later.

When I was in Key West, in the hospital, I was drugged

most of the time. They eventually took me off the harder injections of narcotics and put me on pills—codeine. I acquired a drug habit and they gave me no drug treatment therapy or physical therapy. They just gave me a brace and a cane and told me to go home.

Mr. Reynolds used these excerpts from Alton's letters to put in a biography for the Gainesville trial; he assembled biographies for each of the veterans in case the journalists wanted them. There was not much interest; the case histories were hardly new.

Alton's wife, Paula, wrote in 1975 to Mr. Reynolds that her husband had been apprehended for duplicating a prescription. He was briefly confined. "The day he got out of jail was the ninth anniversary of the ambush in Viet Nam and he's been strung out ever since. You've said before we can't let them take him. If he doesn't clean up, they've killed him . . . There are so few people who can really *see* Alton . . ."

Alton wrote that the doctors in the Gainesville V.A. hospital had amputated the smallest toe on his foot. There had been three earlier operations to straighten that one toe. He was learning carpentry, the letter said, he and Paula wanted a baby. He wanted to forget Vietnam and to forget that he was a cripple-for-life, for what?

In July 1974 Albert Lee Reynolds went to an amnesty workshop scheduled during a large two-day conference of the General Assembly of the Universalist Association at the Hotel Americana. There were only a few people who came that morning to the Chelsea Suite; other educational meetings had been scheduled at the same time. He took two women there to the coffee shop. They were Mrs. Helen Boston of Trenton, New Jersey, whose son Ronald was killed in action in Quang Tri in July 1967, and Mrs. Patricia Simon, whose son David was killed in action at Cu Chi in January 1968, two days before his nineteenth birthday. He knew quite a few women like them, always trying to save other people's sons. Both women work in the amnesty movement; Mrs. Simon is coordinator of Gold Star Parents for Amnesty, with headquarters in Boston. Her son had wanted to go AWOL to avoid being sent to Vietnam, but Mrs. Simon was uncertain of what to advise him to do. She had just moved to Newton Centre, Massachusetts, from Jacksonville, Illinois, with three young daughters. Her husband— whom she had left—wanted the boy to do his duty in the service. Mrs. Simon, once an elementary-school teacher, thought a man should advise the boy but she was uncertain where to find such a man. She went to a minister in Cambridge, who was of no help, who did not even know there was a draft counseling service in the basement of his own church.

"The three of us sat for about an hour . . . And I was rambling on, as usual, and probably saying the wrong things, and not knowing what to say to stop the sorrow, which isn't possible, of course, but wanting so much to stop it," Mr. Reynolds said. Mrs. Simon wrote to thank him for coming. "I wish you joy with your new child," she said. It made him weep. He thought of taking the new child, Patrick Albert, and the others and running away to live somewhere else so the boy would always be safe. He did not tell Linda this, and after a while the idea passed.

On Monday, May 12, 1975, an American cargo ship named *Mayaguez* reported an attack in the Gulf of Siam and seizure of the ship by Cambodian Armed Forces. The next day the *Mayaguez* was sighted by American reconnaissance planes near Tang Island off the Cambodian coast. A land-sea-air assault was launched on May 14; the two hundred Marines landed under fire in Tang Island—but the American crewmen were in a small boat, flying a white flag, in great danger from U.S. bombardments. As the little boat, manned by five Thai fishermen, approached the destroyer *Wilson*, air strikes were being carried out on the Cambodian mainland. The American attack was not halted when

President Ford received word that the Cambodian government was willing to release the merchant vessel and its crew. It has never been explained why air strikes were carried out on the Cambodian mainland at almost the moment the crew members were reaching safety. On May 16 the President appeared on television to announce the rescue was complete. There was elation everywhere.

The Harris Survey showed how dramatically the President's popularity increased after the *Mayaguez*. "The President's decisive action seems to have eliminated the negative effects of Vietnam and at least temporarily restored the confidence of Americans in their presidency," Louis Harris said. The Harris Survey asked a cross section of 1,428 adults across the nation for their reactions. Positive, 79 percent; negative, 18 percent, not sure, 3 percent. Mr. Reynolds felt quite sick.

"By heavy majorities, Americans accept the White House's reasoning in responding to the *Mayaguez* incident quickly, decisively and with force, even if it meant the loss of American lives to rescue the ship and crew. For many people in this country, the incident seems to have provided symbolic reassurance that the U.S. has not 'lost its will to resist aggression,'" Mr. Harris wrote.

Before he moved to Richmond, Virginia, in August 1975, to a new job, Mr. Reynolds had yet another streak of writing, as if he were composing a last will and testament:

> We have rescued the *Mayaguez*. The President's men—in evening clothes—laughing over their victory. The President says "It went perfectly. It went just great." David Hume Kennerly's photograph captures their self-confidence, their assuredness, their glee. "I'm very proud to be an American today," says Nelson Rockefeller. "Damn, it puts the epaulets back on," says a White House aide. "We are not going around looking for opportunities to prove our manhood,"

says Henry Kissinger. "Blow the hell out of 'em," says old James Eastland.

It's a hot Memorial Day weekend in New York and the tourists from Ohio and Pennsylvania and New Jersey are here with their cameras and we have rescued the *Mayaguez*. "There was all these deep bushes (on Tang Island). You couldn't see nothing," says Private Kendrick Deckard, nineteen years old, Nacogdoches, Texas, who was shot in the leg.

The Kennerly picture tells us that we haven't learned anything. Sleek Donald Rumsfeld, thinking about ambassadorships; Henry Kissinger, thinking about power and David Hume Kennerly, who photographed so much in Vietnam, now close to the power. Perhaps the picture tells us that David Hume Kennerly hasn't learned anything, either.

The death toll that the Pentagon chooses to release to us, as of today, has reached thirty-eight dead, with three others missing and presumed dead. Forty-one dead kids. There were thirty-nine crew members on the *Mayaguez* ...

As I watch the reactions, I realize that as a country, we learned nothing from Vietnam. A few—a small group in this massive country—have been driven mad by Vietnam. And the rest of the country has learned nothing.

Nobody wants to listen, Miss Emerson. We are like voices from the tomb. We remind them of death too much. They don't want to listen. It's really too ugly for the mind to comprehend.

It's just a matter of time until we do it again, Miss Emerson. All we can hope to do is postpone it for as long as we can. And all the energy and all the tears and all the grief were for nothing. But, of course, even knowing this, we have to keep on trying to postpone it because nothing else really matters very much, does it.

That's the lesson of the *Mayaguez*. "Blow the hell out of

'em," says old James Eastland, and Alton's dream is almost complete except for the child brought into a world with no more wars. And the *Mayaguez* steams on. And nothing has changed. We have learned nothing.

In Richmond, the Reynoldses' green frame house with its darker green roof is less expensive to rent than the crowded apartment in New York. The children have a large backyard. He still subscribes to the *Elk City Daily News*—Western Oklahoma's No. 1 newspaper since 1901, the banner says—but his letters on amnesty to the publisher and columnist, Larry R. Wade, have not made a dent. OH, GOD, SAVE ELK CITY FROM HER SINS, WE PRAY, a full-page advertisement for the Eastside Baptist Church said in April 1976, but he thinks unless the people of Elk City start caring about Ned Lemley, a draft evader in Canada whose father was Albert Lee Reynolds' Sunday School teacher, the Baptists are wasting time. He wrote the governor of Oklahoma—he had gone to high school with his cousin, Carlton—and several other governors asking them to observe Amnesty Week, February 22 to 28. They did not. His letters to officials are not so pleading now, no longer so certain that these men want to see justice done and the suffering stopped.

He began to see connections between the war and everything else. He read that 24,300,000 Americans—more than 10 percent of the population—were classified as poor in 1974, up from 23,000,000 in 1973. The official definition of the poverty level—an annual income of $5,038 for a non-farm family of four—seemed to him an evil deceit to conceal the real number of the poor which he thought must be closer to 40,000,000. He read that the top 20 percent of the population recieved 41 percent of all income; that the wealthiest 5 percent own 83 percent of all corporate stocks.

"We couldn't have done Vietnam without being this way," he said.

What he fears is that America has become a nation convinced

that the violent sacrifice of its male children is inevitable. War is routine, he says. He thinks Americans tolerate the intolerable. The sales on Veterans Day make him feel furious.

"Honor the dead of Khe Sanh and the blinded and burned of Indochina by saving up to $12.98 on a 12-inch Magnavox Color TV" he wrote on one newspaper advertisement. He thought the men who were war criminals had been forgiven and that Yale had much to answer for because of Ellsworth Bunker and McGeorge Bundy. After Mr. Bundy, chief foreign policy advisor to President Johnson, class of 1940, a former Harvard dean, now president of the Ford Foundation, was invited to speak at a banquet given by the assembly of the Association of Yale Alumni, he protested to President Kingman Brewster, Jr., in New Haven.

"We must think of national problems in university terms," Mr. Bundy said in his address at Yale. *Yale values and snobbery,* Mr. Reynolds wrote across an account of the speech in "News from Yale." *This man helped fill 3d Field.* Mr. Brewster, who had opposed the war, wrote him a sympathetic letter, pointing out that the role of some Yale men in the war did not "tar all Yale men of their alma mater; nor do its vices rob its perpetrators of their virtues in other fields." He reminded Mr. Reynolds that McGeorge Bundy was a "most accomplished, skillful and wise" Dean of the Faculty of Arts and Sciences at Harvard.

"Knowing Mac Bundy as I do, I cannot doubt his motivation, even though I may cavil at his judgment on the war," Mr. Brewster said.

The plan of Mr. Reynolds is to try to rescue people, one at a time. There is sixteen-year-old John Henry Rollins, who was imprisoned for breaking into a school after a long record of minor offenses. John Henry said he was being attacked and abused by other prisoners, so he cut his wrists "to get attention." It was the only way he knew. The boy is slight and considered slow. He was released last March in the custody of Mr. Reynolds and will live with the family until his sentence is finished. There is a deserter—who after spending seven years in Canada gave himself up, received a dishonorable discharge—sleeping in the porch room of their house. A few blocks from where the Reynoldses live is the Virginia penitentiary. He has been there to visit a twenty-seven-year-old veteran named Clifton Powers, Jr., who has thirteen more years to serve. The prisoner said he was in the 101st Airborne in Vietnam, started drugs there, was hit twice, won a Bronze Star for pulling a wounded infantryman out of the line of heavy enemy fire, was hospitalized in Japan four months for what he describes as a "nerve problem." He was jailed for breaking and entering while on parole after serving a year and four months for burglaries. His court-appointed lawyer pleaded there was no excuse for what he had done but that his Army record of service "says something about him." The judge thought not.

"Twelve million men served in the nation's armed services in World War II," Judge William E. Spain said. "I never heard a World War II veteran use that war as an excuse for a drug habit that led to crimes like those this defendant is guilty of."

"I couldn't take all the killings," the prisoner says. Drugs made it easier.

When Mr. Reynolds went to see him, with the parents, the father said Clifton had been "wild as a buck" when he came home, that it seemed as if his son kept wanting to tell him something but he couldn't get it out.

THE WAR BEGAN like this: one man died, then another, then one more, then the man next to that man. The dying was one by one. The war began to finish in January 1975 when the capital of Phuoc Long province fell. It was the first to go. Troops in the Army of the Republic of South Vietnam tried to stop the T-52 tanks of the Vietnamese from the north. ARVN had American-made shoulder-fired rocket launchers. They did not stop the tanks. American military analysts felt that ARVN might have fired at too close a range: a distance of thirty feet is necessary in order to destroy a tank. Then, one by one, the provinces that were threatened caved in. There were no great battles; sometimes men did not even open fire. In Pleiku, the soldiers ran through the streets shouting for the people to run for their lives, quick, quick. As the war rushed to them, civilians and soldiers fled Pleiku, for their own commanders had been told to abandon the city. A Vietnamese journalist named Nguyen Tu wrote this account from Pleiku for his Saigon newspaper, *Chinh Luan,* as he moved with the huge and weary file of people going toward the sea:

> Not a single doctor, either civilian or military, was to be found in the city.... No organization of any kind was set up for the evacuation en masse.... [The exodus] has given me such disgust that I find the slight hope I have been nursing in my inner self since 1954 has disappeared ...

Despair was not what the Department of Defense wished American military men who served in Vietnam to feel. Accordingly, as the country known as the Republic of South Vietnam grew weaker and dimmer, as its death grew closer in April 1975, James R. Schlesinger, Secretary of Defense, sent a message, unclassified, to the members of the Armed Forces:

> As the last withdrawal of Americans from Vietnam takes place, it is my special responsibility to address to you, the men and women of our Armed Forces, a few words of appreciation on behalf of the American people.
>
> For many of you, the tragedy of Southeast Asia is more than a distant and abstract event. You have fought there; you have lost comrades there; you have suffered there. In this

hour of pain and reflection you may feel that your efforts and sacrifices have gone for naught.

That is not the case. When the passions have muted and the history is written, Americans will recall that their Armed Forces served them well. Under circumstances more difficult than ever before faced by our military services, you accomplished the mission assigned to you by higher authority. In combat you were victorious and you left the field with honor.

Though you have done all that was asked of you, it will be stated that the war itself was futile. In some sense, such may be said of any national effort that ultimately fails. Yet our involvement was not purposeless. It was intended to assist a small nation to preserve its independence in the face of external attack and to provide at least a reasonable chance to survive. That Vietnam succumbed to powerful external forces vitiates neither the explicit purpose behind our involvement—nor the impulse of generosity toward those under attack that has long infused American policy.

Your record of duty performed under difficult conditions remains unmatched. I salute you for it. Beyond any question you are entitled to the nation's respect, admiration and gratitude.

On April 29, 1975, President Ford made the official statement: "This action closes a chapter in the American experience." It was not a war. It was an experience. The President declared an end to it on May 7, 1975.

MANY PEOPLE IN the United States, and the government itself, wanted a happy ending to the war which lasted twelve years for the Americans. They wanted to feel we had won something. In February 1973 it was the return of 566 thin and smiling men who had been held in North Vietnam. In the spring of 1975 it was the arrival of two thousand Vietnamese children, described as orphans, who were rushed here just before the Communists prevailed. In June it was the rescue of a cargo ship. But each time the illusion of winning was questioned and attacked: The *Mayaguez* was used as an excuse to bomb Cambodia and punish the victors. The Vietnamese children were snatched out of their country, when peace seemed certain, to reassure us what very nice and decent people we are. The prisoners of war would not have been captives if we had not bombed a small rural Asian country, and they were fewer in number than the Americans who died at Hamburger Hill. We needed something alive to forget the dead. These were the arguments.

Eight times in one day I saw on TV the prisoners of war returning and heard the little speech of the man who had been for seven years in prison, ending with "God Bless America," and hearty reply of the admiral, "God Bless America." It is perhaps my fault but I cannot help asking, in all sincerity, for what?

The writer of the letter was Maurice Braddell, of New York, who said he was seventy-two years old and had "got bombed and bombed and bombed" in England during World War II.

Each year that it lasted Americans who took opposite sides on the war seemed to hate each other more than the Vietnamese who opposed us. The quarreling was fierce; sometimes it did not seem as if the war alone could be the reason for the hatred. I have a box of this bitterness: they are letters written to Seymour Hersh, who in 1969 was the first American journalist to write about the My Lai massacre and Lieutenant William Calley and Charlie Company. In 1970 he won a Pulitzer Prize and his book describing the massacre and the participants, *My Lai 4*, was published. He often appeared on national television. Some letters said he had written about the massacre of the Vietnamese because he was a Jew. Condemnations were often written by other Jews, who thought he would make trouble for all of them. Mr. Hersh read each of the letters once and did not answer any of them.

A woman named Rosenfeld wrote she had seen Mr. Hersh on NBC. "You Jewish boys are well known for making a buck on our poor fighting boys," she said. Another woman in Beverly Hills, California, asked: "How can you live with yourself when you are a Judas to our Army and country. Your face shows it! I'll bet you and your family never went to war." From New Orleans still another woman wrote: "How much did Hanoi pay you?"

One letter said: "You are a lousy stinking anti-American and should be kicked out of the U.S. You went on an ego trip on the My Lai affair, just to get your name in the papers. All lousy jews are alike. Give them protection and let them come into the Country, and immediately they start an underground revolution. Heads of every country know this and Hitler was wise to the Jews. Too bad he didn't get rid of them all—what a lovely planet this would be without them."

A retired captain in the Air Force wrote that his son had served with the Americal—the division of Lieutenant William Calley and of Charlie Company—in Chu Lai. His son only saw Jews at desk jobs. The father said: "One cheerful possibility remains however, that if and when we are attacked and overwhelmed by the Reds, the potion to be meted out to you so-called Jewish intelligentsia could well be another holocaust even as your widely-shouted six millions in Germany."

A letter from a doctor and his wife in Albuquerque, New Mexico, said that they "never for a minute doubted My Lai . . . We are sure there have been tens of thousands of similar 'atrocities' committed by our GIs and other fighting men in the history of this great Nation. A soldier is a murderer only when he kills his own allies, not in the line of duty." It was their feeling that President Nixon should award Lieutenant Calley the Medal of Honor and a presidential pardon. As for the protests over the bombing of North Vietnam, the couple wrote that in World War II the bombing of little German villages like Hildesheim ultimately "broke the spirit of the German people and won the war."

The most desperate letter came from Mrs. Anthony Meadlo from New Goshen, Indiana. Her son had been in Charlie Company when they went through My Lai and left hundreds of dead civilians. She said her son "looked just like he had been whipped" when he came home missing his right foot. Paul Meadlo told everything, first to Seymour Hersh, and then, in a long interview on the air, to Mike Wallace of CBS. His mother wrote: "I only hope and pray that there will be a day coming that you will suffer for what you have done to us . . . You are so rotten you surely don't have a mother or heart . . . so now you got him in all this trouble, now see if you can get him out of it. Your no good your filthy low down. I only hope I meet you again someday."

ON A SATURDAY in January, in the year 1973, there were many Americans who believed that Vietnam had finished with us at last. The peace agreements were signed on January 27. When it was dark, or nearly so, in most of the country, the cease-fire had begun. Here and there, church bells and mill whistles, fire horns and tornado sirens sounded. But in so many more places there was nothing at all, none of the shouting or singing of people who have finally had their way. An elderly woman in Virginia, who wrote poetry as a girl, said it was not a night to put flowers in our blood. She remembered the strutting, the thumping, the kissing when other wars had ended.

There were no speeches. It was America's tenth war and the longest of them all. Reporters were sent out to ask people how they felt. Some felt nothing. A black mail-room clerk said the war had brought the South Vietnamese their freedom and given us inflation, high taxes and unemployment. A New York jeweler, Michael Berkowitz, said it was the only war he was old enough to remember. It made him feel "really bad" that he would not see a victory parade down Grand Army Plaza in Brooklyn, Mr. Berkowitz said.

Not everyone was indifferent, wistful or depressed. A New York executive on a travel magazine saw a bright future. "The end of the war is going to mean an increase in the travel business," Richard Gollan said. "There's no doubt that Vietnam is a tourist destination for the future, along with mainland China. If you have a lot of money to invest, Vietnam has beaches second to none," he added. "Watch the Holiday Inns move in. People will want to go to Saigon, which has the reputation of a lively city, and any American who gets there will want to see Hanoi."

There were no tourists during the war. Congressmen came, and student delegations; scholars and writers came, and once a delegation of clergy, who tried to chain themselves to the gates outside the United States Embassy to protest the war. They were quickly taken away. There were no tourists but there were postcards to send home to prove you were in a combat zone. It was the first war to provide postcards of American troops, in black and white or in color. There was "Mine Detecting" and "Street Fighting" and "Night Convoy Moving Cautiously," among others. Sometimes the postcards showed South Vietnamese troops, but the Saigonese did not like them much and they were expensive.

ALL OF US lived comfortably in Saigon; it was easy for well-paid civilians. In 1970 there were more than 2,100 Americans working for the United States Mission, the name for the embassy, the consulate and other government agencies such as Agency for

International Development and United States Information Services. It was the largest U.S. mission in the world. There were Western restaurants on or near Tu-Do Street, the pretty little spine of downtown Saigon, which once had trees that caught and held the rain. They were cut down to widen the street for military and civilian traffic. The good places to eat included Aterbea and Ramuntcho's, where Americans could have Bloody Marys, good steaks, salads that were safe. The doors of the restaurants were locked, even at noon, so the Vietnamese could be kept out. The fear was that Vietnamese soldiers would demand a table, eat, be unable to pay and make a scene before they left. There was the chance they would throw grenades or shoot. Perhaps the real reason was that it would make the Americans—the constant clients—uneasy to eat with them. Only the richest Vietnamese, or the most powerful, were looked upon with favor, but most of them ate at home. In the months before I left Saigon, the restaurateurs seemed more nervous. In February 1971, at Ramuntcho's, three Vietnamese officers did get past the man who let people in after peering at them through a peephole. The Vietnamese lieutenants were polite and solemn. There were white airborne wings on their shirts. One man was missing a leg but had pinned his trouser up rather neatly. His crutches seemed too high for him. The owner of Ramuntcho's, a short and swarthy fellow who was always amiable with us, spoke harshly to the officers and said there was no table. It was untrue; there was space upstairs. It made the officers very angry. They did not move. One of them—not the man with the leg gone—looked around the room, at all the foreigners, and said long and ugly things to the restaurant owner. None of us spoke or moved or looked up. The military police came and forced the Vietnamese out. We did not go on eating until they were gone.

Saigon was never a city that loved its own soldiers; they were too poor, there were too many of them.

The Americans endlessly entertained each other; there were many parties for those who were departing or arriving. Invitations were engraved. The June 1971 issue of the *Yale Alumni Magazine* had a playful letter from Ambassador Ellsworth Bunker, who was then seventy-seven years old. For seven years he had never faltered in supporting and augmenting American policy in Vietnam. He was thought of—in the kindest terms—as a fierce, brilliant, cold, stubborn man.

Sirs: This is in reply to your letter inquiring into the activities of the Saigon Yale Club.

Like the Yale band at half-time, we are strong on spirit but weak in form. We have neither an executive committee nor a headquarters—although one disappointed Saigon visitor did call my office recently to arrange for overnight accommodations at the Saigon Yale Club. There are also no dues and no obligations other than attending an annual dinner at my residence and a passing acquaintance with Yale songs. We have established the minimum in this regard as an ability to render at least one verse of the "Whiffenpoof Song" and the opening lines of "Bright College Years."

For want of permanent location, the Yale Club of Saigon is temporarily quartered in my residence, where we held our initial gathering on December 18, 1970. Fourteen Elis attended and were duly inscribed as charter members of the association.

The group was refreshingly diverse. It included representatives from our diplomatic and military services, private citizens, an academic, a vice minister and one member of the sixth estate. There was much talk of bridging the generation gap, Yale's football season, a few comments for the benefit of our brethren in Cambridge and, I must admit, a rather patchy rendition of Yale songs. Unfortunately, no photographers were on hand to record the event.

Membership in the Club has now grown to twenty-four

*and we would like to have as many associates as there are
in Elis in Vietnam. Regrettably, our list for the first gathering was quite incomplete. To correct this situation, I wish
to encourage all Vietnam Yalies to send me their names, in
care of the American Embassy, APO San Francisco 96243.
All are welcome, but we are especially interested in tenors, as
we would like to do justice to the songs at our next meeting.*
Ellsworth Bunker, '16
United States Ambassador, Saigon

In December 1971, much to Ambassador Bunker's pleasure, thirty-three men attended. Thirty-three Yalies, as they are called, came in sports shirts, except for a Buddhist monk with shaved head who wore saffron robes. He was the Reverend Quang Lien, a high school principal in Saigon. The ambassador was in an excellent mood. He spoke of the Class of 1916 warmly and his recent trip to New Haven for the fifty-fifth reunion. The Class of 1916 was behind the war, the ambassador had said, on his return to Vietnam.

There was one enlisted man, Specialist 4 Joseph H. Flynn.

When the ambassador took the floor after dinner, he said that the Vietnam alumni chapter had grown 250 percent in the year since its inception. The Yale Club of Saigon was up from twenty-one to forty-eight men. The growth rate, he said, was faster than any other program in Vietnam. There was gentle laughter. The Minister of Finance, Ha Xuan Truong, smiled too.

The ambassador told the men of his own military carrer after Yale: he had joined an artillery unit during World War I that was not sent to the front but south to Mexico to fight Pancho Villa. The ambassador said he ended up cleaning stables, much against his initial intentions. He added that he had been cleaning up after others ever since. More laughter.

The first song they sang was the "Whiffenpoof." No one could lead the singing on the piano but one man managed on a guitar. Voices rose and grew loud. "We're poor little lambs who have lost our way: Baa Baa Baa," the men sang. "We're little black sheep who have gone astray: Baa Baa Baa." The ambassador looked happy.

THE SEVENTEEN-DAY PERIOD of bombing began in December 1972. It cost $25,000,000 a day and sixteen B-52 bombers and two F-111 fighter bombers were among the twenty-eight aircraft lost, a man from the Defense Department said. The American bombing of North Vietnam was so precise that Hanoi residents felt it safe to come out and watch the attack on military targets, Dennis J. Doolin, a Deputy Assistant Secretary of Defense for International Security Affairs, told the House Armed Services Committee. No one hooted.

In Hanoi, Vietnamese officials were quoted as saying that from December 18 to December 29 about a hundred thousand tons of bombs were dropped on their capital. The Bach Mai Hospital in the center of Hanoi was bombed on December 19 and again on December 22. The hospital was destroyed. It is believed that twenty-five doctors, nurses and pharmacists were killed. When asked why the B-52s had damaged a hospital, Jerry Friedheim, the Pentagon spokesman, said, "We don't know what went on in that place."

A report based on a preliminary survey made by the North Vietnamese, and quoted by Hanoi radio on January 4, 1975, said there had been more than five hundred B-52 attacks against the North Vietnamese capital. The North Vietnamese asserted that the United States had razed what it described as economic, social, educational and cultural establishments in 353 places. Some areas, it was said, were hit as many as ten times.

The report claimed that 1,318 people were killed and 1,261 wounded by the United States bombing raids on Hanoi. The workers' quarter of An Duong was said to have been obliterated on December 21 by six hundred bombs dropped by B-52s. The bombs cut a swath more than half a mile long and half a mile wide in this section, destroying two hundred homes and schools, day nurseries, kindergartens, food shops and grocery stores. According to this report: "Kham Thien Street with nearly thirty thousand inhabitants, most of them working people, was attacked on December 26 by thirty B-52 bombers." The investigation said that 534 houses were destroyed, 1,200 others damaged and "dozens of food shops, pagodas, temples, kindergartens, reading rooms and libraries ravaged."

The bombing spoiled the Christmas of some Americans. It was reported that in Fort Wayne, Indiana, for example, nearly five hundred parishioners of St. Mary's Roman Catholic Church took away their big, gaily decorated Christmas tree from the altar. They tore the branches off and smashed the pretty little lights and decorations. The mess was stuffed into a large box and mailed to President Richard Nixon in Key Biscayne, Florida. He never knew about it.

IN PARIS THE cease-fire agreements were signed in the forty-foot-square ballroom of the old Hotel Majestic under a ton of crystal and gilt chandeliers. One wall was covered by a three-hundred-year-old Gobelin tapestry with hawks, doves, swans and other birds in it. Enemies and allies sat at the gigantic table—whose shape had once caused the Vietnamese delegations to quarrel—which was covered in yards of green baize. It was here, at the Centre de Conference Internationale, a six-story stone building on Avenue Kleber, that Ho Chi Minh had met with the French in 1964. On that Saturday in Paris, Secretary of State William Rogers signed sixty-two documents. "It's a great day," he said later at Orly Airport.

But the Vietnam cease-fire agreements were signed in what one observer called "an eerie silence, without a word or gesture to express the world's relief that the years of war were officially ending." The negotiations had taken nearly five years. The morning ceremony on January 27 lasted eighteen minutes; the afternoon ceremony, eleven. Madame Nguyen Thi Binh, Foreign Minister of the Provisional Revolutionary Government of the Republic of South Vietnam, provided a small surprise. She was dressed up for that day. Madame Binh wore an amber-colored ao dai, the Vietnamese tunic, with some glittery embroidery below one shoulder. She looked handsome and calm, a symbol of what 2,300,000 Americans who served in Vietnam called the Viet Cong and often thought of, the way one GI put it, as "runty people, with not much flesh and bad teeth."

Many Americans believed the Christmas 1972 bombings of North Vietnam led to the Paris Peace Agreement. Few knew that the Vietnamese Communists regarded it as a victory for them, for the agreement provided for the withdrawal of all U.S. troops, military advisors and military personnel associated with the pacification program, armaments, munitions and war matériel of the United States. It defined the military demarcation line at the 17th parallel as "only provisional and not a political or territorial boundary." It did not specifically prohibit military traffic between the two regions and it permitted civilians to move freely across the 17th parallel. It referred to "two South Vietnamese parties" as established governments without conferring sovereignty on the government of President Thieu, who had very much wanted this, wanted the total withdrawal of North Vietnamese troops, wanted the 17th parallel to be clearly defined as an international political frontier.

A majority of Americans, perhaps because the Paris Peace Agreement provided for the return of our prisoners of war, thought that President Nixon had achieved "peace with honor" and that the bombing of North Vietnam had done it.

IN ALBANY, IT made some people cross to see how Theodore S. Adams was carrying on about the cease-fire in Vietnam. A few seemed vexed by his good spirits. They told him the cease-fire meant nothing at all, that it was naïve and foolish to believe the United States was really getting out, that the bombing of Cambodia had not ended. Vietnam had been changing his life for so long, no matter how he tried to turn from it or keep it away. The war was like a wild and brownish wind, smelling bad, touching and pushing him even in rooms he knew and loved. He was forty-six years old on the day of the cease-fire, the husband of Rezsin, father of Frances and David, seventeen and twelve, an assistant professor of American Literature at the State University of New York, in Albany. He wanted to rejoice on January 27, even if it was just for a little while.

"It was like the day the children were born," Mr. Adams said. "You felt like rushing out to embrace the trees."

The pleasures of Mr. Adams were many: the writings of Willa Cather, some paintings in a local museum, and washing the dishes at night in the old-fashioned double sink, singing, as he mopped and rinsed, "Death and the Maiden" or "Yes, We Have No Bananas" or "Don't Go in the Lion's Cage Tonight." He had never wanted more than he knew in Albany: the family, the three-story old house on Chestnut Street, where he had a room of his own to work in, left quite undusted by Rezsin, who was too busy; his books, the library nearby; and teaching, which he considered an honor and a privilege. He loved doing lesson plans. Nothing in his life bored him.

It was easy when the war was still small not to think of it at all. But Rezsin, who was named for a Hungarian grandmother, did not wait to be told what to do. There were demonstrations, marches, vigils, visits to politicians, letters, peace groups. But he did not want to hear or see an inch of the war. The Adamses had no television set—just as they saw no need to own a car—so he was safe there. He was cautious listening to the radio. If a magazine showed six pages on the war, he skipped over those six pages.

But it did not work.

"I like American modern poetry. But every poet who was any good wrote about Vietnam. Even Marianne Moore, who approved of it, wrote about it. Every single one did. Conferences on the study of metrics would become a discussion on Vietnam."

The name dropped like a stone, again and again. He turned to short stories. Reading "The Greatest Thing Since Custer" by William Eastlake he calmed himself by saying that the author was using symbolism, the American soldiers had not really cut off and collected the ears of their enemy, such things were not done by Americans.

"It was a perfectly clear story," Mr. Adams said. "I just didn't want to accept what was happening."

Nothing had stayed the same at SUNY, where the middle-class children of middle-class people began to heave and yell, threaten and be rude. He did not know, having a slight aversion to most newspapers except for the *Christian Science Monitor*, which was always several days old when he read it, that other campuses were more chaotic. He had no idea. Although he approved of the anti-war activities at SUNY, the students often angered and touched and grieved him. He was damaged by them, as the war grew bigger and the draft grew deeper, taking a hundred thousand men a month. It became impossible to abide by his standards of marking fairly. He could no longer be scrupulous and just, when that was what had always mattered the most, even more than sharing "My Antonia" or "Shadows on the Rock" with them.

"I invented this crazy mark," he said, sitting in the little dining room of his house where the Great Books Club meets, confessing at last.

It was a B double minus. In those days young men would say to him "Are you going to give me a B or are you sending me to Vietnam?" He had wanted to tell them off, to say "What the hell do I care? Your work is poor work. I'll send you to Vietnam." But he could never have spoken like that, and he did not do it, even with the dumbdumbs, as he privately called them. The B double minus was to distinguish between the student who had a genuine B minus and the boy who must be kept back from rice paddies and guns and cutting off ears.

He had never wanted that kind of power, or even dreamed that such decisions would come before him. He knew the students were trapped in the university.

"In other words, they were saying 'Since I'm a prisoner here, you have to make it easy, and you have to make it fun,'" Mr. Adams said. "It was a terrible thing, it was a terrible thing."

He felt it debased him. Sometimes he would call in a student to whom he had given a B last semester and tell him that the mark was undeserved and that he would have to do better this time.

"If it was a cheaty B, I shouldn't ever have given it," Mr. Adams said. "What did I mean by demanding more work of him? Sometimes he would be resentful, and then I would be so impossible and angry, he would get yellier and I would get yellier, I would think what's wrong, should I go to an analyst?"

For the first time in his life he had put up a big sign on his office door: "Here is my phone number. Call me any time between eight in the morning and ten at night." They did. They wanted to tell him how upset they felt. He was kind, he said he knew, and did not give them advice, for he really had none.

He is a tall and slender man who walks on the balls of his feet, so it makes him bounce a little, like a pleased and eager child. Sometimes he wears a red bandana around his neck or a long scarf when it is cold. Rezsin is very small and round, with clear skin and a lovely smile. When friends drop in everyone sits in the kitchen, unless it is the Great Books Club, which always meets in the dining room.

She traveled often during the war. The telephone began to ring quite early in the morning. She belonged to the Capital Area

Peace Center, Women's International League for Peace and Freedom, the New York State Legislative Forum and Albany County New Democratic Coalition. He had never minded all that. He was proud of her. But he had never stopped teaching during the war even when there were picket lines and demonstrations. Nothing in the world could have persuaded him to cancel a class.

"For I had said I'll teach when I feel like coming to the classrooms and I'll teach when I don't feel like it," Mr. Adams said. "I felt the students had given no such promise. They were free to leave. I was not."

He had stood vigils with Rezsin and her friends, but it was hard to do and sometimes, after half an hour, he would think: Well, let the damn war go on.

On a Saturday, April 15, 1967, they had gone to an antiwar march and meeting in New York. In Central Park, where there were speakers, he had wound his scarf around his chin and worn earmuffs, for it was cold. He had a book with him, *Little Dorritt*. He did not see the seventy students who burned their draft cards. Next to him, on the ground, was an old lady of some eighty years who had a long snooze, which pleased him. People came and took his picture—he was not sure why, so he went on reading.

"A black man came up and shook my hand in the oddest way, in some sort of brotherhood way. It was very pleasant. Students came by and congratulated me, saying they were glad I was supporting them. All I had to do was sit and read *Little Dorritt* and I was supporting them."

He saw all the huge, foolish flaws of many of the antiwar groups, who often opposed each other on how to best oppose the war, but nearly eight years after it happened he could not, without his face changing, speak of a meeting at Union College.

"We ate a sacrificial meal of rice, and the ladies who cooked the rice were afraid it would be too bleak, so they dressed it up with something. There were six priests, two nuns; there were ten

Quakers and Rezsin, atheist priest of the Albany region. There was a woman who sang an ancient Hebrew song without accompaniment," he said. "It was a ludicrous affair and very moving. Perhaps it was the acme of the converted preaching to each other. And I felt something strange—severe, exalted, ridiculous."

He had cried violently.

When the war was very old, he asked the students what they thought of the December bombings of North Vietnam in 1972.

"There was a kind of rationed silence that you feel in a Russian play. It isn't that somebody's forgotten his lines or that something has halted. I would ask about the Christmas bombing, and a fierce silence, a fierce silence, would fall."

He had never been too fearful for Rezsin, who went to many marches, in Albany and in Washington, where no one seemed to intimidate her. A million voices raised and nothing coming back, he had said. She kept working. There was even a mimeograph machine in the downstairs hall near the kitchen. She was jailed once for three days. In his diaries he noted it all, briefly and without comment, making the books beautiful by pasting in pictures or illustrations which caught his fancy. But he had worried.

"I thought: She'll go all day, she won't be able to go to the bathroom and she might lose her lunch and have nothing to eat, she might not have a chair to sit down in, she might want to phone me and not be able to."

When the protests were still new and startling, there had been nasty telephone calls. Once he wrote a letter to a friend describing it all, on the back of a Democratic Sample Primary Ballot dated June 20, 1972, for he hated to waste anything. The house was always stacked with such papers that could be used.

"Some people would begin to rant right away. 'I want you to know how I hate your wife and the filthy rotten anti-patriotic activity she is engaging in. We're going to run her out of town, and that means you, too, Buster.' When I would interrupt to say

'Who is speaking, please?' they would reply '*Never you mind who this is.*' I would tremble a bit," he wrote.

It had exhausted and troubled him, making him see clearly that he was a man apart from the age.

"Any idea of any importance bores me, generally. I don't care who's President. I know Nixon's bad, but don't tell me about it. I know Dow Chemical is bad, but don't tell me about it. If Rezsin wants me to run to the post office at midnight, or lick envelopes, or fold mimeographed sheets—thousand of them—I'm willing, especially if the radio's on," Mr. Adams said. "But I want to give my mind to Emily Dickinson and Sylvia Plath. I know I ought to think about Dow and Nixon and Kissinger and the rest of it, and I can't. I'd rather cut out paper dolls, look out the window, day-dream. I know it's dreadful, but that is the way it is."

He left it to Rezsin, who had always understood. It did not in the least frighten or worry her after the cease-fire that the government appeared even worse, not better, than it had been ten years ago.

"We pushed and we pushed," she said. "So they stiffened." She knew there were people in Albany who had made fun of her, a middle-aged woman dressed in blue jeans and sweat shirts, but she did not care. It had been many years since she wore dresses or used make-up. It was easier to keep her long grey hair loose. She knew there were people who despised her, were startled by her, or astonished, or thought she was goofy and naïve. The war did not ever go away. It just became other places and other problems.

At the last vigil she had held up a sign that a Quaker had handed her, not even seeing what it said. The sign read: WITH MALICE TOWARDS NONE. It was the wrong sign for her.

"I don't feel that way at all," she said. "I see absolutely no reason we should forget or forgive those bastards."

In his classrooms he went on teaching, but sometimes he tried to poke the students very softly, to feel for a tiny gland that was not there. He wanted them to stand up for themselves. Do not pay

$1.50 to the film groups here to see movies that are badly projected and have bad sound systems, he would tell them. Don't pay, or if you do, go up at the end and say you want your money back.

Or he would urge them to refuse to let the registrar use their Social Security numbers and tie them into the 1984 world system, as he put it, reminding them of their Orwell, which not all of them had read.

"Just tell them they have to stop all that nonsense, I would say," Mr. Adams said. "But they only answer 'It wouldn't be of any use, they've got our numbers now, they've used them but they wouldn't tell us.'"

The new students were not ones to complain.

SOME PEOPLE WHO knew and even liked her thought that Mary Jane Nolan Kelly made such a fuss about the war because she hadn't found a good job with a future and wouldn't have a baby. Their feeling was that other people no older than she—the Vietnam generation who came of age during the war—had gotten over it and moved on. Mary Jane, however, did not settle down. The war caught and held her like a giant hook going through the chest; she heard Vietnam not as a name of a country but as a word for death and disgrace. She did not know many people who agreed because she lived in Bay Shore, Long Island.

On the night of the cease-fire she said the war had been won by the Vietnamese who had fought us, whose names we would never know. The honor and glory was theirs, she said, the ruins were us. That was the way Mary Jane talked; some people thought it was her Irish blood which made her excitable.

In Brightwaters, Mrs. Yale Solomon wanted to share a gift, which was a case of Piper Heidsieck, to mark the American departure from Vietnam. She and her husband, an ophthalmologist, invited Mary Jane and her husband, Peter, to dinner on the night of the cease-fire; three other people from the peace movement also came. Isobel and Yale Solomon were Mary Jane's best friends. They were so well known for their long opposition to nuclear weapons and war that at a Long Island bar mitzvah in 1972 one of their four sons was asked if his father was the "Ban-the-Bomb" Solomon. Mary Jane liked that story; it made her smile.

That night she kissed Michael Solomon, the youngest child, harder than usual. He was ten years old. "He had never been alive a day of his life when we were not bombing or killing someone in his name," she said.

There are a good many people in Bay Shore, a community of forty thousand in the town of Islip in Suffolk County, Long Island, who could not stand that kind of talk or such a peculiar pitch of emotion. She did not have many friends except the Solomons and some others who had also worked as volunteers for McGovern. In 1972, seventy-two percent of the voters of Suffolk County, which takes in the eastern two-thirds of Long Island, were for Nixon, which made it an unbearable place to live, she always said.

At the Solomons', there was nearly a whole bottle of champagne for each person. That was nice, Mary Jane said, but it had not been a gay, or even comfortable, evening.

The war was the hardest test that everyone in the Solomons' living room that night would ever have to face, she said, and they hadn't made it. With each march and each rally, she had grown less hopeful that anything would change.

"It didn't and it didn't and it didn't," she said. "So we ended up talking to each other because no one else would listen."

At times she exasperated and even bored her husband, Peter, although he, too, thought the war was wrong. But he didn't think of it that much, not all the time, as she did. He asked her why she took it so hard and why she felt so guilty. She never knew. Once Mary Jane Nolan Kelly said of herself that maybe "some of the right pieces were not nailed on."

That night, in Bay Shore, when she and Peter got home, Mary Jane began to look in her dresser drawer for something she suddenly wanted. It was a button that said CAMBODIA NO. She had first worn it in the spring of 1970 when the Americans and South Vietnamese plunged into Cambodia. For the next eight months she often wore CAMBODIA NO but no one really noticed one more button. She had thought of Cambodia as a plump and gentle country where there were small houses on stilts and yellow pagodas. She remembered reading of the confusion and fear of the Cambodians on the day they saw the war come to them on Highway 1, how some had bowed with folded hands to armored personnel carriers while others waved little white flags, unable to look into the faces of the foreigners. On the thirty-sixth day of the bombing of Cambodia by the United States, she put the button back on.

She and Peter met as undergraduates at a small Franciscan university in Olean, New York, called St. Bonaventure. It was a peaceful campus: no sit-ins, no panic, no fury, no threats to burn the place down. The males wore jackets and neckties, women wore skirts. The students were white, Catholic and mostly docile. She came there, not knowing much, from Butler Area Senior High in western Pennsylvania where she grew up, the oldest of ten children who learned early on how to cook, clean, sew, pray and not to be selfish or lazy. She was a pretty girl, very small and gay, with huge blue eyes and blond hair that she washed a lot and let grow very long because Peter liked it. At the university there was a mandatory ROTC program, considered the best route to avoiding a war which no one thought could last much longer. Peter joined ROTC because he felt it was an obligation he owed his country.

Some St. Bonaventure students surrounded the Administration Building with squirt guns to protest the war, but she thought it was a dopey thing to do. In 1967, teaching a class on the New Testament, Father Aeden Duffy, a middle-aged priest who had once been a military chaplain, was asked what he thought about the war in Vietnam.

"We were talking about the Sermon on the Mount and blessed are the peacemakers because they shall inherit the earth," she said. "Father Duffy told us 'If Christ were alive today, he would be a Marine carrying a rifle.' If I had been braver, I would have spit on him and cried out 'Shame, shame.'"

She transferred to another class, but the memory of what Father Duffy had said, and what she had not done, provoked her for years. Peter, who was in the same class, could not remember any such remark made by the priest.

Peter was inducted in January 1970 and assigned to Fort Sill in Oklahoma as a second lieutenant in an artillery unit. She had been working as an assistant buyer in a department store in Rochester, New York, until they were married on July 4 of that year. Mary Jane was always warning him about the war. "I said to Peter 'If you ever go to Vietnam, I will leave you. I will not stay married to you, that is my feeling.' Fortunately, Peter broke his leg playing soccer for the Army, so then they sent him to survey school, not to Vietnam as a forward observer."

He thought she was worried that he would be killed. But it was more complicated than that: she did not want him to have any part in the death of those small-boned people with black hair who never seemed to grow fat. They lived in a small apartment in a village called Medicine Park because she did not want housing on the base. In Rochester, she had once been on a peace march during her lunch hour, and had gone to the memorial services at the University of Rochester for four Kent State students killed by National Guardsmen.

She never saw the war on television or read much about it, but every day at Fort Sill she heard it. There was the artillery, the big 155 howitzers, firing on the practice ranges, so there was no escape from what she called "the booming and the crashing." In the summer of 1970, when Fort Sill seemed to swell and shine from the heat, there was a Firepower Demonstration Day. Wives and children of officers sat with them in a grandstand to watch a little parade and see the weapons working. There were old, wrecked cars, painted red and yellow, as targets for the artillery. Everyone cheered, even the very small children, when a car was destroyed.

"All those little babies around us kept yelling 'Hey! hey!' every time a car was hit," she said. "And I kept getting colder and colder, and I was shaking more, because there they were hitting cars but somewhere else those things were going into people."

Peter was always patient and kind when she acted like that. He liked the Army and working with enlisted men back from Vietnam because he felt it was a challenge to try to help them. After his discharge, at the end of 1971, they moved to Bay Shore. She did not get a job with a decent salary or a promising future, for in the spring of 1972 she went to work as the coordinator for the McGovern campaign when Isobel Solomon said everyone was needed. Peter was not pleased. Their total income for the first ten months of 1972 was $1,300 until he found a job in November. She was rarely home and he complained she was too wound up and working too hard. Peter thought some of the other McGovern workers were in it for a lark, and did not much like them.

Her mother was puzzled and asked Mary Jane why she wasn't doing anything. Mary Jane, who was working ten hours a day, had no answer. On election night she went to the McGovern headquarters in Bay Shore to watch the results, and a long time later she could still tell you what he had said in the little television speech he made acknowledging his defeat. She had not expected any of it to turn out so badly.

She sat watching television, drinking from a bottle of Boone's Farm Strawberry Hill wine, looking at Senator McGovern. "I don't think I'll ever forget his face," she said. "He said that he wanted us to remember that if we had made peace come any closer by an hour or a day, then every bone-crushing minute had not been in vain. I think I started to go down. And somebody came over and held me up so I could see the rest of it."

In February 1974 she saw Senator George McGovern in person for the first time when he made a speech at Brandeis University. She was startled, then angered by a sign in the auditorium, a big hand-lettered sign: "LIBBY STRAUSS SAYS HI TO SENATOR McGOVERN.

The sign did it. The students near her, squeezed together on benches, were puzzled by such unhappiness. Mary Jane Nolan Kelly, who was then twenty-seven, did not cry quietly, covering her face. The noises she makes are harsh and loud. That night her face was all wet and some of her hair too. She could not seem to stop.

She thought it was the cruelest of all endings: McGovern in a school auditorium telling the kids not to despair or give up, when none of them looked as if they had ever been tormented—a cool and critical audience who was not pleased with him for losing, and among them, Libby Strauss saying Hi.

"I don't like to cry, but it's something nobody can take away from me yet," Mary Jane said. "They can't stop it yet. No one can come to me and say, 'All right. You've cried your last.'"

In 1974 she went to a conference in New York sponsored by the journalism review [MORE] too see Dr. Daniel Ellsberg speak. When the panel was finished she went up to him and thanked him for letting the country see what was in the Pentagon Papers. He was polite and shook her hand. She took the sign with his name on it from the panelists' table to take home. Watergate, the tapes, the prison sentences, the resignation of a President did not make her gloat. Nixon had used up too much of her energy, she said, for hating always made you tired. It all came too late. It did not save a single life. She wondered if the disgrace was our punishment for a war. She did not think it was enough punishment.

"It's giving Congress too much credit to say they acted on Watergate to make up for the years they did nothing to stop the war," Mary Jane said. "They felt threatened but they didn't before because the blood didn't go on them or on their sons. It would have been easier, it would have taken less guts on a practical political level to stop the war. They could have done it without a lot of clanging and banging."

She never did meet Father Daniel Berrigan, whom she had admired so much for opposing the war. She thought that if she ever had been able to talk to him, she might have said: "Lead me, I will do anything that you say, what is it we must do?" The change never came. It made her angry when people said they were bored with the Berrigan brothers, that they were men whose time had passed, but it did not surprise her much.

After the war ended in January 1973 and ended again in August after Congress voted on June 30 to stop all bombing in Cambodia and then did not seem to end at all, she still could not look for a job. She was the campaign manager for a Democrat named Tom Downey when he ran for the county legislature, and won. Later, at the age of twenty-five, he became the youngest man ever elected to the House of Representatives. She was not proud of him. His voting record in the House was good, but she thought all Congressman Downey cared about was being in the news. "Mr. Hit-and-Run," she calls him. She quit politics, saying she was not meant for that kind of work, for caring so much about how people voted. At the end of 1974 she found a job in a large literary agency in New York although she could hardly type a letter; she had never wanted to know how. She still prays to St. Anthony when she cannot find something in the files.

In 1976 she was given a large black-and-white poster of Ho Chi Minh, sent from Bangkok, which she put up over her desk. The face of the dead Vietnamese so upset one of the older women that it had to be taken down.

She and Peter still live on Smith Avenue in Bay Shore, in the little shingled grey house that fills with sea breezes in the summer and is damp in winter. On one wall of their bedroom is an immense sign, meant to be pasted on a billboard, which says McGovern-Shriver. If it were on a billboard, the headlights of trucks would make the names glow at night. Underneath it is the name card for Daniel Ellsberg. She has no intention of removing them.

Their lives are safer now. Her husband has a master's degree in health care administration and supervises a Suffolk County methadone maintenance clinic. They have a car, an Irish setter, a decent income.

But there are days now when she wonders if she will ever put her own touch on the world. She does not drink Gallo wines—no more Boone's Farm Strawberry Hill—because of the boycott called by Cesar Chavez' United Farmworkers Union. It has come to that: the things she will not drink, the lettuce and grapes she will not buy. When the troubador, the child of the sixties, Phil Ochs died, it was a death that made her reel. The singer hanged himself at the age of thirty-five. She felt related to him, the man who wrote "Draft Dodger Rag" and "I Ain't Marching Anymore."

"I will never be the person I probably started out to be," Mary Jane Nolan Kelly said.

Yet no one could call her a sad or spent person. Just the other day she was talking about baby oysters being found again in the Hudson River. She was really pleased about the baby oysters.

"The one thing that's still walking from the sixties is the ecology movement," she said. "They can't knock it down or kill it." Otherwise there was not much left, she thought.

HE HAD ONLY a flashlight to wiggle on the night of the cease-fire. There was nothing else. Earl E. Rhodes, a fifty-seven-year-old bachelor of Durham, North Carolina, did not know quite what to do at first. He did not have a car with a horn he could blow. It was too dark to hold up a sign. He had always made his own, very carefully, on the biggest sheets of white cardboard, taking care that the letters looked as big and black as possible. It meant spending money to have the best marker, but he was always willing.

His favorite sign, which no one could say was inspired by Communists, was SEND LIFE NOT DEATH TO INDOCHINA. The last one he had made was much more daring: IMPEACH DO NOT INAUGURATE THE MAD HOSPITAL BOMBER. But there was not a suitable sign ready for this occasion and it was too dark to show one.

There was only the flashlight.

Once more he walked from Cleveland Street to the corners of Main and Morris, where five streets came together. It was always here, at Five Points, where the peace vigil had been held in a little park. He had stood there many times before, on Thursdays from twelve to one, often the only one to show up.

Mr. Rhodes was alone that night too. There were no pedestrians in that neighborhood. He waved and circled and moved the flashlight and made a peace sign with his other hand. Quite a few cars drove by. Some people honked for peace. He found that quite nice.

After an hour or so he went back to his rooming house, where he is one of twelve boarders but pays no rent in return for doing the chores of a caretaker. It is one of many in an old neighborhood of big crooked trees and dusty cut-up frame houses that have porches and very large cupboards. In his room there is a brown rocking chair, two other chairs that are stuffed, a high and neat bed, with Christ on the cross over it, and the first television set he has ever had in his life. There are some paintings he likes, and the calm of the room helps him to write his poems.

The retired clerk and schoolteacher, the survivor of five nervous breakdowns, the poet and the caretaker, was glad he had not just stayed in his room that night. Other wars had always meant disgrace and isolation, except for this one. He had been a pacifist since 1933, when he was a freshman in a Southern Church College.

In World War II he had been a conscientious objector who had been scorned and put away for not wanting to hurt or kill. He had been kept in three detention camps for four and a half years, places meant to punish and humble men like him. They were called Civilian Public Service camps and were often administered by church groups, although the entire conscientious-objector program remained under essentially military control and was subject to the whims of Selective Service, whose officials, throughout the war, reflected the attitude that such men were criminals. His home had once been in a village called Newport, in the eastern part of North Carolina. He was the son of a gentle, very uncertain schoolteacher whose condition was politely described as high-strung and a high school principal who was a self-made man of harsh and hammered ways. No one in Newport, aside from his parents and an older brother, tried to understand why he refused to fight. Other members of the family were aghast. The death of a first cousin, who had joined the Navy, raised their level of bitterness and kept it up there, like a black and crooked painting on every wall.

Twelve years after World War II ended, he came back to Newport to nurse his mother, who had Parkinson's disease. But there was no forgiveness from them. "Some of my closest and dearest relatives wouldn't speak to me," Mr. Rhodes said. "They were so intolerant. They still are. Still."

He was never violent or threatening during his breakdowns. He simply could not sit still, or lie down, as other people did. He could only keep walking, like a man with secret orders never to stop moving. Once he had been told that his illness was an acute and chronic anxiety with panic agitation.

But to see him is not to think this at all. He looks like a small American walnut of a man, with his precisely parted white hair and firm voice and lovely manners. He remembers trying to defend himself from his father when he was very small, but how the man would whack and hit him with almost anything, even a coal shovel, while his mother could do nothing but plead softly for it to end. She was more afraid than the child.

"I remember my father killing chickens," Mr. Rhodes said. "I used to run and hide because the chicken was me. I would feel like that chicken."

It had weakened and wrecked him for more than five decades, making him unable to teach, unable to work, unable to write as much as he wished. The most he could do was lead a small life, taking tiny and careful steps, staying away from what he called conflict or crisis.

But when he moved to Durham in 1969 things began to happen to him which he liked. He came to know young Quakers in the peace movement, who told him about bombing and antipersonnel weapons which are meant to injure, not kill, because the wounded are more trouble than the dead. He saw Senator George McGovern on television, and was so moved and so pleased, he rather rapidly composed two poems and sent them to Washington. He even tried to work in a local McGovern for President campaign office, where they had posted one of his own poems on a sheet of red paper as well as the senator's acknowledgment.

"There were telephones with many buttons on them. I didn't know how they worked," Mr. Rhodes recalled. "I knew so little. Another thing—they had this map showing where people could register. I could not read the fine print. I could imagine people calling up to know where to go. I wouldn't be able to tell them."

He spoke to a lady about his nervous troubles, and she excused him. No one was unkind. He joined the peace vigil and went to demonstrations. Once he was even called upon to make a speech at an antiwar rally in April 1972. It was most frightening, but he had tried to speak very clearly, in a distinct voice, so that everyone could hear.

"I did not know if I appeared absurd, but I wanted to partici-pate," Mr. Rhodes said. "It was not noisy or raucous."

For what he most feared and disliked were belligerent crowds who shoved and screamed. He had never pushed anyone or been insulting. No matter how dreadful the war was to him, he never said, "Down with us," or wanted the government overthrown.

Some of the old fears began to lift. It was not just the tranquiliz-ers which he had been taking for years. He did things which would once have been unthinkable and made him ill. He had, for exam-ple, organized a fast against the war for more than fifteen people. For nine days he ate nothing, only drank fruit juices. The twelve dollars he saved—later he was not certain if the amount was not larger—had been donated to a fund to help Vietnamese children.

The American Friends Service Committee in Durham went to Washington in January, and he went, too, for the first time. There had been a huge gathering in a church. For the first time he heard Joan Baez sing. He had never heard such a voice. It made him shiver. It made him want to get on his feet and holler his pleasure, but of course he did not. The next day he went, with others, to visit their congressmen, wearing his best suit, a brown one, and a good necktie. Representative Ira Andrews, newly elected, made some people in the delegation unhappy when he told them, rather wearily, that he would ask for a special briefing on the war. A red-headed woman told him sharply that neither the Pentagon nor the State Department would be the place to go to for the truth about Indochina. The face of Representative Andrews relaxed when Mr. Rhodes rose and spoke of their desire, as his constituents, that he vote to end the war, or to, in any way, help shorten it. Rep-resentative Andrews looked relieved as he listened to such a polite man who looked so respectable, whose demeanor was so pleasing.

In the office of Senator Jesse Helms, also newly elected and a man Mr. Rhodes feared to be of a reactionary disposition, an assis-tant told the group that they could not be given a hearing.

"He said the office was too small and that we would disrupt the work," Mr. Rhodes said. "By that time I felt my self-confidence coming along, so I spoke. 'Sir, we have come, some of us, hundreds of miles because of a feeling. We wish to express our thoughts and feelings about this matter, and if it is customary to give priority to the clerks in your office . . .'"

So the assistant to the senator heard them. Before they left, Mr. Rhodes shook his hand and sent his best wishes to the senator, whom he considered less than perfect but still a human being.

Long after the cease-fire, before the Congress ended the bombing of Cambodia on August 15, 1973, he still held vigil at Five Points. He had learned to speak his mind. A man walking by looked annoyed at the group and said: "Well, what will you have to complain about when they stop bombing Cambodia?"

Earl Rhodes broke the silence for once. "Sir, we are not complaining. We are witnessing. It is you who is complaining."

Sitting in the brown rocker, he said to me that the last few years had made him a happier man than he had thought he could ever be. People were beginning to speak out and to question. That was a marvelous thing for him to see. "I think my age saves me from the depression and cynicism that the young people might feel, for they see so little seemingly come from their efforts," he said.

It was different for a man of his age who could remember how he was raised and who had seen blacks working for old clothes and warmed-over food. He could still see them, sitting on the doorsteps, with the Blowing Flies around them, the name Southerners used for the flies that left their eggs or maggots on meat, the flies that always were close to the poor.

The last few years in his life had been brightening, Mr. Rhodes said. Brightening years, he called them.

I NEEDED TO find other women who knew what I knew, and more. I needed to talk to women who had seen unspeakable things, who were without self-pity, who had faced the liars and lunatics, who had survived all of it and, in surviving, made a difference. The second summer back, although she did not know my real reasons, Lillian Hellman said okay, come to see me. I was to do an interview, but I arrived on the wrong day and stayed for lunch, stayed for dinner, which she cooked, and stayed for breakfast. In Vineyard Haven, Massachusetts, the house with its rosebushes is on the edge of the ocean. In the living room is the high, stiff sofa with a carved wooden back which came from the set of her third play, *The Little Foxes*, which opened in 1939 when Lillian Hellman was quite young. Years later she taught the writing of fiction, not of plays, because she thought drama students were apt to be the show-offs. She was at Harvard in 1961 and again in 1968, at the University of California in Berkeley in 1970, at Hunter College in New York two years after that. She had been close to students in the antiwar movement, and gone on liking and caring for them long after those defiant and excited days.

"I never thought I'd live to see any kind of student movement in America. I don't think there had been one before," Miss Hellman said. "It was a great pleasure to see. There was a good generation in the sixties. The student movement is completely dead—I realized that at Berkeley—but I still think it deserves a lot of credit and did a lot of good."

She said: "It took me quite a while to realize they meant what they said. I don't think I ever recognized its importance. I know I didn't. I am sorry to say I learned a kind of caginess during the McCarthy period."

The fifties were a damn dull time, except for McCarthy and his purges, with a dull and stupid generation, she said. Her own generation had not been too great either. It annoyed her in the summer of 1973 that so many people were beginning to say they were terribly tired of everything they had been through in the last ten years, tired of Vietnam and tired of Watergate.

"Yes, but I wonder what they are tired from," she said. "What have any of us done to be tired? What are we tired of? We wear out very fast when it comes to something we don't like."

Some students surprised her in the early 1960s by asking about the Spanish Civil War—she had supported the Loyalists, the anti-Franco forces, and written from Spain—and later, in the same decade, there were students curious about the most bitter period in her life. It was the years, in the fifties, when the late Senator Joseph McCarthy publicly accused hundreds of Americans of pro-Communist activity and disloyalty to their country. She became well known for her refusal to give any names of any persons to the House Un-American Activities Committee. Others had.

"We forget everything. I think as a people we can remember almost nothing. That was one of the reasons I was sure the McCarthy period was going to be over, if one just had the courage to wait it out. Because we don't remember anything. We have no national memory," she said. "Maybe it's a good thing. Maybe it's a mark of a young and vigorous people. Maybe it has great virtue. The day he was over, he was over forever. I think we've already forgotten Vietnam. It's over there. It's as far back as Korea, except for the poor bastards who were hurt."

Sometime that afternoon, before she went for a swim, Miss Hellman asked me how many men had died in Vietnam. I told her.

"My God, that's the size of a town," she said.

The total number of Americans who died from January 1, 1961, until April 13, 1974: 56,555. There were 7,198 blacks. Sixty-four percent of the men who died in action were twenty-one years old or younger. Dead officers: 6,892. Dead enlisted men: 49,639.

There were two kinds of death: 46,229 men died from enemy action or, as the military describe it, hostile causes. Deaths from non-hostile causes, which are those that did not result from combat injuries: 10,326.

If a man's death happened because he ran into the blades of a helicopter, was shot by mistake, fell from a watchtower, sank in a river, was blown up by his own explosives, the Army said, in effect, his death had nothing to do with combat. The implication was that the war was not the reason.

The most common hostile cause was gunshot wounds: 18,447. Multiple fragmentation wounds: 8,464. Grenades and mines: 7,428. Non-hostile deaths by drowning or suffocation: 1,017. Suicides: 381.

Among the soldiers who died in Vietnam:

12	were seventeen years old
3,092	were eighteen years old
14,057	were twenty years old
9,662	were twenty-one years old

General William C. Westmoreland, who had constantly asked for more American troops in Vietnam, said in October 1975 that the press was sometimes "untruthful, arrogant and hypercritical" and that it "needs to examine itself as never before." He said he had no animosity toward the press as an institution.

"I did not exactly cherish some of the verbal flak my colleagues and I had to endure in Vietnam," the general said when he was on a panel of prominent people who had themselves made news at the Associated Press Managing Editors Convention in Williamsburg, Virginia.

He complained of inaccuracies in coverage of the war. For instance, he said, there were not 55,000 combat deaths, a figure he thought was widely circulated and reprinted.

The general pointed out that about ten thousand of those deaths could be attributed to accidents or natural causes. That many young men would have died on the highways or in other ways even in the States, the general said, but he added that to observe this was not in any way to minimize the losses "which we all regret."

In January 1976 the Department of Defense issued an updated fact sheet called "In Connection with the Conflict in Vietnam," which included casualties incurred in the *Mayaguez* incident. Total deaths due to hostile and non-hostile causes were raised to 56,869. It gave: 2,802 who died while missing, 80 who died while captured or interned, 798 men listed as still missing as of December 31, 1975. The wounded totaled 303,704. Hospital care was required for 153,329.

The Department of Defense does not give a breakdown of the serious injuries, so no one knows how many blind, how many burned, how many paralyzed, how many amputees there are.

II

FAMILIES: TOGETHER AND NOT TOGETHER

When American troops first arrived in Vietnam most of them were sent to the 90th Replacement Battalion at Bien Hoa, twenty-two miles northeast of Saigon, for what the Army called "in-country processing." One of the first things they were ordered to do was to write their parents immediately saying they had arrived safely in Vietnam. Later, when they were no longer new troops, soldiers wrote home to their mothers to send them all sorts of things: garlic salt, machetes, wire cutters, wading boots, tennis socks, pickles and certain knives. Many of the mothers sent cookies; I saw a lot of chocolate chip cookies. In the rear, on the big bases, the PXs seemed bloated; at Cam Ranh Bay soldiers could buy Koolfoam pillows, Shag Time bath mats, brightly colored oversized beach towels, Chun King chow mein and garlic sausage. Vietnam was never the same place for the million six hundred thousand men who were sent to Vietnam.

There were always soldiers who found it hard to write home; it required too much concentration, it was too hard to explain what was happening or not happening, they did not know how to say it. In the field the soldiers wrote the names of their girl friends and their wives on their helmet liners or on the soft jungle hats—they were Phyllis, Monica, Susie, Wendy, Linda, Maryanne. They wrote too on the camouflage covers of their helmets: F.T.A. meant Fuck the Army. Peace, Peace, Peace, said the helmet covers, Love,

Love, Love. It was sometimes a gaudy army: the soldiers wore love beads and peace symbols, crosses and bracelets woven out of black bootlaces, folded scarves or woven headbands around their foreheads, tinted sunglasses.

It was a defiant yet dispirited army. They were against the war, not because of political perceptions, but because it took away too much, it put them in danger, and they hated the nagging, the bullying, the hassling of the military. Everywhere we waved to each other by giving the peace symbol, the V, which meant getting out. The infantrymen—the 11 Bravos—liked to wear soft camouflaged hats; some hung the rings of grenades above the brim to show how many they had thrown. It was not permitted for the men to wear these hats when they went to a stand-down area or to the big bases. It meant they were out of uniform. It made them hate their superiors, who became the immediate, the visible enemy. On a C-130 from Cam Ranh to Saigon, just after Christmas, a Specialist 4 named James Blunt in the 23d Division, the American, kept talking about his boonie hat, as the infantrymen called it. Nothing he owned was so important. We were packed in as usual, shoulder to shoulder, knees almost touching in the long rows of web seats facing each other. Almost everyone except Blunt was going to sleep; there was no snoring, they all dozed quietly, like men who had been chloroformed.

"They're always trying to take it away from me but I won't let them," he said. Blunt was twenty-six and his platoon had called him the Old Man. The hat was discolored and smelled damp. "One lifer at Long Binh said to me that I couldn't wear it on the base and I told him I'd kill him on the spot if he tried to make me. He looked kind of startled. They won't let me wear it lots of places but I don't give a fuck. I do my job—I won't let anyone else walk point, only me, that's the way it is. This here"—the little hat was lifted up for me to see again—"is a kind of memento. There's my wife's name. She's my second wife. It's Donna, see. Well, when I wear it walking point, she's kind of leading me, see."

When Blunt the Old Man was wounded the platoon got the hat to him in the hospital.

In Saigon, I sent a telegram to the United States for a Lieutenant Alsup from Asheboro, North Carolina, whose wife had just given birth to a daughter whose name he did not know. The lieutenant was worried; his tour in Vietnam was almost over but he felt he should stay longer to be with his platoon to keep them alive. If the platoon got a new officer, a fool, or one who wanted medals, the men might be pushed hard to find the enemy and engage them. The lieutenant did not want any of his men put in greater risk. No one used the words "die" and "death." A man was hit, not wounded. If he was killed, they said wasted or blown away. He bought it, or he bought the farm. He was greased or lit-up. Death was the Max. Each year the language of the soldiers changed a little as the new bunch came in.

Even now, so many years later, I still have the scrap of paper the lieutenant wrote his message on. It says: "Michelle, I am thrilled about the baby stop I live day to day thinking of you stop I cannot bear to even peek two days ahead for there are so many left but not as many as before stop I love you Bill." But that day he could not make up his mind: to stay with the platoon or to go home to his wife.

The soldiers had a year in Vietnam, sometimes a little less. Over and over they counted each day gone and all the days left to get through. They counted all the time and told you fifty days were left, ten days, three days. The Army counted everything else, insisted that all things be counted, until the numbers meant nothing—but still the counting kept on. Sometimes there were contests for the troops which were based on points to be won and points that could be taken away. One contest in the 25th Division in 1969 called "Best of the Pack," was for the best rifle and the best weapons platoon in the 1st Battalion, 27th Infantry, which was known as the Wolfhounds. One award was a two-day pass for best weapons in Dau Tieng; the other, for best rifles a three-day pass in Cu Chi. "The platoon will also have exclusive permission to wear a special marked camouflaged jungle hat when not on operations," the announcement said. "Points will be awarded for the following":

> 5—Per man per day above 25 on an operation
> 10—Each possible body count
> 10—Each 100 lbs. of rice
> 15—Each 100 lbs. of salt
> 20—Each mortar round
> 50—Each enemy individual weapon captured
> 100—Each enemy crew served weapon captured
> 100—Each enemy Body Count
> 200—Each tactical radio captured
> 500—Each individual weapon captured
> 500—Perfect score on CMMI (inspection)
> 1,000—Each prisoner of war

Points will be deducted for the following:

> 50—Each U.S. WIA (wounded)
> 500—Each U.S. KIA (killed)

If a man was killed, his platoon was penalized and had less of a chance to win the pass.

Many men were desperate to get out of the field, but until they were sick or wounded there was nothing they could do except go crazy, but there was punishment for doing that. I knew some who drank bad water hoping to get a fever of unknown origin, others would not take their malaria pills. There were men who felt terrible, but it had nothing to do with their bodies. At Chu Lai, headquarters of the Americal, there was a mental hygiene clinic and a psychiatrist who saw men on the base and those who had been on the line. He had a tiny room: a table, two chairs, and another chair where I was allowed to sit in a corner. Each man had ten or fifteen minutes with the psychiatrist—a captain— who was young and had never seen combat. He had been drafted under the Berry Plan, which allowed him to finish his residency in psychiatry before induction. At any rate, the doctor let me sit in the room and take notes. The soldiers were asked if they minded this, but all they cared about was talking to him. Not one of them said they were ill from facing their own deaths, they only said how something was wrong. It did not take long to realize the doctor could only follow Army procedures, assure them that it was normal to be under stress, and let them be sent out again. Perhaps there was nothing he could do but give them ten or fifteen minutes, and some pills.

A platoon leader said he had been very dizzy and almost fainted during an attack and that an enlisted man had taken over. The doctor said that when you suffered from hyperventilation, it was good to do breathing exercises with your face inside a paper bag. The soldier looked hard at the doctor, turned his head to look at me, then we both looked at the doctor again.

He said: "Doc, we were taking fire."

"Yes, I understand, but how do you know this won't work unless you try it?" the doctor said. He told the platoon leader how to do the breathing—puff puff out, puff puff in—and that was that.

There was a very pale boy with blond hair that stuck up in back. He could not speak distinctly and for quite some time the three of us sat in the little room waiting for him to be able to begin. His trouble was that his best friend had been killed, but since then he had seen the best friend twice, standing close to him, smiling, looking as he had once looked. The doctor decided the boy should be put to bed for one day and one night and sedated so he could sleep.

"I want to call my parents," the boy said. He was not told yes or no. The psychiatrist said it was okay to let the boy go to bed for a while, but that was as far as the Army could let him regress. After that, the boy would have to go back on the line again.

MORE THAN MOST men he could make the other soldiers laugh. But he did not really joke or act playful. What came from him were huge, leaden outpourings of menace and of mockery. The other soldiers liked to hear it; there was nothing else to entertain them. Boredom glazed their dread and made their faces sink. In January 1970—when the war was nine years old and he was twenty—Michael Garrod of Palatine, Illinois, carried a light machine gun, the M-60, which weighed twenty-seven pounds. He was a grunt. This is what an infantryman called himself, but the officers preferred "trooper." What the soldiers did—the walking, the searching, the hiding, the waiting, the ambushes and the shooting—was known as humping. Humping the boonies, they would say, hating it. To meet the enemy was to have contact, to be in a firefight. It did not matter if the boonies was elephant grass or a rubber plantation with slender, sticky trees, if it was the great tangled blotches of jungle or flat, scratchy land. It was all of these things and more. After a few months the canvas in their boots turned a sickly orange color. When the boots looked old and deformed the men loved them at last. They were proof of the ordeal.

In an army of big men, leaving such footprints as no one had seen before, Michael Garrod was very big indeed. He wore out five pairs of boots in Vietnam. He had worked as a bricklayer after high school. In Vietnam he was called Cy for Cyclops, a name he chose because it seemed so fierce. Around his neck Cyclops wore a jumble of small charms on chains: a religious medal, a ring, a peace medallion and a shiny little swastika that looked like a bright and pretty thing until you came close. No one knew, no one cared, whether he wore the swastika as a joke or because it was an ancient symbol to the Buddhists, whom he had been sent to kill, and was often seen on Vietnamese graves.

Cyclops talked a lot, even to strangers, and he liked to say that ever since he could talk he could joke. A favorite theme of his was how the Army was screwing the men. "A thousand screws a day," Cyclops would bellow. The others did not disagree; soldiers are rarely bored to hear how pitiful and insane their lives have become. At the end of that January, when Alpha Company was sweeping north of Saigon in an area called War Zone C, Cyclops was no more or no less what he had been for quite some time: an unhappy man of great competence with weapons. He did not trust the M-16 rifle: it fired too fast, the rounds were so small you could hardly see where they went. But the M-60 moved him, it earned his love. Sometimes he would pat the M-60 as a hunter might lightly slap a favored dog. He was not eating much. At home he weighed two hundred and fifteen pounds; Vietnam took away thirty of them.

"We fight for each other. We're really tight here," Cyclops said. "Nobody else cares for us." They often spoke like this: in the killing zone, among their own, they were not lonely or selfish any more.

There was nothing special about that day; the heat stuck to the soldiers as if it was paint. They rested by a road in the shade, their helmets off. Only then could you see that their foreheads were not yet lined. Cyclops had a crew cut, and wore very dark sunglasses when he was at ease and did not have to shoot. He was quite frightening-looking, but all of them could be. There were two stories he told once again. The other soldiers laughed, for they made fun of civilians, that strange and fussy race of people who were always somewhere else, clean, rested, fed, fat, unknowing.

The first was about his older brother, Steven, who had spent six years in college and in graduate school. The two brothers were drafted at the same time. It was expected that Steven would be the first to go to Vietnam and that Cyclops would then not have to go. The military did not require two brothers to serve in Vietnam at the same time unless one of them volunteered. The reason was always clear: they both might be killed. But Steven bolted from the Army and went to Canada with his wife; he was AWOL for thirty-two days.

"Instead of staying in the Army and getting some good friends, he fell in with a bunch of shaggy peace demonstrators who talked him into it," Cyclops said.

This was the joke: Steven wrote Cyclops for a letter to show the military that his brother was already in Vietnam, in case he decided to give himself up. Cyclops did not answer the letter. He did not even keep it.

"Man, I burned that letter," he said. Steven then turned himself in and received lenient treatment. "He's in Germany now, sitting around, having a ball, and I'm here," Cyclops said in War Zone C. "But I'll get him. I'll make him suffer in one minute what we have to suffer in a year in this rotten place."

But the insistent clamorous dispute inside him kept leaking out; he always began to defend and explain the man he wanted to punish. "He was just telling the government to get fucked," Cyclops said with approval.

But you had to stop communism somewhere, you really did, and Cyclops said he did not have it in him to run to Canada. So many of them said this; it did not matter whether they believed it or not. The Army did not reward men for trying to find the sense, the reason, for what they were doing; the idea was not to think at all, not to have a poet with the M-60, not to have a platoon that read Carlos Castaneda. It was all right for the clerk typists because not as much depended on them.

The other story he told was about the head of a dead man, a skull. He sent the skull as a Christmas present in 1969 to his mother in Palatine. It cost $1.50 by APO surface mail. There was a Big Red One patch stuffed between the stained, uneven teeth.

"I didn't get a letter from her in two months," Cyclops said. "She didn't like it." That made the men laugh, too. They could almost see the woman's face, the way her mouth and eyes would change, when she saw what she was pulling out of the box.

Mrs. Garrod said it was quite a shock. More than three years later she still remembered the nastiness of it. "You know, I just couldn't take it out of the bag, I just laid it down and put it on the floor," she said. "I couldn't touch or look at it. I had to wait until Bud came home."

But Bud, her husband, had only laughed and put the skull on a shelf in the living room. It stayed there for a long time. Mrs. Garrod became quite used to it; her younger son was always a practical joker. She adored him, she forgave him, she wanted him back. It was typical of him to come back from Vietnam, without a word of notice, pulling up in a taxicab on an August afternoon.

"When I grabbed him his whole body was shaking," Mrs. Garrod said. "It took him three days to eat something. He just couldn't eat."

Mr. Garrod asked me if I wanted to see the skull. Mike—no one at home called him Cyclops—had taken it back. The Garrods lived in a ranch house; perhaps it looked so grand because Mr. Garrod did some of the work and knew what should be done. He was a construction engineer, an architectural draftsman, who liked to make his own wine and wanted you to try it. They had built a studio apartment for Mike right next to their house. He put the skull by his bed, with a decal on the forehead. It said: THE GRATEFUL DEAD.

His platoon had wired an ambush; a Vietnamese had tripped it and died for being in the wrong place at the wrong time. The Americans called it a free-fire zone and it did not matter what the

Vietnamese had wanted there, what he had hoped to find, if once it had been his village. They robbed him.

Cyclops said: "He was a Viet Cong. He had money. All of us got money out of it."

It was not a confession, he did not seek atonement. The dying and the killing had not bothered him at all, he said. Friends would come into the room and see the skull and go Wow, wow, what's that, as if they did not know. In the Big Red One he had gone out on shotgun operations where six men were dropped into an area for a week, not to fight but to find out enemy movements, then call in the howitzers, the cobras, the gunships to do the work. "We saw trees become toothpicks in front of us because we saw somebody moving out there with pajamas on," Cyclops said.

After Vietnam he had married a woman named Jan, who had written him so often when he was in the Army, but it had not worked out. Cyclops did not want to talk about it. He would tell you about the war, about dead friends, about torturing prisoners with cigarette butts, but he would not speak of her or why she had to go away. "She was something, she really helped when I was there," he said. "It wasn't her fault. I had so many diseases. Jesus, the diseases. Bamboo poisoning, two ingrown toenails, urinal infection four times!" More than that he would not say; the subject made him sad and sullen.

"I don't want to use Vietnam as a crutch," Cyclops said.

Before the war he had used grease on his hair and hit people and busted up stuff. Now the hair is soft, fine, long; it falls like strange ferns around the big, rough face. The skull was not his only souvenir; he has a collection of hats worn by Vietnamese soldiers on the other side, and there are his photographs of captured and dead Vietnamese, women and men, neatly arranged in a scrapbook with white covers and clear plastic pages. On one page you see the foot of a Vietnamese woman who was badly wounded, then shot through the head by an American lieutenant. Another shows a Vietnamese woman on the ground, the rounds of an M-16 in her legs, looking at the camera. A GI stands behind her. Her face looks bruised and her long black hair, in a bun, has not yet come loose. The Americans were always taking photographs. They could not stop themselves; it was an obsession they could not explain. At home the pictures went into scrapbooks arranged by young women, usually their wives. If the films had been developed on a U.S. Army base in Vietnam, any part of a photograph showing a wound or mutilation was blacked out.

I had it wrong, Cyclops said, he had nothing at all against the Vietnamese killed in the ambush. Nothing at all against the man whose piastres the platoon took, the Vietnamese whose head had been mailed to that big comfortable room.

"He must have been great to take all that shit he was getting from us," Cyclops said.

But he did not want to get rid of the skull. I thought we should bury it in the backyard. The Vietnamese who were deprived of burial or a fixed grave were called "wandering souls." There was great pity and worry for them. On a day of remembrance even the poorest Vietnamese offered prayers, food, flowers, incense for the wandering souls who could never rest. The graves of their relatives and ancestors were so important to the living. There was a poem Luong knew, written by the great Vietnamese poet Nguyen Dzu, about the wandering souls. He recited bits of it once in a café in Hue. It was most dreadful, Luong said, for a Vietnamese to be buried when his body was not whole.

Cyclops did not listen as I said all this, how I believed that the Vietnamese would have their revenge on us. He needed the skull. I thought it would bring bad luck. There was nothing to do.

CYCLOPS DID NOT ever attack his brother. When he was out of the Army in 1970, he went to see Steven, who lived in Birmingham, a Detroit suburb, with his wife. Cyclops described Steven as a high-strung man, a quiet one, who never raises his voice. "It was good, a very good reunion. I didn't feel like I had felt before. I really love him," he said.

During his tenth, perhaps eleventh, month in Vietnam, when Cyclops had been transferred from the Big Red One to the Americal Division, when the war became so very much worse for him, he thought of what Steven had wanted to do by going to Canada. "I kept saying to myself, 'If I had to do it all over again, I would have went his route.' I wish I wouldn't have went to Vietnam. I didn't care for the country itself."

The brothers did not talk about the war. Nothing was asked, nothing was told. It occurred to Cyclops that if Steven had been the one to go to Vietnam, he might not have made it back.

Their father: a large, hearty man, a buck sergeant in World War II, wounded by shrapnel in December 1944, hospitalized for four months. He wanted both his sons to enlist during the Vietnam war so they would get "a better shake." His boys are very different, he says; Steven took to the books and Mike was the rebel. He was proud of Cyclops, who had been promoted from private to buck sergeant and won a medal, for the father was once sure he would end up in the guardhouse. Both men had had basic training at Fort Polk, Louisiana, both were in the 1st Infantry Division, both were in combat. It made Mr. Garrod glow.

"Mike and I talk about combat, my war and his war," he said. "I'm glad I was in the 1st. Mike was in the mud, all right, he was in the middle of it." What happened to Steven—the student, the gifted potter, the gentle man—made him uneasy. It was Mr. Garrod's belief that Steven had been manipulated by the "peace people" into going to Canada. A very bad bunch.

"They were totally against this country," Mr. Garrod said. "Totally against." Mrs. Garrod said nothing. I thought she nodded, but her head did not really move.

The homecoming of Cyclops had been dramatic at first. "I've seen him sleeping—shortly after he came back I used to see him sleeping—and he'd be talking about things, yelling 'Get it over there, get over here,'" Mr. Garrod said, laughing. "He was still fighting it. That's the way he used to talk. Boy!"

The father did not stay in the room to hear Cyclops speak of the war, answer the questions, push himself back into War Zone C, Happy Valley, LZ Stinson. His mother stayed, but she had heard it all before, none of it was new: the ambushes, the snipers, the booby traps, the Chicano who once tried to take some chocolate chip cookies away from him.

At home he stopped paying attention to Vietnam, the protests and the fighting. The night of the cease-fire Cyclops was at the home of a girl friend, watching a National Basketball game with the Los Angeles Lakers, when the program was interrupted. He was indifferent about the interruption. "It wasn't peace with honor, it was just that we lost," Cyclops said. "We lost the war. They have a goal, they have the initiative, something in their hearts that says they're going to win. They don't even have anything to fight with; compared to us they're throwing pebbles."

But he wanted no part of it and he did not care what happened. The people or their history did not matter to him. "I hated them," he said of the Vietnamese. He meant all of them, except for a few prostitutes. One girl had given him a thin metal bracelet which he still wears. The women gave him decent memories; with them there were lots of laughs, he said.

When he was in Vietnam, Mrs. Garrod thought that if he was killed and she was given a medal, she would refuse it. She remembered hearing of a young woman who refused to accept the flag from her husband's coffin, and she understood this. She saw the big demonstrations on television. "We used to see those things on TV and we'd say well, that's good, bully for you, but it won't do a bit of good, and it didn't," she said. "It never did.

It took a while for Cyclops to calm down after the Army. He traveled around—to Memphis, to Detroit, to Gainesville and to Daytona Beach. There were a few mishaps. In Palatine he once tried to carry off a red velvet and wrought-iron chair from a local spaghetti joint called the Imperiale. In Daytona Beach he made a racket trying to kick down the door of a woman's apartment and the police were called. He had been drinking Ripple, a cheap red wine; in fact, he had finished two bottles before he kicked the door. In California he went to Oakdale to see a friend from Vietnam who made his living by feeding earthworms. In Riverdale he went to the address he had for another veteran who had driven a deuce and a half in Vietnam. But the house had burned down; there was a burned basketball in the swimming pool in back and furniture piled out in front. The surprise was that his friend still lived there although his mother had moved out. The house burned down because his friend had started to cook French fries and then fallen asleep watching television.

"The French fries blew up. About a week after the house burned down he smashed his mother's car," Cyclops said. "His mother told me that. We lived in that house for four days—he and a buddy and me. We were cooking in the fireplace. We went through about three loaves of bread. It was great. But the house smelled of smoke, there was smoke every place. But he lived there and he had a little dog, a puppy."

He missed the men he had known in Vietnam; the ones at home had stayed the same and it was hard being as close to them. Cyclops worked as a laborer for $245 a week; it was heavy work and boring, but he did not seem to yearn for much more.

The last time I saw him he was drinking margaritas in Chicago, wearing shoes with high thick heels that made him walk in a slower, more uncertain way. He was tired of being interviewed, tired of so much talking about the war, and the margaritas made him sleepy.

The trouble was that he had not made up his mind. It did not seem important, not even necessary, to have a distinct or coherent point of view. Vietnam was something that happened to him, it was not happening anymore, he did not want to keep going over it. What he could not say, but what he felt, was there was nothing clear or sensible to say about the war. It was too weird, too strange, it did not neatly fit into an explanation.

He was angry about the fuss made over the returned prisoners-of-war. "They were clean when they got shot down, clean and well fed," Cyclops said. "Way up in the air, they dropped all that tonnage. They just happened to get out of the air."

It did not impress him that many of the senior officers who were prisoners described how they had been tortured by the Vietnamese. "So what?" he said. "We did it to them."

There are things he remembers and wants back. There is the M-14 rifle, which he liked best of them all, and his M-60. Before he went to Vietnam he was a hunter; he shot rabbits in the backyard and birds with a shotgun. "I'd like to shoot up old cars, maybe an old tree," Cyclops said. "Instead of using a chain saw, just shoot the tree down. Shoot something, see what it does to it. That's one thing the war taught me, really. But I'm not into shooting something alive. Not even an animal."

In July 1973 Cyclops wrote me a letter enclosing the photograph from his war scrapbook of the Vietnamese woman on the ground with the shot-up legs. All you can see is her face and the GI legs behind her. The woman is not screaming or pleading, she is just looking at the camera. I don't know why I wanted the picture, but now I have it in a frame next to a photograph of Luong, his wife, Mai, and their three small daughters. The woman is in shock; the bad time has not yet begun for her.

In his letter Cyclops said that he had been traveling around a lot: "I've had a heavy thing hit my head and my life—my wife died in Oklahoma City two weeks ago and it is something very hard to

conceive—I try not to think about it but it's a real mind-wretcher."
He signed the letter "Love, Mike" with a little peace symbol by his
name. I assumed his wife was killed in a car crash. I wrote him I
was awfully sorry. That was the last I heard of him.

TWICE HE CAME to my room at the Hotel Continental and sat
in the old green armchair. He had been a soldier in the army
of North Vietnam. It was how he thought of himself. Luong
arranged the meeting. He knew of the soldier through relatives
of his wife, who knew the aunt of the boy, an aunt who had left
the north to come south many years before. The green chair was
strange to him. At first he was suspicious of its fat arms and high
back and its deepness, for in all his life he had known only benches
or straight-backed wooden chairs.

His name was Tien. He had been captured in a "liberated"
village in Quang Nam province a few months earlier while he was
convalescing from malaria. He was put to work in the rice fields
while recovering. His face was very round, not like the boned,
sharp faces of northerners; it was the illness that made it swell so
much. His hair looked very dry and stood from his scalp like the
bristles of a used-up brush. He could have been sixteen. He was
twenty-one.

So ill had Tien been that he could not walk quickly up the
stairs of the Continental.

It was his legs that startled me, not the illness that had almost
killed him. From his feet to his knees there were scars from the
ulcers and sores no man could avoid moving down the Ho Chi
Minh trail through the jungles of Laos. For three months, in a
company of one hundred and fifteen men, he had made the long
march south. "We walked eleven hours a day and the longer
we walked the more bored and morose we became," Tien said.
"There were many things I missed. First I wanted a real cigarette.

Then I wanted to see my mother, to be close to her. And then what I wanted badly was a whole day of rest."

After his capture he had been flown to Tam Ky in a *truc thang*, the Vietnamese term for helicopter. The words mean up and straight. Tien had felt a fear he could hardly describe. "The first Americans that I had ever seen were the two pilots. They looked unbelievably tall. So very huge. But they smiled down at me. I don't know why. Some of my panic went away."

I could not imagine chopper pilots smiling at any prisoner, but that is what he said. Then Tien asked if he could ever ride again in a *truc thang*. I said it was not likely.

He had dreaded being beaten by the Vietnamese who interrogated him at Tam Ky, but they were nonchalant and gave him a Salem cigarette. He was even allowed to contact rich relatives in Saigon who had left the north many years before, and it was decided that he would declare himself a *hoi chanh*, an enemy soldier who defected under the Open Arms program and was not treated as a prisoner of war. Tien had not defected to anyone, of course, he had simply been too weak to run away from a South Vietnamese platoon.

The last time he had seen his parents was on a June day in 1968 in his village, all that he had ever known, which was fifty miles south of Hanoi. "They gave a small feast for me the day I left home to go into the army. My father, who is a farmer, was unable to speak. There were no words in his throat. My mother could not help weeping. And I wept, too. As I left, she said: 'You must go, I know that, but try to come back.'"

In his village there were no men who had come back. There were no letters from any of them. Before 1968, men going south had been granted fifteen-day leaves, but after the Tet offensive these were canceled. No family knew, or wondered aloud, who had been wounded or killed. The soldiers who did return acted like men with stirring futures. They would boast about their weapons; it made the children feverish and dreamy to hear such talk.

A member of the People's Force, Tien was given a Russian-made K-44 rifle. Every day the villagers expected American bombings. Boys and old men passionately perfected their marksmanship. Targets were decoy F-105 U.S. jets, made of wood or bamboo, hanging from the branches of trees. Farmers practiced during their leisure time; so did students.

"The young did not take the war seriously. The only opportunity for us to use our guns was when American planes flew over. We were really disappointed when they did not come or if they only bombed another village in the neighboring area."

Mrs. Nguyen Thi Ho, a widow with five children, was a most prominent figure in the Fighters Mothers Association in his village, which all women were required to join. Tien remembered how she said to the others: "If all three of my sons are sacrificed in the battle, it is not the end of the family because I still have three grandsons, and at least one will survive the bombings of the north. If my three sons die, I will suffer as a mother but I will also be proud of what they did." Not everyone spoke that way, felt that way, he said.

All Vietnamese children in the north belonged to a Labor Youth force, were lectured twice a month by village cadres or political agents responsible for government propaganda. Over and over again he was told of crimes committed by the Americans and the victories of their soldiers in the south. After each meeting the hatred felt by Tien for the Americans soared and made him desperate to do something. "I thought that it was easy to fight against the Americans because even simple villagers could shoot down American planes flying over the north," he said.

Yet when his turn came to join the army, Tien ducked it. It was easy to do. Many others also avoided conscription, he said, usually at the insistence of their parents. For while the older people never openly said what they felt, they feared seeing their sons leave, since none were coming back for years, if ever.

"In my hamlet I knew of at least eight other eighteen-year-old boys who delayed going into the army, but the grownups all pretended they knew nothing. Some boys just moved to other villages to live with relatives. Others put off the army by reporting to the village chief. You could say 'I am planning to get married next month' or 'You see, my mother is very ill, so although I really want to go into the army this very minute, who will care for her?'

"I did not intend to delay joining the army, but my parents insisted I postponed it," Tien said. "I could not decide what to do. On one hand, I knew it was my duty to report to the army, to fight alongside the Vietnamese people against the American imperialists, to go south to see what it was like. But I did not want to leave my parents. I was afraid of being away from home because I had never been away from home before."

Finally, Tien, with a friend, had walked two miles from their village to the district town to report for duty. After four months of basic training in Hoa Binh province, the young soldiers were restless to start their war, nervous that it would be over too soon.

It took ten days for Battalion 1071 to cross the Annamite mountain range to reach the border of Laos. They passed by tree trunks on which thousands of men before them had stopped to carve their names, their villages and the dates of going south. Even battalion and company commanders had carved their names, Tien said, and the sight of those trees warmed him and made him feel less alone. I tried to smile to show him yes, I could understand that.

It was 6 A.M. when they finally reached the frontier. The soldiers crossed a rope bridge over a ravine. Go quickly, quickly, they were told, for the Americans often strafed and bombed here. Do not look back. But Tien did look back, he had to, and all he could see of his Vietnam was a blurred mountain range in the mist. He was told to move faster. Many of the men disobeyed, as he did, turning their heads for the farewell look.

The trail, to the surprise of Tien, who expected to see a wide road, began as a small lane winding through a bamboo forest. At first, after the days of wetness crossing the mountains, the soldiers were pleased that it was hot and dry in Laos, and Tien threw away his sweater so there was less to carry. The company moved apart from the battalion in case of B-52 bombings, but in the first days they were not fearful men.

Each soldier had a diary and could hardly wait to fill the blank pages. "The first day we cooked our rice in a rush in order to have time at night to write the first page in our diaries, how we felt being on foreign soil," Tien said. "I wrote pages and pages about the terrain, the scenery and my impressions of being on foreign soil. Some of us exchanged our diaries to read. A few wrote poems. We were all tired but too excited to sleep easily that night."

On the tenth day on the trail, the American bombers came.

The soldiers had heard about the B-52 strikes from some wounded soldiers who passed Tien's company on the trail. These men were Viet Cong, or southerners, who told of the terrible sounds and destruction of the giant planes. "One man told me 'You will never hear the approach of the B-52s. Suddenly there will be great undreamed-of noises around you, but still you never see the planes. If you are in the middle of where the bomb lands, you will die. If you are close, you will be deaf for the rest of your life.'" But an older veteran cheered up Tien by telling him, too, that the mountains and forests in Laos were so wide it was very hard for the B-52s to hit men. "He said to me, smiling, that the Americans used to kill trees instead of us," Tien said.

On that day when there was a B-52 bombing it killed two and wounded four. It was the beginning. The effect of the first bombing, Tien felt, made the soldiers move more slowly, as if, in some way, they had all been hurt. The cadres saw this. A few days later the entire battalion grouped together on the trail for their first meeting. "The cadres took one of the poorest soldiers and praised him in public for his efforts to keep up with the other comrades even though he was so small and feeble," Tien said. "Each leader of a company, of a platoon and of a squad then selected, and praised aloud, one man in his group for commendation by the battalion commander."

The only Laotians the North Vietnamese saw were waiting on the trail to trade their cucumbers and bananas for the salt or needles and thread or combs of the soldiers. The North Vietnamese never saw a Laotian village. Tien had hoped to learn something of the Laotians and their lives. He never did.

There were two possessions that Tien, and his friends, loved and cherished in the long days of the march. One was his diary—it is lost now—and the other was his hand-carved walking stick made of *song*, a special kind of bamboo in North Vietnam. All the soldiers had competed to make the most artistic sticks. Most men carved their names, while some preferred the words *Hoa Binh*, which means peace. "The stick was precious to me because it was one of the few personal possessions I had," Tien said.

The soldiers needed their sticks to ease their exhaustion while walking. In small passages the sticks helped them keep their balance. They could also be used to measure the depth of a spring they had to cross. When a tired man wanted to rest, he propped the stick up under his pack, so for a little while the weight was less.

"We called it our third leg. There was even a song sung by soldiers about these sticks," Tien said. "I sang these lines many times." And he did once more, in a high small voice, looking at the ceiling:

> *"It trains the legs for the long march*
> *without letting them get away.*
> *It trains the spirit to go forward only,*
> *never backward . . ."*

When Tien was tired of talking, when we could hear no more, I showed him my Philips cassette player and we listened to Country Joe & the Fish.

But not even Luong, who could dance back and forth between the two languages, could quite explain that music or why the American soldiers liked it. Tien thought the cassette player was a marvel, and looked at it carefully.

On the trail the soldiers passed different North Vietnamese who were stationed there. Liaison scouts met them and guided them down another portion of the paths, telling what dangers to expect, where hiding places such as caves or bunkers were located. The soldiers were often warned by the scouts to beware of what they called "leaf mines." These antipersonnel mines, dropped by U.S. planes, were no larger than a pack of cigarettes wrapped in nylon cloth that was the color of the brown earth or leaves on the ground. When stepped on, they could seriously injure a soldier's foot—and he was more trouble to his unit than if he was a corpse. This was the point.

"We walked eleven hours a day, always on the alert for antipersonnel mines, and the longer we walked the more bored and morose we became," Tien said. "So we became quiet and paid less attention—we just walked, walked, and sometimes the cadres started singing and we sang, too. But after the song, there was quietness again, only the sound of our footsteps and the wind running through the trees."

In his dreams he was a small boy again, standing next to his mother leaning against her, as she cooked.

The soldiers slept in hammocks, taking turns to cook their rice. They moved for seven days, then had one precious day for washing their clothes and their bodies. Their daily ration was 0.7 kilograms of rice, dried lettuce, dried pork or beef or dried fish. On rest day, as they called it, the men would catch fish by tossing a grenade into a stream, although it was prohibited. Only officers—or cadres—had cigarettes. The soldiers smoked water pipes with the tobacco they brought with them from the north.

Their company commander had sugar, tinned milk and vitamins as well as cigarettes, but his men did not resent it. "If you had better food, you had that much more responsibility," Tien said matter-of-factly.

His company survived three B-52 bombings. The worst enemy turned out to be the growing malaise of the soldiers, their exhaustion and malaria. "We were all fed up with walking—we wanted to get into combat," Tien said. "I stopped paying attention to the beautiful landscape—all my concentration went into keeping on walking, lifting my feet. Sometimes I saw nothing around me. Nothing. We passed many ravines, many waterfalls, many springs, but we thought only of one thing: washing our sweat off."

The soldiers had medicine, water-purifying pills and antimalaria pills. Tien said the malaria pills were not good. Out of one hundred and fifteen men in the company, twelve were so seriously ill from malaria they dropped out and never finished the march. Every man had malaria by the time the battalion entered the south, through Kontum province in the Central Highlands. The battalion split up; Tien's company went to Quang Nam province and separated into groups of five and six men. He was assigned to a "liberated" village to recover from his malaria. There was no time to say goodbye to his dear friends.

He did not easily speak of them, for the separation still pained him. "There was Hong, who was twenty-four, skinny but stronger than all of us. He was in love with his fiancée and every night he would stare at her picture. She would not marry him until he came back from the south when the war was won. Hong thought that meant only a year to go," Tien said. "The other soldier was eighteen. Ngoan used to dream all the time, he sang well and he wrote fine poetry. He was not much interested in politics, but people excused him, saying, after all, he was an artist. He hated

Westerners as we did, but there was always a little shade of doubt in his voice when he spoke of war. He told me that his two older brothers went south three years before. He felt they were both dead."

Once, on the trail, they passed a group of wounded southerners —soldiers in the National Liberation Front—who teased them. "Some of them told us 'Go fast or the liberation will be finished before you get there,' and this worried us very much. One man told me that it was easy to fight the Americans. 'They have very weak eyes,' he said. 'If it is sunny, they cannot see well.'"

Tien never did find out if the Americans were made helpless by the sun. He never fired an AK-47. His malarial attacks, which lasted two to three hours, were so intense that two soldiers had to hold him up as the company kept moving.

In Saigon, for the first time in his life, he owned a wristwatch and a pen. He wore white shirts. What Tien really wanted was to have his diary and his walking stick again, and to talk with his friends, the soldiers Hong and Ngoan.

He said wistfully he would like to find out where his unit was and rejoin it. But he knew it was not possible, he knew it very well, yet still he made this request. His relatives sent him to be an apprentice in a Honda repair shop, but he stayed listless and sad, a man of longing and few words, who did not seem to understand where he was.

THIS IS HOW Mrs. Joseph Humber of Westborough, Massachusetts, found out what had happened to her oldest son, called Teddy.

THE SECRETARY OF THE ARMY HAS ASKED ME TO EXPRESS HIS DEEP REGRET THAT YOUR SON, SERGEANT JOSEPH E HUMBER, JR. WAS WOUNDED IN ACTION IN

VIETNAM ON 19 OCTOBER 1969 BY FRAGMENTS FROM
A BOOBY TRAP WHILE AT AN OBSERVATION POST. HE
RECEIVED WOUNDS TO BOTH LEGS, BOTH ARMS, THE
CHEST, FACE, ABDOMEN, AND GROIN AREA WITH TRAU-
MATIC AMPUTATION OF THE RIGHT LEG BELOW THE
KNEE AND TRAUMATIC AMPUTATION OF THE LEFT
LEG ABOVE THE KNEE. HE HAS BEEN PLACED ON THE
VERY SERIOUSLY ILL LIST AND IN THE JUDGMENT OF
THE ATTENDING PHYSICIAN HIS CONDITION IS OF SUCH
SEVERITY THAT THERE IS CAUSE FOR CONCERN. PLEASE
BE ASSURED THAT THE BEST MEDICAL FACILITIES AND
DOCTORS HAVE BEEN MADE AVAILABLE AND EVERY MEA-
SURE IS BEING TAKEN TO AID HIM. HE IS HOSPITALIZED
IN VIETNAM. ADDRESS MAIL TO HIM AT THE HOSPITAL
MAIL SECTION, APO SAN FRANCISCO 96381. YOU WILL
BE PROVIDED PROGRESS REPORTS AND KEPT INFORMED
OF ANY SIGNIFICANT CHANGES IN HIS CONDITION.

KENNETH G WICKHAM, MAJOR GENERAL, USA,
C-2179, THE ADJUTANT GENERAL, DEPARTMENT OF THE
ARMY, WASHINGTON, D.C.

Then she found out more, and still more.

ADDITIONAL INFORMATION RECEIVED STATES THAT
YOUR SON, SERGEANT JOSEPH E HUMBER, JR. CONDI-
TION REMAINS THE SAME. HE IS STILL VERY SERIOUSLY
ILL. PERIOD FURTHER HOSPITALIZATION IS UNDERTER-
MINED AT THIS TIME. EVALUATION IS NOT CURRENTLY
CONTEMPLATED. YOU WILL BE PROMPTLY ADVISED AS
ADDITIONAL INFORMATION IS RECEIVED.

ADDITIONAL INFORMATION RECEIVED STATES THAT
YOUR SON, SERGEANT JOSEPH E HUMBER, JR. HAS

ARRIVED AT THE 249TH GENERAL HOSPITAL, CAMP DRAKE, JAPAN. UPON ARRIVAL HE WAS REMOVED FROM THE VERY SERIOUSLY ILL LIST AND PLACED ON THE SERIOUSLY ILL LIST. IN THE JUDGMENT OF THE ATTENDING PHYSICIAN HIS CONDITION IS OF SUCH SEVERITY THAT THERE IS CAUSE FOR CONCERN BUT NO IMMINENT DANGER TO LIFE. PROGNOSIS IS FAIR. HIS MORALE IS GOOD AND HE CAN COMMUNICATE. EVACUATION TO THE UNITED STATES IS CONTEMPLATED IN APPROXIMATELY TEN DAYS. YOU WILL BE PROMPTLY ADVISED AS ADDITIONAL INFORMATION IS RECEIVED.

ADDITIONAL INFORMATION RECEIVED STATES THAT YOUR SON, SERGEANT JOSEPH E. HUMBER, JR. HAS BEEN EVACUATED FROM VIETNAM TO CAMP DRAKE, JAPAN. ADDRESS MAIL TO HIM AT THE MEDICAL HOLDING COMPANY, 249TH GENERAL HOSPITAL APO SAN FRANCISCO 96267. YOU WILL BE PROMPTLY ADVISED AS ADDITIONAL INFORMATION IS RECEIVED.

REFERENCE MY TELEGRAM OF 27 OCTOBER 1969 STATING THAT YOUR SON, SERGEANT JOSEPH E HUMBER, JR. ARRIVED AT CAMP DRAKE, JAPAN. HE WAS NOT REPEAT NOT EVACUATED TO CAMP DRAKE. HE WAS EVACUATED TO CAMP ZAMA, JAPAN. ADDRESS MAIL TO HIM AT THE UNITED STATES ARMY HOSPITAL, CAMP ZAMA APO SAN FRANCISCO 96343. PLEASE ACCEPT MY SINCERE APOLOGY FOR THIS INACCURATE INFORMATION. YOU WILL BE PROMPTLY ADVISED AS ADDITIONAL INFORMATION IS RECEIVED.

YOUR SON, SERGEANT JOSEPH E HUMBER, JR. HAS BEEN EVACUATED TO VALLEY FORGE GENERAL HOSPITAL

PHOENIXVILLE, PENNSYLVANIA. YOU WILL BE NOTI-
FIED OF HIS ARRIVAL BY THE COMMANDING OFFICER OF
THAT HOSPITAL.

Many such telegrams were composed, all with instructions to Western Union not to telephone the messages. All of them used the same clear, correct and faintly solicitous language developed and refined by the Department of the Army for such purposes.

In Westborough, Massachusetts—a town of fifteen thousand in eastern Massachusetts—a notice to call Western Union for delivery of a telegram was left at the Humber house on October 30, 1969, at 8 A.M. No one was home. It was a small two-story frame house on South Street which the Humbers had been renting for five years. Stacia Humber was already at work that day; for fifteen years she had been employed as an assistant launderer at the Westborough State Hospital. Her husband, Joseph, had worked there as a handyman, but when I visited the family in late April 1973 he had been retired for some years—and it did not seem to suit him. His expression was suspicious and abused; when he spoke it was in short claps of thunder. His very bright blue eyes looked watery and accusing.

On that Tuesday when the notice of a telegram came, Mr. Humber was in Essex Falls, Vermont, visiting the couple's oldest daughter, Rosemary, who was married to a medical student named William Notis. It was Billy, one of the Humbers' three sons, who took the notice to his mother in the hospital and went with her to a telephone booth. Mrs. Humber had a lot of trouble. The Western Union office in Worcester told her they had no telegram for her. When she called Westborough no one in the Western Union office there could locate the telegram. Billy was a great help in keeping her calm and providing dimes. Finally she spoke to one man who seemed to have a more helpful spirit.

"I got real upset," Mrs. Humber said. "I said 'Look I have a son in Vietnam and this telegram is worrying me.' I demanded that something be done. He was gone for several minutes and came back and finally said 'Oh yes, I located the telegram.' I asked him to read it to me. He said 'Ma'am, I'd rather not.' 'What do you mean you'd rather not?' I said. He said 'I think it would be better if you read it yourself.' I said 'In other words, it's bad.' He said yes."

Teddy, who is Joseph Humber, Jr., had enlisted in the Army before he finished high school, after eleven years of education. He did well and was promoted to sergeant. He was an expert marksman and a parachutist. He was in Vietnam with the 173d Airborne Brigade for four months when that October he stepped on a mine near Bong Son and lost most of both his legs. At that time he was twenty years old. In November 1972, at Thanksgiving, he came back to Westborough to live at home, after surgery and prolonged hospitalization at the Valley Forge General Hospital in Phoenixville, Pennsylvania, and additional surgery and hospitalization at the Veterans Administration Hospital in West Roxbury; he also went to the V.A. Hospital in Jamaica Plains. Teddy said he was on his third pair of artificial legs.

All the children—except Jeffrey, a twenty-year-old college student—were at home that Saturday night when we talked. Billy, twenty-three, said he had wanted to be a conscientious objector but after Teddy was wounded he enlisted in the Army. Rosemary, who had two children, was there with her youngest child, a plump and docile baby. Kathleen, the youngest Humber child, was eighteen and also a student. We sat at the dining-room table, stitched together by Mrs. Humber's cheerfulness and calm, her desire to make the occasion seem normal to the caller. Anyone looking in at us might not have guessed that all the questions and all the answers, all the memories and all the opinions, had to do with Teddy's legs. They did not mind talking about it. Only Mr. Humber, who seemed the smallest and most frail-looking member of the family, glowered for no particular reason. The others did not look at him when from time to time he spoke.

The walls and floors of the house were not very thick. It was easy to hear Teddy moving about upstairs and taking a long time to come down the staircase, making slow, uneven thumps as he walked. His wheelchair was in the narrow hallway. Once seated, the ruined part of him hidden below the table, he was a pleasant-looking man, with dark-brown hair and deep eyes, big shoulders and strong arms. That night he wore a checked shirt with the sleeves buttoned. He rolled up the left sleeve to show the arm which still had dozens of tiny black marks made by shrapnel that had not yet worked its way out of the skin. Before the Army he had wanted to be a forest ranger, and now it was not certain what he could do. He said he had liked the Army.

"No, I would never have discouraged him from enlisting," Mrs. Humber said. "I never discouraged any of my children from enlisting. Just hope for the best." In World War II she had joined the Women's Army Corps and liked it. This may explain why Mrs. Humber is a neat and well-organized woman, why she kept the telegrams about Teddy, his papers and records filed in order in a Christmas box.

"I feel bitter about it, but not that bitter," Teddy said. "I mean, after all, we did save a lot of lives over there and we did save the country."

After he was wounded, Mrs. Humber said very brightly, everyone in Westborough was wonderful, wanting to console her but not quite knowing what to do or how to do it. She is an attractive white-haired woman, with a nice smile, who suggests that she has spent years learning how to keep propped up and cheerful. People in Westborough had started a collection to send her to Japan so she could visit Teddy in the hospital at Camp Zama, but then the telegram came that he was being sent to Valley Forge.

Kathleen, who liked being interviewed more than the others because she had never seen a reporter, was a lively, long-haired girl who held nothing back. She remembered, could not forget, how she had told her aunt when Teddy went to Vietnam that she was sure she would never see him again as he had been. "In the same condition" is how she put it, wanting to be tactful. Even so, Kathleen was not prepared for the news of Teddy when it came. "I think a lot of people were afraid. They didn't know what to say. You'd be on the street and they would face you, they didn't break down or anything, but they were afraid to come into our house."

Teddy did not seem to always know what the others were saying. He seemed busy with something else; perhaps it was pain. He sat at the table without moving, often without hearing. Once when the baby started whimpering, Teddy lifted his arms to take it, but the child was passed by him and quickly handed to someone else to cuddle and soothe.

"I think I can be very truthful," Mrs. Humber said. "I think most people will tell you the same. We realized there was a war on, we thought it was horrible, but actually you don't realize how horrible it is until it involves one of your own. I think any mother will tell you the same thing. Even the people in Westborough didn't realize the horrors of the war until Teddy was killed."

No one noticed that she said Teddy was killed. This is what I heard.

Rosemary said her brother was the first casualty in Westborough, which she described as "a middle-class, an upper-class bedroom town" where ninety-five percent of the students in Westborough High School go on to higher education. The people who were training for jobs, who were headed toward a profession, did not go into the war, she said.

Mr. Humber suddenly came to life, and erupted. "Money talks," he said. "I'll go back to the old saying: the rich man gets richer and the poor man gets poorer."

"Money talks," Teddy said. "People with money, people going to college on an athletic scholarship or something, they went into the reserves."

He knew nothing of the long history of Bong Son, a coastal city in Binh Dinh province, or what Americans had been there before him and the 173d. Few soldiers ever did. They did not care. The war was cut into pieces that never came together for them; all that soldiers knew was what they saw and felt in the months they were there. But in 1966, when Teddy Humber was in high school, the 1st Air Cavalry Division fought its longest and largest operation around Bong Son. The campaign, known as MASHER/WHITE WING, lasted for forty-one consecutive days.

There is a big black volume, a congratulatory record, of the history of the 1st Air Cavalry Division in Vietnam—*Memoirs of the First Team*, it say—that calls the Bong Son campaign a success. "The statistics of the operation were impressive: 1,342 enemy killed by the Cav, with an additional 808 killed by Free World Forces. Five of the nine enemy battalions engaged were rendered ineffective and three field hospitals were taken," the Cav "yearbook" says. No American casualties during MASHER/WHITE WING were given. It was always that way. The names of the different operations are in big black type, those foolish names the generals so loved: SHINY BAYONET, MATADOR, MASHER/WHITE WING, CLEAN HOUSE, CRAZY HORSE, WHEELER/WALLOWA ("the NVA never knew what hit them"). Even President Lyndon Johnson found some of the names grating. In talking to senior American and South Vietnamese official after the issuance of a joint communiqué at their Honolulu Conference, February 9, 1966, President Johnson spoke his mind. "I don't know who names your operations," he said. "But 'Masher.' I get kind of mashed myself." The name WHITE WING was added as a precaution against an unpleasant, or squeamish, public reaction.

It was Binh Dinh province, with its long history of resistance against the French, which became the focus of American hope early in 1966 for their pacification program. But year after year, despite the American occupation of it, Binh Dinh never became a place they could overwhelm and change to be what they wanted. The number of dead Vietnamese and the refugees grew: Binh Dinh was never pacified.

Teddy Humber knew nothing of this, or even which side had almost killed him. It was not so strange for a soldier to be unsure. "It could have been a dead round," he said matter-of-factly. "It could have been planted by an American."

"I think people over there began to live a much better life as a result of the war going on and our boys being there," Mrs. Humber said. Teddy did not contradict her. No one in the family called them Vietnamese, only "those people" or "people over there."

There was still shrapnel in his eyes. He had headaches, Teddy said. But all agreed that the Army had given him marvelous medical care; all praised the Army for keeping him alive.

"Yes, the Army—but the V.A. is very bad," Teddy said. "The people think they are doing you a favor. Even now you go into a V.A. hospital and they will give more attention to a World War I, World War II or Korean veteran than to a Vietnam veteran." Then he told a few stories about the V.A. hospitals he knew, how in the ward the most helpless depended on the other men to assist them, how sad a place it had been, how uncaring the staff was.

Teddy said he was against war, that he thought everybody was against war, and if they were not, they should be locked up. "But those people, they came to the United States for help. If somebody came to you to ask for help and if you thought it was worth it, you'd help them. That's what Kennedy did. Then the United States got more involved—in my estimation the politicians and everybody started to prolong it because the country was making money. America was making money on it."

Mr. Humber brightened. "Money talks," he said. Billy wanted to explain why he had been a member of the Baha'i faith, which he described as a religion of Persian origin that believes in all the prophets and is against violence. His allegiance to the Baha'i had diminished when he was at a community college and had so much work. Mrs. Humber smiled sweetly as Billy went on; she said she tried to be open-minded when it came to the younger children. Mr. Humber looked furious.

"I was against the war and I was for the war. I had a personal grudge against the war because it hit the home front, it hit my brother, okay?" Billy said. "If I had really done what I wanted to do, I would have probably gone over there and shot every one of those people over there myself. But, then, obviously, I was still against it, so there was a conflict. I didn't know which way to swing."

Rosemary said we certainly had no business telling another country how to run their country, but that the antiwar movement had not helped or even made a difference. This reminded Mrs. Humber of something unpleasant that had happened when Rosemary's husband graduated from medical school at the University of Vermont in May 1972. She could not get over the sight of some of the demonstrators, although they were few in number. "They were dressed as Chinese, with grey faces, no, white faces, whitish grey," she said. "With hunched backs and old dirty bandages. Dressed as Chinese, apparently the Communist Chinese people."

Rosemary corrected her mother: the demonstrators were supposed to be North Vietnamese "who were being tortured by the Americans." The demonstrators played a death roll on drums, she said. They shrieked and groaned. They carried fake guns. They fell down.

"I had a camera so, oh my, without thinking, I took a picture," Mrs. Humber said. "There were eight, maybe ten, of them. I think they were young people but they appeared to be very old people. It was eerie, it was frightening, they looked so horrible."

"We were appalled," Rosemary said. "I think there was no reason to demonstrate at this particular graduation. They only chose it because they knew there would be news media there and they could get attention."

Mrs. Humber said it certainly wasn't called for, especially

during such a happy occasion. "I was upset because it was something I wouldn't do, and I wouldn't want any member of my family to do anything that violent," she said. "We all have our beliefs but we don't express them in a way that would hurt people. It was very, very wrong."

Teddy said people should be able to express themselves freely but without violence. Mr. Humber said there were a lot of Communists in the United States making trouble. He said it twice.

"Outside of the family we try not to express our feelings," Mrs. Humber said. There was silence. Then she said it was nice to have a family in troubled times. "Together but not together. It keeps you going."

"On the porch, as I said goodbye, Mrs. Humber suddenly looked less cheerful and serene. She had her head down. A few months later I went back to leave her a plant. Mr. Humber came darting out of the house as if he expected savage intruders and then disappeared again. Teddy leaned out of his bedroom window. His face looked strange and excited. "I'm busy," he called out. I said that was fine and went away.

You kept on seeing Bong Son in the wire service stories from Vietnam, the stories that no one ever read. In January 1975 North Vietnamese forces attacked three hilltop positions west of Bong Son. The military command in Saigon said the enemy fired six hundred shells at government positions, then followed up with an infantry attack. Reinforcements moved in and drove back the attack, the command said. Bong Son fell on a Friday; there was no fighting.

It was ten years after MASHER/WHITE WING.

STACIA HUMBER HAD many things to say when I saw her two years later. The family was no longer in the house on South Street. She and her husband lived in an apartment, but they were moving out because she and Mr. Humber, after thirty years of marriage, were separating. Mrs. Humber had retired from the laundry and at the age of fifty-six wanted to start over. The marriage had not been a tranquil one, she said.

"I think it was worse for the children," she said. Teddy and the other children approved of her decision. Billy had finished college and married a nurse. Rosemary's husband was a doctor on the staff of a good hospital and they now had three children. Jeffrey had married and gone into the Army. "That's my third boy; he's been in for a year," Mrs. Humber said. She regretted that he was not pleased with military life. It had something to do with some training he wanted but was not getting. Kathleen had quit college, gone to work for the telephone company in Boston and then joined the Air Force. Rosemary and her husband were heartbroken, Mrs. Humber said, but Kathleen wanted to "advance."

Her most cheerful news was that Teddy had been married on May 26, 1975, to an eighteen-year-old girl named Bonnie Ryan, whom he had been seeing for a year and a half. "You wouldn't know him now," Mrs. Humber said. "Bonnie gets him up and out every single day. So far, so good."

Only Billy had attended the wedding ceremony, for Teddy had not wanted the entire family to come. At the reception for twenty-five people, all the Humbers had been there. She showed me the color photographs: Teddy with a mustache, standing up, a white rose in his lapel, his hair cut, in maroon trousers and a striped jacket. He looked tall next to his wife, a tiny, dark-haired girl whom she described as ambitious.

"The state took her away from her mother when she was twelve," Mrs. Humber said, "and placed her with foster parents. Bonnie met Teddy through a priest who was counseling her. We had such problems with Teddy. I used to rush home at times and never know what I would find. If she sticks by him, we'll have no more problems. He had nothing to live for, you see; a child needs more than the love of a mother and father . . . He'll always be in pain. The stumps still bother him. He has headaches. But when his stumps blister he treats himself. He hates the hospital. He's scared to death in them. They're not very nice to him—well, a little nicer in West Roxbury than Jamaica Plains, but they have no compassion at all for these Vietnam boys."

The collapse of South Vietnam, the television films of a ruined army and of refugees were depressing. She thought that Teddy was resentful, but of course, his wife Bonnie didn't realize what it was all about. "Teddy is the type of boy that shows no emotions, he was always very quiet," Mrs. Humber said. "But there was so much sadness, the bombed people fleeing their homes, totally poverty-stricken. All those people coming here. America's a lucky place for them. They could never stand on their own."

The Watergate conspiracies, the jail sentences of important men in the government, the resignation of a President had been more shocking than Vietnam, Mrs. Humber said. Her husband came in as she was saying once again how much Teddy had liked the Army. "He wanted to reenlist, he enjoyed it and was doing so well," she said wistfully.

There was nothing wistful about Mr. Humber, who said no son of his would ever go off to war again. He glared. "I went through it once with one boy. I don't care what the President says, they'll stay right here in the United States," he said. "If it costs me the last red penny I got."

Then he began to cry. He kept looking at us as the tears went down his face. He did not wipe them away, blow his nose or cover his face. He did not seem to know he was crying. It was not over for Teddy either, he said. "The doctors told me they don't know where they're going to stop cutting," Mr. Humber said.

His wife protested that she had never heard the doctors say any such thing, but it was no use. Her husband gave her a dreadful look. Mrs. Humber said she didn't quite know what she'd do if another war like Vietnam meant her other sons would be called up. "I wouldn't demonstrate," she said. "I'd go along with it and hope for the best."

Mr. Humber had not stopped crying when I left. He seemed to be talking to himself.

WHAT IS YOUR methodology, a famous professor at the Massachusetts Institute of Technology asked me when I said I was writing a book on what the war had done to Americans. He did not see the joke when I told him half the book would be blank, to show there was no effect at all. Twenty-four states, I said, three years of interviews. He said it did not seem a precise or serious way to go about it. Most of the time I wandered about, talking to those who would talk to me. That is how I found Weasel in Michigan working in his backyard. At first I made a mistake and thought we had met before, on Highway 13, or at the Rockpile, when he was in filthy fatigues and wanted so much to sleep for two days in a bed with clean, cool sheets. Weasel was never there. It is a mistake I often make. A neighbor, who was separated from her husband, said Weasel was an angel, that he often came over to help her with her car, and that because he was so nice she did not mind at all the way his backyard looked, although some others in the neighborhood minded very much.

Weasel liked wearing a big-brimmed black hat, a dusty and banged-up thing, when he worked outside. The yard looked at first like a junk heap: there were beams and sickly-looking cars raised up for surgery, and lots of metal things lying about. The business is called Weasel's Towing. He also does wrecking. Perhaps it is the deep, scuffed hat, the long and very fine brown hair, a deeply ruffled sapphire-blue shirt Weasel often wears that gives him the look of a man on the run, a reckless and romantic quality on a street where nothing else is a surprise. Weasel can even use a blowtorch, wearing that blue shirt, without fearing that the sparks will burn his sleeve or skin. You have to know what you are doing, he likes to say. "I love to work, the harder the better," Weasel said. "In the army I worked KP like it was going out of style. I did it for thirty-eight consecutive days."

They began to call him Weasel early in school because he had a way of sliding out of things, although it is not clear what bored or displeased him, except for sitting still, perhaps, and grammar. Weasel talks in long, fast plunges, holding very little back, but finding it hard work to go much beyond the first bare outline of an idea. "Progress can't presume without war," Weasel said. "We've got to have the rich make war for the poor to fight. It's a hell of a way to put it, but there you are. Since we've had the war in Vietnam we've had more people working. There are more jobs 'cause more guys didn't come back. That is what we call progress."

Weasel wondered if I was the squeamish type. He spelled it out: everyone cared for one thing—it was called money. Their lives went into the getting and the spending of it, see? Men in his city did not hate the war, they hated being out of work, Weasel said. Ten thousand six hundred of them were laid off at the plant that spring; it was worse than the draft.

Nothing in his voice indicated mockery, sarcasm, wonder or sadness. It all works out fine in the long run, Weasel said. Two or three men he had known were shot up in Vietnam and one was killed, but their names did not come back to him. "Well, he died for a cause, didn't he?" Weasel said of the dead man, not wanting an answer. "The only thing that upsets me about the war is the draft dodgers. Those guys that went to Canada were just scared. Maybe the Communists proved a point: we've got more of them than ever right here." It was those Americans who disgusted him, Weasel said. He spoke as if the war—which he saw as a very important test of moral and material superiority—had not gone well because of them, the surrogate enemy.

Talking to Weasel was like watching an interview on television. The question goes out, the person responds, the face is before you, the voice is clear, the speech is simple. But what you hear is language you cannot understand, as if it were baby talk in Polish or Cantonese.

Why should men want to fight a war which, according to his theory, was conceived by the rich for the poor to fight? This was the question. But Weasel moved on, saying it had always been that way, that it made for progress.

Weasel is twenty-eight years old and the father of three children. He has had two wives, three ceremonies. The first was seventeen when they married, and there is a second wife, described not unkindly by Weasel as a Polack on drugs, whom he married twice. Now there is a small brown-haired girl, who wears shorts even on cool days, who carries their son, an amiable and alert child on her hip. A hillbilly, Weasel said fondly of her, and a good housekeeper, but he does not think he wants to go on marrying.

"I never went out on my wives," Weasel said.

This is how it went so often for me: people could not talk for very long about Vietnam any more than they could talk about the weather and the reasons for it. Asking them how they felt about the war, I have heard stories about termites, the evil of welfare, diets that did not work, poor bus service, abortion, the horrible costs of feeding cattle and teenagers, busing, crime, useless back operations, the evil of welfare, whether hair dyes cause cancer, how hard it is to pick tobacco by hand, the danger of eating certain fish, crime, the trouble with a car called Capri, busing, why Coca-Cola costs more than beer, ugly marriages, crime, and even how liquid vitamin E and butter can be rubbed on the arm of an addict to get rid of needle tracks. Sometimes I do not sleep well at all, wondering what it is that I am finding out and why some people insisted that after Vietnam nothing would ever be the same again.

Weasel said his earnings were four hundred dollars a week; fifty dollars is *payroll-deducted*, he said, for child support and is divided equally between his former wives, for each has a child. Weasel's parents had four children. They divorced and each married again. His father had three more children. Weasel left home at the age of thirteen to work for a farmer at seven dollars a week. "When everything here is going too fast I think I'd be happier on a farm," he said. Most of the time it goes too fast for him.

He lives in a city of 85,000; more than thirty thousand work for General Motors.

There had been ugly incidents and small but intense agitation about court-ordered busing, but Weasel did not speak of this. There had been very little overt reaction to the war. It was like the weather; people accepted it. He did not much like the controversy he knew it had aroused.

"It's a shame America is being put to dirt," he said. "Not nobody ever helps us at all."

He was drafted in 1967 and sent to Alaska with the 108th Engineers in the Quartermaster Corps. The Army was a challenge, Weasel said, for any man as competitive as he is. "I took pictures of everything I did," he said. "Everything."

He wanted me to see his house, anxious that I admire the crinkled, tufted, black imitation-leather of a couch, and two chairs, in the living room. Above his bed is the only cheerful and conclusive document Weasel may ever have: it is an honorable discharge from the United States Army, in a frame under glass.

A stepbrother named David, who is nineteen, drove with us back to Detroit. He had a big, dreaming, wide face and a low voice. He and Weasel liked driving around, they did it all the time, David said. He was in the Army on his way to Germany with the 1st Division, the Big Red One, as men have always called it. David had been told the way to get along with the Germans was to bargain with them over the prices in shops. He means to be nice and to make friends. At Fort Knox, David heard older men speak about the war in Vietnam: sharp and ugly scraps of stories whose beginnings and endings he does not know.

"The reason most everybody smoked a weed over there is because nobody could stand all the time to see some kid come up and blow himself up with a grenade," David said. The children would try to kill GIs. Vietnamese did not mind dying, which made it harder for the Americans. "See, the Vietnamese never really had anything nice, so when they see a pine box, when Charlie sees a pine box, he goes crazy to get in it."

Weasel had been talking about Walt Disney, whose death almost made him cry. He was slumped low in the driver's seat, one hand barely touching the wheel, the black hat making shadows on his face. He did not seem to have listened to the coffin-talk. "Them Viet-ma-nese have guts," Weasel said suddenly. "That's for sure."

Many Americans cannot pronounce the name of the race.

IF THE CHILDREN helped the National Liberation Front, they risked punishment, as did any other Vietnamese. If they were caught helping the enemy, there was no one to protect them. Nothing could be done to prepare them to rise above the punishment. It was often a complaint of the American soldiers that the Vietnamese children, whom they found so cute and so lively at first, so pleased to get candy and cigarettes, could not really be trusted. In the swollen, confused cities and near the American bases even the youngest Vietnamese became pimps and thieves. It often angered the soldiers when the children behaved in an ungrateful fashion. Sometimes they did things that led to the sudden death or injuries of the GIs, so even small boys were feared and hated. Many of the soldiers would say this only proved what a lousy country it was because the kids were into the killing. They did not understand that in such a war children are never left out, that in a country of such huge and dangerous disorders, the children do not stay childlike.

In Danang the police chief wanted to show how the local Communists recruited the very young and exposed them to risks. It was arranged that Luong and I could see two prisoners, one of them a boy who had recently been captured carrying explosives and weapons, and a girl who was a messenger for the Viet Cong.

Both came from the same village. Dang Van Song, the head of the Special Police Branch in Danang, supervised the interviews, which took place in an office. He had done many interrogations of youngsters; that June there were still seventeen children being held at the Detention Center. The largest prison for children was at Dalat in the Central Highlands, but reporters were not allowed in.

"During interrogation they know how to dodge questions like grown-ups do," said Mr. Song. "With children the interrogations are different; questions are put in a gentle voice and are simpler." Sometimes, he said the interrogators gave the children money to buy extra food because they were always hungry; Mr. Song said that the officials received only 27.4 piasters, or about ten cents, to feed each child a day. It was not enough.

The boy was twelve, Nguyen Dinh Chinh, captured in Danang, March 28, 1971, when he was carrying a satchel holding nearly twelve pounds of explosives, two detonators and two M-26 grenades. He was on his way to meet an older man, a Viet Cong agent named Huy, who planned to blow up the American headquarters of an Explosive Ordnance Disposal team in downtown Danang while the boy stood guard. In the four months of his confinement the boy's response during interrogations had not been "satisfactory," Mr. Song said, shaking his head.

Chinh shuffled into the room, uncertain where to look, what to do. "I was on my way to meet Brother Huy when I saw a policeman who just got out of his jeep and was staring at me," the boy said. "There was something very strange in his eyes which frightened me. I was in a panic. He was staring at me as if he saw the explosives and grenades in my bag. So I ran away and hid the bag under a garbage heap in front of the high school, but the policeman was still there and he stopped me and said 'What are you doing? why do you run away? where is your bag?'"

The boy was finished.

Mr. Song had heard the story many times before, so he did

not pay close attention to what Chinh said. The story was always the same. He and the other policeman did not try to interrupt or intimidate the boy, who leaned close to Luong, speaking in a low little croak, sometimes whispering—unable to keep his hands still, unable to stop plucking or rubbing his clothes.

"I am so frightened," Chinh said. Four or five times he said this. Even I knew the words in Vietnamese for that. At one point, when Mr. Song and the other policeman were distracted by a messenger bringing in papers for them to look at, the boy whispered: "After my capture I was tortured on the first night. They poured water up my nose. They used electricity on me, too. Very painful, no sleep that night."

He began to quiver and cry again. We had no food with us, so Luong gave him two cigarettes to divert him and fool his hunger. Chinh preferred Salem to Pall Mall. He was kept in a small cell by himself, which Chinh said he could not bear. There were three windows—he called them "holes"—but they were too high for him to reach. Once a week, on Saturday, he was taken out to wash, but he always had to wash by himself, with the guard making him hurry.

"I am very frightened to be alone. I cannot sleep at night because of so many mosquitoes, so I sleep in the daytime. I have nothing to do. There is a wooden bed but I sleep on the floor because it is very hot. The food is very bad, there is no breakfast, not even rice soup or bread. Since my capture I have been given fish only three times."

When Luong put his face down to hear better, the boy whispered to him: please, help me, give me money to buy a can of fish, please do what you can to get me out of that room, I am so frightened, I only wish that I can be out of that room, please.

A few feet away you could not hear him pleading. The child looked very pale, almost waxy, with dark circles under his eyes. He trembled and seemed uncertain each second of what any of us might do to him. At first he seemed worried because Luong was being kind, not sure that it was all right to lean against him, let the arm of the man go around him.

Then he realized that as long as we were in the room, nothing would harm him and he was no longer alone. His father was a farmer in Thanh Phong village of Dien Ban district, Quang Nam province. He had been squatting to relieve himself behind a bush of sugar cane, near a tobacco field, when Americans on operations shot and killed him. Thanh Phong was considered a Viet Cong stronghold. Many villagers had left the area, but his father stayed; he was old and sick, the boy said. He spoke only in whispers, his voice did not work. In 1967 the mother of Chinh went to Saigon, where she and the boy and other relatives lived on Nguyen Van Thoai Street. There were many, many bars there for the Americans and even the children knew what they wanted. There were eight-year-olds who pimped.

"In Saigon, I did very well in third and fourth grade," Chinh said. "I was among the best in the class. Once, once I was rated number two. In 1969 I followed some friends who were making money by leading Americans to prostitute houses. I did not go home. I did not go to school. My mother caught me, brought me home, smacked me and then sent me to Danang to stay with my cousin." He had not stayed in Danang, but went to the village near his home to work as a water-buffalo boy. He was trained for five days in explosives, shown how to make the detonator work by using his teeth, Chinh said. He was told not to tell the other children. He never did. He was sent to Danang to carry out missions.

It was a young girl with long hair who gave him the explosives with instructions for that day in Danang, Chinh said. He knew many older Viet Cong cadres, men, who came to Danang and gave him tiny amounts of money to live on. A man named Sau had even given him a watch, which he needed for his missions. The cadres were patient, affectionate, cheerful with him.

"They were very nice to me," Chinh said. But the man he

dreamed of was not any of them. It was his father who came back to him. "Once I had a dream in which I saw me already dead, I was dead at home in my village. But my father was near me. It was he who was alive. Another dream took me home, too, and my father said, 'Come back quickly after classes.'" When he awoke from the dreams and kept crying out, the guard came in and shouted at him and cursed and kicked him.

The Special Police Branch had made posters showing Chinh's picture with details of his arrest to warn others helping the Viet Cong. When Chinh was shown the poster he cringed, as if now he was going to his own execution. He could not stop sobbing. Mr. Song was used to such behavior and did nothing. The other policeman looked bored.

"I have seen such pictures at Cho Con bus station," Chinh said. "There were pictures of this girl and everybody said now she has died. If my mother sees these pictures, she will think I am dead."

We could not keep him with us any longer. The next child came in as he was leaving. Both lived in the same village. Nothing passed between them. They looked at each other sadly but without recognition, without a gesture or a pause. The girl's name was Pham Thi Hoa, her age was eleven. Mr. Song complained that the girl had not been very cooperative. She had lived with a succession of important Viet Cong members, who treated her like a daughter, he said, solemnly. "This girl is very stubborn. But we have found her weak point. She is very afraid of having her hair cut off. So we say that we will cut off her hair if she is not more helpful."

He spoke in English, but the girl Hoa seemed to understand that he was talking about her hair again. I had never seen a child like that: so fearful yet unyielding. Once I tried to pat her hand to comfort her, but she drew back. Not once did she cry. But the small hands moved and moved as if a separate, frenzied life was in them: fingers rubbing fingers, touching each other all the time, clasping and unclasping. Even when she hoped to make her face look stern, the hands betrayed her. She had been arrested as a messenger for the Viet Cong; there was a letter in her pocket. A defector identified her. She had been in the Detention Center for five months; she did not know the time, the day or the month.

"I have no father. My mother lived in Saigon," Hoa said so softly Luong could barely hear. "My mother gave me to Mrs. Xuan when I was very small. When Uncle Xuan died I lived with Uncle Chi. When Uncle Chi died I lived with Uncle Hien." She was not related to these men: "Uncle" is a respectful term in Vietnamese. The girl looked at no one as she spoke. She did not even seem to see her own hands doing their urgent, strange little dances. "Only Uncle Hien loves me. My mother does not love me. She gave me to Mrs. Xuan. Uncle Hien asked me whether I wanted to go to school and I said no. He said 'You decide. If you want it, I will send you to school. If you don't, stay here with me.' Uncle Hien and the other uncles love me."

She had lived in Thanh Phong village in a bunker under a large bush of bamboo. At night Uncle Hien put up a hammock for her to sleep in. She remembered only one girl her own age living nearby, but then the girl's mother took her to Danang, where she worked as a servant. Hoa was picked up at the Cho Con bus station in Danang; the letter in her pocket for Sister Chin was all the evidence that was needed. Hoa said she had been taken away by the Americans twice in her village but that she had not been afraid at all because there were so many other Vietnamese with her. Each time all the Vietnamese were released after being kept for one night.

It made the girl tired to tell all this again, but she knew she had no choice. None of it was helpful to Mr. Song, who said he used little fish to catch big fish. Hoa was very thin; sometimes she seemed to shiver although it was hot in the police office. Once she whispered to Luong that she had been beaten. There was no time to ask her more questions.

The second police official said he had offered to adopt Pham

Thi Hoa and take her home to live with his own children. He repeated the offer, smiling at the girl.

"I prefer to be in prison," she said. "I like prison." Then she was taken away.

Perhaps because Luong's face looked odd, perhaps because I looked queer, too, and we sat there without speaking, Mr. Song gave some advice, wagging his finger. "Now don't write an anti-war story," he said in English. "Write how the Viet Cong exploit children."

A lot of money was given, not once but twice, to the guards at the Detention Center to pass my parcels of food to the children. I dreamed of helping them escape and knew I never could. In Saigon, I begged a kindly man from the International Red Cross to help improve the conditions for the children, but he sighed and told me of worse cases, of reports that were ignored. It was useless appealing to the Americans. They already knew. It was they who created the Special Police, paid them, taught them, urged them on, expected results. A reader wrote to *The New York Times* complaining that my story only put the children in more peril, and still another wrote to complain that I had not ever written of the children killed in Communist rocket attacks, as if I were cheating at a game of tit-tat-toe and had better watch myself. In Saigon a middle-aged and educated Vietnamese, believed to have contacts on all sides, listened to my story of the children and said there was nothing anyone could do, to stop worrying. Perhaps someday the children would be proud of what they had endured. "I envy them," he said. The man disgusted me.

The boy Chinh must be seventeen now, the girl Hoa sixteen. It is their hands I remember more than their faces.

IN SOUTH VIETNAM the smaller bribes needed to proceed with everyday life were sometimes called "coffee money" by the Saigonese, while the big bribes, the crushing and dreadful ones, had no special name. A male wishing to avoid the draft could buy a forged identification card with a false age, making him younger, if he had one hundred dollars in Vietnamese piasters. This was not "coffee money"; it was the equivalent of a monthly salary of a Vietnamese working as a clerk or the pay of a first lieutenant in the Saigon army. As a precaution, many parents changed the ages of their male children when they were still very small, but the war went on for so long it did no good in the end. Ages went backward: a schoolboy of thirteen was really fifteen; at seventeen he was still safe from the draft because the papers said he was only fifteen. No one felt safe as the war grew older and the inflation swelled. The bribes grew bigger: nearly two hundred dollars in piasters in 1971 to get a soldier transferred from infantry to a desk job in the rear. The poor could never pay; sometimes if they sold all that they owned, the money was raised, but their sons were pulled into the war anyway. There was nowhere to hide, for in each village, in each hamlet, in each neighborhood of the cities were police who checked and rechecked the papers of all males. Those who had none were arrested.

Strange and desperate things were done for money. A family could care only for its separate survival. Each year the fear and the grieving grew stronger as the land held more dead and there was less room in the cemeteries. On the Saigon-Bien Hoa highway, some twelve miles north of the capital, there was a reminder of the great unhappiness in the country. It was supposed to be a war memorial, but some Vietnamese believed it was human while others said it was a gentle ghost who could not rest. The memorial was a thirteen-foot concrete statue of a Vietnamese infantryman, resting, a rifle across his knees. He was ARVN, as the Americans called both the South Vietnamese Army and its soldiers. It was a statue of a spent and haunted man; its name was Sorrow. The figure was put up at the end of 1966, below the entrance to the Vietnamese national military cemetery.

There were people who swore the statue came alive; they had

heard it sigh and ask for water. A Vietnamese military policeman had once seen it step off the pedestal, take off its helmet and pack, and lie down on the grass. There were villagers who believed the statue had moved at night, during the 1968 Tet offensive, to warn people of the fighting. Once, they said, the statue had stopped a twenty-vehicle convoy headed for an ambush. There were even Vietnamese who told you that they had seen the statue cry in the spring of 1971 when the South Vietnamese were sent into Laos to cut the Ho Chi Minh trail and could not do it.

Once, the statue was moved from its site to be sent back to the workshop of its sculptor, Nguyen Thanh Tu, so he could recast it in bronze. Women in the neighborhood thought of the statue as a shrine. They came to see it, very quietly, placing flowers and joss sticks before it, kneeling to pray below its huge boots. The taxi driver in Saigon who drove us to Mr. Tu's house was startled to see the statue again. "I thought it ran away early this year—we heard it was lost," he said.

No one in Vietnam could run away. There were different places but there was nowhere to hide for very long.

IN THIS COUNTRY there were children who remembered how they once thought—as the war seemed to go on forever and each birthday took them closer to it—of running away. The first to tell me was a boy named Michael Silberman in New York, who was eleven but going on twelve, he said. At the time the American troops left Vietnam in February 1973 he liked to read, build model ships and airplanes, and take pictures. He was precise and composed. He said: "I guess I've been conscious of the war since 1968. Before then I probably heard about it, but I wasn't conscious of it and I didn't understand war, not really. I've gotten permission from Mom to let me watch the news when I don't have a lot of homework. My father watched Vietnam on television sometimes when he came home week nights. Mostly all I saw was tanks rolling by. Tanks didn't exactly make me sad. But recently I did see pictures—not running film, but pictures of where the children are fleeing from the napalm, a picture of the little girl running down the road. I thought it was awful that we used this kind of stuff. But this time it was the South Vietnamese who did it; they made a horrible mistake in calculation in dropping their stupid bombs. We used incendiary bombs, atom bombs, five hundred-pound explosive bombs. Incendiary bombs break apart and it throws shrapnel. And they also used fire bombs that have jelly gasoline, which bursts into flames and burns people up. But napalm is chemical burning, acid.

"I didn't really hear about the Christmas bombing of North Vietnam until afterwards because I was mostly involved in playing with my cousins and my sister. Because at Christmas time I'm playing with my toys and everything. But I found out because of news reports on Channel 4 and also listening to WNBC radio.

"I really didn't think anything then, but now I think it was really awful. And in *Rolling Stone*, Joan Baez wrote an article. She was in Hanoi when they were doing the Christmas bombing. She said it was sad and terrible to see the American planes come over.

"In school we've had very interesting discussions about the war, about President Johnson, about President Truman, mostly in social studies, and once, interestingly enough, in English. The teacher, Mr. Hurst, said we are having a discussion and not a discussion of personal feelings; he said you should give facts instead of feelings. He especially said we shouldn't express our personal feelings about the Presidents because, I guess, that's mean after they've died. In the class I said I felt President Truman was not really such a very good President because he did a lot of bad things—for instance, starting the Cold War, dropping the bombs on Hiroshima and things like that that weren't very smart. Also establishing NATO, which wasn't so good.

"I don't really know why the war began. I didn't ask Mr. Hurst. Maybe because we had some important military bases in the islands around there. I don't know. I guess we didn't want the Communists to come and take over our land. President Kennedy decided, well, the Communists must be stopped, Communists aren't very good. But I don't see what's wrong with it. I mean it's probably not the greatest thing to live under probably, but I did study China in the fourth grade and I thought it really didn't seem very bad. It didn't seem great, but it didn't seem very bad.

"I think there are more people against the war now than there were before. Mostly it's old war veterans from the Second World War that are for it really. I really don't know why, probably because they're used to this thing about the American way is the right way and Communists are rotten.

"There isn't any more draft. I was worried that I would be drafted. I started worrying about that about the same time I realized Vietnam was happening. Last year I really thought about it. I said to my parents that I probably wouldn't want to get drafted and would probably resist. Mom and Dad said they would shelter me if I did resist. I don't know if I would have gone to Canada. I don't know what I would do. Most people flee. They get shelter from friends."

SOME CHILDREN WANT to forget how frightened they were that the war would snatch them up. They are older now, not so willing to admit such fears. It was Joanne, my cousin, who told me how her son had begun to cry the day they heard President Nixon on the radio explaining why Americans had entered Cambodia. The child, whose nickname is Tico, cried because he did not want to be a soldier, she said, making a sad face, shaking her head. His mother had taken him and his two older sisters to an antiwar demonstration, but he was too little then to understand.

The war is over now; he does not think about it. His grades are good, he has won a blue ribbon for broad jumping in school. Tico shows me the textbook for the eighth-grade class in social studies.

He is finished with it now. The book is called *Promise of America: Sidewalks, Gunboats and Ballyhoo*. It is one in a series on American history. The book is beautiful with its fine illustrations and layout. There are two and a half pages on Vietnam, a little section called "Idealism and Self-Interest: A Modern Example." The Vietnam part comes after a section, "Taking the Philippines" and "Was McKinley Right?" It says:

> The war in Vietnam is another example of a foreign policy issue that has posed questions of idealism and self-interest. Here are two letters written by American soldiers fighting in Vietnam in the 1960's. Are these soldiers fighting for idealistic reasons (concern for the Vietnamese and other foreign peoples), for reasons of self-interest (concern for the United States and for themselves), or both? Write down the exact words of each soldier to support your answers.

> *. . long hours of sweat and blood*

> *Hi Mom, Dad, and all,*
> *. . . It's hard to sleep, eat, or even write any more. This place has definitely played hell with us. It's been a long hard road, Mom and Dad, and I think I've proved myself so far. I know you all have a great confidence in me, and I know I can do any job assigned to me. I've engaged with the Vietcong and Hard Core [communists] so many times, I lost track of them. I've got a right to boast a little cause I know I was right in hitting the licks, just like other good Marines have done and are doing and always will. We've put long hours of sweat and blood in this soil, and we will do our best to get these people freedom. Also protect America from Communism.*
> *I only wish I could do something to encourage the boys that are burning their draft cards to stand up and take their*

responsibilities for their country, family, and friends. You can't defeat Communism by turning your backs or burning your draft cards. Anyone who does it is a disgrace and plain yellow. They haven't got the guts to back up their fathers and forefathers before them. Their lives have gone to waste if the sons today are too afraid to face the facts. . . .

There, I've said what has been on my mind! I hope this doesn't bore you, but I just had to put it down on paper.

Mom, Dad, and kids, whenever the national anthem is being played, whether over TV, radio, or at a game, please, please, *stand up. Show your patriotism. After all, I am not fighting for nothing.*

Am I ?!!

We've got to have a flag, also; do we have one?

Dad, try in every way, whether little or big, to push a little of the patriotism kick into Bob and Ron! Please! *Also religion.*

GO TO MASS . . .

Goodbye for now, and God bless you all.

I love you all.

Doug

Yesterday I witnessed something . . .

Dear Mom,

. . . Yesterday I witnessed something that would make any American realize why we are in this war. At least it did me. I was on daylight patrol. We were on a hill overlooking a bridge that was out of our sector. I saw a platoon of Vietcong stopping traffic from going over the bridge. They were beating women and children over the head with rifles, clubs, and fists. They even shot one woman and her child. They were taking rice, coconuts, fish, and other assorted foods from these people. The ones that didn't give they

*either beat or shot. I think you know what I tried to do. I
wanted to go down and kill all of those slant-eyed bastards.
I started to and it took two men to stop me. These slobs
have to be stopped, even if it takes every last believer in a
democracy and a free way of life to do it. I know after seeing their brave tactics I'm going to try my best. So please
don't knock [President] Johnson's policy in Vietnam. There
is a good reason for it. I'm not too sure what it is myself,
but I'm beginning to realize, especially after yesterday.*

Love, Bill

QUESTION

The two American soldiers both supported American involvement in the war in Vietnam. Here are some statements by critics of the war. Which say that the United States became involved
for idealistic reasons? Which says that the United States became
involved for reasons of self-interest? Which say both?

a. "The United States became involved in Vietnam to protect
   the supply of Indochinese rubber, tin, and other materials
   that American corporations need."
b. "President Eisenhower, Kennedy, Johnson, and Nixon all
   tried to prevent a communist victory in South Vietnam
   because they believed that people are better off under any
   noncommunist government, no matter how bad, than under
   any communist government."
c. "The United States government supports all anticommu-
   nist governments in Asia so that it can continue its policy of
   expansion. The United States wants to keep Asians under its
   thumb."
d. "The United States became involved in Vietnam to prevent
   Communist China from taking over all of Southeast Asia.

American officials believed that if China gained control of Southeast Asia, it would be in a better position to attack the United States."

e. "American policymakers thought it was their duty to stop communism from spreading. They believed that each gain made by the communists further weakened the power of the democracies."

Some letters will never appear in the series *Promise of America*. This is one of them. On February 27, 1970, a nineteen-year-old named Keith R. Franklin of Salamanca, New York, wrote to his parents just before he was sent to Vietnam as a medical corpsman. He asked his parents to open the letter only in the event of his death. Less than three months later he was killed in Cambodia, May 12, 1970.

> *If you are reading this letter, you will never see me again, the reason being that if you are reading this I have died. The question is whether or not my death has been in vain. The answer is yes.*
>
> *The war that has taken my life and many thousands before me is immoral, unlawful and an atrocity unlike any misfit of good sense and judgment known to man. I had no choice as to my fate. It was predetermined by the war-mongering hypocrites in Washington.*
>
> *As I lie dead, please grant my last request. Help me inform the American people, the silent majority who have not yet voiced their opinions.*

"Consider the pathetic irony of all those peace movement leafletters, sign carriers, letter writers, petition signers, speechmakers, demonstration-goers, writers of articles and teach-in participants in having their children read in school textbooks that 'their country came to the defense of democratic South Vietnam,'" a forty-seven-year-old professor of philosophy of education wrote.

The professor is William Griffen, who teaches at the State University of New York at Cortland. He and two other men, John Marciano and Robert Knowles, also teachers, have analyzed interpretations of the war found in twenty-eight textbooks used throughout the United States for secondary education.

They found the textbooks written and published between 1961 to 1967 tended, in general, to be more conservative, taking the view that the United States was standing firm against Reds from North Vietnam who were invading "free" South Vietnam and that this invasion was instigated by the "red" Chinese and the Russians. More liberal, dovish textbooks, written and published between 1968 and 1973, were often apt to depict the United States as having honorable motives in Vietnam while becoming entangled in a war that could neither be understood nor won despite these good intentions. One brief report, written by the three men, said of these textbooks:

> The textbooks thus exclude, *even as a valid thesis for examination*, the position that the conflict was a logical conclusion of racist and imperialist policies which brought the United States to China, the Philippines and Korea; that our efforts were simply an extension of earlier French colonialism. There is simply no recognition that U.S. involvement was one continuous litany of lies and distortions designed to hide the invasion of a peaceful and enlightened civilization. The perspective of radical historians such as Gabriel Kolko, who argues that U.S. policies provided overwhelming evidence of "how devious, incorrigible, and beyond the pale of human values America's rulers were throughout this epic event," is simply outside the limits of debate.

While the earlier conservative-hawk texts viewed South

Vietnam as a "Free" nation under attack by the "Reds," the liberal-dove view freely admits the corrupt nature of the Diem family and successive regimes, but in a manner which does not shed any substantial doubt on the fundamental causes of the conflict nor of U.S. motives in supporting such regimes. While the massive destruction and death is covered, carefully balanced by tales of North Vietnamese and "Viet Cong" terrorism which equally blame both sides for the violence, the later texts basically reveal a pathetic tale of the kind-hearted but stumbling American giant becoming trapped and manipulated by South Vietnamese allies— wishing to help but held back by the likes of Diem, Ky and Thieu. . . . American high school students could thus read twenty-eight leading social studies and history textbooks without considering the possibility that they lived in the nation which had committed the most blatant act of aggression since the German invasions of World War II.

In another textbook published in 1970 by Ginn and Company, a Xerox company, called *American History for Today*, there are nearly six pages on the war. Some captions on photographs say: "Vietnam: something new and something old. Helicopters were something new in the war. Refugees and heartache were something found in all wars." The book says:

> . . . The Viet Cong used terror tactics in an effort to win. They raided towns and killed men, women and children. Often they blasted heavily populated places with bombs and mortar shells . . .
>
> Most Americans found themselves somewhere in the middle. They wanted the war to end. But they did not want to abandon the South Vietnamese to the Communists.
>
> In noisy demonstrations, war protesters brought pressure

on President Johnson. But the President would not change his stand. He insisted that for its own safety the United States must help the one billion people in non-Communist Asian lands to defend themselves.

Secretary of State Dean Rusk also remained firm. He warned that if the United States did not live up to its promises, no other nation in the world would ever trust us again.

Such textbooks do not point out that a poll taken in Sweden in 1973 by the University of Göteburg showed that a large majority of Swedes thought that United States policies were a greater threat to world peace than those of the Soviet Union. The poll conducted among a cross section of 2,500 Swedes in conjunction with the 1973 general election was not released until the summer of 1975.

Mr. Griffen and his collaborators—who said they had no illusions about what they would find in existing history books—have written their own history of the war in Indochina but they have not yet found a publisher. They had been told it is too "soon" for such a work, or there is no interest. The men want schoolchildren to be made familiar with the Pentagon Papers.

"It isn't a question of our propaganda versus their propaganda," Mr. Griffen said. "The case for what really happened will be made by presenting the war-makers' own words, own cables, their own planning documents not for our eyes. For most Americans and for almost all the young, the Pentagon Papers are still unread and still a secret."

On the list of the twenty-eight textbooks the men compiled is the first edition of *The Free and the Brave* by Henry R. Graff, identified as a professor of history at Columbia University, which was shown to me by a seventh-grade student in a junior high school in Long Island. In referring to the Paris peace talks, the textbook says: "A series of determined efforts which aimed to make known that the Americans wanted to end the war met with no response from the 'other side.'" The students are informed that President Johnson tried "all the time he was in office to get a peaceful settlement."

"Many South Vietnamese officials were corrupt," this textbook says. "They used American money to enrich themselves . . . In spite of the graft, much good was done. Hospitals were set up and teachers, nurses and even a police force was trained. Americans taught new farming methods to the Vietnamese. New officials who would serve their fellow countrymen were honestly trained. All the steps taken in the 'other war' were to prepare the Vietnamese to run their democracy once peace came." The point is emphasized again: "Even as the fighting went on, the United States trained the South Vietnamese in the ways of democracy."

It is an astonishing assessment; it has nothing to do with the country and the war I knew. I remember the elections in South Vietnam. They were required exercises, having little meaning to the Vietnamese, for many realized going to the ballot box was simply another gymnastic to be performed for the benefit of their superiors. The Americans were very keen on elections, because they appeared to be proof of their claims that South Vietnam was a free and just society where the people determined who would lead them. But the Vietnamese who won seats in the lower house, or the National Assembly, and tried to oppose President Thieu and the war, ran the risk of being imprisoned. If they were effective opponents, they knew their careers would be short.

The seven million registered Vietnamese voters in the south had no choice but to go to the polls. If their yellow voting cards were not punched by officials at the polls, they were warned they would be punished. In the August 1971 elections for the lower house of the National Assembly—the parliament of South Vietnam—voters were required, in one district in Gia Dinh, near Saigon, to pick six candidates out of seventy-eight who were running. None of the candidates who ran from forty-four provinces were required to be residents in their local constituencies, so often the local Vietnamese did not know who they were. It was harder for the soldiers who had not seen any candidate on television or heard speeches on the radio.

In the presidential election of October 3, 1971, there was only one man to vote for. He was Nguyen Van Thieu, who was already President and wanted to be reelected. Despite the last-minute, intense attempts of Ambassador Ellsworth Bunker to persuade and recruit another Vietnamese, Major General Duong Van Minh, to run against Thieu, "Big Minh" refused, and later said that he did not choose to be used for the convenience of the Americans who had no intention of permitting a free presidential election. Hoang Duc Nga, a relative of President Thieu who held a position of high importance in the Saigon palace, told the bureau chief of *The New York Times*, Alvin Shuster, that the President would be reelected by a vote of 94.6 percent. Mr. Nga was amused as he confided this on the telephone. The Vietnamese were advised that if they chose not to support President Thieu, the only name on the ballot, they could make a cross or another mark, or tear part of the ballot.

"Everyone understands what Thieu is up to and his stupidity in being alone in a democratic election, but the people don't know what to do about it," a sergeant in the Popular Forces, a paid and armed home militia, said. "It is safer to have an attitude that is noncommittal in such uncertain times. Yes, the people know they can tear the ballot or mark it, but they are ignorant and afraid, so they will vote for him."

Some Vietnamese tried to protest the one-man election. It was as easy as it would be for Americans to try to dismantle the Dow Corporation, or Honeywell.

A group of Catholic priests, politicians, intellectuals, Buddhists, disabled veterans and students burned their voting cards as a symbolic gesture of contempt for the October 3 elections. Students tried to demonstrate, but the police were too numerous, too fierce and drove them back. One Catholic who taught philosophy at the University of Saigon, Professor Ly Chanh Trung, explained the resistance to anyone who would hear him. "For the older Vietnamese, religion once came before the country," he said. "Now for the younger Catholics the nation is just about as absolute as the religion. Nationalists are those who cannot accept dependence on foreigners, and more and more Catholics are saying no to the Americans."

A deputy in the legislature, Mrs. Kieu Mong Thu, who opposed the war and Thieu, said that to attack and destroy Thieu it was necessary to attack those who kept him alive and propped up: the Americans. A group of university and high school students organized hit-and-run teams of four members to burn American military vehicles and the American soldiers who were driving them. They used plastic bags of high-octane gasoline, which they threw in the vehicles, then tossed in burning matches. The students claimed they had burned more than fifty vehicles; one American in the Navy received second-degree burns. We heard that he died.

One of the leaders of the student group was a twenty-three-year-old woman named Vo Thi Bach Tuyet who claimed the organization had burned more than thirty-two American military vehicles in six weeks. "I do not think the Americans understand the war in Vietnam and many of them perhaps feel that their soldiers are here to fight under a good banner, to fight Communists," she said in Vietnamese. "So if the American people see that it is the Vietnamese people in the south who are hurting the American soldiers, they will better understand the situation."

They were not Communists: they were only part of Vietnam's sentenced generation—children of refugees, of the displaced, of the dead, of the very fearful, who at fifteen and sixteen saw themselves as resistance fighters. It was hard to understand why the older students had waited so long to act if their convictions were so powerful. The student leaders said they had not dared do anything in earlier years, when the American troops were more numerous, because they would have been accused of being Communists, but now, now, it was different; the people were with them. This is how they put it. Why had they not joined the Viet Cong if they opposed their government and loathed their American allies?

"It is not a question of ideology," a twenty-five-year-old University of Saigon student said. "We don't exactly know what the other side feels, you see, and this way we know what we are doing and it makes us feel useful to the people."

I went out with a team of four Vietnamese on a fire-bombing mission to write a story. The students went on two motorcycles to a busy downtown street where Americans often drove by in jeeps. We waited nearly twenty minutes. I remember praying that no one would come, praying that no American would pass by us, warning myself over and over again to stay out of it and not to interfere, not to remember the crusts and the smell of burned men I had already seen in hospitals. The plan was for one Vietnamese to run out in front of the vehicle, waving his arms, so the driver would stop. Then another student would hurl the plastic bag of gas inside the vehicle. The third Vietnamese would toss in the lit matches.

After fifteen minutes, perhaps longer, an American Army half-truck was spotted. As it came closer, you could see the face of the GI, who must have been whistling. He looked sleepy. There was that second when I could have screamed, yelled, rushed forward to warn him, given the plan away. But the sixteen-year-old student moved too fast for me. He threw, but he aimed badly and the plastic bag of gas hit the windshield. The GI veered, shouted out "you fucking idiot," and drove away from us so fast that people on the street knew something had happened. "Bad shot," said the law student who held the matches. The four Vietnamese were not pleased with their failure. They needed more practice, the sixteen-year-old said. It must have been a few seconds before my legs would work again, before I had a voice that sounded like my own.

The people were not always grateful to these students. One September night, no later than 6 P.M., a U.S. Army van near the Tan Son Nhut airport was set on fire. But the driver was Vietnamese, an employee of the Americans, and the crowd was sympathetic to his dilemma. He would be dismissed, the driver said, and blamed. A neighborhood woman said she had seen two boys speeding by on a Honda and thought they must be students. A neighbor turned to her. "Dumb woman," he said angrily. "What else can they be?"

No one knew how many Vietnamese were supporters of Thieu or how many despised him or felt nothing, or only feared the Communists. All you knew was that most Vietnamese wanted the war to end: it was choking them. They wanted an end to their unhappiness, to their fear of hunger, their fear of dying. They wanted only to be themselves. One professor who taught political science at the National Institute of Administration said of course he would vote for Thieu. There were others like him: bright, cultivated, ambitious men, who liked to say that no democracy was perfect.

"We have to choose the least of the bad possibilities," Professor Nguyen Ngoc Huy said. "What can those who are critical of democracy in South Vietnam say about the assassination of Robert Kennedy? Is that democracy? In a country with two hundred years of democracy? A man wanted to run for the presidency and he was assassinated!"

He did not wait for an answer.

The fire-bombings by the students, and their demonstrations, very much displeased Professor Huy. "I would say to these students, if I could speak to them," he said. "'Why don't you march in bare feet, not ride on your motorbikes? Why don't you stop buying such modern clothes and dress as the peasants do? Don't they realize that eighty percent of our needs are covered by American money?'"

Not all the Vietnamese who burned their voting cards, who risked detention, imprisonment or beatings, had strong political convictions or philosophies. It was that they could not bear their lives or the lives of those whom they loved. They did not want the war and they suspected Thieu did, that it was the only way he could stay in power and that without such momentum, he would shrivel to nothing. Sometimes it was the Vietnamese women who spoke more fiercely than the men and could not be easily shut up.

One of them was a housewife named Tran Thi Bich. She was fifty or fifty-one that year, a widow, with a fine, intense face, a high forehead and thinning hair worn in a bun. She was a Buddhist, who had publicly burned her little yellow voting card. The monks had approved. "I hated it," Mrs. Bich said. "It stands for nothing. The government wants the war to go on because officials get fat and rich from it. Oh, anyone is better than Thieu. But whoever is in power, the Americans will do something to bribe him. The people don't have faith in any individual at all."

She was a talkative woman, not made shy by a foreign reporter. When Luong took her picture, she put on her only pair of beads and showed her profile, which was handsome. She kept standing long after the picture was taken, not knowing how much time it required. "When Thieu first took power he promised peace. Where is it? Since he has been in power, prices have gone up and up. And there is so much robbing and snatching nowadays. Peace for what people? Every day I see more of the young arrested on the streets because they do not want war, but they are taken and forced in the army."

Then, to make it quite clear why she hated the war, in case we knew nothing, she began a precise recital of her reasons, not asking for pity or help, only describing what had happened to each of her five sons, who had all been in the army. The eldest, who was thirty-two, was wounded in a mortar attack. Part of his face was missing and his left hand was useless. He could not find work, perhaps it was because of the horrible new face he had, but then, many veterans had no work. The next reason: a thirty-year-old son who had become a madman who could do nothing for himself. "A bright child, a nervous child, a good son," she said of him; he was the one she had loved the most. The third son was a lieutenant on active duty. A fourth son, a twenty-three-year-old soldier, had been missing for "a long time," she said. The last reason was the youngest boy, a deserter from the army and in hiding. All this she told us matter-of-factly, always circling back to the son who had gone mad.

"He became strange after a battle, a fierce battle—and he came home two years ago with this look on his face," Mrs. Bich said. "He wouldn't eat anything I cooked for him. He sat there and wept. Then we wept with him. A friend of his told me that my son saw too many men die, and that for three days and three nights he was unable to move away from the corpses."

Luong went on translating, making his notes, a bit more slowly this time, while I took my notes and kept asking questions. We had done it so many times before.

The woman did not know what mental illness was, nor if there were doctors who could treat it. She took that son to the largest military hospital in the south, called Cong Hoa—just outside Saigon—but she was never able to find out if the son was treated, or how, or by whom, or where they kept him. She was not allowed to visit him, to talk to him, to hold him, to bring him food. On visiting day, relatives of men in some mental wards were allowed to line up and see the patients. But there was barbed wire between them, Mrs. Bich said, so they could not even touch each other or speak, only look. The visitors, nearly always women, could not even stand there too long because guards kept the line moving. There was not quite a minute.

"He knew me," Mrs. Bich said. "He always knew me. He would try and come to me, but that was not possible. He would stand there, his eyes always on my face, calling out to me."

She could do nothing. Then the woman sat there, quietly,

finished with the story of the second son, who kept calling out Mother, Mother, until the guards hauled him away. She always heard his voice.

Afterward Luong and I did not speak. We went to the tiny soup shop, down an alley off the street, called Pasteur to have *pho*. It was a way of steadying ourselves, drinking the noodle soup with beef and red peppers. From that time on, I began to count the days I had left in Vietnam, just as the GIs always did, for I was stupid enough to think that leaving would be the cure. There were times when Luong and I tried to help: I brought back two wheelchairs from Hong Kong to give to paralyzed men in one ward at Cong Hoa Hospital and it was he who did the paperwork for permission, took days to make sure the wheelchairs would not be confiscated by the customs at Tan Son Nhut. It was never enough. I did not know that for the next five years I would suddenly think of that woman, putting on the amber-colored beads, telling us the story of a second son who wanted to put his head in her lap and not be afraid of night any more.

The last demonstration against the one-man presidential election that I saw in Saigon was on a Saturday, on the steps of the National Assembly, the seat of the legislature, a curved and fat white building with a more frivolous past. It was once the French opera house. There were nine deputies, a senator and three lawyers; all had opposed the war, the corruption and deceit of the Thieu regime. On that soft and muggy day some of them held up three banners for the Saigonese to see. "The Oct. three elections betray the people's interests and must be smashed" was written on one of the white cloth banners. Another banner said the elections would establish a dictatorial regime "serving foreigners."

The well-armed combat police, with their weapons, their gas masks and their tear-gas grenade launchers, stood and waited for a signal to attack. Behind them, the Vietnamese were bunched in the streets and in the little square facing the National Assembly, many of them quite surprised to see such a spectacle. It was a deputy named Ly Qui Chung who was the first to shout out: "I condemn Mr. Thieu as a dictator!" There were no American MPs or troops around; there did not have to be. The grenades were fired, the khaki-colored canisters made in Saltsburg, Pennsylvania, by Federal Laboratories, Inc. The ordinary Vietnamese were often afraid of the American tear gas—no one was sure if it would lead to the spitting of blood later on, or blurred eyesight, but many deputies, students and the Buddhists of the An Quang pagoda had smelled it many times before and knew you could survive it.

That Saturday was not an ordinary failure that ended with the police squashing everyone. Something surprising came about. Ngo Cong Duc, a Catholic deputy from a wealthy Delta family, the nephew of the Archbishop of Saigon, one of the Vietnamese prominent in the Third Force, as the Americans liked to call it, publisher of a newspaper called *Tin Sang* which was shut by the government for its opposition, did not stand quietly as the tear-gas grenades came at them. Each time the first canisters landed he kicked them back at the police, leaping, twirling, stretching in an urgent and strange ballet. Some Vietnamese, watching it, smiled and looked pleased to see the young man, who was a handsome and strong fellow, kick back the punishment. But it did not last long. The tear gas emptied the streets, the police in their masks and with their sticks and weapons chased the protesters. Banners fell. Later Ngo Cong Duc had to escape from the south before Thieu had him arrested on whatever charges he chose. I saw him in Paris—he cooked a Vietnamese dinner—and then we met again in New York York. Some of us were not persuaded he would want to go back when the war was over. He was not an austere man, not a revolutionary, not someone accustomed to sacrifice. He said himself his family were merchants, the bourgeoisie, not peasants. But he went home.

"It is a Vietnamese government," Duc said. "At last."

For me he was always the man he was that day in Saigon, the hell with the tear gas and all the guns, swinging his leg that high, arms out, his face bright and tense as he kept kicking and kicking.

The demonstration made no difference. President Nguyen Van Thieu was reelected by an impossible ninety-four point something percent. The familiar farce was over. Saigon was so still that day. Only the police and the soldiers were everywhere, looking for troublemakers.

THE VIETNAMESE WHO opposed the U.S. government have their own history of the war. Dr. Nguyen Khac Vien, a northerner and a physician, historian and editor, was asked by a reporter in Paris in February 1973: "Could we try to define the U.S. motives during this war? By definition, isn't this an unproductive war for them?"

His answer:

"Obviously it's not the economic exploitation of Indochina and Vietnam which can bring them back the two hundred billion dollars they have spent. Even if the U.S. exploited Indochina for a thousand years, they couldn't recoup their losses. So there must be another reason for U.S. intervention.

"That reason can be traced to a global strategy of counterrevolution promulgated by Washington at the end of World War II. In 1945 the U.S. assumed the 'white man's burden.' Socialist countries were established, and socialist revolution threatened to spread. National liberation revolutions were growing. Movements for peace and democracy were developing in capitalist countries.

"All of this constituted a world-wide revolutionary movement which threatened all capitalist countries, and the U.S. found itself leading the defense of the capitalist world. Its global strategy of counterrevolution was aimed first against the Soviet Union, which in 1945, greatly weakened by the war, did not have the atomic bomb and was isolated. The U.S. was immeasurably stronger.

"From 1945 to 1950, the U.S. was not interested in third world countries such as India, but in Iran and Turkey, countries having a common border with the Soviet Union, and which could serve as military bases. This strategy became obsolete after the fall of Chiang Kai-shek. Socialist countries in Eastern Europe gained stability, and the Soviet Union developed the atomic bomb. A direct attack against these great socialist countries would have been dangerous for the U.S. So Washington turned its global strategy against the third world countries.

"The gradual reversal took a decisive turn with Kennedy. Reread *Strategy of Peace*. The techniques, weapons and tactics to crush national liberation movements are outlined there. Once third world countries were conquered and under U.S. tutelage, then the socialist camp would be isolated. Hence, Vietnam was a stumbling block. There the war of national liberation took its classic form. It had to be crushed to serve as an example and to test all the various weapons, tactics and forms of military activity. It was necessary to suppress Vietnam so that fear of the U.S. could be maintained all over the world."

SO MUCH WAS said about this war, the words came down like landslides, first pebbles and dirt, then rock and stone and trees. When the demonstrations were over—and indeed they were noisy, for desperate people do not whisper or take soft shapes—the speaking still went on. Sometimes it seemed that those who opposed the war were only speaking to each other, for around them were the deaf and the bored. There are records of what public men in public office said, records of what the outraged said, and what others had to say about them, but it is not likely that any schoolbook will print the words of a historian named Arthur Waskow, who in April of 1975, when the end of it was certain, spoke to a group in Washington, D.C., called Fabrangen. In Yiddish the word suggests "coming together." Fabrangen is the name of a Jewish community group in Washington, D.C., whose members work to seek a different, a holier life process. In a Friday night service, this man named Waskow, who is both a joyful and scholarly man said: "The war was a great flash of lightning. There we were, sleepwalking in the thick, thick dark, a dark so thick you could touch it, a dark so thick it was the dark itself we kept bumping into, breaking a leg as we stumbled over . . . something—gashing a cheek as we stumbled into . . . something—crying, mumbling, helpless, blind. And then the war: lighting up the knife-edge of the military institutions, lighting up the pit of corporate power, lighting up the ferocity of racism, sexism, lighting up the destruction of the biosphere . . .

"In the glare of the lightning we discovered what country we live in . . . Maybe instead of joining the old May Day, the one our great-grandparents gave the world, we should remake a May Day from our own lives . . . a May Day of the maypole, of spring and sexuality, of women and men—and a May Day that remembers jail in Washington, death at Kent, 'Strike strike strike!' on the lawn at Yale, a May Day that remembers napalm. Maybe the burning draft card is our bitter herb. Scorch our fingers in memory of napalm . . .

"And in every generation, every human being must look upon herself, himself, as if we ourselves had gone forth from Vietnam."

VERY FEW PEOPLE have such an intention. It is easier to claim the war was impossible to understand, therefore Americans need not feel pain or guilt or the necessity to see themselves differently. After the death of President Lyndon B. Johnson—a day before the cease-fire in January 1973—a first cousin named James Ealy Johnson remembered how much the President wanted to see it end. The cousin said it was an awfully difficult war. "Hardly any-one understood it," Mr. Johnson added.

It is a calming theme, used often with rich results. More than three years later a former governor of Georgia campaigning for the Democratic presidential nomination kept reassuring Americans that they were blame-free and had been badly used. At the West Shore Senior Citizens Center in New Cumberland Township, near Harrisburg in Pennsylvania, Jimmy Carter told his audience: "We killed hundreds of thousands of Vietnamese—little babies and children and mothers and fathers. But we never really wanted to fight over there, *without quite knowing why . . .*" No one ask him how the war could have gone on for twelve years if this was so.

The trauma of Vietnam is a popular expression, a convenient one for writers in magazines and newspapers, but the trauma is often as hard to detect as a virus. In "An American Woman's Bicentennial Prayer," the author thanked God because "never have we turned our back on another nation in need . . .

"Help us stop *criticizing* ourselves so much, God," she wrote in the *Ladies' Home Journal.*

A new generation of singers-composers do not care about the war but put it differently. One of them, Janis Ian, said it was boring to "proselytze" in her songs. "Remember when everyone was doing ban-the-bomb songs?" she said. "Bomb-bomb-bomb. Yatta-yatta-yatta. Bomb-bomb. Napalm. Yatta-yatta. The minute you preach, you're interfering with somebody else's life."

Some American fathers put up memorials to their children killed in Vietnam. I have only seen two of them, but there may be others. In North Troy, New York, a man named Raymond Tymeson wrote a poem honoring his oldest son, his twenty-year-old namesake, who died on December 2, 1968, with the Marine Corps on what the father calls "a stinking little hill in Quang Nam they tried to take for three days." Mr. Tymeson, who has three other children, wrote the poem very quickly although it was his first. "It came to me like that—boom," he said. The poem is inscribed in raised bronzed letters on a twenty-foot concrete memorial which was erected on the ground of what used to be the Little League playing field in the neighborhood. The little monument is enclosed by fencing; the American flag is lit up at night. There are two other names on a plaque: Cpl. Peter M. Guenette, USA, January 4, 1948–May 18, 1968, and Cpl. Paul J. Baker, USMC, Aug 23, 1948–March 26, 1969. The poem reads:

> Summer days were little league days,
> When you were a boy of ten.
> The high pop flies and RBI's
> Were all you thought of then.
> The field once more is slick and green,
> Just right for playing ball,
> Where you and your trusty bat went down,
> On many a three-strike call.
> First and second are white and clean,
> The pitcher's mound is high,
> Third and home, so near, and so far,
> That left you high and dry.
> But I remember one sunny day
> When you were on the mound
> And three came up, and three went down,
> With the bases loaded all around.
> It's fun to think after all these years,
> And every now and then,
> I long for those happy little league days
> When you were only ten.
> But now another boy like you
> Stands on the pitcher's mound
> He's tall and straight and eagle-eyed,

His skin is deeply browned.
He burns them in, and they go down
Just like you used to do.
And I know you're pleased from way up there
That every strike your brother throws,
He's bearing down for you, cause
Ray, we miss you so.

I first saw the poem, and wrote it down, on a winter's day in 1972. It was nearly three years later before I had the courage for such an intrusion and spoke to Mr. Tymeson, who was most cordial, even explaining that RBI's, which he used in the third line of the poem, means "runs batted in." Mr. Tymeson loves the game. He said his son was buried close by in St. Peter's Cemetery, and that from their house they could almost see his grave. I said I was sorry a stranger had to speak of the death, but Mr. Tymeson said it was all right, you could say that the family had gotten over it by now. He had been a soldier himself, Mr. Tymeson said, he had seen combat in Europe during World War II with the 42d Infantry.

"I saw what could happen," Mr. Tymeson said. "No one wants war or likes war. But my son gave his life fighting for freedom. And I say this, and I wrote it to Ray in Vietnam: Where you stand, there stands America. Where an American boy stands, there stands freedom."

IT WAS ONLY a sunken fortified room made of packed earth whose walls were planks of rough wood, the kind used in big crates, and strips of metal. Two thick beams ran across the top of the room, which was no longer than thirty feet. Tarpaulin darkened the window and the low carved-out doorway, keeping out the dirt. There were five litters, but a sixth could be squeezed in.

There were three doctors, all with the rank of captain, twelve medics, and a rather shy chaplain who had been raised in Belfast and did not seem very certain how to comfort men unless he was giving them last rites. The place was called B Med. There were no beds, no sinks, no x-rays, no hospital gowns. It was only a room with a crude floor. There were supplies stacked against the walls and tubes hanging down over the litters. At night the bare electric-light bulbs shone too hard on all faces. Only emergency lifesaving procedures were carried out at B Med. The idea was to get the wounded out in twenty minutes, but some amputations could not wait, certain wounds made men choke on their own blood and vomitus, there were hearts that began to give up. Sooner or later they all left as they came, by helicopters, which took them, the living and the dead, to the 18th Surgical Hospital in Quang Tri.

By the middle of March 1971, B Med was three months old; one hundred dead and more than eight hundred wounded had come and gone. They were casualties of the operation called Lam Son 719, the drive by South Vietnamese troops into Laos to cut the Ho Chi Minh trails, to at last punish the North Vietnamese by slashing their great supply route which took their soldiers and their supplies to the south. The Americans, who did not send their troops into Laos, only their helicopters and crews, provided air and ground support from a newly built vast base at Khe Sanh. It was an old name in the war, where, in 1968, six thousand Marines were kept under siege from January 21 to April 26. But the siege had nothing to do with that spring, there was nothing to remind you of them. At first the casualties at B Med were the American helicopter pilots and crews who flew Vietnamese troops and supplies into Laos, then men in the infantry and engineer battalions sweeping and clearing close to the Laos border. There were many cheerful briefings on the progress of Lam Son 719: there was much talk of thrusts, sweeps and pushes; of plunges, drives and growing mountains of captured supplies. There always was. In Vietnam, soldiers never straggled or stumbled into battle, they plunged, smashed, thrust. The truth is sometimes they were tired, so uncertain, their packs so heavy, they moved like sleepwalkers who had forgotten how to find their beds.

At the briefings for the press, there was no bad news. One day a South Vietnamese major cheerfully announced that government troops on a sweeping operation inside Laos had turned up two hundred cooking utensils, two tons of writing paper and pens and two thousand caged chickens and ducks belonging to the enemy. He was not used to the American press, so the major did not know how to answer, and he looked distressed when asked who had counted the chickens and ducks, as if a great discourtesy had taken place. On the days when some of the Vietnamese generals at their different command posts in Khe Sanh would agree to talk to reporters, they spoke fiercely: their troops were sixteen miles inside the panhandle of southern Laos, twenty-two miles inside, going deeper; Tchepone was taken, Tchepone would soon be taken, Tchepone would fall next week. You could not tell anything from the way they spoke or looked as each day their army withered and fell back.

Inside B Med, there was an enlisted man with a thick bandage over his eyes who, for a little while, thought that his girl had come to be with him, for he spoke to her by name. Not all the wounded were critically hurt, but most of them kept their eyes shut when they were brought in and would not look around them right away. On a March morning, still early in the day, a Chicano enlisted man, with long black eyelashes and a clean, sweet face, lay on one of the litters. There seemed to be no holes in him anywhere, but a tiny piece of shrapnel was in his windpipe. They could not save him; one of the doctors banged his chest so hard it seemed as though his ribs might crack and give way. Sometimes Captain Robert Roth, who was a twenty-nine-year-old pediatrician from

San Francisco, still seemed surprised at what he was seeing, even after being there at B Med for more than forty-nine days.

Often at night, when the shelling began, he would wear two flak jackets, so his whole chest and back were protected. It was very cumbersome. He did not care, he wanted to live.

"Who could conceive of this?" the captain said. "Even as a doctor I could not conceive of this." He slept inside a bunker and wrote very long letters to his wife, describing nearly everything. He told her about a twenty-year-old soldier, name unknown or forgotten by then, whose legs and part of one arm had been destroyed by a booby trap while his unit was clearing a landing zone near the Laotian border. They operated on him in B Med. Just before the doctors began, the soldier asked Dr. Roth to pray with him.

"Then he asked me 'Will my parents treat me the same?'" Dr. Roth said.

Some of the wounded felt cold and wanted to be warm. There were men who could not stop talking at first to the medics and those who seemed to have lost all memory of the language they knew. Often the medics took off the boots of the wounded: their feet looked strangely pale and smooth only because the rest of them was always filthy.

"We've noticed the amount of pain," Captain Roth said. "We have to use more morphine than in a civilian practice, sometimes two and a half times the average dose of morphine. I think a lot of it is anxiety—they come in afraid of what will happen."

In the beginning it had disturbed Dr. Roth very much to realize that the families of the men on the litters would not know on that day what had happened to their sons. The families would be watching television, or eating, or going to work.

"I kept thinking here I am, standing here, with their child dying," Dr. Roth said. Then he learned not to think about it except when he wrote to his wife inside the bunker. The other doctors were laconic men but he was not. It still made him angry to think of the day when Secretary of Defense Melvin Laird said in Washington, D.C., that the invasion of Laos was going according to plan. Someone had run into B Med and told them.

"Then the plan must be to get all of us killed," Dr. Roth said.

The little Bible was found inside B Med, but no one could be sure which of the wounded had lost it or where he had gone. A medic asked me to take it to the hospital in Quang Tri to try to find out if the owner was there. It was a pocket edition of the New Testament, with steel-plated leather covers and a message from President Franklin D. Roosevelt for all men in the Armed Forces, as well as these words: "May the Lord Be with You." Inside, someone had written Virgil Carson of Iuka, Mississippi, and the year 1943; much later, another man had written Lieutenant Carson on that same page. He was the son. The lieutenant had the Bible with him, as always, in the breast pocket of his fatigues on the morning of March 22, 1971, when operation Lam Son 719 was crumpling. Three battalions of South Vietnamese troops—anywhere from one thousand to one thousand five hundred men—had been lifted out of Laos on March 18 by American helicopters in a rout denied by both Saigon and Washington. The fighting was described as "bitter" in a headline in *The New York Times*, whose desk men may not use words such as ghastly or fearful, only "bitter" or "fierce." The South Vietnamese were failing in their campaign to cut the Communist supply lines, failing to show that by themselves and without American troops they could win. It was a winning the Americans most urgently wanted. The war, as it always did, refused to stay fixed: it moved back across the border of Laos into South Vietnam. The artillery, rockets and mortars of the North Vietnamese punched and tore earth and men, grass and trees.

He knew nothing of the retreat of ARVN. His unit was near a dirt country road, perhaps one-quarter of a mile from the old colonial Route 9 which ran into Laos, a place thought of as the last secure position near the border. Lieutenant Lane Carson, leader of 1st Platoon, Alpha Company, 1/11 Infantry, 1st of 5th Infantry Division (Mechanized), heard the artillery coming toward his group; they curled up, hiding their faces, trying to make themselves very flat and small, but it was of no use. He felt, at first, as if he had been buried alive, as if he had been hurt everywhere. He was dragged to a bunker, treated by the platoon medic; others kept offering him cigarettes, but he did not smoke. His glasses were gone, he prayed, the helicopter did not seem to come for a very long time, once on it he felt freezing, and then the morning was at last over. He did not remember B Med. He did not know where he had lost the Bible.

I never found him at Quang Tri, or any other hospital in Vietnam, for many of the wounded were quickly sent to military hospitals outside a combat zone, in other countries. It was nearly a year and a half later that I wrote to the postmaster in Iuka, Mississippi, asking if the Carsons still lived there. The answer came in a letter from New Orleans, a polite and neat letter from Lane Carson, saying how much the Bible meant to his family and offering to reimburse me for any expenses incurred in returning it. I was invited to visit them. There was no way of telling, when we met at last in New Orleans, if I had seen him before, among the dozens of men in the place called B Med.

Lane Carson married Laura, a graceful and bright woman, quite slender, who likes buying and refinishing old furniture. The two dated at Fortier High School and at Louisiana State University, where he was a major in business administration, the class of 1969. Their marriage came after six and a half years, after Vietnam, after the open fracture of his left humerus, the wounds in his left forearm, left thigh, left foot, left flank and chest. Later he knew that the doctors considered cutting off one foot and one hand, but it had not been necessary. They only amputated at the joint of his third toe.

He was grateful for the Bible but he did not want to give his opinions on the war. It made him uneasy. In the kitchen he said someday he might try to run for political office in Louisiana. Of course, it was good to be a veteran, but saying the wrong thing, making remarks that might later be a considered controversial, was a risk he did not wish to take. It was all said so quietly, and with such modesty, that no one could have been cross. He is a careful man, a neat and serious person, a Baptist, who was studying law at Tulane University. At Louisiana State University it had been compulsory to join ROTC in 1966 and 1967 in freshman and sophomore years. He had not minded it at all.

His classmates at Fortier High School voted him most likely to succeed. At LSU he joined a fraternity, was president of the junior class, on the varsity debate team, on the committee for the Union of Current Events, chairman of the Scholarship Committee, and his grades had been fine. He knew what NATO was, and SEATO, and some agreement at Baghdad; it all made sense to him. They were commitments to be honored.

"When we were going to high school we spent, oh, I don't know how many weeks, on communism; they showed us people killed by Communists," Laura said. "There was a real big push on—you know, 'you don't want to be a Communist.' Nowadays in high school—my mother's a teacher—they present communism but there's not as much emphasis on it."

The Army sent Lieutenant Carson to Fort Lewis in Seattle; he was an executive officer for a company learning basic combat training. There was too much paperwork to please him and the hours seemed excessive: 5 A.M. to 9 or 10 P.M.

"It was rewarding in many instances, meeting young men and trying to help them," he said. "Basic training was good for a lot of them. Every company always tends to have the big lug, kind of a dumb kind of a guy, and the rest of his friends make fun of him. Well, for the one we had, it worked out well. He felt he accomplished something. When his parents came to see him they were really proud and they said it had really made a man out of him."

He thought so too. There was a lot of talk about Vietnam at Fort Lewis. "A lot of drill sergeants, a lot of people I talked to in the military indicated how much of it was good duty there," he said. "If you got a good position, you could have a tremendously good time. You could get good money, you'd have tax incentives, you could buy stuff cheaply and you could have a good time."

None of these perks interested him; the good life was not what he had in mind. He volunteered to go to Vietnam at the end of 1970, when the war seemed stifled, forgotten, no more intrusive than a day of rain or a commercial for cat food. His parents took it well. Laura was the only one who kept asking why he chose to do a stupid thing like that. After he was there she began to look at a *National Geographic* map of Vietnam, closely and often.

"Sometimes I think it's just essential to have been there, to be able to say 'I was there, I witnessed it, I saw it,'" Lane Carson said of Vietnam. "I've got that experience behind me, good or bad. For whatever it's worth, it's behind me, it's part of me now."

He did not speak of the Vietnamese, for like most soldiers, he was cut off from them and did not, perhaps, wish it otherwise.

"I came in contact with maids washing clothes quite a lot at Quang Tri. They'd wash them but they'd get everything mixed up, of course. Yes, they were a very small people; I think their teeth were usually poor. The women seemed friendly and questioning."

Laura thought it was curious how the antiwar movement had begun with types you might call hippies and then became many other people as well. "After a while it got to be middle-class America, Mom and Dad. It just got to be everyone." But she did not mean that she had done anything in the streets or raised her voice or made a fist.

He was convinced the war could have been won. He spoke of how Lincoln had blockaded the South, how we might have put a ring around North Vietnam and prevented anything from coming in, as if he did not remember China was there.

Lane said he had joined the local Veterans of Foreign Wars—he felt that their lobby in Washington defended veteran benefits—and the American Legion because he wanted to be involved in community affairs. It was too bad that more Vietnam veterans did not join; the older men would die and then there would be no one to take their places.

"I think our intentions in Vietnam were definitely good. I think it was nice for a group of people to try and help another group of people at a tremendous sacrifice, even if perhaps the reasons why may not be perfectly clear to people," Lane said.

He knew what others had said about the war: that Indochina was a testing place for new weapons, that the military-industrial complex needed a war, that there was oil in Vietnam. "No, I don't believe that," Lane said. "Generally I think our motives were good. I admire that aspect of it."

His father insisted on coming to the apartment on South Claiborne Street that night to thank me for sending back the Bible, which his own father had given to him. Three generations of men had cared about it, and two of them had gone to war with the little Bible close to their hearts, hoping the Lord would be with them.

Mr. Carson, an energetic and outgoing man who works as a mechanical contractor, seemed elated by the occasion. He remembered his distress, so deep and wild, when Lane came back wounded. In the hospital the first words the father spoke were: "Oh, my boy, is it all there?" Perhaps I reminded him again of the ordeal. That night I was with a man who seemed to regard his child as a rare and splendid blessing. Mr. Carson, who wanted to make the evening a treat, took us to the Café du Monde, a bar and coffeehouse, an old and famous one. When I was having my second cup of coffee, eating the third sugared doughnut, Mr. Carson looked at all of us, his face brightening, and said: "Isn't this a great country?"

THE STRICKEN MEN wanted to speak. The survivors of Lam Son 719 did not remain silent, they did not care if everything they told Luong he told me, an American who wrote it down, page after page after page, as they talked. They came out of Laos often missing their helmets, their combat packs, their M-16 rifles, with their uniforms ripped and stained. Nothing mattered to them except to get out, nothing. Sergeant Minh, of Battery F of 2d Marine Battalion, said in Laos his unit had orders to withdraw on Saturday, but there was an attack; on Sunday they were ordered to destroy their howitzers, and did so. On Monday, another attack; they were shelled the entire day, with no artillery of their own. Bad weather—fog, rain, thick mist—kept the helicopters from coming in for them. The helicopters were helpless things.

"We knew that was the end for us. For days we were so desperate with their constant shellings and assaults, with their strange attitude of ignoring death and always moving ahead. Never were the Marines in such a situation as this. We were never afraid of the enemy as we were this time," he said. "They considered us to be babies. They acted as our hosts. They knew everything about us. They shouted: 'We know that you are Company One of Battalion Two. Surrender, friends, we have hot meals and tea for you out here.' And hearing their shouts of 'assault, assault' all around us, we almost wet our pants. And the running away— Oh God, I wanted to throw everything down to move faster." Sometimes he could not help trembling as he told all this to us: the running, the thirst, the fear, the tiredness. He had not yet been able to sleep as well as he once had. All soldiers seemed to be able to fall asleep instantly, anywhere, yet Minh said now he could not.

The two armies, American and South Vietnamese, were

chained to each other in the war and loathed it. But during Lam Son 719, the South Vietnamese kept up the pretense that they were in charge of the operation and that it was going well. This time they were a bit freer to show their resentment of their allies by sending away the American reporters, by booting them out, after years of smiling, of being amiable, of straining to speak English. There were high-level orders not to speak to the foreign press corps, and this pleased the Vietnamese command. It was a huge relief. Two miles west of Khe Sanh, the Vietnamese Airborne Division had its headquarters during the operation, and without Americans to run them, there was confusion and carelessness, as though madmen had made the arrangements.

The wounded Vietnamese were laid so close to the helicopter pad when a giant American Chinook came in to pick up the casualties, the fierce prop-wash of the blades blew away the dressings of the nine men who had been left there on stretchers, lifted up their blankets and bandages and tubes as if a forty mile-an-hour wind had suddenly swept over them. Twenty lightly wounded Vietnamese ran toward the Chinook before it landed, wanting the first places on it, not seeing the deathly ill men who were on the ground being washed by grit and dirt. A Vietnamese soldier holding a stick in his hand tried to direct the proceedings. Inside a large tent, half a dozen Vietnamese officers, nearly all of them doctors, were sleeping or drinking from two bottles of Scotch. One bottle had a Chivas Regal label.

It smelled inside the tent. Luong and I stood before them, but no one said we might sit down. No one offered us water or tea, although both were on the table with the liquor and food. Perhaps it showed on my face that I found it strange to find doctors drinking inside a tent, and napping, when outside the chaos was so constant, the cruelty so surprising. One officer addressed me in English while the others teased him in Vietnamese for speaking the foreign language so well. Luong told me all this later. The doctor told me they did not want foreign reporters, only Vietnamese; they knew the maneuvers of the foreign press and how we preferred to write nasty things about them. Another doctor boasted that he had taken away the camera of one American journalist. I must have stood up for ten minutes, and then sat down on the ground because I had not slept for a long time and was starting to wobble. We went to find the Vietnamese officer in charge of press; he was playing cards and said no journalists allowed, leave here, out! I was angrier then than I had been in months and yelled some nonsense at him, saying I wouldn't go at all. But he said get out of here now. I did. The officer behaved correctly; it was I who was outrageous.

But on that March day I felt the hatred the GIs often had for the Vietnamese. The soldiers always told stories of operations with ARVN, how the Vietnamese would whistle, or smoke, or deliberately make noise to warn the VC and avoid a firefight. They always had stories, their own or those handed down from men who had since gone home, of ARVN running away, of ARVN being chicken. Cowards, thieves, cheats, bums, motherfuckers, rats, pure shit, scared rabbits, the GIs said of ARVN—there it is. It was a favorite expression, which sounded theological the first few times you heard them say it in Vietnam. There it is, they said, when it rained, or the beer ran out, or the mortars came in, or their feet began to rot. They could not understand such an army, could not perceive why ARVN was so bad, so flakey, so without pride, so indifferent to American deaths and to their own reversals.

The Vietnamese I despised were never the soldiers, that human and desperate army, an army without a country, a powerless army that was never loved and who robbed and abused its own. They were victims seeking their own victims. The fury I felt that day— which woke me up, made me forget how much I wanted sleep, clean hair, very cold water—was for the Vietnamese doctors in the tent, whose faces were getting blotchy and soft from the Scotch while outside the Chinook made the bandages whirl like stained and tangled streamers.

An American with the 101st Airborne Division at Khe Sanh said it wasn't safe for Luong to stay among the GIs. There was a possibility that he might be shot if he left the press tent at night. The soldiers were keyed up, the sight of any Vietnamese might make them open fire. No one wanted him there. The 101st Airborne— the Screaming Eagles—was being shelled in the morning and at night, sappers had gotten in through the perimeter to the trench lines and bunkers, there were red alerts. The cooks kept cooking; one of them said the shelling was always at 7 A.M. and close to 7 P.M., with God knows what in between. He was right. One night we ate something veal, and cherry cobblers, on paper plates in a light rain before the mortars came in. Soldiers were told to walk, not run, when there was "in-coming," but I never saw one who could. All of us scuttled or leaped. I reached a bunker crowded with soldiers; we sat on benches while a lieutenant—again the southern voice, so new to me, coming from a corner of Alabama or North Carolina—said to expect a ground attack.

We sat in the blackness, pressed to each other, making no sound, as if breathing too loudly, or one cough, might bring death quicker. Next to me was the hard arm of a man whose face I never saw. The lieutenant said our bunker could expect to receive rocket-propelled grenades; still none of us moved or spoke. The bunker seemed higher than the others: half in the earth, half above it. It was an easier target. When the shelling stopped for a while, we ran out, the soldiers to take their positions for the expected assault. "We'll give you a forty-five, ma'am," the lieutenant said. I refused it, and ran to hide. The reason I might have given at the time was that correspondents were civilian non-combatants and that I would kill no one. It was a long time later before it came to me that in refusing a weapon, all I had done was to make it necessary for a GI to do the defending, that to refuse to take part in the killing only meant that others would have to do it for me.

The attack did not come that night.

A PLATOON SERGEANT named Co had clung like an insect to the skids of one American helicopter that came for his battalion in Laos on March 6. Only one hundred of the four hundred got out: there was no room for all of them. As the soldiers raced to each helicopter, shoving and pushing the slower or weaker ones out of their way, the American crews had to use their feet or fists to stop so many men. The Americans were afraid the helicopters could not rise with too heavy a load. The Vietnamese officers watched and could do nothing. No one listened to orders. The sergeant was older, with muscular arms and thicker wrists, with wider bones than the other Vietnamese, who did not often weigh more than one hundred and ten pounds. Few men had been able to hold on to the skids of the helicopters once the aircraft rose and the wind began to slam and freeze them. Sometimes, on the ground, reporters saw the soldiers fall, unable to hold on any longer, but you could not hear if they howled or cried out when they dropped.

He was not ashamed of what he had one, the sergeant said; to be ashamed was a luxury he could not afford. "Each helicopter would have been the last one, so what choice was there for me?" he said. "Only the madmen would stay and politely wait for the next helicopter.

"The wind, the wind, so terribly strong. Sometimes I nearly fell off. Jesus Christ, my hands and legs were dead when we reached Khe Sanh . . . They fired on us night and day, not saving ammunition as they did here in the south. With eighteen years in the army and fighting so many battles, I never had such an experience as this Laos operation . . . Sometimes we talked to the North Vietnamese on the radio. They told us to surrender to survive . . . 'You realize too well that we are all around you, and can move in at any time, not because you are bad soldiers, but because you are so few, so tired, so lonely and a little frightened. We are Vietnamese, why do you fight for the American imperialists? You should be fighting for your country, the Vietnamese people.' This is what they said. And some of us swore and called them names on the radio: 'Sons of bitches, you are working like dogs for the Chinese, for the Russians, you are selling the country to them, motherfuckers.' That kind of talking went on for ten minutes and they used to cut off by saying on the radio 'We expect you to be nicer. Now it's better to stop. We will call you again, friends.'"

There were many such stories we heard in Khe Sanh. Sergeant Co was AWOL, but he did not care.

"All that counts is surviving this Laos operation," he said. "Being absent for a few days, getting some punishment, that is nothing to me." He wanted to sleep, to eat, to drink beer, to be with friends all at the same time.

There was a twenty-two-year-old Marine named Private Moc—he walked through the jungle for two nights and a day before being airlifted back—who kept sucking on one cigarette after another, a man who seemed to be drinking smoke. He could not stop it. His unit had been near a fire base called Delta on Hill 547 about eight miles inside Laos; he wanted to tell why the South Vietnamese troops ran for their lives, each man struggling only for himself.

"The last attack came at about eight P.M. They shelled us first and then came the tanks moving up into our positions. The whole brigade ran down the hill like ants. We jumped on each other to get out of that place. No man had time to look for his commanding officer. It was quick, quick, quick or we would die. Oh God, now I know for sure that I am really alive."

Squatting, he moved his head from side to side as he spoke, sometimes in a voice that became a whisper. "They were everywhere and they were so daring," Private Moc said. "Their firepower was so enormous and their shelling was so accurate, what could we do but run, run for our lives."

There were others—in the 1st Infantry Division, considered a crack outfit by the American advisors, in the Marines, the Rangers and in the Airborne Division—who had not ever imagined such an enemy and who could not understand how they survived American air strikes and B-52 bombings, which they themselves feared so much. Many complained that since the drive into Cambodia in the spring of 1970 had been so easy, there was so little resistance, they had not known what to expect in Laos. The trouble was they now knew what to expect and thought they could never be ready again for such an ordeal.

Corporal Ti—few men wanted to give their full names—was a Marine who fought on Hill 547 in Laos on the night of March 22. Many of his friends had killed themselves because they were wounded. The American helicopters could not extract the injured because of heavy antiaircraft fire.

"The papers and the radio kept on saying there was a Laos victory, I have learned now, but what a joke," Corporal Ti said. "We ran out like wounded dogs."

This was the most heartbreaking thing to him.

Corporal Ti said: "We left behind our wounded friends. They lay there, crying, knowing the B-52 bombs would fall on them. They asked friends to shoot them, but none of us could bring himself to do that. So the wounded cried out for grenades, first one man, then another, then more."

The men who could still stand up and move began to disperse at 8 P.M. At midnight they thought they could hear the sound of the B-52s coming in.

"Some men who were wounded in the arms or legs tried to run out with us, but they could not make it," Corporal Ti said.

Private Binh of the 2d Marine Battalion had the same story to tell about a wounded friend: "He waved me closer to him and told me in whispers 'No way for you to help me out. So please have pity on me and give me a grenade, Binh, don't hesitate, give me it and run out now.' I gave him one. Seconds later I heard it explode. Poor boy, poor boy. There were about one hundred and fifty left behind. They cried, asked to be shot by friends, asked for grenades. And the withdrawal was terrifying. A group of about one hundred stuck to each other and nobody wanted to be first in line. On the way all were afraid of running into ambushes. Sometimes we were fired on by North Vietnamese or by running-away Marines . . . Once Captain Tien had to swear at us loudly and angrily. 'God-dammit, be courageous. Be soldiers. I'm worrying about my survival too, so when I advise you to go this way or that way I think of you as well as me. Okay, move now. Okay, I move first.' And he pulled out his pistol and ran uphill. And we followed him."

There was nothing more Private Binh could tell and nothing more to ask. Lam Son 719 was the death of the army in South Vietnam, and the total collapse came four years later when province after province in the south was pushed and then quickly collapsed. There were no great battles; in some places the armies did not exchange fire. Americans were surprised, some outraged, by the spectacle they saw on their television screens and what they read in their newspapers. The eyewitness reports told of Vietnamese soldiers who seemed to have gone insane as they ran, pleading, begging, pillaging. Soldiers kicked, battered and fired upon civilians to get aboard the last aircraft to leave Danang. There was no pity in them.

Two hundred and sixty-eight people were the last passengers to leave. Only two women and a baby were among the soldiers of the ARVN 1st Division who fought their way on that flight. When the aircraft rose at last, the soldiers did not cheer at their luck. They were silent, for they understood what they had done. When Danang fell, it fell to a thousand Communist soldiers who came into the city and shortly restored order. Even the Vietnamese who won were surprised. In August 1975 Radio Hanoi said an outstanding achievement of the revolution was the stabilization of social order and security in the southern region, where there had been "a mad and disorderly society having the most unruly troops ever seen in the world."

RENNIE PERRIN, A middle-aged Vermont barber, was sound asleep when his wife a nurse, came home from her shift at the Veterans Administration Hospital, so she thought it wiser to wait until the morning to tell him their son, Richard, had deserted. Mrs. Perrin heard it on the radio at the hospital, where she had night duty. The next day—it was in September 1967—Mr. Perrin had to be told, for there was a story on their son, a nineteen-year-old private, in the local paper, the Springfield *Times-Reporter*. Mr. Perrin, a veteran of World War II who had been discharged after a year in the Army because he had tuberculosis, listened to his wife, Betty. Then he began to cry. She stayed very calm.

"Somebody had to," Mrs. Perrin said.

Five years after Richard Perrin made that choice, his parents were still anxious and shy about talking about the son who had so much changed their lives, as if they still feared he might be hurt. For quite some time Mrs. Perrin thought certain Americans might go to Canada and try to kill the deserters living there.

The couple live in a mobile home in Sharon, Vermont, off Route 14, about ten miles north of White River Junction. They moved here in 1972 from North Springfield, where they lived for fifteen years and raised three children. Springfield is a factory town with not more than ten thousand people, known for its machine tools and often called "precision valley," Mr. Perrin said. He had his own barbershop, called Ray's, but he left it at the age of sixty-three. He only says of all this that business was slow because men were letting their hair grow longer and that he wasn't trained to do the hair styling that younger customers wanted. He does not give his son's notoriety as a reason for leaving. They moved to Sharon to be nearer the V.A. hospital where Mrs. Perrin has worked since 1966 in the orthopedic and neurosurgical wards.

It was in December 1973 when I saw them. They are not cheerful now at Christmas. Mr. Perrin speaks with effort, as if his words were little roots that had to be pulled up carefully from hard ground.

"We had a terrible time for a long time," Mr. Perrin said. "As long as he is in Canada, it will never really be over for us." He thought that people whose sons had been killed in Vietnam might find it easier to accept their loss, find it easier to go on with life, than he and his wife did. Their boy was always missing. "You make up your mind they're gone now and you can't bring them back," he said. "But with Dick, he's alive and can't come back."

The unspoken fear of Mr. and Mrs. Perrin was quite clear. It was that one of them—he at sixty-four, or she at fifty—might fall ill and not be able to see Richard before death. The other children would come to them, of course, but without Richard there was always a space and a longing.

"You'd be surprised at how fast things can happen to people," Mrs. Perrin said, meaning the heart-can-go, the lungs-can-go, the-kidneys-or-liver-can-go, just like that. She looked at Mr. Perrin; he looked at her. They did not want to complain about how they had been treated or tell me the names of people who had snubbed or wounded them. They did not want to be considered whiners.

Mr. Perrin was still a member of the American Legion because he paid his dues, but he had stopped going to their meetings. Mrs. Perrin was a member of the Daughters of the American Revolution.

"I've never been back because I know how they would feel. It would be hard for me to listen to them talk—oh, I know how they talk," Mr. Perrin said, "You know they all went to war, and anybody who doesn't do that—well, I feel I'm just as good a legionnaire as they are. I believe in this country. I love this country. Even if Dick did desert, he said himself that he loved this country. There was the time when they asked him if he wanted to become a C.O. and he said no. He wasn't against all wars, just this one. If someone came to attack this country, he'd fight for the defense of it . . .

"In the beginning it was terrible for us. I was very patriotic, like most men are. I used to make statements like those I've heard people say in front of me since Dick deserted. People saying 'Anyone who deserts should be shot.' It's awful hard for people to understand. When this first happened we didn't go along with Dick because we didn't understand it. Like most people don't. But when you're involved in it you start asking yourself questions, why all this happened. Now that we know, we feel a lot better. In the beginning it was terrible."

Mr. Perrin was born in France, in Vosges above Nancy; he remembered his parents talking, with bitterness, about World War I. He came to Vermont as a child, growing up in Barre, but no one could pronounce his real first name, Rene. They called him Re-en, or Rinay, or Rin, so he called himself Rennie, for everyone could pronounce that.

Richard Perrin was nineteen, a tank mechanic in the 1st Battalion of the 64th Armored Brigade stationed in Kitzingen, West Germany, when he deserted and went to Paris to begin an organization called RITA, which stood for "Resist Inside the Army." It was an underground antiwar group of GIs trying to encourage dissension. Perhaps the most shocking time for his parents was December 11, 1967, when they saw their son on CBS television from Paris with the black radical Stokely Carmichael, who had recently called for the defeat of the United States in Vietnam.

I remember the deserters who came to Paris. A very tall boy

from Florida who liked scrambled eggs slept on my living-room floor for three nights, but we thought it better if I did not know his last name. He went on to Sweden, he could not bear being in Paris. None of them were sure if the French government would not turn them over to the Americans, if there would not be a knock on the door at midnight, and the door kicked down. The deserters had pledged that they would engage in no political activity while in France, but their existence was a political act, their being in a room meant the war and the Army were in the room too.

The notorious interview took place at midnight in Paris after long, secret arrangements which took the CBS television crew and a *New York Times* reporter to a middle-class apartment. White bedsheets were hung in one room to shield a Dutch activist who had arranged everything. He stayed behind the sheets as he spoke of increasing desertions. Private Perrin walked through the sheets to sit down and face the camera, which rested on him like a huge, unblinking eye. He was calm and spoke quietly of his life, recalling how at fifteen he had joined a march in Chicago in 1964 led by the Reverend Dr. Martin Luther King, Jr.

"About this time I began thinking that, maybe, everything I was told in school, maybe, wasn't all like that," the private said.

In Springfield, Vermont, his parents were horrified. Mr. Perrin told a reporter: "We don't go along with what this boy did but we realize he has been brainwashed." He insisted that his son had been a "good soldier" when he first enlisted. Local people, who considered Carmichael a Communist if not something even more evil, were very critical and let their opinions be known. A picture of Richard Perrin appeared on the front page of the town newspaper with the headline AWOL GI RECALLED AS AVERAGE STUDENT.

Mrs. Perrin was worried that the two younger children, David and Nancy, would be bullied or taunted. "That day when I sent them off to school—it was David's twelfth birthday—I remember telling the kids to hold your head high," she said. "When David went in his classroom one of the kids said 'Is that your brother?' and David said 'Shut your big fat mouth.' That's the way he handled it."

She is dark-haired, small, quicker to smile than her husband. Both speak softly. Their son once said of them, in an interview with another American in exile, that his parents were outwardly conservative people but more liberal than their Vermont friends.

"With my folks there is a sort of basic humanism which stuck in my head," Richard Perrin said. "They wouldn't tolerate me saying nigger, Polack, anything like that . . . I was always truthful with them, anything I did, I would always go home and tell them about it."

The word "deserter"—the ancient, horrid word with its dreadful picture of a cringing, failing man who flees—made them feel sick. It is a word they still do not like. It makes most Americans nervous, too, for they think of a battlefield and a soldier running from it, leaving other men in a lurch. No one thinks of courage or convictions.

It took Mr. and Mrs. Perrin nearly three years to accept what Richard had done and to see his reasons, although they always defended him even when they disapproved. Her husband was ahead of her on that, Mrs. Perrin said.

After graduating from high school, Richard had been unable to find a job because of his draft status. He went to California to visit his half brother, Ronald, the child of Mr. Perrin's first marriage, who was fifteen years older and always had a stunning and gentle influence on the younger boy. It was he who had worked for civil rights and made Richard see its importance. That year Ronald, who was teaching at the University of California, was in the antiwar movement, but nothing about Vietnam seemed to reach Richard Perrin until after he enlisted and was in advanced infantry training.

While sitting in a PX cafeteria at Fort Leonard Wood, Private Perrin, an E-2 squad leader at the armored vehicles repair shop, overheard two sergeants reminiscing about Vietnam. One described how he had gotten a confession from a captured Vietnamese by pushing the naked prisoner against the very hot engine of a tank so his genitals would burn. The sergeant was talking in a normal voice, not as if he was telling a secret. From then on, Richard Perrin began to pay attention to everything about the war. At the end of June 1967 he was sent to Fort Sill, Oklahoma. Ronald, who had earlier told him not to desert, had heard that a Private Andy Stapp, also at Fort Sill, was organizing GIs to protest the war. Richard later described his good friend Andy, who formed the American Servicemen's Union, as "anticapitalist, antiimperialist" while saying of himself that at Fort Sill he was just "antiwar." But he was that, and he worked hard.

"He was learning and reading about Vietnam. He was really tore up. He called home, very upset, and begged us to see it the way he did," Mr. Perrin said.

"But of course we didn't," Betty Perrin added, "we believed what we were reading in the papers at that time. We wanted him to just get the three years over and get home."

At Fort Sill, during a press conference of antiwar GIs, Private Perrin handed out his own statement, which received considerable attention in the press. He was eighteen.

"I was being trained as a truck mechanic and was on my way to Fort Sill to work on armored trucks and self-propelled artillery," the statement said. "I realized I was being trained to support these atrocities. At this point I decided to find out for myself whether there was any justification for the war. Everyone said there was, but they couldn't tell me what it was."

He ended the statement by saying that he hoped the people in the United States would wake up to the fact that they were being led through a period that would one day "be called the darkest in our history."

For his failure one night to sign out on the pass register, shortly after the press conference, Private Perrin was arrested, handcuffed and taken to the city jail in Lawton, before being turned over to the military authorities. He was charged with an article 15, non-judicial punishment, which he refused to sign. He demanded a court-martial. It was clear to him he was only being punished for his antiwar activities, not for neglecting to sign the pass register.

Mr. and Mrs. Perrin were flown down to see their son and told by officers to try to bring the boy around to a reasonable point of view, that the military only wanted to straighten him out. They talked to a captain, then to a general, who explained the domino theory to them and the importance of South Vietnam being protected. When they saw Richard, who was in the stockade, they could hardly believe it.

"It was an awful shock," Mrs. Perrin said. "His head has been shaved but they wouldn't let him shave his face or change his clothes."

"He didn't look like our boy," Mr. Perrin said.

"He said he was ashamed to wear the uniform," Mrs. Perrin said.

Richard Perrin said later that when the Army assumed he repented, they offered to shorten his sentence of thirty days' hard labor. If he stopped his antiwar work, the Army said, they would send him to Germany, not Vietnam. Perrin agreed, but in Germany the racism on the bases—much more acute than in the United States—the memory of the stockade, his fatigue and disgust with the military led him to desert. He refused, in all ways, to be a soldier any more. In Paris he wanted RITA to inspire soldiers to challenge and harass the military.

"I was sort of hanging on to the old liberal myth: There's nothing wrong with the U.S. . . . . The war is just a mistake . . . We can stop this and elect a new administration," Richard Perrin said of himself in 1968.

In Springfield nothing was quite the same for his parents, or ever could be. Some people wrote letters to the paper protesting what Richard Perrin had done.

"One letter, I remember, said that we or the schools had failed in not having the Perrin boy read the story of *The Man Without a Country*," Mrs. Perrin said. A disabled World War II veteran wrote in his letter that deserters like their son should be shot. The man's wife was a friend of Mrs. Perrin's; they were both nurses. "We never talked about it, we just never even mentioned it," she said.

A lot of people asked his parents about Richard, including some whose own sons had been in Vietnam.

"You've heard me say this, Betty, but sometimes I had the feeling that some people, not all of them, would ask me about Dick because some of them were pumping me and that deep down they were probably hoping he was having a hard time," Mr. Perrin said, shaking his head.

But there were a few people who tried to tell him, when he was still puzzled and sorrowful, that his son had done the right thing. The couple were encouraged to keep in touch with their son, not to turn their backs on him, by Phillips B. Henderson, pastor of the North Springfield Baptist Church, who had known Richard and had liked him.

Mrs. Perrin felt as if she and her husband had lost a child. "If they were mean, it made me mad. If they were kind, it almost brought me to tears," she said.

She was more often on the verge of tears. When Richard wrote from Canada for a grade transcript, the Springfield school board refused to send it to him. One board member was the father of Richard's closest friends in high school. He told his own children never to associate with their classmate again and he forbid them to write the deserter. When I asked them about the reaction of relatives in Vermont and New Hampshire, Mr. and Mrs. Perrin looked at each other but said nothing.

Richard moved to Canada in January 1969, working for a year and a half operating two hostels and a counseling service for the Union of American Deserters in Regina, Saskatchewan. He married a Canadian girl and both worked at a center for retarded children in Moose Jaw. At twenty-two Richard Perrin said that he did not think he would plan on returning to the United States and that he would be of no use there. At twenty-five he was in Regina working as a garage mechanic. He had always loved working on cars, that was one reason he never let his hair grow long, for he couldn't stand having it get in his eyes when he worked. His two-year-old son was named Shayne.

"He was the quietest of the children," Mrs. Perrin said. "There was a wide streak of idealism in Richard, together with an impatience with hypocrisy. Richard was the most quiet, I didn't always know what he was thinking because he didn't talk much, but when he did open up to talk you better be ready to listen . . ."

They are stubborn people, refusing to give in to the strain and isolation they had felt for so long. Perhaps they had not even known how taxing it had been until the Perrins went to an amnesty conference in Vermont in the fall of 1973. It was so new for them to be surrounded by people like themselves, people who were proud of their sons for escaping the draft or leaving the Army. One young man went up to Mr. Perrin to shake his hand because he had a son in Canada. It was a man who had gone to jail rather than to Vietnam. Mr. Perrin spoke of that handshake, and the encounter, as if he had suddenly received an award.

"Even if they did let them come back, maybe it wouldn't be very pleasant for them—there would always be someone saying something and pointing them out as deserters," Mr. Perrin said. "Dick wouldn't want to come back to live."

The couple had visited their son and his family five times in Saskatchewan. The visits had been happy. David, the youngest son, had spoken often of the brother who went to Canada, for he was proud of him. Richard did not become a ghost. Mrs. Perrin showed me some color photographs of their reunions in Canada: there was Richard Perrin, a tall dark-haired man with a face that was a little blurred in the photographs.

"He doesn't look like a criminal, does he?" Mrs. Perrin asked.

ON SEPTEMBER 16, 1974, President Ford announced his clemency program for convicted and unconvicted draft evaders and military deserters, which he said was an "act of mercy." His offer was delayed a week because of the President's pardon of former President Richard M. Nixon, which provoked a furious and inquisitive reaction throughout the country. The amnesty program applied to those men who had evaded the draft or deserted the military between August 4, 1968, and March 28, 1973, the strange and poisonous period bounded by the Gulf of Tonkin Resolution and the withdrawal of U.S. forces from Vietnam. The President's program had three autonomous parts: the Defense Department handled unsettled military desertion cases; civilian draft evaders went to the Justice Department; and a nine-man Presidential Clemency Board handled civilians and servicemen already convicted and punished. The board was headed by former Senator Charles Goodell, a Republican of New York who had opposed the war. His defeat for reelection by James L. Buckley was believed to have been engineered by Nixon forces. The board, a mixture of men of different backgrounds and political persuasions, included a retired Marine general, the thirty-one-year-old executive director of Paralyzed Veterans of America, a former cabinet member and counselor to President Nixon, and the president of Notre Dame University, who had been chairman of the U.S. Committee on Civil Rights.

The program was riddled with inequities, ambiguities and different perceptions of degrees of guilt. The Clemency Board itself disbanded—after two extensions of the program—in a sour spirit, with four of its members refusing to put their names to the final report, which they considered to be too lenient.

Although the President thought the clemency program would heal some of the deepest tears in the country, it only inflamed them and gave fresh energy to antiwar groups, or those who argued for an unconditional or general amnesty.

On the last day of the very last deadline—March 31, 1975—the American Civil Liberties Union bitterly criticized what it termed "the numbers game" of the clemency board:

> In six and a half months since the inception of the Clemency Program . . . the Board claims to have received about 16,500 applications. It has so far managed to process 65 of these cases to date—less than 1/2 of 1 percent. At this rate, the Board's clemency processing will be completed in 125 years, in the year 2110. Mr. Goodell has announced that he is urging the President to double the size of the present nine-member Board. That should cut the time required for processing to about 60 years, till A.D. 2035.
>
> The Clemency Board has received only 8,334 applications from persons whose eligibility has been established. About 4/5 of them come from Vietnam-era veterans with administrative Undesirable discharges from the military. The Board can offer them a) a pardon which they do not need, since they were never convicted of a crime, not even by court-martial for a military offense, and it can offer them b) a Clemency Discharge, which gives them neither greater dignity nor any veterans benefits whatever . . . And for these dubious advantages the Board will require up to two years of alternate service from these veterans. For 80 percent of the Board's applicants, the clemency is a cruel hoax.

More than 750,000 persons were in need of a universal and unconditional amnesty after the decade in Vietnam, the ACLU said, but only 137,000 were eligible under the Ford plan.

There was resentment over the alternate service—up to two years—required of men who avoided the draft and were not convicted and deserters without convictions. Deputy Attorney General Laurence Silberman, explaining the program, said the government would place such men in public service jobs if they could not find jobs themselves which met with the government's approval. Such work wouldn't be hard to find, Mr. Silberman added, "because they are low-paying jobs that many people don't seek."

In January 1976 the ACLU made public a copy of the final report of the Clemency Board and challenged the claim that the program had been a success.

The board's report said that 113,227 persons were eligible for the amnesty program but only 21,729 had applied. Of this group, 5,052 had been recommended for outright pardon, 7,551 had been given varying periods of alternative service and 911 had been denied any form of clemency. There were 8,215 cases not resolved.

The report also said that 10,115 fugitive AWOL offenders had been eligible for inclusion in the program and that 55 percent had applied, that 4,522 unconvicted draft offenders had been eligible and that 16 percent had applied, that 90,000 discharged AWOL offenders had been eligible and that 13 percent had applied, and that 22 percent of 8,700 convicted draft offenders who were eligible had come forward.

"The program has completely failed in all areas," Warren Hoover, executive director of the National Interreligious Service Board for Conscientious Objectors said.

Ramsey Clark, former Attorney General under President Lyndon B. Johnson and one of the few men who had held high office who later denounced the war, said the ACLU gave too small a number. Rather than the 750,000 Americans the ACLU thought would be affected by a general amnesty—which Mr. Clark said did not include hundreds of thousands of men who had not registered for the draft and were omitted from census counts—the number was far greater. Mr. Clark gave the number of Americans in "legal jeopardy" for war resistance close to 2,000,000.

Such numbers—they sailed out like tiny black butterflies. In Washington, D.C., there are quite different numbers and their numbers are in battle with these numbers. I know what I am forgetting now: the face of the boy from Nebraska who hid in Paris, the book he kept reading over and over. His face is not clear, it becomes the face, thin and careful, of Richard Bucklin on the day he had visitors in the army prison at Leavenworth. He said he had left a letter in his shirt pocket, that this was forbidden but that the punishment was not severe.

III

SMALL PLACES

The newest names are going up now on the war monuments in the South. In a small place called Fulton, Mississippi, between Tupaloosa and Birmingham, there stands off Route 78 a newly erected monument made of old uneven bricks of a burned, darker red. On top, the flame rises from a curved and split iron cup; it was this light that made me stop. The men of the county who went to the last four wars, and are pinned to them forever, are listed on granite slabs: nineteen for World War I, ninety-two for World War II, two for Korea, sixteen for Vietnam: Boozer, Clark, Coats, Davidson, Hall, Hodges, Humphries, Izard, Jones, Palmer, Sanderson, Waddle, West, Willis, Worthey and Yielding. Aron Yielding died in World War II; twenty-odd years later Vietnam had Larry T. Yielding.

DURING THE WAR, somewhere in the middle of it, there were men in Washington, D.C., who were bothered by the rising American casualties—not by the wounds they did not see, but by the concern that perhaps the small towns might not keep taking such losses stoically. It was in these places that people knew the boy who had been killed in Chu Lai, could remember how well he played high school football, knew what his father did, the name of his mother's family and if they were churchgoers. It wasn't the same in the cities, where if a soldier from Detroit or Los Angeles or St. Louis got killed, people in the neighborhood would be startled or made uneasy. In Washington the worry was that the small towns would start questioning the war, that the prominent citizens—the banker, the biggest farmer, a principal— would begin to speak against it.

Once, in Missouri, a university student driving me to the airport remembered what had happened in his tiny hometown in that state when there was someone killed in Vietnam. The neighbors took food to the house. It was always done at such times. The neighbors went to the house carrying soup pots, covered dishes and pies to leave on the kitchen table so the woman would not have to cook for her family during the first days, those first white nights of grieving.

The boy, who was gentle and plump, remembered it all. "I bet they had enough food there to last three days," he said.

People used to say that it was in the small places where Vietnam had cut the deepest, that it was in the small places where the war had taken away so much. So this is where I went: small places of all kinds, everywhere.

One of them was Bardstown, in a smooth and fat part of Kentucky. Driving there, you can see the low white fences of some fine stables. I liked the cold and the grass that promised to be greener when it was warm again, a child's idea of green, clear and shiny, not the greens of Vietnam, not the green of the Army.

Few of us would find it an alien or puzzling place; the white curtains in so many windows look as if women washed, ironed and fluffed them up every week. The porches are still there, but people sit inside at night to watch television. The architecture of the oldest houses is neo-Greek, New England Colonial, Cape Cod or Georgian. Families still live in some of them, taking care of the blue or yellow poplar flooring, the hand-carved mantels, the brass doorknobs and the curving staircases. On Tuesday it is ladies night—drinks half price for them—at the Holiday Inn near Blue Grass Parkway, and its Oak Dining Room, with the harsh air conditioning and all the salad you want to eat, is considered by many a fancy and special place to go for steaks. In the summer a sweet and yeasty smell from the eleven bourbon distilleries in the county speaks of money, melted, soaking the bright air. There are three factories, nine churches, an art gallery, a Catholic bookstore, a swap shop, good bowling alleys and a diner still named for a dead owner, Tom Pig, because there is no reason to change it. An award is given to the Outstanding Citizen of the Year from Nelson County at the annual ladies-night meeting of the Chamber of Commerce in mid-January. The local newspaper, the *Kentucky Standard*, runs a picture and announcement if a young man joins the service. It has been like this for a long time. Louisville is thirty-nine miles away; the population here is 5,800; it is the second oldest city in Kentucky.

The town gives its assets, briskly, on a green sign on US 31E: Bardstown, Nelson County, Bourbon Center of the World, Old Kentucky Home, St. Joseph Cathedral.

Just before North Third, a soft and wide street of old trees and white-frame or red-brick houses, there is the building of the Kentucky National Guard Unit based in Bardstown. The war is here, in a small low-lying house with two crossed cannon barrels in front, looking precise and proper. In red and yellow a sign tells you here is Battery C, 2d Howitzer Battalion, 138th Artillery. The entire battery, part of a five-hundred-man battalion, was called to active duty May 13, 1968, by an executive order that summoned 24,000 men to bolster U.S. forces in Vietnam.

Even during that terrible week in June years ago when four men from Battery C were killed on one day in Vietnam—and a fifth did not live another week—no one ever defaced the 138th Artillery sign or said they could not stand the sight of it any more. In Bardstown they are very nice people, not given to messing up property or doing wild things. Nor could it be said that the reporters, with their notebooks and questions, their cameras and television crews, were made to feel ill-at-ease, even as they asked, so many times, how people felt. For a little while the Vietnam war made Bardstown famous for a new, unpleasant reason. The older people, in positions of prominence, were cordial and kept to their cheerful ways, perhaps trying to make the point that good Christians do not collapse in crises. Millie Sutherland makes marvelous chocolate sheet cake and wrote out the recipe for me. Her husband, Judge Sutherland, gave me two boxes of Kentucky Kernel Seasoned Flour, Ideal for Chicken, Chops, Steak, Fish, Oysters and Shrimp, which is made by his family's firm, with very precise instructions on how to make the best batter and gravy with it. It was the judge who called Bardstown "a place of wholesomeness, goodness."

The town has always been used to outsiders; it calls out to tourists—who are usually southern—and does not make fun of them when they come. What draws many people is My Old Kentucky Home State Park, one mile from downtown Bardstown, where each summer a cast of forty-six performs in an outdoor musical drama called *The Stephen Foster Story*. One small Kentucky newspaper called the performance "as merry as a mint julep." The performers sing "My Old Kentucky Home," "Old Folks at Home," "De Camptown Races," "Jeanie with the Light Brown Hair" and "Oh, Susanna." Some are not so sure that the composer wrote his most famous, very sentimental song in Bardstown in 1852 while visiting his father's cousin, Judge John Rowan, in his mansion inspired by Independence Hall in Philadelphia. But it sells more bourbon and country hams, more souvenirs and more meals, and fills the motels where the room clerks referred to the mayor as Gus and know if the corn is doing well. It is typical of Bardstown that there are taxis bearing signs that say "Heaven Hill creates a better atmosphere." It was quite some time before I realized that Heaven Hill is only a bourbon sold in Kentucky, but the point is that Bardstown wants things to be calm and pleasant, and believes its own atmosphere to be very nice.

The past is persistent here, claiming attention even under the plates and coffee cups at the Old Talbott Tavern, which calls itself the Oldest Western Stagecoach in America. For there are paper place mats in the restaurant to remind you that the tavern and inn was opened in 1779 during the Revolutionary War when it was used by General George Rogers Clark as his base. Provisions and munitions were brought overland from Virginia and stored in the cellars. In 1797 the exiled Duke of Orleans, Louis Phillippe, stayed here, feeling rather ill, with a large entourage. Later, when he was King of the French, he sent paintings and church furniture to the Catholic Bishop of Bardstown. The gifts included two paintings by Van Eyck, two by Van Dyck, one Murillo and one Rubens, which were hung in St. Joseph's, the first Catholic cathedral west of the Alleghenies upon its completion in 1819.

Not far from the packages of Old Kentucky Bourbon Candy, $2.95 a pound, on sale in the Old Talbott Tavern, is an eight-inch steel saw which was one of four instruments used by Dr. Walter Brashear in 1806 in the first successful amputation of a leg at the hip joint. The patient was a seventeen-year-old boy whose leg was mangled. Nowhere is his name to be found.

In the Old Court House Square there is the plaque to the surgeon who amputated "without any precedent to guide him," and another to John Fitch, who died penniless in Bardstown, giving him credit for demonstrating a working steam-powered boat more than twenty years before Robert Fulton.

There is the slave block with the notice that upon this stone slaves were sold before emancipation in 1863, and a tribute to Thomas Nelson, a member of the Virginia House of Burgesses and, later, the Continental Congress, a signer of the Declaration of Independence and Commander of the Virginia Militia, who in 1781 was "commended for selfless patriotism in ordering guns to fire on his own home, the British headquarters at Yorktown, 1781." Here, too, is a cool bronze reminder that Braxton Bragg's Army of twenty-eight thousand men camped here from September 20 to October 3, 1862, moved to Harrodsburg, then met Buell's Union Army in the Battle of Perryville, October 8. The language on the plaques is dry, sparse, correct. It is not intended to move the imagination, to depress people or make them proud.

The newest bronze plaque, put in the Court House Square in May 1970, says this: IN MEMORY Dedicated to those men who gave their lives in Vietnam 1969 for the preservation of freedom.

There are seven names on it. Five were National Guardsmen from Battery C whose deaths came from an enemy attack before dawn at Fire Support Base Tomahawk, near Phu Bai, in South Vietnam. Four died there, in a place women could never imagine, but one burned man lived for another five days. In the long war, twelve men from the Bardstown area were killed. The first died in February 1966 and another later that year. Three died in 1968. The last two died on June 24 and 25, 1969. But there was never such a day as June 19, 1969. Some of the dead were from villages close to Bardstown: Cox's Creek, Willisburg, Carrolltown and New Haven. In Bardstown, when you ask about the dead, people nod and speak of the Simpson boy, the McIlvoy boy, the Collins boy; even if they cannot clearly see their faces now, there is a father or a cousin whom they know.

There was only one widow left. The four others remarried. It made her feel more alone. Her name was Deanna Durbin before she married Ronald Earl Simpson, who was killed at Fire Support Base Tomahawk. Other reporters had been to see her. She wanted no more of it; she did not want to see me. A child, whom she named Cheryl Lynn, was born five days before her husband's body was flown home and buried at Bardstown Cemetery on July Fourth in a military service. There were soldiers from Fort Knox, who fired their rifles, and Masons in their white aprons. At the cemetery she sat under the funeral tent, clutching a yellow handkerchief, and afterward she was led away to a car, unsteady, holding the folded American flag.

The young husband is remembered as an easygoing, pleasant man, tall and dark-haired, who did not complain or ask questions when he was in Vietnam. However, Specialist 4 Simpson had been one of the one hundred and five plaintiffs in a lawsuit argued by Nathan R. Zahm, a lawyer from California, that it was unconstitutional to send National Guardsmen overseas. The case was moving slowly to the Supreme Court, but the unit was shipped overseas one day before the court met on October 26, 1968.

Mrs. Simpson did not know what had happened to the case. Nothing about the war, its purpose or its weaponry, or the arguments over it, seemed clear, only that she could not forgive the death of her husband, and the words used to justify it did not calm her at all.

Sometimes Deanna Simpson thought of leaving Bardstown, but it was always the house on West Forrest Street that held her there. Ronald Earl Simpson had built it for them, close to the home of his parents, and they had lived there during that brief marriage, until at the age of twenty-two he was killed. She did not know right away that it happened on a Thursday in a place near Phu Bai. She was not sure what a fire base was. She knew nothing until the following Monday that he was missing in action. The notification of his death came two days later.

The government said it was shrapnel, Mrs. Simpson said. "They bombed the place where he stayed and threw grenades into it," she said.

Two British reporters from BBC had come to Bardstown, where they were looked on kindly as somewhat exotic but affable fellows. To this day Deanna Simpson remembers how Peter Taylor, one of the BBC men, told her of one man in Bardstown who had shocked the British visitors by his reaction to the casualties. It was First Sergeant Pat Sympson of the National Guard in Bardstown, the man who knew the Bardstown boys in Battery C and first trained them, who had even spent ten months on active duty in Vietnam, although he was not at Fire Support Base Tomahawk when the North Vietnamese sappers came through the wire and, at 2 A.M., half asleep, the young men of Bardstown learned, at last, the real purpose of being in Battery C.

"That man, that sergeant, he said 'Well, somebody's got to get killed in a war,'" Mrs. Simpson said on the telephone.

First Sergeant Sympson was sitting behind his desk in an office at the National Guard building. He had his souvenirs arranged around the rim of the desk. There was a grenade and a defused shell casing, which the sergeant said was from a "pineapple." This is a nickname for an antipersonnel weapon. The pineapple was a very small bomb compared to others. It looked like a perforated Sterno can with six steel spring-locked fins on the top and two hundred and fifty pellets in the casing. An American plane could drop a thousand pineapples over an area the size of four football fields. In a single air strike two hundred and fifty thousand pellets were spewed in a horizontal pattern over the land below, hitting everything on the ground. A long time ago I learned about the pineapple, looking at a Vietnamese, lying on a straw mat, whose body seemed to have a thousand cuts.

The sergeant did not want me there. He did not pretend otherwise. There was only one peculiar thing about him: not the face that made me think of rope, not the hair cut so close to the scalp, not the boots shined to a ferocious glare. It was a pair of pinkish earplugs inside a tiny plastic vial that hung from a breast pocket of his fatigues. They are issued to artillery crews, but in Vietnam I did not see anyone who used them; the men simply covered their ears with their hands, except if they had to handle the warm canisters. The earplugs made it seem as if Sergeant Sympson was not sitting in an office in a quiet town pushing papers, but in the field, standing by the heavy 155s as they turned down to fire point-blank at attacking enemy positions.

Do you think that too much attention has been paid to the deaths in Bardstown? It was the only question I needed to ask him.

Sergeant Sympson did not speak; perhaps he had been told to shut up. He only nodded his head, not once, but twice, the big head dipping up and down very slowly, making sure I would have nothing to write down or quote. Then the sergeant, with the tiny pink earplugs hanging in the little vial on his chest, rose from his desk and made it clear my time was up, that I was not to loiter. He escorted me to the door, and stood there until I went away.

THE ARMY WAS wise about death: it understood that the dying soldier, the dead man, could not give them as much trouble, present as many delicate problems, pose such embarrassment as the people who loved or were bound to him. In the Vietnam war they worked a procedure that was quite perfect for their purposes, a better system than the sending of a telegram, although much more troublesome for the military, more dreadful for the men who had to inform the families.

When a man died in Vietnam, his next of kin were notified in person. The notification teams of two men each were from the nearest Army base. An officer informed the family of a dead, or missing, officer, and noncommissioned officers told the families of men whose rank was below first lieutenant. The rules and guidelines were strict: be sure to identify the next of kin correctly, the wife or parents; always ask a woman to sit down in case she faints; if there are children around, take the mother to another room, so they will not learn the death of their father from a stranger; do not touch the woman even if she cries out or trembles terribly. Never touch her. Neighbors can be called in to assist in cases of collapse or hysteria. The fathers of the dead are not expected to go beserk, or weep uncontrollably, so they were not automatically asked to sit down. There were no prescribed formal expressions of sympathy aside from the opening sentence: "The Secretary of Army has requested me to inform you . . ." The idea was to convey regret—deep, official, masculine regret—but not a regret that sounded too regretful, too mushy, as if the death had been a waste.

It was nearly always expected that a woman would weep. The very calm ones, who stayed composed and polite, usually had a hard time after the notification team had driven off and they began to understand. Notification teams only visited survivors between 6 A.M. and 10 P.M. if a death had taken place in Vietnam. The idea was not to wake them up in the middle of the night when there was no reason to do so. I have heard of women who saw the Army sedans outside their door and at first would not let the notification teams inside. But sooner or later they always had to open the door because the notification team just waited there, knocking politely a second time, a third, refusing to go away. There have been cases of women turning on the man who told her she was a widow, times when women got nasty, blaming the Army, shrieking at the uniform, pleading for proof that the dead man was not someone else. Nothing of the kind happened in Bardstown in June 1969, or in any of the little towns nearby, when it became known that within a week, Staff Sergeant Harold Milton Brown, Specialist 4 Ronald Earl Simpson, Specialist 4 David Burr Collins, Specialist 4 Ronald McIlvoy, First Sergeant Luther Malcolm Chappel, Staff Sergeant James Thomas Moore and Specialist 4 Barry Neal Thompson had ceased to exist.

There were four days of mourning, when flags flew at half mast. It ended on the Fourth of July, a day when men usually go fishing, when there are picnics, a day of pleasant slumping. There was a memorial service, sometimes called "the ceremony" by townspeople, in the auditorium of Bardstown High at 9 a.m. There were Bible readings and prayers given by an Army chaplain from Fort Knox, the Reverend Linus Geisler Joseph Cathedral and the Reverend George Lollis of First Christian Church. Several Bardstown choirs together sang "The Battle Hymn of the Republic" and "America the Beautiful." Two hymns were sung. Mayor Guthrie Wilson read the names, ages, dates of death of the slain men—the honor roll, he called it—and James A. Sutherland, Judge of Nelson County, borrowing from the Gettysburg Address, said: "None of us, yes, none shall ever forget what they did there." It was these words, perhaps, which the judge said slowly in his old, clear and important voice, that made many people break down, so that the auditorium was filled with the soft, gulping noises of grief that people could not hold back, could not muffle with their handkerchiefs.

Later it was thought that perhaps more than eight hundred people had filled the auditorium. There were not enough seats; dozens had to stand in back.

Judge Sutherland recalled, in his speech, how a party had been held for the Bardstown National Guard Unit before it had departed on active duty, then praised them: "Our men were met on the battlefield, none faltered, so we now come to dedicate a portion of what we have to them. Our men, our husbands, our fathers, our sons have fallen, and in doing so, did consecrate far above our power to add or detract. Those yet to fall must struggle in the storms of fate. Brave men and worthy patriots are dear to God and famous to all ages. Men do not live by bread alone, but by faith, by admiration and by sympathy. So I strain to convey to you, who have had the supreme loss, our pledge of complete admiration and sympathy. None of us, yes, none of us . . ."

MANY OTHER AMERICANS saw the memorial service on CBS national television, or read about it. Beamis Samuels, of the Bardstown City Hall office staff, was surprised that some letters came from as far away as Wakonda, South Dakota, or Westfield, New York. Mrs. Lillian Thompson of Dayton, Ohio, for example, wrote: "This is just to thank you and the people of Bardstown for the most sincere and beautiful service you held on July 4, 1969 in memory of those DEAR PEOPLE who sacrificed their lives for the U.S. I was very fortunate to have seen this service on the television screen." Mrs. Annie L. Ruckers sent a message on Card-A-Prayer In Sympathy, which said: "To the Grieved Family. Just a word to let you know we are sad in Heart with you all. We are Negroes but we are white with God because we are Christians and the color don't make a person, we have been sad since we heard the news of the loss May God take care of you."

All the letters were answered as soon as possible. Mr. Samuels was helpful, and as detached as if I had come to find out about the qualities of limestone water or farm subsidies. It seemed to worry him just for a second that only Deanna Durbin Simpson wished to be left alone. He thought that even at the end of 1973, she had not yet gotten over it.

"She hasn't made the effort," Mr. Samuels said, but quite gently.

THERE HAS NEVER been a war, except for Vietnam, in which the men of his family did not volunteer, Mayor Guthrie Wilson will tell you. He was born in Bardstown in February 1923, the only son of Frank Wilson, a farmer who was also in the show-horse and cattle business until he went into automobiles in 1918. During World War II Guthrie Wilson spent fifty-three months in the Army, mostly as an infantry instructor of weaponry and later of company tactics, attaining the rank of major. He did not see combat. He was happy in the Army and might have stayed if his father had not summoned him home to join the business, called Wilson Brothers. The generations catch up with you, Mayor Wilson likes to say, every generation. His father was eighty-one years old, he said. Their ancestors were Scotch and English—Archibalds and Camerons—which leads him to a little joke.

"Of course, you don't want to get into your family tree too hard," the mayor said. "Because you don't know how they got here. They may have come out of debtors' prisons or anywhere, you know. That's how we all got here." His wife, Kitty, and their daughter traveled to England twice and to Scotland, too. The mayor was too busy to go.

It seems only fitting that Guthrie Wilson should live in a red-brick house with a green shingled roof and fat white pillars, not surprising that the parlor, a dim and waxed room, is full of very nice antiques, that the couple sleep in a huge, high and very old four-poster bed. They receive guests in a cheerful small room facing the front, a room many Americans call a den. The mayor has been in office since 1965, running as a Democrat because he was born one, because, by his own admission, he would be licked if he ran as a Republican. But his duties are not full time, the salary is quite small, so he is mainly concerned with being a Chevrolet and Buick dealer. He does not look like a farmer, with his unweathered, handsome face and pale, neat hands, but occasionally he speaks for generations of Wilson men who, even before Kentucky was a state, owned land here, raised crops and had cattle, knew how the weather could ruin you.

"When you're raised next to the ground, like we are, you're more conservative-thinking," the mayor said. "People here just don't like big government, they don't like too much liberalism in ideas. As new things come along, good things, they're a little slower to take hold to them. I'd say people in this area probably thought when Social Security started, it was socialism."

But the suspicion does not extend to wars, and Mayor Wilson works hard to make you see that in Bardstown people live by putting fears and doubts to one side when the country calls them. He is an honest man, a relaxed one sitting in that sunny little room with its plants and bright colors, telling you that Vietnam was a complicated thing and not all the town's memories of it were bad. In June 1966, for example, there had been a Vietnam Day party in Bardstown High in honor of Colonel Hal Moore, a local boy who had gone to West Point, a decorated hero of Vietnam, who was home on a visit. The reception, which also paid tribute to other soldiers in Vietnam and local veterans, was from one to three in the afternoon. More than a thousand people came, but Colonel Moore did not talk about the war, and no one pressed him to do so, or asked questions. There had been a sweet and stirring shimmer to that day.

"There was a happy occasion then because in 1966 there was a kind of feeling we were winning, you know," the mayor said. "Gosh, what an ironic thing. I made a short speech, recognizing boys that were in Vietnam, or some that were back. *Life* magazine had two big spreads on Colonel Moore. A very low-keyed fellow. He wouldn't permit us to have any ceremonies. He said no, which I don't blame him."

If people grew questioning about the war, or doubting, it was not their way to speak out against it, or to pay too much attention to the demonstrators they saw on television, who were regarded, for the most part, as lunatics or weak-minded.

"Even though people became very disenchanted, it is still a pretty patriotic town, a very great majority of people still thought 'Well, okay we've got to put up with it even though we've lost our belief in it,'" the mayor said. "And even over those eleven young men being killed, there wasn't any bitterness here. I am sure there were isolated cases, I don't mean to say there weren't, I can't speak for Jane Doe or Joe Blow, but generally there was no feeling of bitterness or anything."

His father, Frank Wilson, who had fought with the Wildcat Division in France in World War I, commanded by General

Douglas MacArthur, was not pleased that his grandson, known as Guffy, was avoiding the war. The young man finished college in the summer of 1969 and joined the National Guard on a six-year basis.

"His grandfather said 'Why don't you go in the Army instead of going in the National Guard?'" the mayor told me. "We never had a war in which a member of my family didn't volunteer. But Guffy said 'I don't want to go in the Army, and the purpose of going into the Guard is so that I won't have to go to Vietnam unless they call this company back.'"

Mayor Wilson thought that was fine. Battery C was not called up again. But the country stayed hitched to the plow, as he puts it, stuck in Vietnam. "You know, like plowing along, and you hit a rock or something and you can't move it, so you have to back the mule up and pull the plow back and start over."

John Laurence, a twenty-nine-year-old correspondent for CBS News, who was well known for his Vietnam coverage, came to Bardstown to cover the memorial service in July. Mayor Wilson had no idea that this slight young man, who looked like a schoolboy until he spoke, was one of the best television correspondents in Vietnam, not only brave (not all were brave), but a fine reporter. The mayor and his wife invited Laurence to have dinner with them.

"We talked till about one-thirty in the morning. He told us 'We can't win this thing. It's useless. There is no way to win it.' He said 'You people are being bamboozled. You're being fooled and you don't know it.' I remember those were just about his exact words."

Mayor Wilson had never heard it put that way before. It had never been clear to him that anyone was lying about the war until that long dinner with Jack Laurence. On the day of the cease-fire, in January 1973, a different CBS crew flew into the local airport from Chicago to see what Bardstown was doing and thinking. They were in a dreadful rush. They only had time to find the mayor and film him in the street. Their speed amazed him. "They just flew in one morning and landed right here. They went back, had that thing edited and on the six-thirty news," the mayor said. "I nearly fell over. I said surely they can't make it, but they did. They asked me what effect the war had on the community."

Not until he saw himself speaking on television did the mayor really know what he had said. But he would not wish to alter it. "I said . . . well, really, I don't think they felt anything," he told me. "Except for a little relief. But I heard no conversation about it."

It was an ordinary day, January 27, 1973.

"It was just this: you got up and went to work the next morning. I guess we felt, well, we're out of it. But there was never any real resentment. Not that."

He did not think the people of Bardstown, the people of Nelson County, brooded much about the war, thought of it as futile or unjust. There was nothing like that.

"I mean, it was over after the ceremony, wasn't it?" the mayor said.

FROM THE AIR, coming down in the UH-1 helicopters that were so open and seemed so frail, the fire bases looked like outdoor prison camps, dried and greyish places where no one could run away, big circles of punishing dullness and undreamed-of noise. When the choppers came down, or rose up, a vortex of dust, twigs, earth, pebbles and bits of nothing whipped the face, coated the teeth, shut the eyes and made you double over. There was so little on a fire base and nothing around it: only the fat black guns, the eighty-pound shells and casings, the miles of barbed wire thickly circling the perimeter, the bunkers and tents. And always there was the promise of a boredom so immense it seemed to flatten or deflate many men, making them dim and dull things, like eardrums that had been punched too often by the ancient noise of cannons. The men were always naked to the waist except when it rained or was cold in the northern provinces. Their faces and chests were startlingly brown; only below their waists did their skin have the paleness of milk. Some fire bases were put up fast, shut down fast; others lasted a very long time. The purpose was to provide support for troops in the area; the self-propelled 155-howitzers could hurl high explosive charges twenty miles away. Sometimes artillery was called in by a platoon that had been fired on by no more than four, perhaps six, of the enemy. The Army did not find that peculiar. All the fire bases had names. There were lots of Bs at one time: Bastogne, Beverly, Birmingham, Buckshot, Brown, Bruiser, Buttons. Others had names that told you a little more: Siberia, Love, Lonely. At night the shells sounded like rushing trains overhead.

There is no reason to suppose that Fire Support Base Tomahawk, twenty miles south of Phu Bai, in Quang Tri province—within the military region called I Corps—was any different from the rest of them. Bulldozers made it, and nothing remained when the men at last left it but a faint raw circle in a place without a name. It was often cold in I Corps during certain months, there was the rain, and a sucking thick mud that made men slide or tilt when they walked in it. There seemed to be no bottom below such mud.

Don Parrish did not mind any of this. None of the Bardstown men in Battery C found Vietnam unbearable; it did not rub them each day like a giant slab of sandpaper going deeper all the time. Artillery was better than the infantry, for they had dry beds and hot food, a sense of power and order and purpose that foot soldiers did not know. The danger was much less. Even Ronnie Simpson, who had wanted the courts to keep the National Guard from sending them to Vietnam, was the same affable and hardworking fellow. He never sulked or pulled back in Vietnam. After all, he had not originated the lawsuit or helped organize such a solemn rebellion. The idea had begun in Louisville, among some of the local Guard units there who wanted support from soldiers who came from the small towns like Bardstown. Don Parrish said the plaintiffs had been organized at Fort Hood, where Battery C was sent in May to train with more modern equipment and to learn urban riot-control tactics. Some of the men had thought they might be sent to Cincinnati, where racial tensions were rising, but Parrish felt it would be Vietnam. He did not think the lawsuit could ever succeed. In Bardstown, many people were distressed by the lawsuit and considered it unpatriotic, but no one mentions it any more now that Ronnie Simpson is dead. No one says he was right or wrong—it was all so long ago.

"I'm really glad now that I'm home that I did get the opportunity to go," Mr. Parrish said. "I do feel like I did my part and I feel like I learned a great deal from such a service. But I'm very sorry that anyone had to die as a result of it."

This is how he spoke on that cold December morning in the offices of his father's firm, Ray Parrish & Sons, which sells concrete products and professional tools. He spoke like a man reading from a piece of paper no one else could see. If you ask him why he feels he benefited from the war, Don Parrish can take you upstairs to a long new office that he designed himself in Vietnam, in his spare time, a tangible gain from the war.

The workday often begins at seven-thirty. Don Parrish is a precise, practical man whose passionate hobby is history. He does not read books about it but rather collects documents, newspapers, and bits of it that come his way. There is an old-fashioned case in his office that has glass windows which pull out and turn like the pages of a huge book. For a little while I stopped asking him to lead me back to the day in June when Battery C was ruined, to look at a list of the valuation of the slaves of Samuel Bealmar from Nelson County. It lists Polly thirty-four years old and child Ellen eight months at five hundred dollars; Old Polly sixty-two years old, sick and diseased and considered of no value at all; Hanora Sunny's child ten years three hundred dollars. Of the thirty-two slaves that Mr. Bealmar owned, the most valuable were a twenty-year-old male Ben, six hundred and fifty dollars, and Isaac, age thirty-three, six hundred dollars.

Able-bodied men have always been of great value, although there must be other people like me who all their lives never thought much about this. Once I asked a black soldier how much his pack weighed—it was seventy pounds—and although I am not a small woman, I could not stand up straight or walk when he laughed and put it on me. Before Vietnam, I never paid attention to the words "able-bodied." Don Parrish, of course, was much older than most of the soldiers then in Vietnam: he was twenty-seven then. But none of the bunch from the Bardstown area were fragile men; they knew how to use their bodies and they could push them a long way. They had a simplicity that might have saved them.

"I learned that no matter how bad things get with me here, there's always someone worse off," Mr. Parrish said. "I observed life in Vietnam. You don't see much of it but you don't have to, just a little, to know you don't want any part of it."

He had heard something, of course, of American troops using drugs, trafficking with pimps and whores, making money on the black market, killing their officers with fragmentation grenades, and in the last years, causing more trouble to the U.S. command than the enemy did, but Don Parrish cannot imagine it. Strangers did such things. Strangers wanted marijuana or heroin, put peace signs on their helmet liners, wrote Fuck the Army on walls everywhere, had clap, refused orders and made money.

"The National Guard managed to attract—well, I hate to classify people, but it seems like they managed to draw people who were not so inclined to do this sort of thing," Mr. Parrish said proudly. "I don't know that there was a single person from Bardstown who made any attempt at all to make any contact with anyone male or female who was Vietnamese."

Battery C had been a good unit in Vietnam, an exceptional one, he said. They had arrived there in October 1968. He and Jimmy Moore, who were schoolboys together at St. Joseph's for twelve years, had sat together on the long, mindless flight from Texas to Travis Air Force Base in California, from Wake Island to Guam to Danang. The unit had been moved around a lot. Ninety-five percent of the battery were from Nelson County, and even now he likes to remember their excellence, how very good they were.

"We fired rounds faster than any 155-howitzer battalion in I Corps," Mr. Parrish said. "We worked together better than any unit I saw in Vietnam. I don't know that there was anyone in the unit who really let a whole lot of things bother him, and that's the reason we worked together so well."

It saddened him when the Army began breaking the unit up, as if no one realized or cared that they were at their best together, the big country boys understanding how it was done, not whimpering or slowing down. He knew why the Army did it, of course, everyone knew. He still regrets it.

"My thinking was that they tried to break up the small hometown units so if one of them was overrun so many people from one town wouldn't be wiped out," he said. "My thinking was that this was, maybe, a good move, but at the same time they were destroying something that we had that no one else had."

The attack, the first and the last he ever knew, began at 1:45 A.M. on Thursday, at Fire Support Base Tomahawk, which sat in a saddle between two small hills. An infantry platoon was on one of the hills; not more than one hundred men were on the fire base. He was chief of the Fire Direction Center and used to sleeping in a bunker with 155-howitzers going off thirty feet from him. What woke him up that Thursday was the sharp, whiny noise of the rocket-propelled grenades coming in. When the attack began the Americans were changing shifts, and the generator, which provided lights in the bunkers where the troops lived, had been shut off for the night. There were eight howitzers on the fire base. The North Vietnamese sappers had silently slipped through the wire, as they always did. Only one bunker was not destroyed by them. It was the one where Don Parrish slept, connected to the Fire Direction Center where his job was to call in air support and medical evacuation helicopters during fighting. They brought the wounded there, to the Fire Direction Center. It was dark. You could see almost nothing. When Jimmy Moore, who was chief of a howitzer section, came in, it was too dark to see him. He was a tall, bulky man whom Mr. Parrish describes "as a real friendly person, he'd do anything in the world for you . . .

"He walked in saying nothing, really. I recognized him because of his shape. I said 'Jim, what's your problem, what's happened to you?' I put my hand on his back and I said 'Jim, what's the trouble?'" But touching the man, standing so close to him, he knew what the trouble was. He could touch it and he could smell it. "He said 'Donald, I'm burned up'—he couldn't sit or lie down, so he just stood there," Mr. Parrish said.

Forty-four Americans were wounded. The primary attack was over by 4 A.M., although thirty minutes later a few mortars came in, landing outside the fire base. One howitzer had been destroyed. The Americans laid out the enemy corpses: there were eighty-five. It was almost 5:30 A.M. when the helicopters came in from Phu Bai for their own wounded and the dead.

Specialist 4 Ronald Earl Simpson had been shot leaving his bunker, Don Parrish said. Specialist 4 Joseph McIlvoy had fallen on a sapper charge. Part of the skull of Specialist 4 David Burr Collins was gone when he was found inside his bunker, and Sergeant Luther Chappel had been shot through the head, he thought.

They carried Jimmy Moore to a helicopter on a screen door taken down from the little mess hall, for there were not enough litters. Five days later the burned man died. The day after, Specialist 4 Thompson, a draftee who was an infantryman in the Big Red One sweeping near the Cambodian border, died. The first man to be wasted that June was Sergeant Brown, but Mr. Parrish did not know how or where in Vietnam.

Battery C abandoned Fire Support Base Tomahawk shortly afterward, although the Army did not choose to put it that way. The fire base was moved to a site which was more defensible, they said. Nothing happened to Don Parrish afterward that he considers important. He had gone to war to stop the spread of communism—he is not certain whether this was done but he wishes now that the war had been fought a different way.

"The biggest gripe I ever had as an artillery man was that I was not allowed to fire into certain areas, knowing the enemy was there," Mr. Parrish said. He said that he knew why he couldn't, there were civilians in those villages, but you could tell that such arguments bored or puzzled him, and had nothing to do with getting the job done.

·The survivors of Battery C raised the money for the memorial plaque that stands in the Old Court House Square. They did not need contributions from outsiders.

"It comes back to me every year on June 19 . . . well, no, I think of it—fleetingly—almost every day," he said.

Then there were his last words on the war in Vietnam. He did not really know how startling they were. "A higher percentage of its population died as a result of Vietnam, more than most small towns, and this was unfortunate," Mr. Parrish said. "But then, Bardstown had a bigger piece of the action, so to speak."

FOR A LONG time afterward it was hard to hear those words "a piece of the action" without thinking of a big man charred and dying, standing in a dark bunker, waiting to be asked what was wrong.

IT WORRIED THE wife of Jimmy Guthrie when their oldest son Michael was sent to Vietnam in 1970, but it wasn't the sort of worry that stabbed her, kept her awake, brought on headaches or dreams. Michael had told her he would not be near the fighting, that he was in communications and the equipment was so expensive, the Army put it way back in the rear. This made her feel calmer. She was never sure exactly what he did there. Michael was a teletype operator, a Specialist 4 stationed near Danang, who did, as he calls it, "secret cryptography."

Mr. Guthrie watched the news from Vietnam on television and hoped it would mention Danang. For years it had been hard to connect all the names of places over there with anything at all, but Danang changed that. At the lumber mill in Bardstown the *Louisville Courier-Journal* has always been delivered each morning and Mr. Guthrie took it home at night.

"I feel Michael was safer there than he would have been at home," he said. "They talk about those fifty thousand boys that were killed there, but I bet half that number would have been killed if they'd been at home, killed in automobiles, cars, that sort of thing." He meant those killed in Vietnam would have died anyway, just differently.

Jimmy Guthrie had enlisted in the Navy at the age of seventeen and served on a transport ship. In September 1948, when he married Shirley Buznick, they were a startlingly handsome couple: it had something to do with his height and his smile, her eyes, her skin. In December 1973 their nine children ranged in ages from twenty-six to five. Mr. Guthrie is a partner with his wife's father and brother. Michael is their oldest son; he is small, like his mother, not a mixer and a joker like Jimmy Guthrie, who belonged at one time to the Knights of Columbus, the Optimists Club, the Poker Club and the Quarterback Club.

It may be that Michael is the child that puzzles him most. Mrs. Guthrie is always quick to defend Michael in her soft, insistent way, and in front of company, he does not go too far in making his points. Some of Michael's remarks do not sit well with his father, who looks bored or irritated when he hears them. He could not know that Michael, for all his mockery and contempt of the Army and the war, the work ethic and materialism, seemed to me a pale and placid creature, quite an ordinary one for his age, compared to others I have known. Michael, with his long hair and sketch pad, was not dancing to a fierce new music.

His mother thought he had changed after thirteen months in Vietnam. "I hate to see him so quiet. He's so much different. But he still is friendly," Mrs. Guthrie said.

It did not please her husband to hear us wonder out loud if Vietnam made Michael different, although he saw no combat, only messages giving the end results of it. "But that's been two or three years ago," Mr. Guthrie said. "Is he going to keep dwelling on that for the rest of his life? Not too long ago he was raving about something up in Washington, why they weren't doing it right. And I said 'Well, how would you go about getting it done?' He didn't know."

"He's twenty-one years old, he's not supposed to know," Mrs. Guthrie said. "I would say the same thing. And I'm forty-five years old."

She made homemade chili, which we ate on top of spaghetti, and a big salad for dinner. Three married daughters live nearby and they come over often for dinner, pretty, quiet girls with husbands and babies; the circle closes when they are there. The men drink and talk to each other. Mr. Guthrie, who towers over all of them, has funny stories to tell and his language is his own. An old car is a junker; right smart of hay means a lot of hay; a group of times means often. "Them Kennedys, they tough," Mr. Guthrie will say, meaning it as the highest, if begrudging, praise. No one, of course, would say that Michael was tough. His mother thinks even at the age of eight he was different from the other children.

"I don't think we were trying to win that war," Mr. Guthrie said. "We didn't send enough. They could have sent two million troops if they had to, if they'd wanted to win it. They could have done it. They could have sent five million. We didn't have the will, I don't guess, to fight like we should have. We could have wiped out fifteen thousand or twenty thousand at one lick. What they were getting was peanuts."

He had read that for each man doing the fighting, there were ten in the rear, Mr. Guthrie said. That was no way to do it. Win it or get out, he said.

He did not know about the machines that were waging the war, doing what troops could never do, making it impossible for the Vietnamese to flee or hide or plead innocence. He had never seen the gunships—AC-47, called Puff the Magic Dragon, the AH-1G known as Cobra, the AC-54, AC-119, AC-130—whose primary weapons were the 7.62-mm Gatling gun and the 20-mm Vulcan cannon, capable of firing 6,000 rounds of ammunition per minute from a single gun. He did not know about the fighter bombers, the F-4s, or the B-52s that operated at 30,000 feet. The sky was crowded: FACs and observation aircraft at 2,000 feet; attack and gunships at 5,000 feet; fighter bombers at 7,000 feet; reconnaissance and electronic warfare aircraft at 10,000 feet, and above them, the others. "When they fire their guns, it looks as if a stream of brilliant candy apples is streaking from the aircraft to the ground," an Air Force sergeant said of the gunships. There were electronic sensors designed to monitor ground movement; ANPQ radar meant to see through trees; infrared cameras intended to register heat emissions at night; giant computers intended to record enemy movement; flares and napalm, Guavas and radar-guided Bullpup missiles.

It was unimaginably expensive; it did not work as well as the Americans had hoped. Some Vietnamese knew why; some Americans gave their opinions. General Julian J. Ewell, often called "Bloody" Ewell by some reporters, who commanded the 9th Infantry Division and then II Field Force, the largest combat command in the Army, was not so sure technology had helped the combat situation. The general, who was famous in 1968 for telling his troops to "get a hundred a day, every day" gave an interview to an Army publication, *The Hurricane,* before leaving Vietnam, in April 1970, for his next assignment as senior military advisor to the Paris peace talks.

"I think some of these technical devices have been very useful, although it is odd that when they're first introduced they're very useful for a period of three to four months and then they begin to tail off. I think the middle-range radar is a good example. When we first introduced them and got them working well, we just shot the brains out of the Communists," General Ewell said. "And then, after two or three months of that, they'd catch on and begin to get lost, and although the radars now are quite useful, they aren't as decisive as they were during their early months.

I think this is true in practically any new technological device. The enemy is quite clever and observant, and as he catches on, he devises some way to guard against it, even if it's just to get lost," he added.

The Vietnamese put it quite another way. In March 1973 Lieutenant General Tran Van Tra, who was then the chief delegate of the Provisional Revolutionary Government to the truce commission, said at a reception in Saigon that "Americans were good soldiers but they fought the wrong war. They did not have the ideals our soldiers have." Asked how the Communists always seemed to know how and when the B-52s would strike, the general—who wore a plain, baggy green uniform—said: "It is our country, the trees and the leaves are ours, we know everything."

THE BOMBING OF Hanoi at Christmas had not upset anyone they knew in town, nor did it bother Mr. and Mrs. Guthrie.

"I think most people thought it was just justified if it got the war *done with*," Mr. Guthrie said. "Anyone who grew up during the Second World War would have felt that way. Do you remember during the Second World War anybody complaining about bombing Berlin? I don't think anybody thought that the Germans were committing atrocities by bombing."

For them only a very dim and tiny memory exists of Americans who protested the bombing, as if Massachusetts was no closer than Danang, as if the marches in Washington were no more comprehensible than the Buddhist monks who burned themselves in Saigon. Mrs. Guthrie, who gives the impression that her husband is too strict with the children without ever saying so, does not think much of people who marched against the war, those demonstrators. We were sitting in the little dining room when she said it in her halting, pretty way; I was eating the chili and spaghetti and looking at a framed illustrated copy of the Ten Commandments on the wall. It is easy to imagine Mrs. Guthrie praying in St. Joseph's Cathedral, her head covered with a scarf, wanting God to consider the children.

"It's because of prosperity," she said. "The younger generation's been spoiled, we've sheltered them, and they are used to having their own way. It was all students, or ex-students, disgruntled students. The demonstrations were a lark for ninety percent of them. I think it was just like the panty raids of ten years before that. Well, maybe a little different, but I don't think there were many sincere ones in the bunch."

Michael might have been one of them if he had gone to college, I said.

"Not if I was paying his way," Mr. Guthrie said.

Mr. Guthrie seemed perturbed, not about the war but about Michael and his attitude toward money. It seemed as if his son had broken a rule, or worse, ignored it. All of us know the rule: money is the measure of our worth, profit is the proof of virtue; people who do not understand this, who do not choose to make money and then make more of it, are flawed. In men it is a disability.

So it did not impress Mr. Guthrie that Michael had once sold his motorcycle and given the money to his married sister, Scarlett, who wanted to buy a sofa. It did not touch him when Michael turned over a calf he owned to his brother-in-law, Bobby Ballard, so Bobby could sell it and buy an air conditioner. None of this cut the mustard with Mr. Guthrie.

"Yes, yes, he doesn't want or need too much. He might seem real selfless because he gives somebody the shirt off his back, but you'd bet it would be warm weather if he did. He gives the other kids all his money. I'm not mocking him because of it, but it isn't near as selfless as you might think because he didn't actually have anything to spend the money on anyhow. He didn't care about it, the money didn't mean anything to him. It wouldn't be like me giving it away, 'cause I want that money."

"PEOPLE THINK I come out here to die, to starve myself," Michael said. His cabin, five miles outside of Bardstown, is in the woods. It is a small thing, a child's dream, with pine walls, unpainted shelves and seats. There is an army blanket on the bed. Michael's decision to "retire" so startled older people in Bardstown they could only think of it as a self-punishing act. They could not imagine what he meant when he said he wanted to "sit out here and get things straight."

At the lumber mill Mr. Guthrie, who took care of customers, saw lot of the men who lived in and around Bardstown; he liked chatting with them. Marchel Simpson, the father of Ronald Earl who married Deanna Durbin, told Mr. Guthrie that his son's death in Vietnam was a complete waste.

"He said if they have another war to stop wars, he said they ought to start with the oldest and come down to the youngest, start with the seventy-years-olds and then work down," Mr. Guthrie said. "He said it like I would have said it hearing some Saturday or Sunday morning that some kid was killed in an accident out here, running into the bridge at eighty miles an hour or something."

He did not think Mr. Simpson was bitter, just sad. "If I had a son killed in Vietnam, I'd be sorrowful but not bitter," Mr. Guthrie said.

Michael was not upset to hear his father's comment. He smiled a little. "I understand *him*. The only reason he would be bitter is because of a feeling my life was wasted, right? But he wouldn't feel like it was wasted if I was killed there, he'd feel it would be worth it. People weren't affected by the war here. You've got *American Graffiti* in Bardstown. Somebody goes away to war. They come back two years later, and they pat him on the back and say 'What the hell's going on, man, it's good to have you back.' Happy times again. It's ridiculous. I don't know what it is, but I guess people are content here. In a weird way I think there is contentment. I don't know why they would be."

He had been stationed at Hawk Hill and then at Freedom Hill, names that mean nothing to us now, and three times he had been able to go to Danang before the city was declared off-limits to U.S. military.

He had come back from Vietnam with $3,500 in stereo equipment, which had been stolen while he was living in the cabin. The insurance money made it possible for him to pay his father for the land, the six acres on which the cabin stood. It had made it possible for him to be quiet and to think and read. He had worked at the family lumber mill in the summers after coming home.

"I tried to fit in, I thought I was going to fit in. You know, come home a different person, fit back into the world a different person but more content. That's the way I thought it was going to work. I got up there and they were crazy. Crazy. Now, my father, he made more sense to me. He tried to teach me the business, he had mellowed. He just more or less told me 'There's a living up here to be made, son.' That's what the told me. 'I've made a good living up here. I've got a lot of things. I've made a good living up here. Stay here if you want.' That's what he told me. And my uncle started driving me crazy, my mother's brother. I mean, he's just got a split personality. As a man I like him, he's a wild dude, likes to go hunting and such things as that. You know, just a man of the world. Yes, he is. But at work he's a penny-pinching dude. He gets out there and wants to load the truck, wants to shove things and just go real fast, and stuff like that. And they wanted me to go up there and be a boss, see? They wanted me to work in an office and not go out and work on the trucks, like I'd been doing."

He did not want to give orders or hassle anybody. He preferred to do things himself, which was inefficient and drove his uncle crazy. "I was out of place out there," Michael said. "After three months I was going nuts. After six months I just couldn't take it no more.

"If I hadn't gone to Vietnam I'd have stayed into the swilling," he said, "I'd be at the lumberyard. I learned a lot; I made a constructive thing out of it. There is no doubt in my mind that the Vietnamese didn't like Americans. They made it clear that Americans were assholes, a lot of them. But they did tell me they weren't prejudiced, they didn't hate Americans like somebody might hate a nigger, be down on a Negro, see. I like the Asian people. I'd go back to South Vietnam, but I doubt I would be able. I'd probably be shot there."

AN ENDING, A consoling one, which made people of Bardstown proud, came at last when its prisoners of war came home after five years in North Vietnam. Once more people came together as they had in 1966 to see their decorated hometown boy, Colonel Moore, as they had in 1969 to praise and pray for the dead. This time it was to rejoice. On Friday night, April 13, 1973, nearly nine hundred people squeezed into the auditorium of Nelson County High School to pay tribute to a survivor. It was, as the *Kentucky Standard* described it in a happy manner, an hour's program that very much resembled *This Is Your Life*. The guest of honor was Colonel James E. Bean, age fifty, of the United States Air Force, a Cox's Creek boy who was the son of a farmer. He had spent nine hundred and fifty-seven days in solitary confinement in an eight-foot-square cell in Hanoi.

They had not given him enough water, that was the most unforgivable thing, Colonel Bean said later in an interview with the *Kentucky Standard*. The food was wretched. He had been given a decent meal on the Fourth of July and again on Christmas, good enough so that at least you could chew and swallow. He said he was not tortured. He never did say much more than that.

He did not speak of the cell that night to the people who came to laugh, to clap hard and to see the giving of gifts. The master of ceremonies, a man known for his plunges into wit, Jack Arnold, had been the colonel's close friend in the class of '42, Bardstown High. Mr. Arnold spoke at length, adding bits of humor, about the colonel's triumphs in football and basketball in those early days. Jimmy Bean had lived with Jack Arnold's parents in town, Monday through Friday, so he could practice these sports in the afternoons instead of taking the afternoon bus back to Cox's Creek. The colonel had always been a boy with a sharp, steady glow to him: he was captain of the Bardstown High football team, which ended its second season undefeated in 1941; he was president of the 1941 basketball team; selected as All-Conference fullback in 1941; chosen state president of the Future Farmers of America; and elected president of the senior class. His grades were very good. He began taking flying lessons while in high school and won an athletic scholarship to the University of Kentucky. You might say that his life was a very pretty story, the kind of story they like to tell in small towns. In 1943 he joined the Air Force, was a pilot in World War II; in the Korean War and until he was shot down on January 3, 1968, he had more flying hours as a pilot of an F-105 fighter than any other pilot in the Air Force.

"President Nixon had to make many unpopular decisions, and I suspect he was a lonely man in December last when the bombing was commenced again in North Vietnam," Colonel Bean said, in a short speech. "But to us in jail in the center of Hanoi, it was the greatest display of mass precision bombing the world has ever seen. It was the most heartwarming sight I have ever witnessed firsthand. At that time I and my captors realized that the U.S. had accomplished its national objective of a free Indochina."

No one was made uneasy in the audience that night, wondering how a man in prison, who saw nothing, could be so certain the bombing had been precise. But perhaps no one cared if the bombing was precise or messy, it was none of their concern, nothing they chose to worry about. They could not question a man who had always made them so proud, whose life had been more stirring than any Western on television, whose family were such churchgoers, and who that night told them all they were loved.

After Colonel Bean thanked them for keeping faith in him, after he promised to again defend American freedoms if he was needed, the tall, pale man stretched his arms open very wide and called out: "I love you this much. God bless you."

Mayor Guthrie Wilson presented the gifts: an engraved silver tray and six engraved silver julep cups, one for each year in prison; fishing equipment, including a tackle box full of lures; an album of early class pictures collected and presented by Mrs. B. L. Beeler, a classmate from Bardstown High; an engraved gold charm bracelet for the colonel's wife, Jeanette; silver cuff links for his two sons; a gold locket for his mother, Mrs. Mary Bean; a picture of the Old Kentucky Home from the Girl Scouts; a lifetime pass to all athletic events in Nelson County High and Bardstown High; life membership in the American Legion Post 121; a season pass to and stereo tape of *The Stephen Foster Story*.

Once again it was Judge Sutherland who spoke, who told people what they felt. Colonel Bean had "deepened our love and belief in God and in country," he said in his speech. He referred to the statements of the returned prisoners of war, who one by one by one, over and over, praised the President and the American people, as having "hushed the critics that were so vocal previous to your release and return," as if the judge himself had never much cared for those troublesome types. He spoke slowly, letting the words wash row after row of people like warm and healing water. Their faces showed they were grateful for it.

He had never known a critic of the war, only the name of Jane Fonda, some Catholics named Berrigan, perhaps a few others, all held in the lowest esteem in Bardstown. Yet at one time even Judge Sutherland seemed puzzled and saddened by Vietnam. After the deaths in July 1969, he said to reporters that ninety percent of the people in Bardstown would vote against going to the war, that the President and Congress wanted to bring about an ending to it. "It brings the question why?" the judge said, meaning the purpose of the war. He was quite good at talking to the press, it did not ruffle him, he spoke in wide, soft strokes, neither condemning the war nor urging men to go off to fight in it. Michael Guthrie used to say that the prisoners of war could not have suffered half as much as the Vietnamese did, but that kind of comment did not reach the judge's ear.

Once he had stepped slightly out of line as a young man and the memory of it is still with him, nearly thirty years later. "After I got back from overseas in World War II, I lived with my first cousin, now a retired admiral. At breakfast one morning I said 'Allen, you people in high military positions are prolonging World War II because you want to remain in the spotlight,'" the judge said.

"That was such a ridiculous statement. I regretted it after I said it. But it seems like maybe this is the way things have turned out to be. Big business—if they've got something going for them that's making them money, they'll go to any means to maintain their position, keep it growing."

Yes, yes, there were people making money from the war; perhaps now China would be our only friend "down the road"; if the United States had not gone into Vietnam, he was sure it would have sent troops to Israel: his opinions are affable, vague, softly pitched. Asking questions is like throwing darts in a bucket of clay. Perhaps the war annoyed and puzzled him more than anything else, for quite a few people had told him firsthand that we could have easily won it.

"If we had just turned our forces loose to go really fight to win a battle," the judge said. "We were always fighting a suppressed-holding area sort of thing. The multitudes around here would probably say 'Use the atomic bomb or the hydrogen, use whatever you've got.' I would not have gone that far. But if I'm going to play mumblypeg with you, I'm going to try and beat you. If we're in any serious body-to-body conflict, I think I ought to try to whip you. I don't think we did in Vietnam."

MRS. MARY POWERS BEAN lived in the same white frame house in Cox's Creek since her marriage in June 1920. In the winter she shut off some of the rooms to save heat. She was eighty-two years old, and that very morning, had baked a jam cake to send to her daughter-in-law, Jeanette Bean, who works in the Pentagon. The four Bean children grew up here, the children of a farmer who did chores, who could not, did not want to goof off. Their father said he always knew Jimmy would be released but that he would not live to see it. This happened.

"Jimmy was very forward as a child, he wanted to go places,"

Mrs. Bean said. "He always wanted to be a pilot. I don't know why, but he did."

She had believed that her son would not be freed. When he came back she asked him when he knew that he would get out of the Hanoi Hilton.

"That was a common question, everyone asked him that. He said 'When the first bomb fell.' That's when he knew. He said those people don't understand anything except explosives and power. They don't understand nice talk. Just power and bombs."

She is a tiny woman who uses a walker, which makes her grumble because it gets in the way; her memory and energy are alarming. The New Salem Baptist Church takes up much of her time. Elmer and Jimmy were both in World War II; she remembers that Elmer, who was a draftee, didn't sleep well when he first came home. He lives up the road, an inspector for Rural Electrification.

"He rides over four counties, so he's busy. Then he has a big hog setup too. He has hogs that are never on the ground, they're in this electric thing," Mrs. Bean said. "Air conditioning in the summer, electric heat in the winter." She and the other twin, Charles, have the three hundred and thirty acres of land, good land for tobacco, cattle, corn, alfalfa, soybeans.

Neighbors thought of her as a stoical woman who remained calm and busy during the five years of her son's imprisonment. Colonel Bean spent five weeks at home, that summer of 1973, farming. His mother said he worked hard, very hard. It was splendid for him.

"He didn't look too good when he first came. He had no coordination, he couldn't play golf. It was humiliating to him not to be able to accomplish what he always accomplished. A neighbor told me that when she first saw him he held on to the steering wheel viciously with both hands. But then she said it wasn't but a little while before he got so he could drive with one hand and wave with the other."

In the prison camps he had farmed every day in his mind, carefully, wasting nothing.

"That's what kept his mind going. He said the boys who didn't, or couldn't, well . . . I think that's a lesson to older people. Train ourselves. We're such poor trainers, aren't we? Our ancestors weren't. My old grandfather was a Baptist preacher and he never forgot anything. You could send him places with a list in his mind."

No one in the Bean family had wanted the celebration for the colonel's homecoming to leave out a reference to the casualties in Vietnam, a homage to be paid to the dead. "We had a little neighbor boy who was one of them. Barry Neal Thompson." She had known his mother since she was a girl. "I helped rear her, I know his whole family. It was hard on that family, and they've never gotten over it. They still go to the cemetery and they still grieve for him. But you know, I think you can do that if you don't get hold of yourself," she said. "A lot of people have troubles, we're not the only ones, don't you know? You have to overcome them. If you don't have faith . . ."

The coffee was ready. She uses instant coffee now only because of her infirmity. She went on to say how she had always had faith, the children had faith. It was what counted, what got you through all of it. There are 2,505 Americans still unaccounted for; of these, 795 are listed as missing in action and the others killed in action.

IN EARLY MAY 1975, when Vietnam was no longer a country at war, CBS went back once more to Bardstown to find out what people thought. Mayor Guthrie Wilson appeared on my television screen—poised, white-haired, well-groomed, solemn. He said the war had not been worth it. Then the camera showed a middle-aged couple. They were Mr. and Mrs. Marchel Simpson, the parents of Ronald Earl Simpson who had died at Fire Support Base Tomahawk.

"If we had done it, if we had won, what would we have?" Mr. Simpson said.

THE ENLISTED MEN did not like the bagginess of their fatigues, so they often had the pants made narrower so they would fit more tightly over the calves, making their legs seem strangely thin. From a distance, with their helmets and packs off, the men with thin legs looked like soldiers from World War I in puttees. There were no trenches, yet sometimes the deep, long bunkers and their ancient, hateful smells, the rats and the different ways the soldiers liked to kill them, the sandbags and the mud spoke of that early war. All I remembered of it was a photograph of gassed men, sightless, standing in single file, holding on to the shoulder in front of them. It was that I thought of when the wounded in Vietnam had thick white bandages across their eyes. You did not understand how filthy the soldiers were until you saw such whiteness wrapped around them. Once, in the field, I saw a boy on a stretcher, his left arm made bigger by those thick white soft bandages, its hand looking huge and very dirty. He was touching his eyes with that hand, although the eyes were sealed with more bandages. He lies on the stretcher forever in a photograph that I used to show to people during the war. The ex-medic David had told me that the English poet and officer in World War I, Wilfred Owen, had more than fifty years ago shown pictures of the wounded to civilians in England to make them understand. But my own photograph had little effect: a lot of people said they had seen it all on M*A*S*H and they were reminded of how much they liked Hawkeye, how cute Radar is, what a really marvelous television program it is.

Americans had only one happy war. It was World War I, the late Governor Roger Branigin of Indiana said, in April 1968. It was a short involvement, the governor pointed out, but the aura of "Gay Paree" and such songs as "It's a Long Way to Tipperary" sung by servicemen created "a nostalgia of spirit." It was a happy war, perhaps the last happy one, Governor Branigin said. A Democrat and one of Indiana's most popular governors, he totally supported President Lyndon B. Johnson's policy in Vietnam. He thought Americans disliked World War II, hated Korea and despised the Vietnam conflict.

The Hines Veterans Administration Hospital, twelve miles west of downtown Chicago, started as a memorial to a young officer in the war that the governor called the happy one. On a bronze dedicatory plaque in Building 2 of the Hines Hospital, the little story is told. The hospital was named in honor of Lieutenant Edward Hines, Jr., the first graduate of the officers' training camp at Fort Sheridan, Illinois, to die in France. He was a resident of Evanston, Illinois, in the class of 1918 at Yale, commissioned a second lieutenant, assigned to 61st Infantry, volunteered in response to a call for officers for immediate foreign service with machine-gun companies, sailed for France, was sent to the Toulon-Troyon Sectors, Verdun, "in the severe winter and spring of 1918."

"On April 4, 1919, while on reconnaissance at Graffier Woods in front of these sectors, Lieutenant Hines succumbed to the effects of the rigors of trench life and to extreme exhaustion and from their effects died in base hospital 15, A.E.F. at Chaumont, France, June 4, 1918 . . ." the plaque reads. President Warren G. Harding designated the hospital be called after Edward G. Hines, Jr. His parents provided over a million dollars.

It is an enormous hospital now—fifteen stories tall, fourteen hundred beds—where nearly three-quarters of a million veterans have been treated. But for those in them, hospitals tend to shrink; beds, rooms, halls become quite small. Building 13 at Hines is the Blind Rehabilitation Center for visually impaired and blinded veterans, the largest of three such Veterans Administration centers in the United States. There are one hundred and twenty beds for them at Hines.

He was having a typing lesson with an elderly woman instructor and not doing very well at it. I was on a tour. Right away the blind boy said he was called Jerry and that he had a good job in an office waiting for him. The instructor looked worried, for he had no such thing and the keyboard was giving him trouble. And right away I said his shirt was a very nice one. It was blue and white.

"I like to dress up," Jerry said. The instructor let it be known in her face that chatting was disruptive. John Malamazian, chief of the Rehabilitation Section, a polite and anxious man, told me what was taught during the eighteen-week course to the blind veterans. They learn how to use a handwriting guide, how to write out checks, home mechanics—how to repair a broken window, fix a bicycle, patch holes in walls, change fuses—how to cook for themselves, how to determine different types of materials so they can buy their own clothes. Mr. Malamazian might be displeased that I have first noted these details. The main purpose, according to all the booklets he gave me, is: orientation and mobility, manual skills, Braille skills, personal and vocational counseling, physical conditioning, recreational activities and self-care. Each man has his own room and radio; he must make his bed, sweep the floor and dress himself.

There was talk of "mobility" techniques, development of tactile perceptions, and the benefit of association with others who were also sightless. I asked Mr. Malamazian if I could spend time with Jerry, who came from a tiny town in the South. Mr. Malamazian looked unhappy. "But he's emotionally disturbed," he said. I should have said so was I.

It seemed that Jerry had been in the Rehabilitation Center before, there had been an untoward incident and he had bolted. Now he was back. Mr. Malamazian, a nice man, overcame his hesitancy and we went to Jerry's room. He was dressed, lying face down on his bed, his arms around his head. When we were alone, Jerry sat in the armchair by the window and was very nervous until he found his lighter, which he had left on top of the dresser. He thought someone had moved it, which was not the case.

"I was wounded in November," he said. "But I can't remember, it was 1968 or 1969." He said he had left Hines the last time, maybe after hitting someone with his stick, or saying he was going to do it. He could not gather together the details. For some reason I laughed, which rather pleased him. He said he liked to laugh. And despite everything, there kept rising in him, above the madness and despair, a spirited boy and a defiant one whose gaiety was of no good to him now.

He did not always finish his sentences; he went in and out of words like a man running in the woods, bobbing and ducking around the trees and then hiding behind them. His father was a policeman, his mother worked in a restaurant, he had three sisters. There were photographs on the dresser: a pretty baby-faced girl, his wife, with children, two chunky sons. One was three years and one was five months old. His wife was in Chicago, staying with a couple they had known in Mississippi, she was able to visit him often, he was allowed to go out. The booklet at the Center said: "Although a member of the veteran's family may make the journey to Hines with him, he is expected to undergo the program, complete it, and return to his home alone."

I do not remember if he wore his Braille wristwatch and knew where he was scheduled to be ("Each man engages in all the activities, five days a week, from 8 A.M. to 4 P.M. There is little free time except for weekends and evenings," the booklet said). But we went off to the cafeteria, neither of us knowing where it was. I asked directions, but it was he who led the way, using the long, light metal cane in a frivolous fashion, like a man whacking at daisies in a field of flowers. He hit a standing ashtray and then a lady on the ankle, but neither of us felt sorry about it. In the cafeteria it went well until we reached the cashier. I carried the tray. But he wanted to pay and he was slow with the money in his wallet. There were two bills and he did not know which was the five and which was the one. The cashier became a little cross, as the line was growing long. She did not know he was blind. There was nothing about his face to make you turn away; he was not like the others I know, with their ruined noses, the mashed bones in their faces, the strange hollows, the paths of scars.

Jerry did not want to eat at all; he only wanted to manage the whole thing, make the voyage. Some of the sandwich went on his blue-and-white shirt and there was trouble with sugar in his coffee. I wrote down nothing. I remember how fiercely he spoke of his own father, and the father he was himself, how his own three-year-old had better behave.

There was trouble when we got back to his floor: he was late for an instruction period in mobility technique with his cane. A small dark-haired woman, Miss Saber, spoke to him quite sharply, and my own attempts to take the blame seemed to make her crosser. Jerry stood still and said a lot of yes, ma'ams as the voice of Miss Saber went at him. Miss Saber wanted Jerry to walk different places, correctly using his cane, remembering to keep the cane opposite the side of his step. "I'd like you to trail the north wall heading west," she said.

Sometimes he forgot to keep the cane out in front of him as he was supposed to do, or he didn't keep the back of his fingertips waist-high or the crook of the cane over his knuckles. Perhaps his trouble was that being a tall and jaunty man, he had always taken long, loose steps. It was still pretty to see him walk. He did not really want to have to keep close to the walls, walking slower, being careful.

At the end of the instruction period, Miss Saber said to him: "Your directions are good." Perhaps the best teachers must be harsh. But I thought then that what all of them wanted was for him to move like a timid and old person, a more humble one, who had given up those long, careless strides.

The next class was to develop tactile perceptions. "It's irrelevant what they make," Mr. Malamazian said. That day it was wallet stitching. Jerry did not want to go to stitch wallets with old men who gave no trouble, who had already begun their work when we walked in. The instructor looked up, and Jerry, who had not yet learned to be passive or to placate, spoke loudly. "This is my girl friend," he said. "You had better watch out for her. She's a shady lady."

I kissed him goodbye. There had been talk of dinner with his wife, but when I called the hospital only a few weeks later, he had bolted again, unable to finish the eighteen weeks.

That day Mr. Malamazian went on being polite and worried. He showed me the room where blind men learn to operate machinery, to take apart and put together things. I was taken to the library, where there are recorded books: *The Godfather* was the most popular one that year. The younger men balked at learning Braille. Mr. Malamazian was not certain that I should talk to the psychologist, the idea seemed almost dangerous to him, but she was a handsome young Brazilian who thought it was a most reasonable request. Her name was Beatriz Klich. Hers was the only voice on the staff that did not sound as if it came out of an old, dented can. She told me nothing I did not know, but it was a comfort to have her voice in that place. Jerry had said he liked it, too, that she was nice.

"Vietnam veterans are prone to be schizoid or angry," she said. "They feel they have been emasculated, that blindness is equivalent to a loss of manhood. It helps them to talk, sitting here; they come in feeling furious. It's very important for them to speak out. They're young, impatient. It makes them bitter that so much was done for the POWs."

Going back to the typing room, an instructor—a different elderly lady—said the new veterans could be very difficult. What she meant was some of them were hateful. Her eyelashes seemed almost wet when she told me of one former helicopter pilot who said, during his third or fourth typing lesson, how many people he had killed in Vietnam and how much he liked it and wasn't sorry at all.

"Can you imagine, can you imagine," the typing lady said. Yes, ma'am, I said, yes, ma'am, the way Jerry does it. A little revenge is better than none.

There were other men I knew who were blinded in Vietnam, who made it through Hines, who could move in and out of airports, who managed the perilous line the fork must make from the plate to the mouth, who could cross streets, write checks, type, heat soup, buy clothes. The war words "win" and "lose" still had meaning for them.

This was the case with John Robert Todd, who wanted to talk about the war and did nearly all the time in discussions and debates. He did not tell stories about what he had done or seen, he argued and wrote about the issues. He did not think that most people were even interested. In February 1973, when he had been blind for nearly four years, referring to this always as his "injuries," Mr. Todd lived in a ground-floor furnished apartment in an East 64th Street brownstone. He had been in New York for nearly two years to consult surgeons privately about restoring some sight in his left eye. "The primary mission of my life is to put myself together again," Mr. Todd said. His manner of speaking was often military.

Most of the time he was busy as the national leader and chief policy-maker for a group called Vietnam Veterans for a Just Peace, whose purpose was to support U.S. policy in Vietnam, to explain the mission of the Americans there and how well it had been achieved. His little group was pitted against a larger, older, more publicized one—Vietnam Veterans Against the War. People often called up Mr. Todd thinking they were talking to VVAW.

His voice is the voice of a pilot. It is calm, clear, low, with a pleasing pitch, a rather lovely voice for a man. He was often in demand for radio and television shows; it was easier to find a veteran to denounce the war than to find one who would support it. The newspapers and his mail were read to him by a pleasant middle-aged woman named Janet Martin. They met in the residential hotel where he lived during his first days in New York. He was also taking French lessons at the Alliance Française, four blocks from his apartment. There were mostly women in his class. He thought they came from nice houses in Long Island and wore fur coats: this is how he imagined them. Once the teacher asked the students to say something of their lives in French, expecting shy, soft little sentences to come forth. When it came his turn, Mr. Todd, making a few mistakes in grammar, blurted out: *"J'étais aviateur en Indochine et un jour j'ai reçu un mission de combat, et j'ai engagé l'enemi et j'étais fusillé."*

It must have gone around the room like a whip, touching all of them, making the women suddenly stare at the tall young man who wore such dark glasses and moved a long white cane in little arcs when he walked. It was not a typical thing for him to do, he did not often mean to startle people.

But he always calls himself an aviator, not a pilot, even in English. "I could fly very well, I thought," Mr. Todd told me. "I made life and death decisions and I thrived on it. I was never more proud to be an American man that I was in Vietnam. I'm very grateful for the role I was able to play."

All of their lives were little before the war; you can sum up the histories of veterans very fast. He was the first of five sons born to a construction contractor in Michigan; he was drafted and volunteered to fly; after six months in Vietnam, where he flew a Charlie-type gunship, his aircraft was hit by a .51-caliber antiaircraft gun northwest of Phan Thiet. He was shot through the nose. The co-pilot was uninjured and got them back.

"I'd like you to underline, to place asterisks by, to put in capital letters, that my views on the war are not new to me, that they are not a result of my injuries, that I have felt a consistency about the war all my adult life," Mr. Todd said. He knew that people of his own generation who opposed him said he was trying to rationalize his condition. It bothered him a lot.

In Vietnam, he flew support for the 101st Airborne and the 23d ARVN, a South Vietnamese division. Helicopter gunships were used to give close support to troops in battle by hovering above them or to stalk mobile targets. Their rockets, which were delivered singly or in bursts, came from tubes mounted under the aircraft. They could also dispense small bombs that on bursting sent out barbed nails which ricocheted through a human body, destroying tissue and organs; the nails could even penetrate trees. Incendiaries fired by the gunships included white phosphorus that burned on contact with oxygen and could not be extinguished until it had burned slowly to the bone. The pilots called white phosphorus Willie Peter and also used it for target designation for further strikes.

"Twenty-eight days out of the month I flew in support of U.S. infantry; one day out of the month I was flying in support of the Vietnamese. I found this wrong for both countries—wrong for them, wrong for us. Vietnamization was good for both countries—you had to give the South Vietnamese that bullet-type choice: if you want to support your type government, take this M-16 and fight."

He thought that many people on the fringes of the antiwar movement did not realize that the hard core of the movement wanted a Hanoi victory and that many of them had been deceived. "What they wanted was, let's just say, a plain end of the war, an end to the killing on both sides," Mr. Todd said. "I don't think they espoused victory for Hanoi."

He flew more than four hundred and fifty hours of combat missions in Vietnam before the last one of them all. For some time he did not know how hurt he was. The damaged eyes and nose did not give him pain: he recalls how the nurses and doctors at

Long Binh and then at the 249th Hospital in Osaka, Japan, had to convince him that he had taken a "pretty bad hit." He was thankful to be alive, deeply, deeply thankful to have had no brain injury. For a year and a day he was in Ward 2, the officers' neurological ward, at Walter Reed Hospital in Washington, D.C. Across the hall was Ward 1, where there were other aviators, he said, and infantry, the lieutenants who had been platoon leaders. Nine out of ten men had agreed with his views on the war, Mr. Todd said. Then he had gone to Hines, which was so different, not like Walter Reed, where the men had bought champagne and given parties, invited the nurses and had "great, great times." He had done the eighteen-week course at Hines in twelve weeks, skipping the cooking course, wanting to be out as fast as possible.

There were people his own age who opposed the war, who voted for George McGovern, who wanted an end to support of the Thieu government, and he did not despise them or think of them as fools. One of his friends had gone to Canada to avoid the draft; they were still friends. He was not combative. "I don't see any reason to cut off a friendship if the other person is sincere," Mr. Todd said. "But those people nineteen years old who start discussing the high morality of it all, coming on as though they were the monopolists of conscience, really perturb me."

There was a framed letter from the White House, dated June 21, 1974, in the apartment, signed by Richard M. Nixon, praising him for forming Vietnam Veterans for a Just Peace, urging him to speak out on "every forum and every occasion."

He was hopeful then that an operation scheduled for the following month would let him see. A corneal transplant had already been done on that left eye and it gave him some vision. "It really zooed me out," Mr. Todd said. "I could see." But the vision could not be sustained. It lasted for three weeks and then he lost it.

"I wish I could show you a picture of myself before the injuries; people said I looked like Robert Wagner," Mr. Todd said. He asked me what his face looked like. He took off his dark glasses and I said it was okay, there was a big scar, the nose was a little crooked, but nothing alarming. We talked again about the operation.

"It would help my social life a lot," he said. "People are afraid of a blind man."

Almost four years later much had changed for him, but the operations had failed, the sight in his left eye could not be restored. He is still legally blind, although he can make out the shape of some things. He still uses the cane for walking. He married a woman named Joyce, they have a daughter named Lacey.

"She was a blind date," Mr. Todd said. "We went to a dinner together in Washington, D.C., given by the *late* Mr. Agnew for the *late* Mr. Ky." He had never much liked Nguyen Cao Ky, who had been premier of South Vietnam when he was flying the gunship out of Phan Thiet. The couple live in Ypsilanti, outside of Detroit. He said he was building a patio deck out of wood; Joyce cut the pieces and he did all the work. But there was no way he could fix the lawn mower, which was not working. He is at the University of Michigan getting his undergraduate degree in political science. Joyce has long been a member of the Church of Christ; now he has also joined. They both plan to go to law school together and then work as attorneys, in public service, being useful. It was a word he had used before: useful. The disability payments he receives would make it possible for them to do public service, Mr. Todd said.

The ending of the war upset him a lot. "The attitude of so many Democrats, the men who put us there, led to the retreat and collapse of the South Vietnamese, a Democratic Congress led to their downfall by the decision to not send them more bullets," Mr. Todd said. "All this occurred because of Watergate—if Nixon had still been in office, he wouldn't have let that Congress do it."

Most people had forgotten about the war, he said. "The apathy has continued, furiously, but it's a landmark as far as foreign policy goes. The politicians misread what the people would tolerate; it was a limited war and the people still wouldn't tolerate it. There'll never be another one like it, never another Vietnam."

He had stopped speaking about Vietnam when he went to Columbia University in New York in the fall of 1973. There was no point to it. "I didn't talk about the war because I thought I might be ostracized. I wasn't ashamed, I was just very quiet. But the students couldn't have cared less. They wouldn't even have been mad at me."

IN A TOWN in Oklahoma named Cheyenne, where 892 people were counted in the last census, club women made ditty bags for soldiers during the Vietnam war. I never heard the expression or saw a ditty bag in Vietnam; the soldiers had deep pockets on their jackets and low on the legs of their fatigues, which, when filled, gave them strange lumpy lines. Nonetheless a sustained effort was made by these women, including one with the pleasing name of Laurabel Lemon, who helped head the ditty-bag drive. By 1968 ninety-two ditty bags had been dispatched. This was noted briefly in the *Cheyenne Star*, which runs county news. Back issues of the newspaper are bound in huge books, the war threading lightly through its pages among other announcements of weddings, illnesses, meetings, auctions, sales and gatherings. There were lists of local servicemen in Vietnam and their APO addresses so people would know where to write Pfc. Tommy O'Hara or Pfc. Roy L. McDaniel. There were bits of news that revealed Sgt. Donnie Walker had a Purple Heart and an occasional snapshot of a grinning GI, like Kenneth Kirk, sitting on his heels somewhere in Qui Nhon.

The Redden brothers publish the Cheyenne paper. W. J. Redden, who is known as Joe, served on the local draft board. The war disgusted him. "We could have walked through them real easy," Mr. Redden said. His face has the contours of a clean, dependable engine: parts of it move only if necessary. It is a peculiarly dead and correct American face, the kind that men are supposed to need when they play five-card stud, a handsome face for some women.

"Fathers who served in World War II expect their sons to serve," Mr. Redden said. His son had. Mr. Redden did not disclose his son's unit, where he had been in Vietnam, how long, or very much about what he had done or seen. Perhaps he did not really know, perhaps he thought it was none of anyone's business. "He was in rockets," he said, the way people might say a man was in textiles, in construction, in advertising.

Cheyenne has a deserter: his name is William L. Males. His father is a banker, L. L. Males, whose nickname is "Red." No one held it against his parents, Mr. Redden said; you could not blame it on his father, it was nothing against a man like Red Males.

People held the banker in the highest esteem. He was one of the men who had turned that part of the dust bowl into a dairy center, and in Cheyenne he is often called the "father of upstream flood control."

"If everybody is left to decide when to fight for their country, we won't have a country," Mr. Redden said. It is a sentence that has come at me so many times, I need now only write down the first words "if everybody" and the rest I know by heart. It was all right with Joe Redden if that Males boy wanted to come back; nobody would try to keep him from coming home. "Of course, there are not too many who would socialize with him, he wouldn't be welcome in our homes," Mr. Redden said.

He did not ask me how I knew about William L. Males in Sweden. The subject is a touchy one in Cheyenne, not something to be discussed with outsiders. I knew about the deserter from an article, a long interview in which the writer asked William L. Males in Stockholm why he had left the Army. "Because I knew too much. All of us here knew too much," Mr. Males said. There were five hundred deserters at that time in Sweden.

He called himself Willi. He spoke Swedish well. He was a student and worked in a hospital, even doing chores like emptying bedpans, which he liked very much because it gave him a chance to touch people. He wanted to touch people. He did not want to hurt or abuse or frighten anyone, the deserter said.

From Cheyenne he went to Yale, where he was fearful that he could not fit in. But then the university made him as uncomfortable as did his hometown. He tried to run away, to go home, but then he bolted from Oklahoma too.

"Cheyenne made things worse because it just reeked of dreams that failed me," he said. Ashamed of trying to escape from the Army, he joined it to become a medic. After a year he deserted.

"You can't guess the evil of the Army unless you see it," Willi Males said. "The thing that bothered me most about the Army is that it's based on hate . . ."

IN THE CHEYENNE lunchroom a waitress named Tennie Dale Campbell introduced me to her father, an eighty-one-year-old farmer, who had a lot to say about the Great Depression but nothing about the war. I always wanted to talk to farmers. In Texas, in Iowa, in New Jersey and in New Mexico I went to them, pushed on by the sentimental persuasion that these men, above all others, would see the cruelty of driving the Vietnamese from their land and water and rice into the towns and cities where they were degraded and lost. I was quite persuaded that American farmers would not approve of the forests and farms and rice fields of Vietnam being put to death. But the men I met had their own worries; some had doubts but turned from them.

Early in 1967 Senator Richard Russell, born 1897 in Winder, Georgia, spoke his mind to a young member of the White House staff, a speechwriter for LBJ who often wrote on the war and was leaving for a two-week trip to at last see it for himself. "Look into that free-fire zone business. I don't like the sound of it," the senator said. "The Vietnamese people are animists. They feel very deeply about the land where their ancestors are buried. I suspect we're alienating them by moving them away from their homes, even if it's for their safety. I know how Georgia people feel about that. When a big dam is dedicated down there and a lot of farmers have been moved out to make way for the reservoir, I don't go to the dedication. I don't want them to see me up there on a platform built over their land."

It was good advice, surprising advice from a man of such power who headed the Senate Armed Services Committee, who always voted to keep the war going.

IN THE CHEYENNE lunchroom, of all places, over pie and coffee, I remembered for no reason a man who had lost his garden. It was the garden of a Vietnamese named Le Van Phuoc; Luong and I saw him on the afternoon of a Christmas Eve, a year in Vietnam where that month meant the Bob Hope Show more than Bethlehem. This man, Phuoc, called himself a farmer, for he had been one nearly all his life, but he was then surviving as a carpenter in the city of Can Tho. For five years there had not been a single day or a single night when he had not thought of a village called Long Tri. His family owned a little land there; their house had been built by his father. It was a simple story, many Vietnamese had told it before; one out of every three Vietnamese in the south felt themselves to be refugees, even if they were moved less than thirty miles from their homes. There was nothing unusual about this man and what he told us.

It had always been a deep pleasure for Mr. Phuoc to go out to his garden every morning, even before it was very light, to stand there for a minute, in the lifting darkness, before he left the house and joined the other men in the walk to their rice fields. He could still remember each shape in that garden, even when he was nothing but a refugee in a houseboat that smelled of the brown water of a canal.

Americans had destroyed the village of Long Tri from the air with rockets and napalm. Some Viet Cong—our word, not his—had, perhaps, fired on something to provoke this punishment. He was not clear about this, not wishing to be clear. All Vietnamese knew it was safer to say very little. Speaking of his village, he sounded like a man who had found himself pushed across a fearful frontier, no longer living or sleeping under the same sky. We sat cross-legged on mats in the only room of his houseboat, a low and dark place where I was too tall to stand up, a houseboat that rested on stilts in a canal.

"The wood columns of the house burned for seven days," Le Van Phuoc said. "And, after, all we had was a basket of nails."

All of us pretended not to see that his wife was weeping. She kept lifting a checked cloth towel to wipe her eyes and sometimes press against her mouth, although she made no noise.

It was always this way when she thought of their son, Mr. Phuoc said to Luong. He had been killed as a soldier in the Saigon army, in Cambodia, a place his parents knew nothing about. Every sentence seemed to jab the woman into remembering the boy although his name was not mentioned, for we spoke only of the lost village. I knew better than to reach over and touch her hand; they never could bear it.

"Sometimes I cannot sleep at night," Le Van Phuoc said. "I think of the hamlet, and where I made grow a certain plant, how such a tree grew in the garden, and how we set off early in the morning for the rice fields." Even if they had to get up so early, and even if there was never enough rest in those days, Mr. Phuoc said, it was a good life. "Everyone felt fine," he said. "We were very strong."

His village was only twenty-five miles away, a tiny distance for

an American, but there was no way for him to return. He heard
the war was always there. There were mines; the land was hurt.
Nothing was as it had been. Official permission would be needed
to go back, and it was impossible to get—the area was not safe. He
did not say that without a son he could not manage to farm again.
Instead he showed us a photograph of the dead boy, with his small
face and huge smile, which was framed and hung on the wall of
the houseboat.

LOVE YOUR COUNTRY, the Vietnamese in Paris said. In Tennessee there were the trees and their names to learn: beech, maple,
elm, ash, hickory, buckeye, tulip poplar, redbud. In Smith County,
cattle and tobacco country, there are villages called Carthage,
Defeated and Pleasant Shade, Horseshoe Bend, Brush Creek and
Difficult. On Main Street in Carthage, a woman on her front lawn
said these are the boxwood bushes, this is lily of the valley, there is
dogwood and mimosa. Old men sit on the benches in the court-
house square of Carthage, with their suspenders and shapeless
hats that shade their faces, chatting with each other. In the library,
which was opened in 1941 for the county and has fifteen thousand
books in all, there were a few books on Vietnam, less than eight:
Hell Is a Very Small Place by Bernard Fall was borrowed by five
people from April 1967 to 1973; fourteen people read *No Place to
Die* by Hugh Mulligan, an Associated Press reporter from 1968
to 1973. *Behind the Lines* by Harrison Salisbury of *The New York
Times*, the report of the first American journalist allowed to visit
North Vietnam, where he saw that U.S. bombing targets were
civilian as well as military, had not been touched.

The younger librarian, a bulky woman in a flowered dress of
thin, light material, seemed to find it odd that I would even ask
about the library books on Vietnam. She said she had a brother
who had been in Pleiku. "Most people like me don't want to read

about it," Claudia Dillehay said. "I have no desire to read about it. I don't want to read a whole book on it."

One of the leading citizens in Carthage was Judge Clint Beardsley, who was born in 1898, was appointed judge and took office in 1930, then stood for election and went on for more than forty years handling juvenile and nonsupport cases as well as being county fiscal agent. In his law office, in Court House Square, Judge Beardsley, a small white-haired man whose favorite poem is "Annabel Lee" and who wore a diamond and gold ring of the Blue Lodge, a chapter of the Shriners, seemed fit except for a slight sinus condition. He called me "honey" or "my friend," or "my little queen" when he thought I was being slightly sassy.

The judge said: "I know that from the beginning I thought we would have no earthly business in this war, if that's what you want to know. I would say the vast majority of our people just had no interest, no concern for the war excepting they didn't think we should be in it.

"Going to Canada—well, I don't think that was the right route to take. No, I didn't approve of it, no. Just to be frank with you, there again I would say that by a vast majority our people object to all types of demonstration, especially if there's any violence attached. The mob has never been right. Mobs just don't do the right thing. They're not at heart bad, vicious people by any means, I don't say that. They're opposed to violence, I'd say, they'd tell you they were opposed to violence but they become excited."

Napalm, white phosphorus, cluster-bomb units: that was the violence that I knew, not the inaugural weekend in Washington in 1973 when I kicked a policeman *hard* and he returned the kick *hard*. I asked the judge in that small, orderly room, with its leather law volumes behind glass and its venerable clock, that if he thought the war was ill-advised and if the antiwar demonstrators thought the war was wrong, then they had something very much in common.

The judge said: "Now wait a minute, my little queen! I'm a

strong believer in constitutional society. Even though I don't like certain things, if I don't like certain laws, I think I'm duty-bound as a good citizen to have due respect for the law. I believe one of the worst problems we have today in this country is not teaching young people to have proper respect for constitutional authority."

Vietnam was a bad experience, it divided the country, but the judge was not worried. "People forget—fortunately they forget the bad things. Back when I was a child the Civil War was still being talked about. In some cases people were bitter towards the North. And if they were not bitter, they certainly were strong for the South. So people forget. Now, back when I was a child I didn't think they'd ever forget. My own grandfather fought for the Confederacy."

The judge, who is married but has no children, said he thought of himself as "typical pacifist, if you like. In other words, I'm against wars and I'm against fighting and I'm against feuding, and I believe in people living together in love and peace and harmony."

I said: "That's lovely."

The interview made the judge twenty minutes late for lunch. He was very nice about such a delay. He always went home and ate a chopped egg salad sandwich with olives, coffee and canned pears. Then he took a nap, and went back to the office.

"As a matter of fact, it's hard to describe, but people here have not discussed this war much—that is, on the street corners. Or, if they do, they must make a few 'cracks,' as I'd call them. Make some cracks, wisecracks, and that's about it."

Six miles from Carthage, in Gordonsville, Mrs. Orion Key had been the secretary of the local draft board, which is now closed. The board had met once a month in the Federal Building, in a room over the Post Office.

"The Korean war was a nightmare, I was much busier," Betty Key said. "The Vietnam war, well, this is a patriotic country and few cases caused me any heartache. Five died, but they were all volunteers, none of them draftees. Isn't that marvelous?"

Men who thought they would get drafted volunteered because they hoped it would give them more of a choice about what might happen to them. Sometimes it did.

"Everybody knew my home, I had calls on Saturday," she said. "The worse thing about the war is that we've seen it in the living room. We see murder on TV."

Her usual day went from 6 A.M. to 11 P.M. Mrs. Key was secretary of the First Baptist Church, cleaned a six-room house, and was secretary for Mixon & Key, which she calls a motor company but looks like a garage, next to her house on Main Street. Mrs. Key is a dark-haired woman—the mother of a thirty-four-year-old son—who does nothing slowly or sloppily, although she made fun of her "in-and-out method of bookkeeping" for her husband's company. There was something cooking in the kitchen for supper, which she raced in to stir.

The draft boards did not have to see each man who received notice from his Selective Service Board to appear; they saw only those who wanted deferments for one reason or another. One of the three men on Local Board 87 was Lewis Parker, assistant mortician of the Bass Funeral Home in Carthage, and a coroner. He was a large, calm man who did not want to be interviewed and had his own almost admirable methods of protecting his privacy. He would say "I guess it was" or "I reckon that's the way you could put it" or "I just don't hardly know how to answer that question" or "Well, now you know, that's the sixty-four-dollar question." Yet he did not tell me to go away and stop bothering him. For an hour we faced each other, like two foreigners, in the Bass Funeral Home on a quiet day when there was no business at hand.

"Nobody don't want to go," he said of the draft. "You bring your child up, you want your child deferred. But we didn't have too many who was nervous up here. But the majority of them was leaving home when they ought to be at home. It was a hardship on the family."

He was on the draft board for four, maybe five, years. There was no reimbursement. It was clear that Mr. Parker was a man with a regret.

"I got on it when I should have stayed off it," he said, and would explain nothing more. It made him glum. "It was hard. The biggest thing is your friends. There you are, lots of times your friends, you see, some of them you was raised up with, you know, and then their children come in."

Those who asked for deferments were mainly college students or hardship cases where a son was needed to help his family. Mr. Parker knew the draft was harder on the children of poor families than on those who could get deferments as students. "Yes, that's true, but there's a lot of things you wouldn't think was fair in the deal but we just had to go by that law they had on the books," he said. "I don't remember if there was anyone that wanted to be let off because of what they felt about the war, see, I've been out of that thing now and it's slipped my mind what all did go on."

During World War II he had been exempt from military service because of a job with the railroads. Both of his two sons, aged thirty-seven and thirty-five, served four years in the Air Force after high school. There were moments when, if Mr. Parker's large seamed face had changed slightly, become more intent, he might have looked like Lyndon Johnson. But he did not joke or look menacing.

He had never settled the reason for the war in his own mind. "Well, I still don't know what it was all about, the way I look at it," he said. "I done my duty without having it settled, I guess that's it. I don't feel nothing in favor of it."

He thought that the men who volunteered had wanted to get it over with. "But just like Betty told you, we lost some, but they volunteered. That wasn't on your shoulders, don't you see? If one of them had got killed that I had sent, that would bring more on your shoulders than if he's volunteered. See what I'm talking about?"

I did not see.

Then Mr. Parker suddenly relented and shared a memory. "I just had one lady and she worried me to death, she'd call me at home in the evening, she'd be cryin', carryin' on, all this stuff, this, that and the other. The boy was already drafted, he went off, did his two years, got out. No, no, he's not dead. If he was dead, I'd know it. He's here. There's not many that dies that I don't know or hear about."

He knew what I meant when I asked if the country had been deformed by the war, but he had not heard the fury and the shame firsthand, only knew the worries that being on the draft board could lead to hard feelings among old friends.

"I think we'll get back on the right track," Mr. Parker said. "I do believe we'll all get back to pulling together."

People did not try to save their sons from the war because "they just want to keep out of trouble," he said. People went along with what they had been told: the fighting in Vietnam was to save a country from the Communists. "But I don't know whether I do believe that or not now." Mr. Parker spoke as if it did not make such a difference; a judgment was not required.

We drove through Gordonsville again; I said goodbye and thank you to Mrs. Key. She asked me if Mr. Parker had told me why he quit the draft board, why he had been so upset and felt he had to resign. "Well, I suppose it's all history now," Mrs. Key said. Mr. Parker had been shocked by how Lieutenant Calley was treated, how they were blaming him for all those killings. Mr. Parker could not take it. That is how I found out the sad, small secret he wanted so much to keep from me.

Of them all, only Mildred Davis had some questions to ask me. Harrison, her husband, a fifty-four-year-old sharecropper and farmer who takes care of the one hundred and eighty cattle and the thirteen thousand chickens, and grows an acre and a half of tobacco, on Gore Farms, was the one I approached, but he was watching *Maude* on television and had to get up at five-thirty.

"Well, why not me, I'm the one with book learning," Mrs. Davis said.

The Davises were married in 1939, had five children, all of whom were born at home, wherever home was. One of them, a plump girl named Brenda Kaye, a pillowy girl with skin as white as eggshells, is still at home. The house has four rooms; a giant color television set goes on during the day and at night. Mrs. Davis said her brother, Virgil Hobbs, was a retired staff sergeant who had been in two wars and said that people who went through wars did not like to talk about it.

"Do you like to talk about what you went through while you were in Vietnam, do you like to?" Mrs. Davis said. Even Virgil could not explain why the Americans went to Vietnam or stayed there.

"I read any paper I can get. I don't know about the Christmas bombings—a good idea or a bad idea. I just don't really know, 'cause you read things like that going on and you don't know whether to really believe it or not, so you just go on to things you like to read better."

She thought if George Wallace had not been wounded, he would be a good President, but she didn't know any women who voted. "I never voted for nobody. Don't reckon I've got a cousin or an aunt or anybody like that who did, I never knew none of them voting."

Mildred Davis went through the seventh grade; her husband has lead schooling. She remembered when he had made only seventy-five cents a day, now he was on salary, perhaps making as much as a dollar fifty an hour, and they had a decent place to live.

"Back then when you had big farms to look after, well, the older generation felt you didn't need much schoolin', you needed to be home working," she said. "Once when the five children were at home a lady came to the house, for the Red Cross, mebbe, asking some questions. I said 'I've got the best occupation in the world, I just don't make no money at it.' She quit writing, she looked up at me and said 'Well, you got the best job in the world, keeping these children in school.' And I thought 'You don't know what you're talking about. I don't make a thing. Everybody wants to make a little money.'"

She did not know about the Vietnamese, allies or enemies. "Let them fight their own war, it's the north and the south, just like the other war, our war. But I think the United States won most of it over there because they had the most equipment and the know-how and more troops than the other country does."

Brenda Kaye, whose silence was quite stunning, spoke at last to say yes, the United States won, but the war did not interest her very much. Her mother thought maybe the antiwar people wanted to be on television.

If there were people in Tennessee against the war, Mrs. Davis thought they probably kept themselves quiet. "They didn't want to get involved, most of them don't want to get involved in nothing. 'Fraid to speak out," she said. "But me, I never did meet a stranger. I can always talk—I may not talk plain every time, but I never did meet a stranger. I can always get up a conversation with somebody. Can't you?"

She was sorry people didn't have time to visit each other as they had once done; she did not deny her loneliness.

"Are you married? Well, you have been married, then. You know how men are whenever the football season is on and the basketball season. Why, you know they're glued to that on Sundays, so you don't have much conversation with a man on Sundays. I rattle off all the time, and Harrison, he listens if he wants to, if he don't, well, he gets up and leaves. He says I talk too much."

She seemed pleased that I had been told the very same thing, and many times.

It was not until the end of our talk that she said her son-in-law, Rufus Melvin, who married Helen, had been in Vietnam. Mrs. Davis brought out the box that held a card for Tet which said "Cung Chuc Tam Huan" and letters. She had never thrown away the card. Brenda Kaye, who had been deeply bored but could not summon the energy to leave the room, said Rufus couldn't get used to the weather. "It was so hot over there," she said.

"He used to wake up hollering and hollering when he came home," Mrs. Davis said.

A few miles away from Carthage, in a small place called Donelson, Rufus Melvin said he had never been taught anything about the war, he knew nothing about it, perhaps because he didn't care for book reading.

"I thought it'd be ended before my time, but it wasn't," Mr. Melvin said. We sat at the table near the kitchen in his little ranch house. Helen, the daughter of Mrs. Davis, sat with us, but like Brenda Kaye, she did not speak or hear or even squirm. Mr. Melvin was a construction worker. He had been married before and had two children, which gave him a draft deferment. When he divorced and married Helen, he lost it. "They went ahead and got me," Mr. Melvin said.

He spoke sorrowfully, in a low voice, a shy man with tight curly brown hair married to a woman with ice-blond hair that was so neat, so landscaped, it might have been a wig. Helen looked at her fingernails a lot.

"I was wounded in Mo Duc," Mr. Melvin said. "We took a little red hill." The Americans had made a combat assault into a hot landing zone. His platoon was walking a ditchline; there was an ambush. The South Vietnamese troops made the men in the platoon nervous, made Mr. Melvin nervous. "I felt right fearsome. One day it seemed to me we'd fight with them and the next day we'd fight against them because they all looked the same to me. They couldn't control their weapons. They'd start running out in front of you, them ARVN, you'd better step aside because they just liable to shoot you in the back. Because it would just get away from them on automatic."

Helen did not move. Perhaps she remembered her father telling her mother not to talk so much, perhaps she knew what the words LZ and on automatic meant.

Mr. Melvin remembered basic training at Fort Campbell when he was scared of shooting so many guns. It made him jump every time he pulled a trigger, but then after a while in Vietnam such things did not bother him any more. Taking the little red hill in the ambush gave him some shrapnel and later he hurt his ankle. In between he had been sent to Mount Baldy to be an aide for a brigade commander. He spoke in knots. I did not try to get the dates straight. Mr. Melvin said he never really knew who he was fighting.

"To me Charlie was North Vietnam and VC. I thought they was the same thing but I didn't learn the difference until the other night on TV, when they signed the peace treaty, that they was two different things."

When he came home, there were a few who asked him if he had killed anybody. It brought back to him the man he had once been; it made him take account of himself.

"I always said that I would never be able to kill a man, I never thought I could kill anybody," Mr. Melvin said, looking at the table.

I looked at the table. Helen kept looking at her long frosted nails, fussing a little with the tips.

"When I was over there I couldn't understand why them people here was protesting. To me they were showing their hind end. If they cared anything about their country, then why ain't they trying to straighten it out? When I was over there, well, now, I never thought about nothing that happened back in the States except for the war protesters. Because you can't have too much on your mind and stay alive over there," he said.

If the police had been rougher with the war protesters, who he thought were trying to take over the government, then America would be in better shape. "That's what I think. I have been taught right from wrong. Mom had always, Daddy had always, taught me that if I wanted anything to ask for it. Why, I was eighteen years old before I even had my first date," Mr. Melvin said.

On his second night in Vietnam in the field, only the second night, in the dark at a listening post in Pleiku, six years ago, he and two other soldiers were sitting out in front of some huts. He remembered hearing the crying of babies when shooting broke behind them, in the place where the huts were and where the people lived. When the attack came, it came from Vietnamese in the hamlet they were guarding.

"One of them went right on top of me. We shot him through the back of his head, all three of us. We put sixty rounds in that man before he fell. We called for those lights, those flares. And so the way he died, you know, he died with one leg up in front of him like he was trying to crawl. And every time one of them flares went off, it looked like that man was moving and we just kept pumping them out. The next morning we went out there. He had an M-1 carbine and we shot it all to pieces and everything. We shot it through the clips and everything. I took it out of his hand. We shot him through the back of his head. It all come through his nose and took all his head out right here. Then the captain come out there and said 'Good work, good work.'"

He didn't think the South Vietnamese were grateful. "I would feel the same way if this country got into a fight and another country come in," Mr. Melvin said.

Then it seemed as if he could not stop talking, not yet, because he was listening to himself for the first time, hurrying as he heard. "I done try to forget most of it, everything I done seen or heard and everything," he said.

But that was not the end of it.

"I think the war took a lot of morale out of the American people," Mr. Melvin said. "For me it was mostly the killing. My worstest mistake one day was when we was near a bunker, we had gas grenades and frag grenades. Them Charlie, the VC, were in the bunker and I threw in a grenade. It weren't gas, the mistake was it was a frag, and there were people in there, and out comes a grandfather holding a baby in its arms, near dead."

Mr. Melvin looked at my face, but there was nothing for him to see.

The Americans used different gases. If they used too much CS at close range, it gave the Vietnamese burns. CS was wretched for the Vietnamese with lung diseases: it made them choke and squirm and throw up. Luong was persuaded that any American gas had lasting effects and would rot something inside the chest. He had very fixed ideas. There were different gases to induce nausea, irritate the mucus, tighten breathing and sting the eyes. If the gases were combined, or fired in canisters from an M-79 or from the rocket pods of gunships, the Vietnamese were sure the gases were meant to disable or kill them.

"There was lots of mistakes, see," Mr. Melvin was saying.

There was a noise then, something no louder than a sigh, but much harsher. Perhaps it came from him, perhaps it came from me.

Mr. and Mrs. Melvin stood outside their little house when I left them. She moved her hand in a single wave, but he stood still, an ordinary man with big shoulders and quiet ways, whose name was written in a family Bible when he was born, who trembled in basic training, who used to yell and shout in his sleep and warn his wife never to come up behind him too quietly. But standing there in the sun, he looked like everyone else, a man with nothing special to say, no more dangerous than the rest of us.

HE REMINDED ME of a woodcarving, nice in its way, for Kenneth Morris was a slight, steady, neat man of tidy ways. He teaches what he calls a survey course of the whole spectrum of American history in the high school in Carthage to juniors who are usually sixteen years old. He has five classes a day, no more than twenty in a class. There were five girls in his first class of the morning who were already married. By 1973 there had not been a day in the eight years he taught there when boys, like the ones he faced, were not in Vietnam. Yet the war had not been of that much interest to his pupils, Mr. Morris, a forty-three-year-old Tennessean said. Oh yes, there were boys, mostly boys, who got riled up, not because of the war but because of acts of Americans who opposed it.

Mr. Morris said: "If they were talking about those people lying down in front of troop trains, you know, they said they ought to execute them, shoot them, that's right, shoot them. I said 'Well, we're not at war, if it was a declared war, then they could.' Then the students said Well, we should declare a war. I didn't know what to say. I didn't feel hardly that strong about it, because of the nature of the war. In World War II certainly they should have. They were also strongly against people dodging the draft, they thought that if a person's time comes to go to war, then they shouldn't run off."

It was an act people associated with "sorry-ness," he said. "That's not a word you use up North. Sorry-ness: somebody's no good. And people here have a very low opinion of people who disputed the President and the leadership about the war. I'd say that the position here were ninety-eight percent in favor of Calley, that they shouldn't do anything to him. And I said to the students Well, he lined up all these little children and tied their hands behind their back and killed them—women and everything. They said they were the enemy, that they'd read about these children tying bombs to themselves, that the children were the enemy too, in an enemy area, everybody was the enemy, Calley should have killed them all.

"That kind of struck me because I'm a Goldwater man myself,

but I'm not that much. I think Calley is a criminal. No, I didn't put it that strongly to them. I really didn't take a strong position with the students, I just gave them the facts on both sides, you know, that perhaps Calley was wrong, then I took the other position a little bit. That Calley thing, that really got them."

Each year that he taught, the war came closer, but few heard it. Mr. Morris said that he gave some history of Vietnam, but in less than twenty minutes; there wasn't time to do more.

"We took over the vacuum where the French left. They were colonialists and that's the reason why, of course, when they asked for our help at Dien Bien Phu, we couldn't afford to help them because if we took a position favoring colonialism, then it would hurt us in our relations with Africa.

"I started back and told them about Vietnam to start with, before the war, about the struggle with the Vietnamese nationalists and the French. And then we'd take it up to the time when the Japanese occupied Indochina. I'd tell them how Ho Chi Minh was against the Japanese at the time and was aided by Americans. We don't make a hero out of him, we say he fought the Japanese and after the war they were trying to get independence. Then in '56 we sent in advisors under Eisenhower. The Vietnamese defeated the French and drove them out, and then it was a struggle between the north wanting to take over the south and make it all Communist. I don't get into that Geneva Convention too much, about the elections they were supposed to have. Oh sure, Ho Chi Minh would have won. Not that the people believed like he believed but because he was a kind of George Washington. I think it would have been a vote for an individual instead of them wanting communism."

He said yes, yes, he knew Ho Chi Minh was loved, still loved. Some of us could have told him that no living Vietnamese had the power of this dead man.

"I don't go into that very deeply because, you know, you teach what you want to teach. You can leave the impression that you want to leave, I guess."

He thought of himself as a conservative man. He had watched the war on television, he had seen the troops, the prisoners, the helicopters, the rifles, the paddies, the jungles, the litters, the wounded.

"Nothing romantic, like you would have had in World War II, putting the flag up at Iwo Jima. It was just a war going on; of course I wanted to know all I could. But I never believed that we should just pull up stakes and just cut. Dealing with Asians is always a matter of losing face.

"I think actually this war caused a lot of people here like everywhere else to lose the romance of war. It's no good any more, there's no romance. The war wasn't fought for any purpose except to more or less prevent somebody else from doing something. America's gain in it was nil. This war it's probably done more to prevent wars than anything that's ever happened in this country."

A brother was the postmaster in Carthage and owned interest in a store on Highway 25, which sold $126,000 worth of beer in 1972. The shop was near the Green Hills Golf and Country Club. It was a nice place, Mr. Morris said, there were dances. It cost three hundred dollars to join, fifteen dollars a month for members. There was a bar that didn't serve drinks: you had to bring them and mix them yourself. He was one of nine children born in Monterrey, Tennessee, he was a member of the Baptist faith but leaned a little toward the Methodists, whom he considered a bit more liberal about their views of Christian behavior.

"I think no one actually won the war, but certainly the Communists came out on top because of their superior dedication," he said. "I think we met our commitments and got out."

He knew of no boy killed or badly hurt in Vietnam; there was one who drove for a general, but he did not always know what happened to any of them after they left school.

"I'd tell the students that the Vietnamese are a very warlike people and have been all back during the history. They've always picked on their neighbors—the poor Cambodians and the other tribes in that area. They've always been that way. While the Chinese haven't."

The students did not much read newspapers, but he remembered a girl who once in the sixth grade read both *The Banner* and *The Nashville Tennessean*, who once read 112 history books in one year. He thought that boys on the whole were more disinterested than girls in schooling.

"You'll always have that," Mr. Morris said. "They're interested in other things. A lot of them work after school, work at nights. The factories are working a lot of the boys."

THE VIETNAMESE PEOPLE were many things, but I did not think of them as warlike, the word used by Mr. Morris. What runs through their history, like a coarse, brilliant thread of crimson, is opposition to foreign rule. After a thousand years as a Chinese colony, they were independent—except for a brief period of Chinese rule in the fifteenth century—under their own sovereigns until the mid-nineteenth century. As of 1887 Vietnam had ceased to exist for all practical purposes, as one historian wrote, "except as a memory and a rallying cry to revolt." In its place a French decree established the Indochinese Union. Three parts of it were Vietnam split horizontally from north to south into the protectorates of Tonkin and Annam and the colony of Cochin China. Japanese intervention, after France was defeated in Europe in 1940, broke the continuity of French rule, but Japanese domination of Vietnam did not survive after the August 1945 surrender which ended World War II. On September 2, 1945, in Hanoi, Ho Chi Minh declared the independence of the Democratic Republic of Vietnam, and the war with France began. In December

1946 the Vietnam Doc Lap Dong Minh Hoi, or League for the Independence of Vietnam, was supported by the majority of the nation because, when it went to war with France, it carried on a nationalist tradition that stretched back to Emperor Ham Nghi. He was the very young Emperor in 1884 when the French tried to establish a protectorate over Vietnam, and he called on the people to revolt against the French in Hue.

Early in the fifteenth century the national hero Le Loi, who liberated Vietnam from Chinese rule, issued a proclamation in which it is written: "Our people long ago established Vietnam as an independent nation with its own civilization. We have our own mountains and our own rivers, our own customs and traditions, and those are different from the foreign country to the north [China]. We have been weak and we have been strong, but at no time have we lacked heroes."

When the war with France was over—with General Giap's military victory early in May at Dien Bien Phu in 1954—the French military effort in Indochina was ended. In a final declaration the Geneva Conference of 1954 noted that the line of demarcation at the 17th parallel was a provisional one and should in no way be constituted as a political or territorial boundary divorcing the north from the south. Article 7 guaranteed the right of the Vietnamese people to enjoy the fundamental freedoms guaranteed by democratic institutions, which were to be established as a result of free general elections by secret ballot in July 1956 under the supervision of the International Commission. The United States government announced that it would refrain from the threat or use of force to disturb the Geneva agreements, but the 1956 elections, giving the Vietnamese the right to choose between the governments of the north or the south, were never held, for the Americans would not permit them, nor would the Saigon government of Ngo Dinh Diem, which we had installed and nourished. President Eisenhower, in his memoirs, said that if the elections had been held, eighty percent of the Vietnamese might have voted for Ho Chi Minh.

In the province of Phu Yen in southern Vietnam, famous for its guerrilla fighters in the nine-year war against the French, I met men who did not dare speak to their children of what they had helped win. They were Viet Minh soldiers in the movement to liberate their country from foreigners; if the movement was Communist-led, it meant nothing for many Vietnamese because it drew the proudest and most hopeful men to its side, the patriots who did not wish to be ruled by whites. After the partition in 1954—when each Vietnamese was to decide whether he wished to live north or south of the 17th parallel—those who stayed in Phu Yen were denounced by the Saigon government and viewed with deep suspicion by local officials during the American presence, when there were monthly quotas and constant pressures to round up any Vietnamese who could be accused of sympathizing with the Communists.

This is why, in the little town of Tuy Hoa, Luong and I waited for hours to arrange to meet the *chien si*, the Vietnamese word for fighter, men of the Viet Minh. There were handwritten messages to be sent through an intermediary, messages to come back. Luong went out for hours, and only when it was dark did a student arrive to lead us, as silently, as gravely as if we were departing on a night ambush. It was a great risk for the veterans of the Viet Minh to meet with us, when anyone could be arrested under the Phoenix program—arrested, held, abused, bribed, jailed—whose purpose was to round up the Viet Cong and its sympathizers. All were suspect.

The first man was known to us only as Tai. We went down little alleys to find his house—a frail thing, as they all were—and then sat close together by a kerosene lamp. Tai spoke in whispers. It was always the lowest, softest voices in Vietnam that seemed most drilling. Once he moved in that blurred light and I saw that he was not a strong man, that his thinness was not just a matter of small bones and hard work.

"I will never regret it," Tai said. "I will never be ashamed of it. What we did in those long nine years led to the independence of half of our country." The half was the north. His own family in Tuy Hoa were not peasants: his father taught school and owned two buses. In the early meetings of the people, Tai told us, all swore to rid themselves forever of the French. No one held back or could not make up his mind, so they were moving times, not like the meetings held now for the people by the Saigon government officials, which made them all sleepy and dull, Tai told us.

On that October night in 1972 he remembered how thirty years ago he and nineteen other youths from the area fought near a bridge nine miles south of Tuy Hoa. The bridge had recently been blown up by Viet Cong guerrillas. Luong and I had seen it. No one spoke of repairing it and no travelers loitered by it.

The day that Tai left Tuy Hoa he told his parents to think of him as their dead son. Twenty of them made the march from Phu Yen province to the U Minh forest at the southern tip of their country, where their mission was a French naval installation. The men crossed through the area of Nha Trang, the coastal city, down to the Saigon-Cholon area, through the Plain of Reeds, crossing the Mekong River to Tra Vinh province, the old name for Vinh Binh, and then on to Tan Bang, Thoi Binh, in the U Minh forest which was never a forest despite its name. There were ambushes by the French, there was malaria, there was a tiredness he had never dreamed of, different dreams and fears.

"The most terrible was moving through the jungles in central Vietnam and those swampy areas in the south. The hardships only sharpened my hatreds, especially when movement exhausted me and I saw airplanes in the sky, automobiles on the road and even trains moving in a distance."

They walked two thousand miles. It took six months.

The French seemed to have everything: weapons, artillery, planes. Tai remembered the foreign names of the planes: the Morane, an observation plane; the Spitfire, a fighter bomber; the Dakota, a transport and supply plane.

"But anywhere I went the local people considered me as their son and there was no moment in those years when I had the slightest fear of death," he said. Indeed, he expected it.

During the six-month march his unit never attacked the French, for that was not their mission, he said. His greatest longing was for sugar. Before the march and after the march sugar was never so important to him again, but the memory of it made him ache.

After the Geneva Accords, Tai went back to Tuy Hoa, not to North Vietnam. He said it was his liver which had made him so ill: yellow skin, yellow eyes, a headache that seemed fixed to his skull.

"I was stopped outside Tuy Hoa by police. I resisted arrest by telling them that article 14D of the Geneva Accords allowed me to choose to stay in the south or to go north," Tai said. "I told them if I had turned up twelve hours earlier they might have arrested me, but now you can't do it, I said."

And he was right, for the Geneva Accords protected him. Tai said he knew nothing of the men now fighting a guerrilla war in the south, the men of the National Liberation Front. He did not call them Viet Cong, which to many was considered a bad name. Cong is an abbreviation for Communist, and the designation Viet Cong—or Vietnamese Communist—was used by the Saigon government to avoid the patriotic connotation which the older term Viet Minh had for the people.

"It is much harder for the Front to fight against the Americans. If I were with the Front now, I don't think I could stand it. The B-52 bombings, the M-16 and so many other weapons. It makes it ten times harder, ten times," he said.

The second man, known as Huan, was even bolder; he did not want to be humble about what the men in the Viet Minh had done.

"Former resistance fighters like me were looked upon as criminals under Ngo Dinh Diem," Huan said. "It was an outrage. There is one thing I have—my love of country—and all those government officials can never be as proud of this as I am."

Huan was a tailor and raised pigs in Tuy Hoa; his wife had a stall in the market. They had seven children. He knew all about the Phoenix program. He had been picked up by the police twice and kept in detention for one month in May 1971, then again in September of 1972. He had been freed only for ten days when we met.

"People like me have had no peace in our own life. I built this house in 1969, the police thought, hah, he is rich and tried to get money by disturbing me. Those Phoenix people spent more time extorting money from innocent people! The south can never find its feet if such a wicked practice is permitted to go on and on. During my last arrest, when I was brought before the Province Security Committee, I told the province chief, in front of all members of that committee: 'Do you intend to let innocent people earn their living peacefully? May I advise you never to corner innocent people?' Some men of the committee told me later that they had never heard anyone speak like that."

He was forty-five, not an age to be feared in Vietnam, as Americans fear it. Something of the young man who had led an assault group rose up again that October night in Tuy Hoa. In his army there were boys and older men; each wore his own clothes and only a few had French guns, the *mousqueton indochinois*, which were carbines. Huan explained—knowing we knew nothing— that there were three elements in any attack: the assault group, the unit assigned to stop the enemy's reinforcements and the unit assigned to harass the enemy. He began as an assistant platoon leader of an assault group in what the Viet Minh called the Sixth Military Region. Its five provinces included his own, Phu Yen.

Inside the perimeter of a French outpost, his men always made noises, the same high, piercing sounds that came from the throats of the Vietnamese from the north fighting in Laos during Lam Son 719.

"Yelling was the most important thing. We were at such a disadvantage, for the French had so many more weapons and we had only our conviction. During the assault we would yell, and then, suddenly, the yelling would make us feel very brave." It did not matter what they yelled, but usually the men screamed "*Xung phong*"—Assault, Assault—and Huan thought the French felt weaker just hearing that.

"In the first six months my company fought in sixteen battles. We always tried to carry out the wounded around our shoulders and there were times when the man you were carrying was shot as you ran away with him. In the hospital where I was treated, there was only chloroform for the dying or those who had amputations. The nurses gave us more consolation than the medicines."

His left hand was always still and twisted. It was ruined by shrapnel. It was a useless hand, good only for guiding the cloth when he worked the sewing machine.

"It was a surprise for us that people living near the French outposts had sympathy for us and in many cases helped us a great deal, for we thought they had followed the French. They had not."

His unit made their first attack against the French on a mountain by the bridge Luong and I had seen.

"We were almost naked except for our underpants," Huan said. "We smeared mud on our faces and chests. Each *chien si* carried four grenades and a long knife. But the first attack failed because a deputy platoon leader lost his courage. He was tried on the spot by a military field court and shot. The whole company almost wept with shame, but later we attacked and overran the outpost and withdrew. It was never our policy to seize and to hold."

He was what the Americans called a sapper. A new generation of Vietnamese smeared themselves with charcoal, wore only underpants, and attacked in the darkest dark with satchel charges and grenades. But they did not yell as they came closer. They came ghostlike through the minefields to the barbed wire, sliding and cutting through it, small men who scarcely seemed to make a noise until they lifted their arms and began to throw.

The Viet Minh only intentionally killed those French or Vietnamese in the colonial army who were officers or noncommissioned officers, Huan said. After each attack villagers would praise and cheer the survivors of his assault group.

The new generation in the National Liberation Front had a worse war, a more dreadful one, he said, dreadful.

Huan said: "Our *chien si* could mingle with the people even in areas controlled by the French, but now the Front has to operate underground and it is more difficult. In our time there were French-controlled areas and the rest were *vung tu do*, free places. And the new *chien si* faces American firepower, tremendous firepower—such as we never dreamed of in those days—so the endurance of the *chien si* now is much better than ours was."

Later, when we were alone, Luong told me that Huan had only been freed the last time because he paid a bribe; this one was so large that his wife could not sleep, but somehow she had raised the amount. There was no choice, after all, only the money could have saved him. It was a stunning sum for them, but only forty dollars to an American.

IV

ODD THINGS NOT YET FORGOTTEN

They were afraid of the dark, as they might once have dreaded it as children of five and six. Every day in Vietnam, when it was still light, the dark pushed in too soon, always ahead of itself. You could not drive on any of the highways much after five in the evening; you had to be someplace by six, and stay there. It was no use ignoring the dark, or trying to defy it, or hiding inside it. It was not a loving dark. The fear of the troops was considered a "major deficiency" in fighting the war, something stubborn and childlike which had to be overcome. A veteran lieutenant colonel put it this way: "Night operations don't require comment; they require doing. The average American seems to have an innate fear of the darkness and will avoid night operations when possible. This applies to new recruits and officers in high commands . . . Until we can teach every U.S. soldier to consider darkness an advantage, the night will belong to the VC."

So the night remained theirs, that did not change. Even the Americans who wanted to take risks, who were among the least timid, hurling themselves into the war, feared that in the darkness they would be wasted. Even the calmest of them were impaired by the night and remember it now so many years later.

"I had to move my kids in the dark and they were scared shitless, all of us were scared," Ron Ridenhour, a former team leader

263

of a Long Range Reconnaissance Patrol group, said, calling them kids because he is thirty now.

Sometimes the dark would be pierced by the flares which lit up the landscape like a sickly white sun, leaving small parachutes in the trees that hung from the branches like pale, sleeping bats. Sometimes, late at night, each man fired every weapon around the perimeter, and kept firing, for sixty seconds. This was called "The Mad Minute." Its purpose was to scare off the enemy, in the darkest hour of the night, before the light came. The soldiers looked pleased, the extra noise excited them, no one out there came closer, nothing came back. In the light of the flares they looked like ghostly, busy men.

If it was not the dark, there were other things, and each man found a way to calm himself and push back the image of his own death or mutilation. There were things to wear that brought luck: beads, necklaces, tokens, symbols, rings, boonie hats with girls' names on them, scarfs worn like headbands, which stopped the sweat. The Marines, needing to be perverse, liked to wear big disks that spelled out war. Most of the troops wore their dog tags not around their necks but outside their boots, strung through an eyelet. There were rituals and taboos to be observed. A few carried small Bibles; others wore crosses and religious medals.

Some of the soldiers, in the world's richest-equipped army, found a degree of comfort and certainty in what they refused to do. There was a certain squad—a squad is only eleven men— who would not eat apricots. Apricots led to burns, smashed faces, broken bones, to being wasted.

A private named Thomas Hobbs told me about it. He would not touch them in his C-rations. He ate the fruit cocktail, the boned turkey, the spaghetti, the scrambled eggs, the grape jam. But no enlisted man in 2d Squad would touch the apricots. "The day we hit a mine a sergeant ate apricots," Hobbs said. "If a guy eats apricots, he is not coming with us."

It happened like this. On November 12, 1970, their column of eighteen armored vehicles passed over a mine of nearly 175 pounds that did not explode until the third track went over it. Afterward there was a hole about eight feet in diameter in the earth. Hobbs was thrown free, landing on squashy ground. But the driver, who was always holed up in the hatch, had his face slammed into metal.

"When I got over to him he was saying over and over 'I've lost all my teeth, I've lost all my teeth,'" the medic said. His name was Burke. Everyone's name was on a tag over his left pocket, so you did not even have to ask. The sergeant's face—the nose and the chin—were a mess, Burke said.

It was wrong to call it an armored personnel carrier, Hobbs told me, looking at the big, shaky notes I wrote as we moved in that machine, which creaked and lurched and swayed. It was a gun track because it had 81-mm mortar.

All of them were as precise, always at ease with the machinery of murder, understanding exactly how it worked. They knew the arsenal so well: "See, ma'am, that canister round has something like seven thousand oblong bearings in it, with a range of four hundred meters, and it just rips everything to pieces out there, even trees."

Hobbs was a country boy, a Texan, who liked to hunt. He had a cowlick and big feet. He was nineteen. He was exactly what the Army wanted and the Army got. Something about his neck and wrists made me think he might still be growing. You could imagine Hobbs, as a child, wanting to learn to drive and steering the wheel from the lap of a grownup.

For a little while the men in the squad came to life, pleased to be talking to someone new. The war had blunted and dulled them, teaching them what it was to be helpless and how to wait. They rarely saw the North Vietnamese, or any Vietnamese. It was hard to write a letter, to read a book, to think of anything, the medic said. He gave out tranquilizers. The squad knew nothing about Vietnam, or what was happening in the war, or what had happened a year ago. They did not see themselves as men who had burst into history.

The area of operations was near Nin Hokai Ridge, below the Demilitarized Zone which cut Vietnam in two. Circling those hills in their huge rackety machines, they could see older ruts made by the Americans before them and by those who had been there the year before. Hobbs did not care. He had only three hundred and one days to go, he said. That is how it went: each day had to be killed.

The column stopped for lunch. Someone had a transistor radio—someone always did—and it gave us "Baby, They Are Playing Our Song." It was very still in that grey place whose birds and animals had gone. A Vietnamese in Paris had once told me there had been cattle grazing in Quang Tri, and wild animals, but I wondered if he had dreamed it. Hobbs thought that he had once seen wild geese which pleased him. Private Patrick Sand hoped to dry his socks over a small bonfire of litter. But he only scorched them. No one spoke again of the canned apricots.

In Saigon, I wrote to Hobbs' mother, said he was fine and sent her a photograph of her son and his friend, Nate. Her answer came on pink paper from Junction, Texas. He had hit another mine on January 16. It was nice of me to write for she was always worried, always.

Now, so many years later, watching a television commercial, I was reminded of Hobbs and his friend Nate and the apricots and the man who lost his teeth. The little commercial was for a game called Tank Command, described as the strategic military game from Ideal. The two men playing it make a lot of faces to show you that it is an exciting, tough game. The man who has just been outsmarted looks up and says: "War is hell."

We are an odd people with odd playthings, odd ideas of what is good for our male children. In June 1968, after the great Tet offensive in Vietnam, when American and Vietnamese casualties rose, George Gallup, founder of the American Institute of Public Opinion, concluded in an article called "What Combat Does to Our Men" that combat was beneficial. The Gallup Poll had analyzed the answers of 140 veterans of Vietnam in a survey to find out how they were affected. Mr. Gallup wrote: "In summary: These 18- to 25-year-olds command respect because they respect themselves. They have gained self-confidence, firmed up their goals. They have learned to follow and to lead, to accept responsibility and to be responsible for others. While only 26 percent wanted to go to Vietnam in the first place, 94 percent having returned, say they are glad for the experience. What kind of citizens will they be? Judging by the cross section we talked to, the answer is: superior."

Quite a few veterans laugh when I show them the poll. It is not just that their benefits are mean—much less under the G.I. Bill of Rights than those given to World War II veterans—or that jobs are hard to find or even that the war was lost and they are uncomfortable, sometimes embarrassing reminders of it. Something is missing in them. I ask David, the ex-medic, who likes his job, his friends, the place where he lives. He killed no one. "It's hard to be hopeful about anything," he said. There it is.

In a later, more profound, study of college and noncollege youths done by Daniel Yankelovich between 1969 and 1973, the public-opinion analyst reported that the attitudes and characteristics of the Vietnam veterans were generally comparable to those of their peers. One important distinction did emerge. The veterans were markedly less optimistic about themselves and their society.

In January 1973 the Reverend Billy Graham, a close friend of President Nixon, said that he had avoided making public his personal reservations about the war in Vietnam because "then I would be forced to take sides in every war in the world." He said that over the years he had kept his reservations about the Vietnam war quiet because "all through the period I have not been sure whether our involvement was right or wrong." He "didn't want to get involved on either side," Reverend Graham said. Nevertheless, he told a reporter that the war in Vietnam was "a judgment of God on America" and that from the beginning he had "grave questions." It was an odd interview, with the Reverend leaping from one answer to the next.

"A thousand people are killed every week on American highways, and half of these are attributed to alcohol. Where are the demonstrations against alcohol?" Reverend Graham said.

In the December 1975 issue of the *Ladies' Home Journal*, during an interview in his home in San Clemente, California, former President Richard M. Nixon said: "We are so cynical, so disbelieving, it may take the shock of another invasion—in Korea or in Thailand. If American lives are threatened, we may regain our sense of belief in our country and our need for strength."

What the former President is saying is that we need another war.

In the Dynacopy shop in Columbus Circle, the men who work the duplicating machines do not read what they copy. They are too busy and people resent it if they do. I invite them to look at my lists. NUMBER OF CASUALTIES INCURRED BY U.S. MILITARY PERSONNEL IN CONNECTION WITH THE CONFLICT IN VIETNAM BY HOME STATE OF RECORD and MILITARY SERVICE from 1 Jan 1961 thru Sept 1975.

"How many in New York," the grey-haired man asked. He found out. Then he wanted to see New Jersey, where he lives.

"Oh my God, the cream of the crop," the man said, looking at New York.

ALABAMA	1,181
ALASKA	55
ARIZONA	604

ARKANSAS	579
CALIFORNIA	5,448
COLORADO	608
CONNECTICUT	589
DELAWARE	120
DISTRICT OF COLUMBIA	235
FLORIDA	1,897
GEORGIA	1,548
HAWAII	271
IDAHO	207
ILLINOIS	2,876
INDIANA	1,510
IOWA	818
KANSAS	613
KENTUCKY	1,037
LOUISIANA	870
MAINE	331
MARYLAND	992
MASSACHUSETTS	1,300
MICHIGAN	2,597
MINNESOTA	1,043
MISSISSIPPI	627
MISSOURI	1,380
MONTANA	259
NEBRASKA	385
NEVADA	143
NEW HAMPSHIRE	218
NEW JERSEY	1,435
NEW MEXICO	391
NEW YORK	4,033
NORTH CAROLINA	1,573
NORTH DAKOTA	192
OHIO	3,021

OKLAHOMA	973
OREGON	686
PENNSYLVANIA	3,066
RHODE ISLAND	200
SOUTH CAROLINA	883
SOUTH DAKOTA	187
TENNESSEE	1,274
TEXAS	3,316
UTAH	353
VERMONT	100
VIRGINIA	1,268
WASHINGTON	1,012
WEST VIRGINIA	713
WISCONSIN	1,131
WYOMING	117
CANAL ZONE	2
GUAM	70
AMERICAN SAMOA	4
PUERTO RICO	342
U.S. VIRGIN ISLANDS	15
OTHER	120

The article on a veteran in the official newspaper of North Vietnam, *Nhan Dan*, on June 2, 1974, was called "Living in Between." It was written by a man who signed the article Nguyen Khai.

A few years ago I made the acquaintance of a young poet. He came to see us after he returned from the battlefront. His complexion was dry and sallow from malaria, but his voice and his eyes seemed to throw flames onto his listeners. He told stories about the battlefields, he read poems—hundreds of poems he had composed during the years he was in there [in the south]. Some of the poems were beautiful, others were violently emotional. He lauded a way of life and a style of action, and condemned another way of life and another style of action which was alien to him. It was very interesting to listen to him, but it was difficult for me to embrace it whole-heartedly. I even felt concerned for him. He was still too innocent, too naïve, and was still unfamiliar with the ways of life. During the few days he spent in Hanoi, there was not one single night when he could sleep peacefully. Every night he went to see his friends and read his poems to them. Then he asked them to play music and songs for him to listen to; he wanted to be told about the situation in the field of arts and literature, the problems that existed, and about the difficulties and potentials of this field. During the day, while his friends were at work, he sat in one place and continued to write poems. He wanted to know everything, experience everything, to have an opinion on everything, and he wanted to be the most productive and best writer around. While he was living in Hanoi, he became even more emaciated and his hands were burning to the touch, as though he was in a fever. But his eyes were ablaze with fires, his voice was full of fire, and his movements radiated a fiery energy. Each of his days was filled with so many hopes, so much passion. He lived to the fullest.

Though I was very fond of him, I found his style of living very strange. It seemed eccentric and arrogant. When I communicated my observations to my friends, it turned out they too shared the same view. This friend of ours, this poet, was not only out of his mind but also arrogant. He was talented, but he was deluded by his immature talent. We concluded that there was not much we could hope for in this man. His was the first success, but that was all, and would not lead to anything.

I do not know whether our secret observations reached his ears or not, but when I saw him again sometime later, some changes had taken place. Recently, he had changed completely. His movement became hesitant, his look became hesitant, and his voice also became hesitant. Not only did he no longer read poetry to anyone, but when asked, he answered in a noncommittal manner: "I'm still writing, but it's going very slowly!" Observations about him immediately changed. He now knew how to think with maturity and to live with modesty; he had become realistic in his assessment of his own and other people's work. That is to say, he had become exactly like one of us, neither too passionate nor too indifferent, neither too happy nor too sad; he did not ask too much either from his friends or from himself.

So another person had found a pleasant way of life, one that was peaceful and "in between!"

David Elliot, who had worked for The Rand Corporation in Vietnam and was now doing his doctorate at Cornell, sent the article to me. In an accompanying letter he wrote that his wife, a Vietnamese named Mai, translated the article, and offered his understanding of it:

It requires some reading between the lines. My own interpretation is that he was a wounded veteran (hence he returned to the north 'a few years' before the large-scale troop rotation of 1974, and does not go to work). He has probably been away for some time, hence his passionate and insatiable curiosity about what has happened during his absence. The "fire in his eyes" is clearly due to the intensity of his relived experience. His inability to communicate it to his friends (who merely view him as "naïve" or "crazy" and "arrogant") finally extinguishes the spark. This is one of several illustrations about how the youth (in North Vietnam) is living a life that is bland, and neither here nor there. Hence the title "Living in Between."

Needless to say, the author feels this attitude should be overcome by a more positive attitude. But the description of how he and his friends drained the juices out of this vibrant, returned soldier and left him a vegetable is remarkably frank.

I wouldn't draw any sweeping conclusions from this episode—the only one of its type I have ever run across. But it has an unforgettable poignancy. I'm sure many American Vietnam veterans would recognize the syndrome . . .

They did.

THE CRUELTIES WERE so constant, the weapons so huge, the victims so many, as the war drifted everywhere, that no one could pay much attention to a single incident.

It was often the Army which unwittingly provided examples of how the Vietnamese stayed loyal to each other and helped those who defied the Americans. Sometimes a little story would turn up in the river of press releases written by GIs working in the information offices of different units. It was their job to make the press releases both lively and flattering to the Army, in the hope that civilian reporters would pick them up. In November 1970 many correspondents in Saigon were mailed such a release.

Release No. 1111-70-546

INFORMATION OFFICE
AMERICAL DIVISION

FOR IMMEDIATE RELEASE   11TH INFANTRY BRIGADE
APO San Francisco 96217

LADY SAYS "NO BIK"   Tel: Bronco 148
SERGEANT HARD TO   26 October 1970
CONVINCE
by Sgt Chuck Merdzinski

FSB BRONCO, Vietnam (AMERICAL IO)—A carefully devised ruse, developed by a sergeant of the AMERICAL Division's 11th Infantry Brigade, met with success recently by nabbing two hard-core VC sympathizers in the act of hiding the "enemy."

While searching for rice caches, Sergeant Rick Hupp (Newark, Ohio) of Company A, 1st Battalion, 20th Infantry, and his comrades passed through a small village where a poker-faced woman passively told them that she knew nothing of VC activities in the area. Her performance wasn't convincing enough to satisfy Sgt Hupp and a lingering doubt remained with him as the men left the village.

He evaluated the situation and came up with an idea that later confirmed his suspicions. Hupp removed some VC clothing that the men had procured the day before and persuaded a Popular Forces (PF) soldier to don the enemy attire. The next step of the plan took place 20 minutes later when the PF soldier, disguised as a VC and carrying an M-2 carbine, wandered into the village and talked to the same woman.

He asked her if any U.S. soldiers were in the area and she replied, "Beaucoup GI." In a worried voice, the allied soldier asked the woman if she could hide him from the American soldiers. The woman willingly led him to a concealed spider hole beneath the floor of her hut and told him to get inside. Minutes later, Hupp entered the village for the second time and asked the same questions. Again the woman denied knowledge of local insurgents.

Hupp then yelled "La Dai," and the South Vietnamese soldier continued to play the role of a guerrilla by answering with "Chieu Hoi!" He came out of the spider hole with raised hands, surrendering his weapon to Hupp. The woman never found out about the hoax until she was escorted to Mo Duc for a questioning session by Regional Forces soldiers.

Much to Hupp's delight, the trick worked again in another village a short distance away. The men of Alpha Company had a lot of chuckling to do that night over the incidents, and with any luck at all they'll continue to chuckle their way through the hamlets of Quang Ngai province working their ruse.

No one knew what happened to the woman described as poker-faced and who was supposed to have said, to another Vietnamese, "beaucoup GI" when, of course, "beaucoup" was a French word used only by the Americans. It is an odd story as written by Sergeant Merdzinski, who thought "No Bik" means *"No biet"* or "I don't know" in Vietnamese, who did not understand why the woman would hide the man, just as I would hide an American who was running from foreign troops. The press release did not attract much attention.

THE ARMY HAD its own green matches. On the cover it said: "The matches are designed especially for damp climates. But they will not light when wet or after long exposure (several weeks) to very damp air." So they did not light.

BLOOD: SOMETIMES A GI would complain that the Vietnamese fighting him did not bleed enough. One man from North Carolina told me that when he cut himself shaving, he bled more than a "dink." There were soldiers puzzled by this; it seemed to bother a few. The reason was the Vietnamese did not have as much blood, for they were much slighter, they did not consume the vast amounts of food the Americans do. In the field, it was not special for infantrymen to be supplied by helicopters with hot lunches every three days, whose odd diet for the tropics included barbecued beef, cabbage, potatoes, two kinds of soft drinks, milk and two kinds of ice cream. Some units were allowed beer; others were not. It was too hot for the men to often want second help-ings, and too much food made them sleepy. They had so much to carry: packs that weighed sixty-five pounds or more, nine quarts of water meant another eighteen pounds, one hundred rounds of ammunition were another six. The Vietnamese never ate like that, could not have as much blood in their smaller bodies, which did not bulge or thicken as ours do.

The blood of the soldiers and civilians never looked the same red. The shade changed with the wounds. Sometimes blood com-ing from the eyes or the skull looked a bright, fresh pink, but the blood was dark and browner if the wound was in the stomach. In the heat the blood seemed to dry in greenish ribbons on the clothes of the Vietnamese. After a while the blood did not matter unless a man drowned in his own; it was the wounds the blood concealed which were worse. Once in a ward of the provincial hospital of Quang Ngai, where the Vietnamese went, where the smell was that of a wet and rotting rag pressed over the face, among the patients was a man with no blood on him at all, although so red were his eyes, which he never seemed to blink, that blood might have been inside them. He sat on the edge of a cot in that dark-ened room, wearing undershorts, no inch of his skin as it once had been. He was covered with small black marks—ears, lips, hands, neck, wrists—made by shrapnel, almost as if he had been a target in a shooting gallery, unable to get away, being moved forward again and again to be hit by steel. He was waiting for a doctor, but two days later a doctor had not yet come.

IN NEW YORK nothing worked like a liver. Jill Seiden Mahoney found out that if you mushed the liver on bandages, it made stains that looked like seeping, untreated head wounds. It looked ghastly and the smell was repulsive, which was fine. The liver was useful for the "die-ins," the name for reenactments by the antiwar movement of Vietnamese villagers receiving brutal injuries from American weapons, chemicals, bombs.

Mrs. Mahoney, who was single then, and her friends made up what they called the Emma Goldman Brigade, in honor of the anarchist. Before they demonstrated, the Brigade went to some trouble to make their faces look as if they had been scarred in the war. Their favorite method was to use a mixture of oatmeal, ketchup and liquid make-up foundations, which they put on their faces after twisting their skin with strips of Scotch tape. The effect was exactly what they wished: shocking.

The targets of their protests were often business corporations; in the spring of 1972 it was the ITT Building on Park Avenue. The ten women in the Brigade, dressed in black pajamas, with the liver-stained bandages on their heads and their faces deformed, rushed into the lobby when it was crowded in the morning with people coming to work. The first thing they did was to put up posters of wounded Vietnamese children on the marble walls.

"Then we started dying, we started our blood bath. We threw Baggies which had red stuff in them. We were screaming, yelling, dying, very dramatically. Here's the sick part: the janitors started ripping down the posters of those fucked-up hurt little babies. After fifteen minutes the police came. They seemed sort of scared of us," she said. "We were rolling on the floor; it was all they could do to get us to stand up and shut up. Each of us had a flare for drama and we were trying to imagine what it would be like for a Vietnamese woman under bombs. We had fun. It sounds childish to say that now, but it was exhilarating. That day we felt we were in control. If you're rolling on the floor, screaming, nobody wants to get near you. When we finally limped out, some people applauded.

"I never knew if they applauded because they enjoyed the show or because we were leaving or they thought they were brave," she said. "It was meant to disrupt; everybody was talking about us. Energy that might have been used in their jobs that day was going into talking about our demonstration.

"Oh, sure, I know that it is said that doing things like that alienated people. But look, any action will alienate somebody. You have to expect it."

In the sixth grade in P.S. 104 in New York, she knew that her IQ was over 130. Her parents were not surprised. After graduating from the University of Pennsylvania in 1967, she worked for an advertising agency, Cunningham & Walsh, in the city. "I was a Jewish princess," she said.

In the streets young people were passing out pamphlets denouncing the war in Vietnam, and from them she learned about it.

"I would take time off to go to antiwar demonstrations; it shocked some people, who called me a Communist. The antiwar movement was personally and socially fulfilling and it was lots of fun. I miss it very much but I'm glad the war is over. I miss the commitment and the urgency—the commitment to selflessness. When it happened I thought we were all just the greatest, as a group certainly more generous than the people in the advertising agency."

In those days she often wore a T-shirt saying "The East Is Red, the West Is Ready," while her friend Coke, an unusually pretty blonde, wore one saying "The Vietnamese People Are Not the Enemy." Both women did not care if people stared at their ample chests; they wanted the T-shirts to be read.

Some of their exploits were daring: ten of them bought tickets, at fifteen dollars apiece, to attend and disrupt the National Women's Republican Club lunch in March 1972, which honored Patricia Nixon as the Woman of the Year. It was crucial for them to look like ladies. They obliged.

"Everybody still had one good dress," Mrs. Mahoney said, who wore a pink-and-brown suit from Saks Fifth Avenue. Coke even had a fur coat which she had stopped wearing; it was skunk. The plan of the Emma Goldman Brigade was for five of them to release the rats they were carrying with them, healthy rats that had been secured from laboratories so no one could accuse them of using animals that might spread disease. They were always careful about small things like that. It went wrong in the lobby: a man she calls John Finnigan of the New York Red Squad, who was watching radicals, stopped seven of the women from going into the ballroom. Three of the rats had to be released in the lobby. Inside, Mrs. Mahoney, who did not have a rat, rose and in a strong voice spoke against the war, saying nothing—on the advice of a lawyer—that was either treasonous or obscene. Then she left, leaving the ladies at her table, who were Republicans from Westchester County, in an unpleasant, if not agitated, state of mind. Two more rats were released in the ballroom, causing some consternation, but the lunch and ceremony continued.

"The antiwar movement made a difference in me and in everybody who participated. I think if there had not been such a movement, they might have nuked Vietnam off the face of the earth," she said. "It forced people to recognize what was going on or to become totally, unnaturally, blind."

It still puzzles her why other people do not understand very much, do not even know that GVN meant the Government of Vietnam in Saigon, that DRVN meant the north, or the Democratic Republic of Vietnam, that ARVN was the army in the south.

"They can tell you someone's batting average from 1948, or who hit the big homer in the 1932 World Series, but they don't know the difference between the NLF and the NFL."

The blindness, as she called it, always surprised her. On the day of the Emma Goldman Brigade's die-in in the lobby of the

ITT Building, it was raining. The group worried that the rain might wash off some of the mess they had put on their faces. It was decided to take taxis.

"We were totally mutilated. None of us were recognizable," she said. "We got into two cabs at Fifty-third and Third. In each cab one person had to sit in front, so the drivers had to see what we looked like. We told them where we wanted to go and they didn't say a word. Remember how we looked and what we wore, and besides that, we all smelled, it was the oatmeal and the other stuff. We smelled horrible. Neither driver said a word, or even did a double-take. And in one newspaper, I think it was the *Daily News*, they described us as 'slovenly hippies.' They just thought we were dirty."

The Emma Goldman Brigade did not hold together but the women have stayed friends. Her marriage in September 1973 to Peter Paul Mahoney peeled apart. They had met in the anti-war movement, gone through the hard days before and during the Gainesville trial, endured all of it, only to find out how different they were. In those days she saw him as a valiant fellow who stood out for her among all the other veterans going to war against the war.

Even when the war ended and she needed a job, Mrs. Mahoney was not one to jump over her principles. She now works for a small trade magazine, having refused to consider better-paying jobs related to the military-industrial complex, the stock market, or the manufacture of foods or consumer items she thinks are dangerous. She does not want to ever contribute in any way to the misery of any people.

She will not eat bacon or frankfurters because they contain nitrates. She is even beginning to cut back on pastrami. She will not eat canned tuna fish because she deplores the killing of the porpoises caught in the tuna nets and she thinks the waters are filthy. She is quite specific about insect parts and rodent hairs in some American chocolate. When she has time she makes her own cosmetics, but she hardly wears any.

There are no regrets, just a tiny afterthought.

"The Brigade should have used indelible red ink for blood," she said, "instead of Rite-Dye."

IT BECAME QUITE commonplace in the antiwar movement for bags of "blood"—red tempera paint—to be thrown at structures which symbolized the war, or whose offices made the war possible. They were thrown, over and over and over again, in the names of the people of Vietnam and Cambodia and Laos and their victims. On a Good Friday, April 20, 1973, to commemorate the shedding of the blood of Jesus Christ, bags of blood were thrown at five Boston institutions. Four people who threw blood inside the JFK Federal Building were charged with willful destruction of government property before a federal magistrate. The government claimed it took five men working for three hours to clean off the paint. The defendants were allowed five minutes for a summation statement. One of them, Madeleine Cousineau, pointed out that Pope Paul VI, in his encyclical "On the Development of Peoples," stated that property must never take precedence over the common good of people, that peace is not merely the absence of war—and that she felt Americans who continued to commemorate Good Friday and to call themselves "one nation under God" had to reexamine "our way of dealing with our fellow human beings . . ." She was fined thirty-five dollars.

Then the paint seemed trivial and false, so the blood of humans was used. On a Saturday at the end of April in 1973, six vials of it were splashed on the tables and walls of the State Dining Room during an ordinary public tour of the White House.

"Claire got the tables and I got the walls," Steve Cleghorn said. The woman was his wife. Both were in their twenties, described as Christian/Catholics who wanted to serve humanity. The couple both worked in a soup kitchen operated by the Community for Creative Non-Violence. Friends donated the blood to fill the vials. Nearly fifty people were in the room where White House dinners are given when the couple went to work. Some screamed out "Please don't, please don't, you awful people," "Kooks" and "Bastards!"

The man and the woman each said the same thing as they emptied the vials. It was: "This is the blood of your victims." Their manner was unperturbed and thoughtful.

"The blood is seeping through the walls and the blood is coming from underneath the varnish of the tables. It's not that we have put it there. It's already there," the woman said later.

"In some sense, what we did is cast in Gospel terms," Mr. Cleghorn, who had once studied in a Paulist seminary, explained. "The table of state is where the buying and selling goes on, internationally."

In a handwritten statement that was only published in *The Daily Rag*, a community newspaper in Washington, D.C., which ran a long interview with them, the couple said: "There is no sanctuary from this blood. This is the blood of our brothers and sisters. We affirm this blood and life. We resist waste and death. We mark these walls and this table with the blood of your victims."

In the White House, when the State Dining Room was blood-splashed, they were arrested by Secret Service agents. One of them asked Mrs. Cleghorn if she meant to embarrass the President.

"That wasn't my intention; my intention was to speak the truth. If that embarrasses the President, let it be," she said.

RALPH BLUMENTHAL, WHO was a young *New York Times* reporter in Vietnam for fourteen months, did a story for the newspaper on military chaplains in June 1971 after he returned to the

United States. He covered a convention in Washington, D.C., of the Military Chaplains Association, composed of two thousand of the thirty thousand active and retired chaplains. The members cheered Senator Sam J. Ervin, Jr., of North Carolina—who two years later became a heroic, winsome figure in the Watergate hearings—when he said in a speech: "I think if you get in a war, you should get in to win." The chaplains loved it.

"That's not our job," said Lieutenant Colonel James E. Shaw, a chaplain at Fort Lewis, Washington, when the reporter asked if he would preach to his troops against the slaying of innocent civilians. "I thank God we come from a country with rules of engagement," he added. "The Communists don't have that."

Nearly three thousand chaplains served in Vietnam. The chaplain's job was to perform the religious services of his denomination, provide ecumenical services for other faiths when necessary, and offer counseling on faith, family and personal problems. Mr. Blumenthal interviewed about fifty chaplains and commanders in a four-week tour around the country which included visits to Washington and various bases.

Lieutenant Colonel Reinard Beaver, a Roman Catholic who was head chaplain of the 4th Infantry Division at Fort Carson, told the reporter he did not agree with Christ saying that greater love hath no man than that he lay down his life for his friends.

"He was wrong. Greater love hath no man when he lay down his life for a stranger," Colonel Beaver said. "That is what the United States is doing in Vietnam."

One of the chaplains, Major Emlyn Jones of the Church of the Brethren, who was then stationed at Fort Bragg, recalled his tour in Vietnam with vehemence. "It gave me sorrow," he said, "but most of all it gave me a tremendous hatred of Communists. Man! I hated those spastics!"

Later, at Fort Hamilton in Brooklyn, where he was assigned, Major Jones said to me he was in Vietnam from December 1966 to the end of December 1967, at Tuy Hoa, where there was the 17th Aviation Group, an engineer's battalion, an artillery battalion and a Korean infantry unit. On his return to the United States after a tour in Germany, the major said how shocked he had been by the reporting on the war on television and in the newspapers.

"They embroidered and embellished their documentaries with downright lies," Major Jones said. Certainly he was very anti-Communist, he added. "Since Vietnam! Because I've seen Communists in action. I've seen them cut off fingers. Well, north of Tuy Hoa, in that area, down near Ninh Hoa. I've seen Communists get outside a city and throw in two hundred buzz bombs on children. I saw two hundred Communists one day—*well, I didn't see them do it personally*, but they went into a little Catholic village where the priests and the nuns live, right outside of Tuy Hoa, and they shot them to death. When our battalion arrived they were dead. For no reason at all."

Question: "You came upon the corpses?"

The major: "Well, they called us in and they dared us to come in."

Question: "They called you in?"

The major: "We had been told by informers, you know. And our battalion surrounded this little village and they dared us to come in. Of course, nobody did because basically Americans are very humane people; there were children and old men in that village."

Question: "The North Vietnamese challenged you, or the Viet Cong?"

The major: "The Viet Cong."

Question: "They called out to you?"

The major: "Well, after they got there, yes. Of course, the entire battalion didn't go up there, elements of it did. And they called, daring the men of the battalion to come in there and get them. They called by loudspeaker. They were calling insults."

Question: "In Vietnamese?"

The major: "Well, I think it was Vietnamese because we had a Vietnamese who was a captain. Our people are very basically humane people. There are a few who are not, of course, but basically the American soldier is a very humane person. And they stood there, they stood there all day, and the South Koreans went in the next day and took them. No, we didn't call in an air strike. You see, if that would have happened—and I suppose that would happen once in a while—that's what Walter Cronkite would show and talk about."

The South Koreans, referred to as "rock" for ROK, the Republic of Korea, were subsidized for fighting in Vietnam by the United States, who also paid the Thais. The Koreans were often cited by exasperated Americans, who were straining to "motivate" the South Vietnamese army, as a fine example of what an allied Asian army could become. The Korean army had, after all, been trained and built up by the Americans. But the Koreans were very much feared by the Vietnamese in the province of Phu Yen, whose capital is Tuy Hoa. They were much hated.

"Well, the Koreans are a very tough, warlike people," the major said. "They had the philosophy that if you go to war, they wanted to win. There's no sense to go to war and not win."

It annoyed him, too, that a *Time* reporter he met on a flight from Saigon to Cam Ranh Bay did not come to see the Catholic school that had been built for six hundred children in the town of Tuy Hoa, or the orphanage for the Buddhists that had ninety-seven boys and girls in it, and the American-built Christian day school for two hundred kids in the Christian Missionary Alliance Church.

"It's not newsworthy to do good things," Major Jones said.

In Washington, D.C., Brigadier General Gerhardt W. Hyatt, the Army Chief of Chaplains, was asked by Mr. Blumenthal of *The New York Times* whether he and other chaplains were experiencing doubts about the course of the war. General Hyatt, a Lutheran, said: "A man of discernment has to give his government the benefit of the doubt." Part of a chaplain's role as a moral leader, the general added, is not to stir up scandal in public if the matter can be resolved within the military.

Four years after he wrote the story, Ralph Blumenthal said: "I was very surprised that no one else thought the story was surprising, none of the people on the paper or the friends I talked to about it. And the chaplains didn't seem to think what they were saying was unusual."

There was no one to confess to, no one to bestow forgiveness, no one to define a penance, no one who could undo what had been done. The chaplains, who tended to be conventional men, were dependent on the military system for salary, promotion and pension. They did not seem concerned about the behavior of the troops. If they did know something startling, then in most cases they did nothing. Not untypical was the Reverend Carl E. Greswell, an Episcopal chaplain in Vietnam at the time of the My Lai massacre, who told a military court that he had mentioned a report of the killings to army superiors. "In hindsight I feel I should have done more," he said.

There were men who came back from Vietnam with nothing to tell and those who had too much, who were weighted and chained, who needed to confess, who wanted themselves and their country to change. Some of them met in a Holiday Inn in Detroit on January 31, February 1 and 2 in the year 1971 to speak openly of American war crimes. The meeting was called the Winter Soldier Investigation, organized by Vietnam Veterans Against the War. Beacon Press published a small and punishing book of the testimony of seventy-five veterans and four civilians. They were among a larger number who gave firsthand accounts of crimes which they either witnessed or committed. But Richard Brummett, who was attending a small college in New York State, knew nothing of these hearings, knew no one at college who was in Vietnam Veterans Against the War. Instead he wrote a letter on October 27, 1970, to the Secretary of Defense, Melvin Laird. He typed the letter on stationery used by the staff of the yearbook of Marist College in Poughkeepsie. It listed him on the masthead as Photography Editor.

Dear Mr. Laird,

The subject of which I am writing to you tonight is a very heavy one, one which I have had upon my conscience for over two years now. To the point, it is of similar nature of the My Lai incident which is so troubling our nation today.

From July 1967 to July 1968 I served in the United States Army in the Republic of Viet Nam as an armored crewman. During the months of Jan 1968 thru May 1968 my unit, A Troop, First Squadron, First Armored Cavalry Regiment, Americal Division, did perform on a regular basis, random murder, rape and pillage upon the Vietnamese civilians of Quang Tin province. This was done with the full knowledge, consent and encouragement of our Troop Commander, a Captain R_____, and one of our platoon sgts, a Sgt B_____.

These incidents included random shelling of villages with 90mm white phosphorus rounds, machine gunning of civilians who had the misfortune to be near when we hit a mine, torture of prisoners, destroying of food and livestock of the villagers if it was deemed that they had an excess, and numerous burnings of villages for no apparent reason. These are only a few of the many events that have been upon my conscience, I will not go further at this time. I hope that you will act upon my letter and expose those responsible for these acts. If you can not I must attempt to do so myself, my conscience will not allow me to do otherwise.

I hope that you do not think of me as one who is so bitter

that he is attempting to destroy our nation. I have great faith
in our democracy, it has the greatness to accept the fact that
it is not perfect and to correct itself. Before the war I had an
unquestioning faith, now I question. Over four years ago I
joined our Army in a time when it was unfashionable to do
so. I volunteered for Viet Nam when it was not necessary for
me to go. The Americal Division changed much of that. You,
Sir, I hope, by your desire for the truth will change it back.

So that you may identify me I shall give you my serial
no. etc at the time I was separated from the Army.

Sp/5 Richard H. Brummett RA 12762829
A Troop 1/6 Cav, Ft. Meade,
Maryland

He gave the full names of a captain who was his commanding officer and a platoon sergeant, which are not used here. Mr.
Brummett was informed by letter that the matter was being
investigated.

On November 30, 1970, an investigator for the U.S. Army CID
Agency, which stands for Criminal Investigation Division, questioned Richard Brummett in Champagnat House, where he lived
at Marist College. The questions and his answers were typed on
Witness Statement, file number 70—CI0052—06312.

Q: Mr. Brummett, did you write a letter to the Secretary
of Defense stating that during the period of January to
April 1968, members of your former unit A Troop, First
Squadron, First Cavalry Regiment, Americal Division,
did perform random murder, rape and pillage upon
the Vietnamese civilians of Quang Tin province?

A: Yes, I did.

Q: Would you relate what the incidents were and where
and when they happened and by whom they were
committed?

A: Yes. On approximately 22 January 1968, in the vicinity of Tich An, VN, a mortar track, vehicle number A-18, hit a mine, blew up and killed two men. I heard Cpt R_____ on the radio in my tank order the 1st platoon to "take care of that village." Psg B_____, in charge of the 1st platoon, had his men burn and level the village and shoot into the village area.

Q: What type of weapons were the 1st platoon using?

A: .50 Caliber machine guns and M-60 machine guns.

Q: Did you see B_____ or any of his men actually shoot into the village or burn it?

A: I didn't see them light the fires, but I did see them shooting into the village.

Q: Did you recognize any of the personnel firing the machine guns?

A: No, I didn't know any of the 1st platoon well enough to identify them.

Q: Did anything else happen at this time?

A: Yes, I was told that a young man who was standing in the vicinity where A-18 blew up ran and was shot. I saw the body of this young man, and saw Psg B_____ beat up an old man who furnished the young man's identification showing he was loyal to the Vietnamese government. B_____ took the ID card away from the old man and threw him in to the mine crater.

Q: Was the old man killed?

A: No, but the ID card was placed on the engine of the blown up track and blown up with the destroyed track.

Q: Did you see any incidents personally?

A: Yes, sometime in mid-March 1968, in a village West of our base camp, B_____ threw an old man down a well and then dropped a hand grenade down the well. This failed to kill the man so B_____ then took his pistol out and fired three shots into the well.

Q: Did you see that the man was dead?

A: No, I did not.

Q: Did you check the well?

A: No, I didn't.

Q: Were there any other incidents?

A: Yes, the day after the above incident B_____'s tank
    hit a mine and he was injured. The gunships flying cover
    for us worked the area around us over machine guns
    and rockets. I heard on the radio the 1st and 2d platoons
    firing on a village. They were talking about shooting
    the animals in the village and burning the village.

Q: Did you see anyone actually shoot the animals or set fire
    to the village?

A: No, I just saw the results as we moved up to the village.

Q: Did you see any other incidents happen?

A: Yes, in April or May 1968, we were West of our base
    camp and we stopped at a small village for a routine
    check. Cpt R_____ walked up to the cattle pen
    with an M-16 carbine and started shooting the cattle.
    Cpt R_____ had us gather all the rice in the
    village in to a pile and then placed 2 blocks of C-4
    explosive in the pile and blew it up. Then in May 1968,
    Cpt R_____ ordered us to run through a village
    with tanks to knock all the buildings down, a small
    boy was standing in front of his house and jumped
    at the last minute to avoid being crushed by a tank.

Q: Do you know the names of any of these villages where
    the incidents happened?

A: No.

Q: Did you see anyone actually kill any Vietnamese villagers?

A: No.

Q: Did you see anyone actually rape a woman?

A: No, I did not.

Q: Do you have anything else to add to or delete from this statement?

A: No.

In February 1972 the matter was closed when Mr. Brummett received this letter from the U.S. Army CID Agency, Washington, DC.

Dear Mr. Brummett:

The Secretary of the Army has asked that I further reply to your letter of 27 October 1970, to the Department of Defense, concerning alleged atrocities committed in Vietnam.

Investigation by the U.S. Army Criminal Investigation Command revealed that at an unspecified time, date and place, in RVN, during military operations mounted by your former unit, A Troop, 1st Squadron, 1st Cavalry Regiment, American Division, an unidentified person threw an unidentified Vietnamese National into a well. Subsequently, a hand grenade was heard exploding and an undetermined number of shots were fired. Of the numerous witnesses interviewed, only one stated that he observed the incident, but was too far away to determine the identity of the perpetrator. It could not conclusively be determined if the unidentified Vietnamese National died as a result of this incident.

Investigation did not support your allegations that former members of your unit committed murder, rape and pillage upon Vietnamese nationals at random.

Further investigation disclosed insufficient evidence to substantiate that the Commanding Officer of your former unit conducted himself in a wanton manner regarding his responsibilities as a commander; or that he, in fact, ordered and/or participated in the unwarranted destruction of Vietnamese property, to include livestock.

The letter ended with an unforgettable sentence: "Your interest in the military is appreciated." It was signed Henry H. Tufts, Colonel, MPC, Commanding.

Mr. Brummett kept going back to Vietnam with his cameras. In 1970 he walked into *The New York Times* office in Saigon wanting to tell a reporter what he had seen as a Specialist 5 in I Corps. His memory was very good. Twice he came back to Vietnam as might a man who was looking for something, found it, then forgot he had, only to begin looking again. He seemed content to be in the company of journalists and other photographers; he was less stiff and forlorn when he was with them. Perhaps it was like being with his platoon again, among others he could trust and like. He took nice pictures. Go back to school, his older friends kept saying. He did, and has never seemed to be able to leave. In 1974 he received his B.A. in history; now he wants a Master of Fine Arts degree.

"I try not to think of the war, but I do so incessantly," he said. "I feel cut off, I am out of touch. I just want to make beautiful photographs for their own sake. Even my few small victories over other photographers in Saigon brought me no joy. I can remember your saying in exasperation that I was too slow. I am."

IN VIETNAM THEY all knew the name of the book; no man was so dull he did not recognize the shorthand of *Catch-22* even if he had not read the novel by Joseph Heller. It meant lunacy, greed, a cluster-fuck, idiocy, farce, the Army. Few of them talked about the horror in *Catch-22*, the way Kid Sampson died in the scene on the beach. They liked to think of Yossarian rowing to Sweden and making it. Sometimes a soldier would say how really weird it was that *Catch-22* was written before Vietnam.

I wanted to tell Joseph Heller this when he appeared at a fund-raising party in Easthampton that the food writer Craig

Claiborne had been asked to give in his pretty modern house. The party was to raise money for opthalmological supplies for the Bach Mai Hospital in Hanoi. Too many of us were standing on the sun deck of Mr. Claiborne's house, drinking the punch he had made himself that morning, when I was introduced to Mr. Heller after waiting for more than half my life. As one of us said "Hello" there was a warning noise, a long and high gurgle of distress, growing louder on my right. People were sinking. One woman seemed to have lost her feet, then her ankles, and a bit of her shins. The grey boards of the sun deck were ripping and gaping under the enormous, jovial weight of the party. No one shrieked or began to moan and bleed. The evacuation was swiftly carried out as the men assisted the women to the stairs. There were no injuries, no bodies on the ground. Mr. Claiborne remained composed; when it was clear that no one intended to sue him he seemed quite cheerful about the damage, although he had no insurance to cover it. Mr. Heller disappeared. There were short speeches by the swimming pool. People really paid to come to the party to see what Mr. Claiborne's kitchen looked like, to inspect all those knives and pots, but a decent amount of money was raised.

THERE WAS AMERICAN music everywhere in the Vietnamese cities, like a constant humming beneath the louder, deadlier noises. In the nightclubs of Saigon, Vietnamese rock groups and singers imitated the Americans, pushing out "Proud Mary" and "Have You Seen the Rain" as hard as they could in their high, thin voices. They called themselves the Magic Stones or Elvis Phuong or Candy Xuan, dressing and moving and arranging their hair as the American stars did. It was often too difficult for them to do, for Vietnamese is a tonal language, its music has different scales, but they were not easily defeated. In Saigon some of the cleverer foreign service officers wrote their songs about the war, in the spirit of "Country Joe & the Fish," and copies of them were easy to come by. The songs were inspired by military advisors to the South Vietnamese with MACV (Military Assistance Command Vietnam) or the older civilians who worked for USAID (United States Agency for International Development). There was even a song about bulgar wheat, a type of grain grown in this country that was sent in massive shipments to feed hungry Vietnamese under the Food for Peace program which reportedly cost $18,000,000 a year. There was a rumor that an official said the Indonesians liked it, so the Vietnamese would, too. But they detested it and fed it to livestock. The Vietnamese did not want to eat bulgar wheat any more than you and I want to eat the flesh of horses or dogs. It repelled them even when they tried to cook it.

Young men who lived in villas or modern apartments and worked in offices wearing jackets and ties wrote their silly, thin songs and made each other laugh, having a secret little war of their own with the older powerful men in the U.S. Mission, and in the Army, who knew best. They did not resign and leave, they just had their little jokes.

The younger Americans found comfort in mocking the war, as if they were not to be held to account for something so clumsy and going so wrong. It was the Vietnamese who wrote the wild and sad laments, the poem-songs not meant to make you laugh. The finest of them came from a young Vietnamese from Hue—the haunting and beautiful city in the center—named Trinh Cong Son. He was a guitarist and a composer who between 1958 and the end of 1970, when we met, had written more than one hundred and fifty songs, becoming a heroic figure to the young Vietnamese when he was in his early thirties. He had rough hair and wore eyeglasses with big black frames that seemed too heavy for such a face. He was their Dylan; there was no one else like him. His most famous music was banned by the Ministry of Information in 1968, but the ban was not rigidly enforced, for it could not be. In that same year an official of the national police asked Trinh Cong Son to write an explanation of his antiwar songs so that radio and television audiences would be enlightened. The request amused him and he refused, saying that explaining his work was not his job. It would have been foolish for the Saigon government to arrest him. They knew it.

Even in October 1970 he was still not afraid to speak about the war. "It is for nothing and it is idiotic," he said in French. "Politicians—even the most intelligent of them are imbeciles. I call them inspired murderers."

Tapes of his songs were played in the little coffee shops of Saigon and in the nightclubs where the young Vietnamese officers went in bunches if they were able to afford one or two soft drinks apiece. All wanted to hear his earlier songs about the war. On a Saturday night in October 1970, Luong and I, with three American men, went to the Queen Bee nightclub to hear a girl named Khanh Ly—a famous name in that city—sing his songs. No one sang them as she did, knowing so well what he meant them to say. Years before, the two of them had wandered from place to place performing for students wherever they found them. She did not sing in English, or tease her hair, or wear padded brassieres, or bend and wiggle when she sang. She stood quite still. That night in the Queen Bee, Luong wrote a note in Vietnamese to Khanh Ly, asking her, as a great favor, to sing "Love Song of a Woman Driven Mad by the War." It was risky to sing that song—his most famous—but that night Khanh Ly did, and as the lovely voice wound and curled through the noisy dark room, the young Vietnamese lieutenants at the table next to us sat very still, stopped smoking and drinking.

> *I had a lover who died at the battle of Pleime,*
> *I had a lover who died at Battle Zone "D,"*

Who died at Dong Xoai,
Who died in Hanoi,
He died far away on the distant frontier.
I had a lover who died in the battle of Chu Prong,
I had a lover whose body drifted along a river,
Who died in the dark forest,
Whose charred body lies cold and abandoned.
I want to love you, love Viet Nam,
The day when the wind is strong
I whisper your name and the name of Viet Nam,
We are so close, the same voice and yellow race,
I want to love you, love Viet Nam,
But as soon as I grow up my ears are accustomed
To the sound of bullets and mines;
My hands are now free but I forget from now on the
    human language.
I had a lover who died at Ashau,
I had a lover whose twisted body lies in a valley,
Who died under a bridge, naked and voiceless.
I had a lover who died at the battle of Bac Gia,
I had a lover who died just last night, a sudden death,
With nothing to say, feeling no hatred,
Lying dead as in a dream.

All wartime capitals are gay cities, a famous writer in Memphis said, meaning it. Even Belfast was a gay city during World War II, even Belfast, and no one who had been in London during those years would ever forget it. The writer—a courteous and brilliant man who writes about one war better than anyone else in the world—is without deceit. He had supported the war in Vietnam for many years, he said, until the end of it when he knew the Americans could not win and should not win. He told about having lunch with President Johnson in the White House, a grand lunch which left him with a huge, affectionate memory of a President. His generation knew what it meant when an army invaded a border, the writer said, they knew you had to do something. He meant Hitler sending his army of Germans into Poland, into Czechoslovakia, into France. There was no border, I said, for the 17th parallel was a thread laid down in 1954 and made into a dead man's zone with the land bombed into mush, Vietnam was one country. But he was thinking of London in the war years and Belfast, where the poor still live in old houses as close together as teeth.

Saigon was never a gay city during the war: it was malignant, cruel, crowded, costly and furtive, but never gay. That night in the Queen Bee, when a twenty-three-year-old woman sang in Vietnamese and finished the song of the mad woman, no one clapped. It was not a song to applaud, not that night in that year when all of us feared in the shadow side of our minds the war would go on forever, be such a long and greedy war there would be no one left to smile if it ever came to an end. I needed to persuade the writer in Memphis that Saigon had not been romantic, remembering the woman who asked me what I wore to officers' dances and the others like her with fixed images: pilots dancing with women in black dresses and hats with little veils, an orchestra playing "We'll Gather Lilacs in the Spring Again."

NO PRISONER OF WAR can tell us everything. There is no language easy enough for them to use. Yet, in the Dunes Motel in Aurora, near Denver, for three days in July he tried to make clear what had happened in those five years. At night he went back to sleep at the army hospital, Fitzsimon General, where he was on convalescent leave. That first summer of release in 1973 he had the rank of staff sergeant. At the hospital, once the tests were done, they had the good sense to let him come and go. He was not a sick man in any way the doctors could perceive: his left leg was about one and a quarter inches shorter than the other and between fifteen to twenty percent out of alignment, but there was nothing to be done. The high school hurdler and high jumper walked with a limp. They checked all of him. It pleased him that the dentist could not dig out the old-fashioned filling which was done in North Vietnam to put in a new one. The hospital made him nervous. Once, standing by the laundry chute that suddenly made a sucking, whooshing noise, he flinched when no one else noticed it.

In the sitting room of the Dunes Motel the twenty-eight-year-old man sprawled on a couch, long legs pulled up, holding on to one ankle, answering the questions that were pushed in him like thumbtacks. Sometimes he seemed to stammer very slightly, or speak in circles. He would wind the different months together, circle them, go back, sort it out, begin again. There was nothing he forgot. It was a long story to tell and he could not take a shortcut. Sometimes, in remembering, he would pull his dark-brown mustache, which was new, or he'd play with the metal horseshoe on a chain around his neck, which he had just bought. He did not eat much, he shopped often, he drove too fast. Possessions seemed to confuse him, so there was always a bit of delay when he had to find the car keys and his sunglasses, which he needed because bright light or glare hurt his eyes after such a long time in dim rooms.

"I don't regret none of it," John Young said, of the 1,811 days as a prisoner of war of the North Vietnamese. When he broke down it was not because of the bad leg, which was almost cut off; it was not because of the five birthdays lost in the prison camps, or the letters from Erica he never received, or the son born to them that he did not see until the child was five. It was not hard for him to speak of pain and maggots and hunger, of dreams and a vision of his own death. What made him weep in the motel room were the memories of kindnesses: a Vietnamese medic, a Christmas dinner, a

prison official named Cheese, a flower given to him by a Vietnamese priest which he kept long after it died, a composition he wrote
in prison. And he wept again remembering how he had wept such
a long time ago on a September day hearing of the death of Ho Chi
Minh. It seemed better to leave him alone at those times: he did not
want anyone to touch him or say "There, there." When it happened
he did not try to hide his face or put his head down, like the GIs in
South Vietnam used to do so you would not see them crying.

John Young was freed, with close to thirty other prisoners, on
March 16, 1973. It was not the happiest day of his life. The day
before his release, the Vietnamese called Cheese said goodbye.
"He told me 'Do not lose your determination and do not forget us,
for we will never forget you,'" Young said. There was a large Air
Force colonel at the Hanoi airport who saluted him and shook his
hand and said something like "Welcome back," although the men
still stood on the soil of North Vietnam. Young did not believe
the colonel was at all glad to see him. He had made antiwar statements as a prisoner and he did not intend to say he was sorry or
that he did it under torture.

There were two American soldiers to escort each prisoner of
war to the big C-141 at the Gia Lam airfield. "One would grab
your bag and one would hold your arm—they thought we were
weak," Young said. "I guess it was for show mostly. I told them
'Hey, don't worry about it, I'm all right, let me walk by myself.' I
just left them behind. I just went and went by myself."

He did not make trouble, his behavior was correct. He did not
wave or call out to any of the Vietnamese he cared for. He did
not falter as he walked away from them. They had asked him to
behave correctly and he did not disappoint them.

"I think walking up the ramp on the back of that plane was the
hardest thing I have ever done," Young said.

When the airplane rose, most passengers began to cheer and
laugh and roar.

"No, I didn't, I didn't. I don't think anybody of the eight of us cheered," Young said. He had not stopped biting his nails.

The Eight: enlisted men who while in captivity made tapes and wrote statements for the North Vietnamese and the National Liberation Front which condemned the war and the American role in Indochina, deplored the deaths of GIs. Young had even appealed to American soldiers to stop fighting.

They were charged on May 30, 1973—by Air Force Colonel Theodore Guy, a senior officer who had been imprisoned at the same camp called Plantation Gardens—of collaboration with the North Vietnamese, of aiding the enemy in return for preferential treatment.

There were eight, then there were seven. One man shot himself on Wednesday, June 27, 1973, with a .25-caliber pistol in the house of his father-in-law in Commerce City, a Denver suburb. He was a Marine. His widow was twenty-two years old—Mrs. Abel Larry Kavanaugh, expecting a child.

"The North Vietnamese kept him alive for five years and then his own country killed him," Sandra Kavanaugh said.

Six days after the death of Sergeant Kavanaugh the Secretaries of the Army and Navy both found on July 3 that there was insufficient evidence to take any cases of former prisoners of war to courts-martial. Colonel Guy's charges against the eight men were dropped.

A coroner's jury, in ruling that the accused former prisoner of war had committed suicide, criticized the military for its handling of the case. The jury said it felt that upon his release Sergeant Kavanaugh could not manage the readjustments necessary for his new life and its unfamiliar pressures, particularly the charges brought against him by the military; it was also of the opinion that Sergeant Kavanaugh should have received much more follow-up care by the military when he returned to Denver. In his testimony to the jury, Dr. James Selkin, a psychologist and director of Denver

General Hospital's Center for the Study of Violence, said Sergeant Kavanaugh was "unable to distinguish fantasy from reality." Dr. Selkin had studied military records and interviewed the other former prisoners who knew the sergeant, and members of the Kavanaugh family. On his first night home with his wife and daughter after five years in captivity, Sergeant Kavanaugh packed his bags and said he was leaving the country, but his wife persuaded him to stay, the psychologist said to the jury. The former prisoner of war was deathly afraid he would be unjustly convicted and sent to prison by the American military. He said he would die before he went back to prison.

It was the opinion of Dr. Selkin that Sergeant Kavanaugh had been interviewed twice by an inexperienced military psychiatrist who did not appreciate his pain and confusion.

John Young was captured on January 30, 1968, only six weeks after he had arrived in South Vietnam and just before the Tet offensive. His first assignment had been in Danang, with Charlie Company, 5th Special Forces Group, working in security. Three days before the end of January he had been sent to Lang Vei, a small Special Forces outpost near the Laotian border, off Route 9, the French-built highway that cut across the frontier. There was a bigger Green Beret outpost near his; they called that one Lang Vei II. He was an advisor to Laotians, the 33d Battalion of the Royal Elephant Brigade. Young thought the Lao soldiers had been pushed back into South Vietnam after a beating.

On patrol there were seventeen Laotians, including one of their own lieutenants, and Young, who carried the radio. The Laotians could not speak English. Young used hand signals with them. They were moving southeast between Khe Sanh and Lang Vei to check out a village.

Young wore his tiger suit, those tight-fitting camouflage fatigues, and his hard black jump boots, not the softer and easier boots issued to GIs that had holes in them to let the water squish in and squish out. He loved his boots because they told you he was Airborne. He would not wear a helmet; branches scraped against it, making noise in the jungle.

The ambush came after they had crossed Route 9 in two columns. The point man suddenly went down and was only a small heap. Young went to him and knew then how close the North Vietnamese were to have been able to shoot the point man right between the eyes. The Lao soldiers fled. Young was trying to get to a clump of trees when he was hit twice by the same round. It came from an AK-47 rifle, or an AK-50, the 7.62 machine gun.

They saw him and kept firing: mortars, machine guns, AKs and SKSs, he said. He was afraid they would use grenades and get him.

"I figured, well, I am going to die so let's go down fighting," Young said, in the manner of men who are trying to describe a peculiar, passionate moment of panic. He fired fifty to sixty rounds from his M-2. He was still lying on his stomach in the gully when he felt the bayonets in his back. It was about nine o'clock in the morning. He had not even noticed how much he was bleeding or the pieces of bone that had pushed through his skin and were sticking out of his leg like huge toothpicks. He thought that he had tripped on a tree stump, until he tripped to get up. "It just cracked, crumpled, gave way," Young said.

After his capture he was carried for a day and a half to a North Vietnamese base camp in South Vietnam, on the side of a mountain. He was given morphine, penicillin and a tourniquet. North Vietnamese officers interrogated him. He would tell them nothing except his name, rank, serial number, date of birth. They yanked his leg and hit him with the butt of a weapon on the head and in the back. He does not think he screamed when the Vietnamese twisted and bent his shattered leg. He hated them too much, Young said, to do that, so he stayed silent and let the pain shine.

Speak now or we will shoot two men, they said. He said nothing. They brought forward a young Laotian soldier and shot him in the head twenty-five feet from where Young sat. Twenty minutes later another Lao was killed. Young does not know why they spared him. He thinks they may have realized he was only at Lang Vei for three days, and they wanted information on the bigger Special Forces outpost, Lang Vei II, of which he knew nothing. The North Vietnamese were planning to overrun it at Tet. They did.

A long time afterward, when he had grown to like and respect some Vietnamese in the prison camps, he mentioned how the two Laotians had been killed. He was mistaken, the Vietnamese said. It could not have happened, their forces did not do such things.

The early days of capture were so clear to him, so much sharper than the days in prison camps, where small things did happen, but then they happened over and over again. The operation took place out of doors as he lay on a bamboo table. The doctor took off his tourniquet and Young saw the maggots that had been eating the decaying flesh around the wound and making him itch. The maggots looked like very small white grubworms. He could feel the maggots falling off.

The interpreter for the Vietnamese doctor told him: "He is not so sure he can save your leg but he will try." Yeah, okay, do what you can, Young said. The doctor gave him Novocaine with a huge syringe. It surprised Young that a Vietnamese guard came to the operating table, took one of his hands, and did not let it go all the time the doctor worked on the splintered bone, put in the drainage tubes, fixed the bandage and the splint. It was the first of the kindnesses. Young says he did not feel great pain. But he was glad for that hand holding his, it was a help. They gave him twenty-four bottles of penicillin before he was moved, saying he must ask medics to give him shots whenever it was possible. Such a precaution astonished him.

For two weeks he stayed in a Bru village on the border. He lay inside a small peasant house on stilts, a typical Montagnard house. It did not hurt too much until he turned on his side or moved by propping himself on his elbows and sliding his body. There was a small fire in the room at the base of a pillar. He relieved himself by making a space in the bamboo floor and then he would sprinkle ashes down the little hole. Two girls brought him food: rice and soup. After a week the cast felt mushy and the leg began to speak with a foul smell. Two Vietnamese medics made him a ladder splint of wire with bamboo, but it cut his foot. He made his own splint—remembering the first aid he had learned in high school and in the Army—which went from the hip to the ankle.

The villagers moved up and down on a path outside the house. Sometimes they would wave at him and leave food for him. It was often sweet potatoes or cassava, which he would try to cook. He was glad to have the foot-long tobacco leaves that he could tear in pieces and smoke.

There was a small Montagnard girl, perhaps five, who came and sat by him, saying nothing. She played an instrument that looked like a one-string guitar. She would sit for several hours, playing and singing.

He stopped being terrified. Sometimes when he woke up the room would be full of North Vietnamese soldiers sleeping on the floor, their weapons right next to him, the loaded magazines near his body.

"If someone walked in with a weapon—well, I wasn't even shaking or anything," Young said.

They moved him to Laos, to a new prisoner-of-war camp for Americans captured in the south. A small medic named Thanh would often sit by Young and teach him to count in Vietnamese. *Moit, hai, ba, bon.* The American would count for him in English. They liked each other. The counting lessons went on. The little friendship made the sick and filthy prisoner feel better.

"It was so different—I never had this happen," Young said. "I taught him hello and thank you and how are you. He remembered pretty much of it. He was trying to help me. You know, he'd give me part of his ration to eat. Every day he'd try and give me a little something extra. In fact, he went to the commander of the camp and got me a little bit of milk."

It was powdered milk, wrapped in a piece of newspaper. The day Young was moved out, Thanh came to say farewell, but could not bring himself to say he would miss the American and the lessons. The two men shook hands but were unable to speak or hug each other. Goodbye to the medic Thanh. Sometimes Young would think of the Vietnamese soldiers captured in the south and how they were treated by Americans. "I know exactly what I would have done to them. I probably would have beat the hell out of them or shot them."

He was carried up the Ho Chi Minh trail in a hammock slung on a bamboo pole. At first, South Vietnamese soldiers, also prisoners, carried him and hated it—the huge American who was so helpless he could not do more than open his pants when the dysentery came. They even had to lift him to a spot on the road. His leg stuck out of the hammock and sometimes it would swing into a tree or a rock, and when Young shrieked, the soldier hit him with a stick under his back to make him shut up. Once the bamboo pole for the hammock snapped. Young could hear it cracking and tried to brace himself as he tipped back and fell. There was no bamboo in the area, so the men cut down a hardwood tree. The new pole was much heavier than the bamboo one. The North Vietnamese then began to carry him. They did not complain.

"It really ate away at their shoulders," Young said. "They were bleeding and they had huge blisters."

They would move up the trails for nine or ten hours a day, stopping before it got dark. They walked on earth, on dirt, on gravel, on asphalt. In an area where North Vietnamese troops were bivouacked, a company commander came to the American prisoners and asked if they had everything they needed. He talked mostly to Young, telling him what a beautiful city Hanoi was. The officer had children and he showed his pictures of them. The North Vietnamese troops moving down the trails looked young and anxious. They stared at the prisoners but said nothing and kept going. Sometimes they gave Young cigarettes when he held out his hand and begged for tobacco saying: *"Thuoc, thuoc."*

Perhaps, at the age of twenty-two, he almost died. The dysentery grew worse and he saw the feces were bright green. The leg was infected. He could not eat. His weight dropped to a hundred and ten pounds from two hundred. Young began to remember children who had been in kindergarten with him in 1950. He thought of his father and wanted to be with him. They stopped at the border of North Vietnam and put him in a hut. They persisted in keeping him alive. Medics came with precious things: sugar and water, penicillin and vitamins shots.

An artist came into the hut to sketch him as he lay on the floor on a straw mat. Young thought the charcoal drawings were good; no one had ever sketched him before and he rather hoped he might keep one. But the artist was sorry, he could not give Young a sketch to keep. They moved again after two weeks. A B-52 flew over and dropped bombs about three hundred meters from where they were resting off the side of a trail. The pilot only made one pass. Young had seen it all before. In Laos he had survived two B-52 strikes. He remembers the deep shaking of the earth and the sound of trees burning.

He entered North Vietnam in a truck. There was nothing to see but craters and land that was dead, land that looked like oatmeal. There were no birds or trees or people; no rice, no gardens. Nothing moved. "For hours and hours we'd travel through areas and there would be nothing but bomb craters. Just completely destroyed. In every direction there was nothing. Nothing."

On the morning of April 15, 1968, the long voyage came to an end. He was in the prisoner-of-war camp in Nhi An province that the Americans called "Bao Cao." It was a joke. The words mean "to report." The prisoners had to tell the guards "*bao cao*" in order to do anything, even to go to the latrine.

The North Vietnamese seemed insanely curious. There were endless questions, and so many forms to fill out. How much money did you make, how many cars do you have, how big is your house, how many rooms, what kind of furniture, are you married, does your wife work, how much money does she earn, are there children, what are their ages?

Young and another American, who also resisted answering the questions, were told to report to another building about twenty-five yards away from their room. No one helped them. Neither man could walk. "We crawled. I crawled. He crawled," Young said.

An officer with a pistol said they would have to cooperate. The prisoners looked at each other and one man told the other of the military regulations: Don't do anything that will cause you harm or abuse. This is how they remembered the phrase from the Military Code of Conduct for prisoners of war. Then they talked: cars, wives, money, furniture, children houses, lawns, television sets . . .

The Vietnamese asked him to write his feelings about the war. He wrote that he thought the Americans were in Vietnam trying to fight communism and help the Vietnamese people. No one shouted at him, or struck him, or took away his food. He is not sure he really believed what he wrote, but this is what he had been taught by the U.S. Army.

He was twenty-two when he was captured; his twenty-third birthday was September 9, 1968. He hardly had a past, there was nothing splendid or surprising about his life. Words do not work well for him, for when he was growing up it was not language that mattered. Grammar was for old ladies and spelling was for girls. He did not read. He was a poor student, restless and inattentive. What seized him and filled him with longings and excitement were cars; it could be said he only cared for cars. His parents, of German and Dutch descent, considered him the baby, the wild one, and when things went wrong they would say it was "Dear John" again. Edward, his brother, was two years older and quieter. Their father, a big man with a strong voice, often went hunting in the woods; he had a Mauser, a twelve-gauge shotgun and a pistol. His sons did not sass their father nor did they have much to say to him. In their five-room boxlike house in Third Lake, Illinois—forty-five miles north of Chicago—no one else sat in the white-plastic recliner, only the father. He was an electrician. Dinner was at five, always.

When Young was a boy competing in school athletics, his father would always say: "Go out there and get it."

He always did. The young, hard body never failed him. It was easy to race and jump, just as, years later, Advanced Infantry Training at Fort Knox and jump school at Fort Bragg would be easy.

"By the time I was through grade school—you know, eighth grade," he said, "I had my whole chest just covered. With blue ribbons and red ribbons and yellow ribbons."

He dropped out of high school in June 1963, in his junior year. He was seventeen and he joined the Army. He was stationed in Germany from November 1963 until May 1966. He reenlisted so he could marry Erica, a German girl, in October 1965. He wanted to stay in Germany, but the Army was pulling troops out to send them to Vietnam.

His father died from cancer of the lungs in November 1967 when he was at Fort Bragg. It changed him, Young said. He began moving away from his wife, feeling restless, wanting to leap anywhere. He was not a very good husband. That made him sorrowful when he was a prisoner. When he telephoned Erica from Clark Air Base in March 1973, Young said to his wife: "Are things still all right between us?" She said we'll see.

He was always stubborn and proud, wanting to go places and

get there fast. When the twenty-eight American prisoners, and North Vietnamese guards, left "Bao Cao" on the twenty-ninth of August at 7 A.M., Young refused to be carried any more. He was sick of that; he would do it himself. The wound was still open on his leg. The pain was so brilliant he had to ask for Novocaine. Young walked with a bamboo pole, but he could not keep up. The Vietnamese did not push him. Rest here, they said. Do you want to smoke?

They had just crossed a river and were moving onto a dike when fifteen Vietnamese guards suddenly came back and surrounded him in a circle. Then he saw the villagers yelling and throwing stones. They hit the guards with sticks; it was the American they wanted to beat. The guards kept moving, slowly, with Young looming up in the center of the fierce little circle they made, shouting to the villagers to stop at once, to go away. Those who came too close were knocked down.

He had almost reached the road where the other prisoners were waiting in trucks when he heard the sound of a Phantom, or maybe it was a 105, the jets that drop the big bombs, the 500- or 1,000-pounders. The first one hit the other side of the dike, behind the trucks. He heard three bombs explode. He had walked through the area and he knew there were no military targets, only a river and the dikes and the rice fields and the village. It was an ugly day. He never knew if any of the villagers were killed.

D-1 is thirty-five miles east of Hanoi. He spent two years there. The interrogations started again. He wrote his autobiography over and over. Young called them off-the-wall questions. How many girls have you slept with? Do you enjoy sex, do you enjoy sports, what recreation do you like? Describe where you live, how big is your village. Much later he realized the questioning was being used to teach the new interpreters, who had studied English for only six weeks. Every day different interpreters took turns reading reports from AP, UPI and the Hanoi news agency to them.

The Americans captured in the south were always kept together and were subject to the rules and policies of the Provisional Revolutionary Government, even though they were being held in North Vietnam. In late September, Young lived with Specialist 4 Michael Branch and Private George Sparks. Each one was given two cigarettes a day. They saved the tobacco from their butts as carefully as beggars working a hostile neighborhood. The trouble started when the men tore a copy of *Vietnam Courier*, an English-language newspaper printed in Hanoi, for cigarette paper. The Vietnamese asked who had done this. Young said he did it. Sparks said no, he did it. Branch said it was him.

Their punishment was having to stand up with their arms straight over their heads every day from 6 A.M. until 9 P.M., when they went to bed. They were given thirty minutes to eat at noon. They were on half rations—water and bread—and there was nothing to smoke.

It was not torture, it was punishment, Young kept saying in Aurora, Colorado, and long afterward. "Torture is . . . is . . . is getting your fingernails pulled out, soap and water, a knife to the belly, electrodes to the testicles," he said. "But nobody was touching me. Sure it hurt. It hurt my back, my knees, my arms, my shoulders, everything. But the next day, if the punishment was over, you didn't feel it at all. It's gone."

Sometimes, when the Americans knew the guards were elsewhere, and not looking in the room, they could lean against the wall and relax. The punishment changed. They were ordered to kneel on the concrete floor, arms raised straight up. On some days one man would be excused and would be permitted to smoke and eat while the other two still knelt. Young thought it was done to divide them.

Cheese called them into his office. He was the officer who dealt with the prisoners. The Americans thought of him as the head cheese; they had nicknames for all the Vietnamese. The two prisoners explained they had wanted cigarette paper. Cheese said no, you did it to defy camp regulations and the Provisional Revolutionary Government. It was true in a way, Young said. They said okay, okay, that was it. The punishment was ended.

"We looked at each other when we got back to the room and just busted out laughing," Young said.

Cheese was something. He was a Vietnamese in his forties, who looked frailer than most of them to the Americans. His English was not fluent, but Young said Cheese knew the grammar better than he did.

"He was real thin. I mean, there was nothing on his arms," Young said. "If you seen him in shorts, you'd think he had two toothpicks for legs." It was a long time before Young became attached to Cheese. "At times he'd get on our nerves. But when he was gone awhile you'd start to wonder—damn, where the hell is Cheese at, he's supposed to be here. He grew on you." Not all the other men felt so warmly about Cheese.

They dared Sparks to break wind in the face of a guard. He did it, standing on tiptoes, through the little window in the door. The three men were put in isolation. Young was alone, back on his knees again. He began yelling at a guard one night that the NLF was a bunch of liars, all of them, all they did was lie, and they were a bunch of Communists, too.

Cheese called for him. "He asked me what I had said the night before. I started telling him what the hell I thought. He had a real strange look on his face. He got up and he walked around and he just knocked me off right off the chair. He just nailed me one. He picked me about a foot off that chair."

The night he was so angry at Cheese, Young accused the National Liberation Front of using torture and lying about it. He hoped it would stop the practice of making the men stay on their knees. "We do not torture," Cheese told him. "We criticize."

In isolation, Young was allowed to go outside to wash, to empty the bucket he used as a latrine, to sweep an area. He slept on a small wooden bed. There was a mat and blankets. He liked to talk to the Vietnamese interpreters or cadres. There was not much to do but think and sleep. It was 1969. He always kept track of the months.

He could not do complicated mathematical problems, or remember poetry, or build houses in his mind, as other Americans have said they did during captivity. "What I was doing was trying to understand. Why didn't they kill me, beat me, take tire irons or water hoses and stuff like that, when asking me questions. I just started thinking."

At first it was like chewing fog. Cheese came often to talk to him. Young was still arguing a little.

"I was taking a look at the war. What did I see happen in South Vietnam? What was I told when I was in the United States and what have these people told me? Who was telling the truth?"

He was not scarred by combat in South Vietnam. He did not see any American friends die. What he remembered was the bombing he saw in I Corps, the northernmost provinces of South Vietnam; the removal of Vietnamese civilians from villages; the collection of ears from Vietnamese corpses owned by a sergeant. And the three fishermen who were picked up on the beach near Danang although they said they were only there to catch crabs. All had the required ID cards.

The Vietnamese were beaten and put in a Conex, a closet-sized box of corrugated tin. "It must have been a hundred and five degrees in there. They didn't have any place to defecate or urinate. They had been given no food," Young said. He ordered the fishermen freed.

In September 1969 he was at D-1, in a room by himself. He could not see or speak to another American. Ho Chi Minh died on September 2. There was a most terrible hush, as if the Vietnamese had stopped breathing. Young heard of the death over the camp radio. There was a speaker in each of the prisoners' rooms.

He wept. The Vietnamese named Cheese came into his room, asked him quietly why he was so upset, then left. To this day Young remembers his grieving. You only had to see him in the Dunes Motel to know he could not be cured.

"He freed the country from the French, right, and the Vietnamese really loved and respected this man," he said. "I think a lot of people around the world did. Even I did. I mean, I'd never known him. I'd just read about Ho Chi Minh in prison. But talking to the cadres . . . they'd talk about him with such esteem, such respect. You know, you don't ever hear people talk about our President, any of our Presidents, as highly as the Vietnamese talked about him."

He wanted to have someone like that; many people do.

In the fall of 1969 he read about the antiwar movement's Vietnam Moratorium in the United States. There were Americans who really wanted the war to go off, Young said. He asked Cheese if he could write something to help the antiwar movement. Cheese said no. But Young tried to put down some of his feelings on paper. "I knew what the consequences would be with the U.S. military, but I says, well, I got a conscience," he told me.

Cheese looked at it but did not praise him. He was always critical of his spelling, handwriting and sentence structure. "He said it was very bad. He said it was very sloppy," Young said. Cheese always seemed disturbed by Young's education. No one had ever paid that much attention to how much he did not know and could not do.

He was never allowed to study Vietnamese in the camps but he learned words and tries now to remember them. Once, shaving and looking into a small mirror, he saw that his face was not the same any more, he saw how all of it had changed.

It was a Christmas he could not believe. The Americans were always given a special dinner on December 25, but in 1969 there was a Christmas Eve party. The prisoners sang and laughed and could not stop talking. They went in shifts: fifteen men at a time. It had been six months since Young had talked to any Americans. It had been years since he had heard a roomful of men laugh like that. He was so happy to be with them, happy that for once no one was depressed.

The Americans had been allowed to decorate a Christmas room. Young had been given permission to whitewash it by himself. Others had made the green-paper wreaths that looked like holly, the snowman pasted on the wall, the paper fireplace and the big Santa Claus. There was a program, too, of poems, essays and singing. Young recited a little essay he had written on the meaning of Christmas and how he had spent it in Third Lake, Illinois. In Aurora, he remembered how people at home had stopped hollering at each other when it was Christmas, but he did not put all that in his composition.

The Vietnamese had sent someone to the mountain to cut down a tree, and the little white bulbs hanging on its branches had been painted different colors. Cheese had told them all that there would be photographers present, but none of the Americans seemed to notice, or much care.

He and Branch sang "Jingle Bells" and "Noël"; some officers sang "Rudolph, the Red-Nosed Reindeer." They sang wonderfully. At one end of the room was an altar. A church in North Vietnam had sent a cross and candlesticks. There was even a little crèche showing Jesus and the manger. He remembers an incense burner, too. The Americans went, two by two, to the altar to kneel and pray.

On Christmas Day he had a present: he was no longer alone. Branch moved in with him, this was the gift. Eight prisoners had their dinner at noon together. Young remembers how the tomatoes and carrots were shaped into flowers, something he had never seen before. He had been so hungry for so long, but that day he could not eat all that was given him. There was soup, turkey,

French fries, hard-boiled eggs, bread, vegetables, beer and coffee. As a treat, American rock music was played over the speaker for the prisoners to hear in their rooms. He wanted Erica. New Americans came into D-1 that day.

Cheese looked very tired and his eyes were bloodshot. He asked Young to help him. The problem was a young prisoner—whom I shall call Banks—who was trying to kill himself and could not be left alone. Banks had been a prisoner since 1966.

Young asked him to play ping-pong. "He said they were going to castrate him," he said. "We were playing ping-pong, but then he shut everything off and asked to go back to his room."

Banks was hoping to die by biting through his wrist and cutting the veins with his teeth. He had gnawed through that arm quite deeply. The Vietnamese gave him iron and vitamins because he had lost quite a bit of blood. "He looks at the pills and he looks at me. 'They're trying to poison me,' he says. But he took them," Young added.

Banks moved in with Young and Branch so they could watch him all the time and keep him from chewing his wrist. One night Young dozed off and heard the guard calling his name. He saw that Banks was huddled in a corner, trying to get at his wrist. There was blood on his teeth. Young grabbed Banks and threw him back against the door and hit him.

Cheese was very angry at Young. "He said I had no right to do it." Cheese did not punish him. He only said he was disappointed in Young.

THEY MOVED TO Plantation Gardens in Hanoi on the night of November 22, 1970. He does not remember how many anti-war tapes he made. There were a lot. In one broadcast for the Provisional Revolutionary Government, Young said in a letter addressed to President Nixon:

I no longer want to fight for you, or anyone like you. In fact, I won't ever again fight for your kind of American democracy. I will, as I said, fight for my real American people and country. Not you, Mr. President, because you don't represent the real America.

It was much better for the Americans at Plantation. There was a volley-ball court and a courtyard where they could exercise. Young liked to listen to the train that ran in back of the prison. If he was outside, he could even see the passengers.

"We always knew there was a possibility that we'd get into trouble with the military when we got back, but it didn't make no difference," Young said. "We wouldn't have changed what we were saying. We weren't ashamed of what we were saying."

Cheese had gifts brought to them in the room. Young thought that other Americans were always there when the gifts arrived and that perhaps this was planned by Cheese. At first there was Kool-Aid, candy, milk, sugar, cigarettes. After 1971 there were no more American items, just ones made in Vietnam. That made Young feel more uneasy. He and the others had complained to Cheese. "We'd tell him, look, we don't need it. We aren't doing this because you're giving us all this stuff. At first we refused it. Then Cheese says the camp commander says you have no right to refuse anything that we give you." Young admits he was glad to have the cigarettes; so were the other heavy smokers.

"We felt guilty because we knew that children outside the fence were having a hard time getting this stuff and that they needed it more than we did. When we started getting Vietnamese stuff, why, their soldiers weren't even getting what we were. We had enough sugar in our diet already. We had sweet rice on Sunday and sometimes they'd give us sugar with our bread in the mornings."

Young claims that the men tried to share their extra food with the guards, who had been generous and polite to them. But the guards would always say no, no, the milk will give us diarrhea, the candy will be bad for our teeth, too many cigarettes make us cough.

It was early in August 1971. Young and four other men were walking across the compound to the kitchen where food for Americans was prepared. The five washed the pots and pans and dishes. Some senior officers were outside, shaving. Suddenly Captain Edward Leonard, Jr. shouted: "Kavanaugh, you and your men must stop all communication and collaboration with the enemy."

One of the five yelled back: "I'll protest this war until I die."

Another officer later said that on that day one of the enlisted men also shouted: "Who's the enemy?"

Young does not remember. He was watching the Vietnamese guards, who were always armed. The Americans were forbidden to talk, and for a second he thought the Vietnamese might open fire. It was an "asinine" thing for Leonard to do, Young said, it made him furious.

Major Edward Leonard, Jr., had his turn in July 1973. The thirty-four-year-old Air Force officer, who had been promoted on his return to the States, filed mutiny charges against the seven men under Article 94 of the Uniform Code of Military Justice. The long list of offenses included attempts by the seven to "advise, counsel, urge and to cause insubordination, disloyalty and refusal of duty" in another prisoner of war "by stating to him that the United States should not be in Vietnam, that the United States was committing atrocities against the Vietnamese people, that money to keep the war going was going to rich Americans and that American soldiers were being killed for no reason . . ."

The charges also accused the men of making a poster that said "Nixon Sucks," of singing the anthem of the National Liberation, and of seeking political asylum from officials of the Army of the Democratic Republic of Vietnam. The Army dropped these charges too.

• • •

IN 1972, AS a prisoner of war, John Young read *War and Peace, Romeo and Juliet, And Quiet Flows the Don,* and *The Arrogance of Power* by Senator William Fulbright.

THE BOMBING OF Haiphong came on April 16, 1972. Be prepared, the Vietnamese told the prisoners in Hanoi. The siren went off the next day.

"I think the bombing was the most horrifying thing in my whole life. Worse than when I was captured, because I understood it," Young said. The first raid was a short one. The men in his room sat on their beds and waited after the siren sounded. "We waited and waited and waited. It was only about five minutes but it seemed like an eternity. All of a sudden you could hear it off in the distance, you could hear the jets coming. Then the antiaircraft in the distance. Boom, boom, boom. Then a terrible and thunderous roar over the building and the shaking of everything."

The bombers came during the day, and during the night, for more than five months. Young swung between outrage and fear and a terrible pity for the people of Hanoi. Six times he had been taken out of the prison camp on trips through the capital, dressed in a Western suit and flowered tie provided by his captors. He had been to the Museum of Natural History, to Unification Park, to the circus. He loved the circus, he can talk for a long time about that circus.

"We were feeling what the people of Vietnam were feeling," Young said. You could smell the smoke in Hanoi after the raids and hear the ambulances and the fire trucks. He hated the delayed-action bombs, those that went off after the all-clear when people thought it was all over and they were safe. He hated President Nixon. "We called him every name in the book," he said. "It was murder, that's what it was."

In October, the month when Henry Kissinger said that "peace was at hand" and that a final agreement on a cease-fire and a negotiating settlement with the North Vietnamese was only three or four days away, there were quarrels among the twelve men living together. Young says The Eight moved out and left the four men alone, because it was felt the attitudes of the others were too conciliatory. They thought the war was over.

"These men were doing an about-face," Young said. "They figured they'd be going home soon, so they didn't want to do anything. I says okay, if you want to cover your ass, you cover your ass."

It was not over. The B-52s came back over Hanoi on the night of December 18.

"The Vietnamese always told us that when the U.S. government destroyed Hanoi, there will be nothing left to destroy in Vietnam, and when they destroy Hanoi, they will have to get out because at that time they know we will never give up. They will have to kill everybody in this country," Young said.

First you could hear a distant rumble of the B-52s, a steady rumble which got closer and closer.

"It got closer and closer and closer, and you could look out the window and see where they were, for the sky was a fiery red. Then it was like an earthquake," he said.

The prisoners dug shelters in their room. They could see the SAM missiles hitting the planes.

"It was worse than hell," Young said. "I've seen so many of those planes go down, and I've seen so many of these bombs exploding, and it's just at times unbearable. You want to lie down and die. Die. You do. Because you know the pilots didn't have a chance, I mean, it hurt just as much to see them die as to know the Vietnamese were dying. They were our people, they were Americans too. And there was nothing you could do. You knew you were helpless and it just eats at you, it does."

They moved to the Hanoi Hilton on December 27.

HIS OLDEST SON, John, who was born in Germany, was two years old when Young went to Vietnam. In spring of 1973 the child asked his father about the war that kept him away for such a long time.

Did you win or did you lose, the child wanted to know.

"I told him I was on the side of the winners," Young said.

AFTER I CAME back from being with Young, another returned prisoner of war called me at eleven-thirty at night. I was asleep. He was a polite and determined man, with the rank of captain, who was getting out of the Army. He knew I had spent three days with Young. It was wrong of me to write only about Young, the captain said. That was only one side of the story and I must talk to other POWs. It wasn't just that Young and the others were against the war, so were most prisoners, the captain said. I said I thought this was not so. He went on: But The Eight had taken gifts, accepted special privileges. It was bad for the morale of the Americans, it was bad for camp discipline. You had to have discipline.

For two weeks each time the telephone rang I dreaded speaking to another officer, back from D-1 and Plantation and the Hanoi Hilton, wanting to give me the full picture, ma'am. Each man has his own story, each man knows whom he cannot forgive.

Young and I met several times in the next two years. He grew more hair, the mustache was longer and thicker, the sideburns more bunchy. His deep-set eyes looked strangely bluer. He gained weight. He was going to Harper's Junior College, giving antiwar speeches, and working with a local chapter of Clergy and Laity

Concerned. Shortly after the first of the new year in 1974, five of them had their first reunion in northern Kentucky, in the home of Michael Branch, who lived in Highland Heights, across the river from Cincinnati. The first to arrive was Frederick Elbert, an ex-Marine from Brentwood, Long Island, who had been a prisoner for fifty-five months. Elbert said he had spent fifteen hundred dollars on new clothes, which looked a little snug because he kept gaining weight. He bought new furniture for his parents, a good stereo, a console TV and car. He spent eight hundred dollars on Christmas presents. Sometimes when he planned to go out at night his father wanted to go along with him.

His parents were not curious. "They never asked me a single thing," Elbert said.

Mrs. Earl Branch, the mother of Michael, who was twenty-six and had been a prisoner for fifty-eight months, showed me the rosary that he made in captivity and gave to her. He had used the cord from the drawstring pajama bottoms the prisoners wore, and carefully knotted it. The cross was made from bamboo and old toothpaste tubes. The rosary looked very old and delicate, like something dug up two hundred years ago. "He only did what he had to do in order to survive," Mrs. Branch said mournfully.

She did not understand that her son, or any of the others, regretted nothing and kept insisting they were not tortured into making antiwar statements. No one had explained this to her, or perhaps, considering her nerves, she did not want to hear it. Mrs. Branch said that she wished she could have answered all the letters people wrote to Michael welcoming him home. Young girls and lonely women wrote him. One letter read: "Dear Michael, Just a note to say I'd like to meet you sometime if you are not married. I heard you were married then I read how you were divorced so I'm a divorcee and would like to meet you. I would love to meet a POW and just talk . . ."

Elbert and Branch sat with William Hagedorn in the Gladiator cocktail lounge of the Travelodge Motel the first night of the reunion. He was Branch's lawyer, who liked to drink with, and show off, his most famous client, who seemed to both like and be repelled by the attention of reporters. When Branch was a prisoner, all of his pay was sent to his wife, who had written him when he was a GI that only his daughter really missed him. That letter made Branch go berserk. He was captured the week he received the letter; he read it over and over.

Local television described his homecoming, the ruined marriage, the stalled life, the collaboration charges. It was voted as the best news story of 1973 in a local poll of television viewers and the film on Michael Branch was shown again. The lawyer was delighted.

The men moved around to drink in different places. They were joined by a doctor with a large local practice who said in World War II he had been a prisoner of the Germans in a camp between Berlin and Breslau. It was not of much interest to Branch or Elbert, but they had learned to listen politely to such stories.

The Americans and the Germans were much more alike than Americans and Asians, the doctor said, because Asians had little regard for human life. Everyone knew that.

"What about the six million Jews?" Branch asked. The doctor said something about a law being passed by the Germans. Branch said a law didn't make it all right, did it?

The lawyer wanted to know something about the needs of the former prisoners of war but he didn't want to know very much. "Listen, were you guys able to masturbate?" he asked. "I mean, that must have been the only way to get to sleep."

Branch and Elbert laughed just a little, but they did not like the question much, perhaps because women were at the same table.

The men wanted Elbert to see the Beverly Hills, a huge place on a hill that looks as if it had been yanked out of Las Vegas and put down in Newport, Kentucky by mistake. There was a bar, a nightclub, a garden room, a ballroom and a wedding chapel. In the gift shop Elbert bought a little plaster statue bearing the words: "Somebody has to say it first—I love you." He was going to mail it to a girl.

John Young was the only man who came to the reunion with a wife, although the others are all married now. Erica, a pleasant, pretty woman with blond hair and nice legs, was at ease with the other men and with Branch's family. She spoke and wrote English more correctly than her husband, or any of the others. I asked if her husband was feeling steadier.

"He still has his moments," she said. She joked about the posters and pictures he hung on the walls of a room in their house in Arlington Heights, Illinois. "There is Easy Rider on one wall and Ho Chi Minh on the next," Erica said.

When her husband first came home he could not sleep on the big soft mattress after such a long time on floors, boards and concrete platforms, so he asked her if she would sleep on the floor with him. Erica said she would rather not. She kept on working, as she had when he was a prisoner of war, because they needed the money while he was at school. Young made so many speeches he became very good at it; his grammar improved and his speech was clearer. He would tell students that nobody wanted the war in Vietnam except the Army and big business, that he wanted Nixon impeached for keeping the war going another four years when he could have ended it, that the bombing of North Vietnam was mass murder.

At the reunion, Branch told Young what the doctor had said about the Germans and the Americans.

"He is right. We are a lot alike," Branch said.

"No, Americans are the most brutal people in the world," Young said. The booted motorcycle police in Chicago, dressed for winter, reminded him of the Gestapo and SS troops.

When we met again, it was in February 1974 at Iowa State University, which was having a week of speeches and seminars on Vietnam. In one class Young spoke to a handful of students but he did not mention his own personal experiences. When he finally mentioned his captors, finally spoke of Cheese, he slowed down, and those who were close to him could see his eyes were filled.

Everyone has theories about these prisoners of war. It has something to do with their fathers, a man in New York said to me, but almost everything does. A psychologist thought perhaps these particular prisoner might have had damaging or disruptive childhoods and that perhaps the Vietnamese, even when punishing them, gave them more time and attention than anyone else in their lives had provided or been willing to give. Maybe I said, maybe. A teacher said American education had failed them. A woman in the antiwar movement said they had understood the truth about the war and acted on it. Maybe, I said. Another woman said the split between the eight enlisted men and the other prisoners of war—the officers, the careerists—was only a sign of class war that would soon make itself felt in America despite all the "pacification" programs to keep the poor alive in line, and silent. But I know who can give us the answer. It is in Hanoi with some Vietnamese whose names we will never know.

He never thought of himself as a man to be pitied. He was glad he had been a prisoner.

"I don't think Americans really know what love is, or what it is to love a country, or to love their own people," Young said to me. "The Vietnamese in the north do. It's unbelievable. They'll do anything for each other."

In December of 1975, when I telephoned, Erica Young said John was no longer with her and the boys. He had left in May, saying he had to get "all away from everything." He asked for a divorce. Mrs. Young was composed but sounded clenched. She was thirty and their marriage was ten years old. She did not know why he had to leave. We remembered: how he had said how much he owed her for waiting five years for him, how much he wanted the marriage to be a good one, how hard he had worked to end the war and to make other Americans see they were the wrong side. She said his work at college had not gone particularly well but that he had liked becoming involved with the students' senate.

"He wanted to do so much good," Erica Young said. "And it was easier for him to do it in prison."

LUONG ALWAYS SAID the same thing when the village dogs got closer and I wanted to run. It was this: Stand still and they will not hurt you. Sit down quickly on the ground if a dog begins to bite you, he would say. The dog would then feel bigger and act nicely. Luong believed in his advice. The young dogs and the old dogs, in a fury, would come racing out as we walked up the paths to all the Vietnamese villages where I wanted to ask questions.

The dogs were always the same dogs, overwrought, with crooked tails and watery eyes, dogs who had no names, for the Vietnamese did not consider animals to be equal with children. I was afraid of being bitten because I did not want to have so many shots in the stomach for rabies.

But perhaps there was another reason. The proud and worn village dogs, of all things Vietnamese, seemed free to show who was not wanted. I always understood this. The villagers had no choice: Americans could not be sent away, or told they had no right to ask so much.

Dog-fear was wasteful, Luong said. He meant foolish. Other things were to be feared: helicopters flying in a fog and crashing, helicopters being shot down, cluster bombs, white phosphorus, mines and booby traps, mortars, rocket-propelled grenades, and riflemen in all armies. But even after the ambush, the firefights, the American artillery that fell short and almost killed us, the helicopter being hit, I could not trust the dogs, any of them. It was not unusual to devise imaginary threats, or enlarge the littlest ones, in order to be distracted from the real dangers that were so constant and so brutal it was better to ignore them.

The American troops loved Vietnamese dogs. It was what they loved the most in that country. They adopted dogs, none of them very big, who grew fat and playful. They were cuddled, scratched, teased, talked to, wormed, washed, and overfed a good deal of the time. There were puppies everywhere: on fire bases, where they learned not to mind the great slamming noises of the howitzers; in base camps; in mess halls; at headquarters; in trucks and in tents.

There were dogs called Dink, Gook, Slut, Pimp, Scag, Slit, Rat, Zip and Trouble. Despite the paperwork, which most soldiers loathed, in 1969 GIs took home two hundred and seventy dogs, thirty-three cats, nineteen reptiles, twenty monkeys, twenty-six birds, one fox and three lizards. In the same year slightly more Americans—four hundred and fifty-five of them—received permission to marry Vietnamese women and take them home, which required more paperwork and unending bribes.

At Long Binh Post there was a Military Dog Hospital for the animals that were used as trackers, scouts and sentries. GIs were allowed to bring in their pets to a small, gleaming dispensary. It was a far better hospital than most Vietnamese could hope for. When there was a rabies threat, the head veterinarian, who was a kindly captain, had to tell quite a few GIs that their healthy dogs would have to be killed. The problem was that the dogs had not been vaccinated before a date determined by the Army.

Some of the GIs had to be told this several times, and then once more. They knew, even the dimmest man among them, that it was useless to argue with the Army. Some of them stood in the hall, holding dogs, trying to arrange their faces. Cats were brought in to the hospital too. A young sergeant, with the name of Kirby, walked by holding a two-month-old kitten, named Re-Up, that he was going to put down. The animal was very sick. "I have nightmares doing this," Kirby said.

There was no one nightmare for all of them. For one man, Vietnam meant killing small cats; for others, it was something else. It was an army all to its own.

The scout dogs were German shepherds, held by their trainers on very long metal leashes. Something about them looked wrong, as if too many tiny wires inside their heads touched and smoked, making them mean and unhappy. Some acted as though they smelled a peculiar scent on me which made them more alert, and I tried to comfort myself by saying it was nail polish. The GIs had the same PX deodorants that I did, and used Desenex foot powder. There would be huge dark circles of sweat around their shoulder blades. Sometimes the infantrymen, the 11 Bravos, had bamboo poisoning, rotting feet, or boils on the backs of their necks from the heat and dirt. They called them dink sores, and would cut them open for each other with Schick razor blades. The animals did not bother them; the dogs were on their side.

The dog trainers seemed to be set apart. None of the wild bitter talk came from them or the sense of ill-usage which made men sullen, murderous or frantic. Once a trainer told me, as we waited for a helicopter, that when it was that hot the scout dog panted so much his tongue was apt to get sunburned. That worried him. Some Americans were very happy in Vietnam, happier than they might ever be again. They knew exactly what to do.

Later I knew I was right, when Luong and I talked to some Vietnamese who swore they had seen an American let loose his German shepherd to attack a man riding on a motorbike, an ordinary man on an ordinary road. Later we knew without any doubt that dogs had been used on some Vietnamese prisoners. There was nothing to do but stay as far away from them as possible, which I do even now.

THE GI WAS trying to explain to an older American civilian why he had given up marijuana for heroin.

"Grass is loud," he said.

The soldiers liked heroin because it had no smell and did not give them away. The officers could not tell who was smoking or snorting it in 1971 before the Army started drug checks, raids and testing men's urine.

"You can salute with your right hand and take a hit with your left," a draftee said to me. He thought it was a splendid revenge. He saluted often when he smoked it.

In the third week of February 1971 a lieutenant told me that heroin was being sold everywhere in Vietnam. Luong and I went to find out and buy some. We bought more than forty dollars' worth. Alvin Shuster, the bureau chief in Saigon, was nervous when he saw me come back with that heroin—it was the proof I needed for my story—so I flushed it down the toilet in *The New York Times* office. On the fifteen-mile Bien Hoa highway, which ran from Saigon north to Long Binh—the largest U.S. military base in South Vietnam—we bought the first vial from a little girl sitting alone under an Army poncho held up with poles. It cost three dollars for a vial about the size of a salt shaker served with meals by the airlines. Sometimes the price went up to six dollars. Across the highway was the entrance to the headquarters of Lieutenant General Michael Davidson, commander of II Field Force. The little girl sat there alone, humming, with a monkey on a rope and a bird in a cage.

In areas outside of Long Binh, called Ho Nai and Tam Hiep, Vietnamese sent children to sell the stuff to GIs driving convoys; it was easier for girls because the Americans were suspicious of all males, even small ones, who they felt could be Viet Cong. The Vietnamese called heroin *bach bien*, or "white opium." The children were very clever. They never kept the heroin on their bodies or in the little boxes they held up which displayed sunglasses, Seiko watches, billfolds and headbands. They hid the drug in a nearby bush until the sale was made. One of the best routes to work was between Binh Duong and Ben Cat; sometimes the little girls went to Tay Ninh or to Long Khanh, for they knew the convoys stopped there. The little girls did not know where the heroin came from but they thought it came from Cholon, the Chinese twin city of Saigon. There was a pretty one, with a wide smile and coquettish manner, who lied about her age. She said she was seventeen, but Luong thought she was much younger. Her business was very good.

"More white Americans buy heroin than black Americans, but I don't know why. If you see an American sniffing *bach bien*, you would certainly die of laughter," she said. "His hands shake violently when he is given it. Then he immediately sniffs it, even poking it in the nose. Then he closes his eyes as if he faints. Some minutes later he wakes up and looks more intelligent."

I HAVE MADE many people angry. Once, after speaking at a small lunch given at the University of Missouri, a woman came up to me and said it was shaming to have had to listen to what I said, when everyone knew the Americans were a kind and generous people—and I spoke so harshly of what they had done in Vietnam. Her son was in the Special Forces, the lady said, and all he had done was try to help poor weak backward people defend themselves.

The lady—who would certainly not want her name set down in these pages—spoke of orphanages, churches, schools and cleanliness. She spoke loudly because she was deeply distressed. People like me worked on her like sand in the eyes. "Is there nothing we did over there that you have the fairness to acknowledge?" the lady in the red dress said.

I have been thinking about it, needing to explain why even the most well-meaning plans and gestures did not help the Vietnamese, since, nearly always, it was we who had injured them and made them helpless. The wooden chests, for example, made by industrial-arts students in Pulaski County, Tennessee, which were sent to Vietnam in 1965, were filled with school supplies. Included also were softballs, baseballs, almanacs, world atlases, books of American geography and, sometimes, high school yearbooks. They were, of course, in English. I saw a child in Anh Giang province looking at a book from America that was a beginner's manual on carpentry. He was holding the book upside down. The children of Vietnam did not need maps of the United States, or yearbooks, they needed to know how to find their own country.

It is true that there were small boys in Vietnam who imitated the GIs and were overwhelmed by them; it is true that there were women who did love some Americans. But so huge, so powerful, so rich were the foreigners, their presence became a poison in the Vietnamese blood. Even the garbage of the Americans was a garbage the Vietnamese had never seen; the children dug in it for food. All that was certain was the great wealth, power and the strangeness of the foreigners who were at the same time persuaded of their own kindness while being persistently cruel. A fourteen-year-old girl in Saigon wrote this poem; nearly all Vietnamese write poetry and there is nothing unusual about it. The title is "Americans Are Not Beautiful."

> They are called My,
> Which my brother says means beautiful.
> But they are not beautiful:
> They have too much hair on their arms like monkeys,
> They are tall like trees without branches,
> Their eyes are green like eyes of boiled pigs
> In the markets during the New Year.
> Their hair is blond and not black,
> Their skin is pink and not brown,
> Their cars frighten cyclists in the streets,
> Their flying machines and their dragonflies

Drop death on people and animals
And make trees bare of their leaves.
Here, Americans are not beautiful.
"But they are,
In their faraway country"
My brother says.

In Duc Duc, in the province of Quang Nam, where I met the captured Viet Cong nurse before she was taken away with the other prisoners, the villagers spoke often, and wearily, of the fierce fighting in March when North Vietnamese troops attacked. One American, who flew over Duc Duc after the fighting, said it looked like an overflowing ashtray. There was a man named Tanh who said he was not for the Communists, but the Saigon government and their own soldiers were too weak. It made him groan: He had *never* seen such a bunch. "The nationalist soldiers are all cowards and their leaders have no initiative. When we were attacked they only stuck to each other, and lots of houses were destroyed by their artillery fired point-blank, not by Communist fires," he said.

That night a man yelled out, but there were always men with nightmares who moaned or called out in their sleep. In the morning we saw that the male prisoners—in the same group with the nurse and the girl—had not been lucky. There were sores, welts, cuts, bruises and a cigarette burn on one farmer's face. The Americans said they had nothing to do with VC prisoners, the South Vietnamese handled them.

A South Vietnamese captain complained that under the Phoenix program he had a quota each month for VC and VC suspects which had to be met. He did not like what I said to him about torture and demanded to know if I was wearing a Viet Cong jacket. The label on my safari jacket was from a bad tourist shop in Nairobi, but the captain was not convinced.

In the only café in Duc Duc, which was a hut with several wooden tables and stools, Luong asked the woman who served us how it went in Duc Duc. He did not ask right away; it usually took him twenty minutes of conversation, if not longer, to come to the first question. Her answer was the longest of sighs; it seemed to touch the ceiling and drift down like smoke. She mentioned the little dispensary the Americans had and how the doctor could call in airplanes to take away the sick and the wounded. He was, in fact, an older man who had once been a Special Forces medic, a man who helped any Vietnamese who came to him. Three more cups of tea, then the new question: How would she feel if the Americans left Duc Duc?

"Bad," she said.

Why?

"No more sick-planes," she said, meaning the U.S. helicopters that came in for the wounded and very ill.

Luong said there would be such planes, only they would be flown by Vietnamese, not by Americans. He did not really believe it. "That will be good, won't it?"

"No," she said. "The Americans run; the Vietnamese go slowly."

THE WOMAN IN Missouri might like that story; some people think it is very comforting. Perhaps this, too, would please them—unless they understand it. In the hamlet of Nhon Hoa, about twenty-five miles southwest of Saigon, it was decided by the Americans to create a Model Sanitary Hamlet. The site was a peaceful, lush, reasonably prosperous place on the Van Co Tay river where cucumbers, sugar cane, thick bushes of purple bougainvillaea and cocoanut trees grew and flourished. The idea came from an American public-health team—the Military Provincial Health Assistance Program Team II—based in the nearby town of Tan An. The head of the team was a major, regular Army, who was a surgeon. He said the Model Sanitary Hamlet was a self-help program and the people *wanted* to do it themselves. These were the magic words of the song that the Americans could not stop singing. The goals for the hamlet were inexpensive toilets, proper storage of drinking water, the penning of animals to keep them out of the houses, the building of sanitary wells, and to persuade women to let their dishes dry in the sun because this was hygienic procedure.

The major did not seem upset that he was not working as a surgeon in a province where the Vietnamese needed emergency medical care. The hospital in Tan An did not need him, the major said. He did not care to discuss the merits of letting dishes drain dry inside dark houses—the Vietnamese kept cooler in rooms where the sun was shut out—compared to the trouble of carrying them outdoors into the sunlight where the flies were thicker, and bugs or bird droppings might land on them. We were driven to the hamlet with a military member of the team as an escort, who was supposed to keep an eye on us.

"Health Is Gold," said a little sign in Vietnamese tacked onto a cocoanut tree. "Sanitation Makes the Hamlet Cheerful."

There were some Vietnamese who were depressed by such devotion to sanitation. A thirty-three-year-old schoolteacher found the plan puzzling because he felt it unnecessary. "Cities and towns are places where this kind of project should be carried out first," Mr. Phu, the teacher, said. "Many people of this hamlet now have latrines, as they were told to, but they never use them." They resented the cost and the work involved.

Other Vietnamese said they were either frightened to use the latrines, which were so constantly inspected, or did not choose to.

"They are good at night but in the daytime people still prefer the rice fields or the riverbanks," one man said. He showed us the latrine he built, which was impeccable. His mother, who was eighty-six and seemed no heavier than a vase of leaves, said she was quite afraid she would slip inside the outhouse. It was very slippery, she kept repeating. Her major concern, which she expressed daily in her prayers to Buddha, was that neither of her two sons, both middle-aged, would ever drink or smoke. Luong and I smelled of tobacco; the fat and wooden American with us had whiskey-eyes.

There were complaints that the hamlet chief, an amiable man, had suddenly grown rather nervous. He had been yelling at small boys who urinated in a stream to stop it immediately or they would be put in jail, although most people knew the chief had been stopping by the stream nearly all his life.

It was a quiet hamlet. There had been no fighting for three years, not even a shiver. The Vietnamese worked hard and bathed several times a day. It seemed like a fine place, except for the unpredictable influx of visitors coming to inspect the hamlet's latrines. It caused the children much excitement although it baffled many of their parents, who were made uneasy by the foreigners' intense interest in their bowel movements. Several mothers told Luong it was unnatural.

As the American and I walked up to the sign of the Model Sanitary Hamlet, two small boys spotted us and began to scream out the news.

"Look, look, more toilet-Americans," the children hollered.

IN THE MIDDLE of November 1972, when the last people I wanted to be with were professional soldiers charting their way up the chain of command, the U.S. Naval War College in Newport, Rhode Island, requested my presence at an unusual weekend seminar. It was called, those two days, "The Military and the Media: Toward an Understanding." The president of the Naval War College, Vice-Admiral Stanfield Turner, an urbane man, wrote in a

"Welcome" to the visitors: "When you think about it, our missions have as much in common as they differ, for both protect the quality of life we cherish."

I could never quite grasp that. I had not thought of myself on a mission while reporting in Vietnam, and the military there did not seem to be protecting any quality of life to be cherished. The admiral, who was no fool, added that he found a certain adversary quality between the military and the media to be healthy. He cautioned us that although some of the questions raised would be incendiary, everyone should work to discuss them both "dispassionately and unparochially . . . This conference will have failed if we allow personal and professional views to dictate judgment and conversation."

But if either group had obeyed him, the officers and the journalists would have stayed silent, the reasons for facing each other would not exist. Some of us were pushed hard by memories and perceptions that were ugly. It was hard to be mannerly, to believe that anything could be shared; even language shoved us apart, as it had always done in the war. Vietnam flooded the Pringle Auditorium like dirty river water, rising to our waists, making us all shift and turn and use voices of different pitch. I spoke—and there were others who put it better—of a lack of truthfulness and honor among the career military in Vietnam, of a tendency in them to cheat, citing how the nation's most esteemed medals were handed out like salted peanuts to field-grade officers. An example was the well-known brigadier general who received a Silver Star for acts of valor invented in a citation written by enlisted men who were ordered to do it. There is no need to give his name once more, in these pages, or the names of the officers involved—all have been printed in *The New York Times*. I grant them amnesty, for a priest who went to jail for his beliefs has told me that true amnesty must not be only for the draft evaders and the deserters, but even for the American Army, who are more in need of it. You cannot want amnesty just for one group of people, the priest said.

Afterward, at one of the War College receptions, where we were supposed to mingle, I was asked if I knew the general who had taken the Silver Star, the general to whom I caused such distress, if not embarrassment. I said no, we had never met. The officer at the reception assured me he was a fine fellow, one of the best, which made it clear that nothing I said had made a difference in the Pringle Auditorium, which was that men who practice deceit with medals or body counts are neither men of honor nor of valor. What I remember most clearly is another officer—most of them wore civilian clothes, which disguised nothing—who rose, after one panel finished, to ask why correspondents were sent to cover the war in Vietnam when they knew nothing about war or the military. It was a stunning question because he asked it sadly and sincerely.

"A sports editor wouldn't send someone to cover a football game who was a novice, would he?" the officer said. He felt it was a shame that the press corps knew so little; perhaps he meant me and guessed I knew nothing of small-unit infantry tactics, of weaponry, or figuring out the range of mortars. I had sat through dozens of briefings in Vietnam and never learned anything, ever.

In the bar after dinner, in the officers' open mess, another man asked me if Seymour Hersh, the reporter, was queer. He did not seem either a stupid or a vicious man. His eyes were a little too large for a correct military face, which should look sterner, more shut-down. I assured him Mr. Hersh was married, had two children, and certainly liked women. Did the officer want to go to the table where Mr. Hersh sat and be introduced? He refused, saying it was a shame what a man like Hersh had done. I do not know if he meant Mr. Hersh's reports on the My Lai massacre, or the story on the massacre at another hamlet called My Khe, his disclosure of the Army's attempts to cover up both, or the stories on the secret bombings of Cambodia. There was no reporter in the United States who had written the stories that Mr. Hersh had written, and has kept on writing, and he was hated for it. The rest of us, even a most famous novelist who were there, did not matter much.

It was a sad weekend with the well-mannered admirals and the promising battalion commanders, for underneath the rich lacquer of the U.S. Naval War College the different shades of anger splattered and smoked. The weekend reminded me—as nothing else had done for many years—how once I had thought of career officers as being grand and stoical men, made of superior stuff. As a schoolgirl I had seen World War II newsreels: the tanks with the long noses that were guns, the air raids, the searchlights moving back and forth like pointing fingers, the people looking cold. It was impossible not to believe in those years that Americans did not make up a warm-hearted, gallant, resourceful army led by officers who preferred to die rather than be dishonored. Each American generation is glued to its own moral imperatives and it is hard to rip them out of yourself. I cannot now understand why I thought for so much of my life that it was a lovable and self-correcting army, could not see the contradictions in this. It surely could not just have been the movie made of *The Young Lions*, in which the terrible sergeant is at last found out and court-martialed for treatment of an enlisted man.

When as a young woman I lived in Europe for nine years it pleased me to hear older people in Belgium and France occasionally say how *gentil* the American soldiers had been, what generous allies. In the villages of Europe, I would sometimes catch the names of men, from places in my own country I had never heard of, who had given away food or a blanket, and never been forgotten. The sight of them had made Europeans rejoice. Only one Frenchwoman complained to me of how clumsily the Americans had bombed in Orléans. She insisted the British were much more precise, and it made me furious. That was in 1964. Korea taught me nothing, for no one spoke of it when I was growing up, except something about how wonderful the girls in Japan were. Vietnam taught some of us more than we perhaps ever wished to know.

THE REVOLT OF the enlisted men in the Awards and Decorations Office, Adjutant General Section, 15th Administration Company, of the 1st Air Cavalry Division's base camp at Bien Hoa began on the night of October 5, 1970. The soldiers who worked in Awards and Decorations were called in and ordered to prepare a descriptive narration of acts of valor so that the brigadier general—who had been assistant division commander for five months—could quickly receive a Silver Star before he left the 1st Cav for another assignment.

"That night I was at a party—a kind of movable feast in one guy's hootch—when I'm called in by the captain. He doesn't know how to do it, so I become inspirational and Napoleonic," Private James Olstad said.

The captain, whom the men liked, appeared bitter about the order but insisted the citation had to be ready by eight the next morning even if the men had to stay up all night. He also said to make it for something done in the Cambodian operation. Specialist 4 George Tillinghast protested mildly to the captain, to no avail. The captain's orders came from two majors at Bien Hoa, who were aware that no realistic records of any kind for the general were available. Specialist 4 Roy Trent, Jr., was so disgusted that he quit the office, leaving the work to be done by the two experts, Tillinghast and Olstad. There was nothing to go on, not a date or a scrap of information or eyewitness reports of what the brigadier general might have done.

Private Olstad, who came from Cashton, Wisconsin, and was a student at Dartmouth College before he was inducted in the Army in November 1969, was an exceptionally clever and poetic fellow whose work in Awards and Decorations was to polish, tighten or rewrite recommendations sent in for individual acts of valor. He had been doing it for four months. They were normally based on eyewitness statements and endorsed at company, brigade and battalion level in the division, which was then the second largest in Vietnam. The twenty-two-year-old private was known among his peers as a man of much talent.

"He's a born artist," Specialist 4 Trent said. He was well-read, mocking, brilliant, and totally unimpressed by the Army and what it required of him. Olstad's face was thin and too inquisitive, too alive, for him to be an acceptable private. Specialist 4 George Tillinghast, who at twenty-six was the oldest of the men in the office, handled special awards and knew the files. He was as intelligent but more conventional than Olstad, who, possibly because of the party and the state it left him in, made sure that the citation bore his special stamp.

That night, to inspire themselves, the two enlisted men borrowed bits from the Silver Star citation awarded to another 1st Cav general who had commanded the five-day task force carried out by the Americans and South Vietnamese troops in the Fishhook area of Cambodia in June 1970. They needed to be reminded of what phrases the Army preferred in such citations. "Dynamic leadership" was always a favorite, so was "courage and devotion to duty." It was axiomatic that the citation would end by stating that the actions of the officer were "in keeping with the highest traditions of the military service and reflect great credit upon himself, his unit and the United States Army."

The men picked the date of June 9 because it was the twenty-first birthday of Specialist 4 Richard Kemkens, who worked with them. It was also the birthday of his wife, so that made it a fine date for made-up history.

The citation began modestly, describing how on June 9, 1970, while flying with a co-pilot in his own command helicopter on a visual reconnaissance, the brigadier general spotted a ground unit near Fire Support Base Bronco in Cambodia taking fire from the enemy.

It was a normal beginning, but then Olstad, the poet and the cynic, went too far and could not stop himself. The citation went on to describe how the general's aircraft, flying overhead as a firefight took place on the ground, made radio contact with the troops, who were perilously low on ammunition. In the draft, Olstad described the general as making "an immediate and flawlessly competent determination on the course of action to be followed."

The general called in and coordinated supporting artillery fire to within one hundred meters of the American troops, Olstad wrote, and ordered his pilot to descend to a lower level in order to make sure his adjustments were correct and that no Americans were endangered. The aircraft came under enemy fire from light automatic weapons and machine guns.

"Ignoring this threat to his aircraft, and disregarding the personal danger to himself, he continued with his observations and adjustments, keeping the tactical situation calmly and totally in control," Olstad wrote. The general flew back to Bronco for the necessary ordnance for the troops, returned to the area of contact, personally aided in the kick-out of the ammunition, and directed that casualties be placed aboard his aircraft. He flew them to the nearest facilities for the wounded. That was the part Olstad liked best in the citation. It was also the most dangerous part, for no records existed of such casualties being evacuated or treated.

"Brigadier General _____'s conspicuous gallantry and decisive leadership were the deciding factors in turning a desperate situation into a defeat of a determined enemy force," Olstad typed.

It was something of a masterpiece as citations go. Although the final version was more compressed and a bit flatter than Private

Olstad's original work, omitting one or two thunderous tributes to the general's abilities, it contained all the information the men had dreamed up. The private kept a copy of the draft so he could prove it was nearly identical to the citation.

Everyone was pleased. At Phuoc Vinh, headquarters of the 1st Cav, the chief of staff, a colonel, was delighted when he read it. It was the colonel who told his own staff to get moving on the citation. They did, by sending urgent instructions to Bien Hoa. When the colonel received the citation he said "Well, by God, it's about time."

"I reviewed it and quite honestly I was elated," the colonel later said to me in Phuoc Vinh. "It read like a dream."

The chief of staff said he had not checked the citation and had assumed there were legitimate records available. He said the brigadier general was such a modest man, he had not wanted to embarrass him by going to his personal crew for details but that he had often heard of the general's exploits. "It sounded exactly like what I expected it to be—you know, what I heard discussed in the mess halls, that he was in the thick of everything," the colonel said of the fictitious citation.

The brigadier general had been given the Silver Star on October 15 at a small awards ceremony at Phuoc Vinh. The Army claimed he did not have the citation and was unaware of how it was prepared.

It was Specialist 4 Roy L. Trent, Jr., who refused to forget and who wanted justice done. In the Awards and Decorations office at Bien Hoa, he sat next to an enlisted man who typed letters of sympathy to the families of those who died in Vietnam. That may have done it. Trent wanted a letter giving details of the incident to go to the late Mendel L. Rivers, chairman of the House Armed Services Committee. None of them knew that Congressman Rivers was hardly disposed to revealing or correcting such a practice.

It was the "born artist" Olstad who composed it, informing the congressman of "a grave infraction of military policy and an abominable insult to the integrity and intelligence of all lower-grade enlisted personnel." Private Olstad wrote that an inquiry should be initiated for several reasons, among them "the vile reflection one can perceive cast by these events on the entire American military structure." It was Roy Trent's letter, but the five others, including Olstad, signed it although some of them knew too well what consequences they might face. Perhaps it was Olstad's idea to send a copy to *The New York Times*. They never did hear from Congressman Rivers' office.

"I wanted to write to Nixon—there are guys in the field getting killed, really acting with valor, and sometimes nothing is submitted for them to get an award, or their awards are downgraded, even if they are approved," Trent said to me.

There was a terrible fuss. It was the strict policy of the *Times* that the accused must be told of the charges and given a chance to reply. At Bien Hoa, I had to track down the two majors who had ordered the captain to order the citation written. One of them stayed calm but his hands began to shake uncontrollably, until he finally put them in his lap where I could not see. The cast of incriminated officers was large. One lieutenant colonel thought the enlisted men had sent the letters because they were "disgusted at having to work late."

The bureau chief of *The New York Times* and I went out to Tan Son Nhut to speak to high-ranking information officers at MACV headquarters and then we flew in a helicopter to Phuoc Vinh to see the colonel who had started it all and whose career was now in trouble. He was charming and controlled on what must have been one of the most horrid days of his life, for he well knew that the Army does not look kindly on chiefs of staff of a division who make a mess of getting one medal to one general. I might have almost liked him if he had not said he thought the enlisted men were being "sanctimonious."

The cruelest part of the meeting with the colonel was when—still insisting that the award was valid—he summoned the general's aide to say yes, yes, it was true that it all happened on June 9. The aide said he was in the helicopter. Even the colonel looked sad as the lieutenant stuttered and moved his feet and half shut his eyes. He tried to defend the general. I did not take notes on the lieutenant's moment of disgrace, I just looked down at my sneakers. I seem to remember that he was a southern Baptist and made some mention of going in the ministry.

When the colonel realized at last that I was going to write the story, his final plea to me was based on everything he thought was decent and maternal in women. "If you print the story, think how it will affect the mothers of all our dead boys who won decorations."

It was a mistake. I was thinking of all the dead, just as Trent and Olstad and the four others had been thinking of them. For a long time I was afraid that the enlisted men would be punished and sent into the field despite being clerk-typists, for even cooks could be shifted around in Vietnam, whose every corner was considered a combat zone and every man expected to fire a rifle.

It was Private Norman Shantz, a New York boy, who during the peak of the Army's frenzy, said what had made them do it. "The lifers lie to us, expect us to carry out the lies for them, and then, see, we can't say anything back to them." I said yes, I saw that. The officers looked on the enlisted men as "nothing much," Shantz said. He and the others saw the officers not as courageous men making lonely decisions but as men willing to accept pettiness, untruths, a rigid and relentless pecking order, and even glad to do it.

When the Army turned its eyes on him, Private Olstad did not wither in the hot white blaze of their disapproval. He was certainly not nervous about any impending punishment. None came. The enlisted men were protected by the publicity they had received. The Army would have risked losing even more by slamming down on the culprits who were telling the truth.

"It is possible that the brigadier general could have seen a lot of action, but he did not see this action and the Silver Star award he accepted is for action that never existed," Olstad kept saying. "He is an accomplice for accepting it." When I asked him for other examples of citations he had written for awards for valor to high-ranking officers, he said he had done dozens of them. He could not remember the names of officers because there had been so many of them. In cases where the Army did not supply sufficient information, he had only one course of action and the Army knew it. He added that he did not claim the recipients of the awards were unworthy in every case. "I just make it up," Private Olstad said. "I don't know what they did."

Olstad said he did not believe in the concept of medals in a war. In fact, he did not believe in war. "Sadly, there are many who believe in decorations and what they mean. I may disagree with them, but I respect the sincerity of their beliefs. Given this difference of opinion, I still do my job. I support that other man's faith to this extent. I have a soft life—I am not being shot at, I am not slogging through mud, I am not sleeping in the rain," he said. "If that other man believes an award is adequate compensation for his sacrifices, I will attempt to maintain the integrity of that belief. If a man performs an act of valor and receives an award for it, I see no justification in an officer, a general, let us say, receiving a higher decoration for no action whatsoever."

That was Private Olstad being openly, unabashedly solemn, but at heart he preferred satire. The Silver Star inspired him to write a poem, which he sent me. It went:

> "Why yes, I earned the medal,
> Of course," the general said.
> He went into his toilet,

He believed it in his head.
With his little wooden soldiers
And his tiny tin-tin men
He crumbled all his enemies
And frightened all his friends.
Behind his bathroom door
He fought his Mitty war,
Emerged again a victor
He came panting after more.
Let me go into battle
A Hero I shall be,
I'm forty-four, I'm still alive,
And the Army's mind . . . is me."

On October 28, 1970, a printed memorandum for correspondents was distributed by the U.S. Army which said that the brigadier general was not aware of the circumstances relating to the preparation of the citation for the Silver Star and that he had not read it until his return from a leave. The general, when informed of the circumstances, left the matter in the hands of Army authorities for resolution, the memorandum said. Action was taken to rescind the Silver Star "due to administrative irregularities" which the Army said had been disclosed by its own inquiry.

The general took over his new job, in Saigon, which was the assistant chief of staff for the agency known as Civil Operations and Rural Development Support. Called CORDS, it was directed by American civilians and military who headed what was called the pacification program and whose stated objectives in South Vietnam were:

TERRITORIAL SECURITY
PROTECTION OF THE PEOPLE FROM TERRORISM
PEOPLE'S SELF DEFENSE
LOCAL ADMINISTRATION

GREATER NATIONAL UNITY
BRIGHTER LIFE FOR WAR VICTIMS
PEOPLE'S INFORMATION
PROSPERITY FOR ALL

There were letters about the medal story from readers, some belligerent, others reminiscent. One of them came from a man named John Maas in Philadelphia.

> Your "Silver Star for General" story takes me back to 1944 when I was a clerk in a Heavy Bomber Group of the Army Air Forces in Italy.
>
> A major had his heart set on getting a "Distinguished Unit Citation" for the Group. He picked out the mission of which we had the best pictures and wrote up a fine presentation. The photographs still did not look sufficiently dramatic, so he had me put in flak bursts with charcoal pencil (I was a commercial artist in civilian life). Then we rephotographed the doctored photos.
>
> We got the Citation and the pretty blue ribbon with the gold border.
>
> I can't say that I was upset at the time. It seemed like a just war. Now I am twenty-six years older and wiser and convinced of the total depravity of the U.S. Army. I am glad you exposed that racket, which has probably been going on since George Washington.

The file is still with me: more than fifty citations for medals awarded to generals in Vietnam; one colonel is included. They are for the Silver Star or Distinguished Flying Cross. Some of them have the flair and drama that Olstad himself quite relished. The generals are always flying their command and control helicopters in extremely hazardous flying conditions, with complete disregard for their own safety, to assist and direct rifle companies on the ground in contact with the enemy. The generals do it all. They arrange for artillery and air support, they sight enemy positions, they order the door gunners to open up, they give tactical guidance, they bring in more ammunition, they get out the wounded. Sometimes they come down and stay. It is, as one citation says of a general, to confer with their subordinate commanders and to urge on the troops in pressing the attack.

Only one general did operate on the ground, so unusual a thing that his citation noted it and said: "It was from this vantage point that he felt he could best estimate and determine more fully the tactical situation." The general is praised. "Regardless of the continuous and heavy volume of rockets, automatic weapons and mortar fire, he was on the ground inspiring and giving confidence . . ." the citation goes on, as if it was much more heroic for a general to put up with such danger than a draftee.

The citations always end by commending the officers for gallantry/ outstanding courage and devotion to duty/ valorous actions/ disregard for personal safety and courageous determination/ selfless dedication to duty and great personal bravery/ extraordinary heroism/ gallantry in the face of withering enemy fire/ in keeping with the highest traditions of the military service and reflect great credit upon himself, his unit and the United States Army.

But it was the draftees who gradually came to represent an increasing proportion of the soldiers who risked the most and whose deaths rose. In 1965 draftees represented only 16 percent of the total battle deaths in the war; a year later they constituted 21 percent. By 1967 they made up 34 percent; in 1969, 40 percent; and in 1970, 43 percent of all those killed in action, according to a Nader report on veterans. By 1969, 62 percent of all Army deaths, due to combat or hostile causes, were draftees. Draftees represented 70 percent of all combat soldiers for the fiscal year 1970.

In 1969 the casualty rate for Army draftees was 234 per 1,000. The lower their education and socioeconomic background, the higher their chances for being wounded or killed. "The Army assumed a remarkable shape in Vietnam," Paul Starr wrote in his Nader study. "In most organizations it is the permanent long-standing members who usually take on the most critical tasks; the more transient and less-skilled members are relegated to support roles. But not so in the Army during the Vietnam war. There the 'regulars' did less of the fighting than the amateurs who had been pressed into the enterprise against their will."

Sixteen million one hundred and twelve thousand five hundred and sixty-six American men served in the Armed Forces between December 1941 and 1946. For a long time I kept asking World War II veterans, especially those who had been enlisted men in the infantry, what they thought of Vietnam, of the ordeal of a new generation of riflemen the ages of their sons. But most did not think about the war at all. In New York the fastest way to meet such veterans was to take taxis, for they are still driving them.

But it became more and more meaningless, and the little talks in the taxis cost too much. The older veterans did not have much to say, they did not have pity for the men doing what they once did, or concern, or fury. They were passive, detached, and usually willing to tell stories of what had happened to them thirty-odd years ago. Sometimes the stories lasted all the way from the 59th Street Bridge to La Guardia Airport. There were drivers who said the GIs in Vietnam had it easier because of helicopters dropping them in or lifting them out of combat. One man laughed and said Vietnam was a better place to be wounded than during the Battle of the Bulge in Belgium, where anyone who could still stand had to go on fighting, even if he was bleeding. It was that way, he said, there were no choppers coming in for them.

Another cabdriver of Italian parentage said that when he

worked at Walter Reed Hospital some nurses who had survived
Bataan were in a special mental ward and behaved strangely. It
was very sad; some nurses screamed and pulled off their clothes.
Lots of soldiers acted strangely too, this pleasant and serious man
said. He had been a medical technician in Italy at a convalescent
center for troops not severely hurt. They all had to go back to
their units. Some of the soldiers pleaded with him to help reas-
sign them to the convalescent center, or not to discharge them
so soon, but he could do nothing. At night they became other
people, the driver said, they seemed to shrink and made noises
when they slept. He should have thought of becoming a nurse
and going to school, but he had not planned enough. He hadn't
paid much attention to Vietnam, it probably cost too much, a lot
of people probably made money, and look at all the potholes in
Manhattan and in Queens which hadn't been fixed. It was the
best work he ever had, the driver said about World War II, just
before I left him.

In Texas, miles outside of Houston, another World War II
veteran—who shall be called Max Wilson—wanted to tell everything, for he saw himself not just as a survivor but as a man who
had profited from the war more cleverly than all the others. He
lives in a fancy residential community where the low big houses
rim a large man-made lake and sit apart from each other in a rich,
solemn stillness. His house, which has several bedrooms, a very
long living room and a kitchen-dining area where twelve people
could easily be seated, is on an acre and a half of land, so the value
of the property could be as high as two hundred and fifty thousand dollars. The house was full of American triumphs. In the
kitchen Mr. Wilson and his wife, who works in his silk-screen
supply business, have the largest and the yellowest refrigerator I
have ever seen. Then there was the Corning stove top, a flat white
surface which has no grill or visible heat, and the trash masher
that does just what its name says. Mr. Wilson demonstrated how

the stove and the trash masher work, showed me the bathroom with a built-in black-marble shower and sink, and his collection of fancy Jim Beam whiskey bottles from the years 1955 to 1975 which were displayed on bookshelves in the living room. The couple have four children, two boys and two girls, ranging in age from twenty-nine to eighteen.

There is night jasmine blooming outside the back door where you walk down to a little pier and the boat they own. The stereo can be heard even here because Mr. Wilson installed an outdoor speaker. No one would simply let the door open to hear the music because the house is intensely, perfectly, centrally air-conditioned.

Mr. Wilson, who spent two and a half years in Army hospitals after he was badly wounded in the right hand, has a good many souvenirs and treasures he collected during World War II. They are a source of deep pleasure. "They remind me of good times," he said. "I like to look at them."

On his left hand he wears a heavy gold ring with an intricate crest that a barber in the United States once assured him belonged to the Royal Family of Italy. The barber, an Italian, was curious about the ring. Mr. Wilson first said the ring was his father's heirloom, but the barber knew better and explained the crest to him. Then he said how he had taken the ring off the hand of a captured Italian officer. Mr. Wilson was not sure if the man had been an officer but he was sure the man had been "something."

"They called me 'Loot' and his Forty Thieves," he said, laughing a little. He was drafted in 1941, trained as an M.P. and fingerprint expert, then went into the infantry where after Officers Candidate School he was commissioned a first lieutenant. He served with heavy weapons, an infantryman in the 3d Division, in General Mark Clark's Seventh Army. He was in campaigns in Africa, in Italy, in France. Mr. Wilson is a large, blunt, hard-working, humorous man with a very military grey mustache that has waxed and curled ends. It looks like the fierce and theatrical mustache of a British sergeant major in World War I. Mr. Wilson called his mustache a "breaker"; it reminded some people of a Calvert's Man of Distinction advertisement, he said. He remembers the Allied invasion of Sicily in July 1943 and the four months at Anzio. American troops were landed there to draw German forces away from Cassino, where the Allied advance to Rome was being blocked. The 3d Division, which could not retreat except into the sea, was trapped at Anzio by intense German bombardments. The Americans were on the flat ground, the Germans above them.

"They had their Big Berthas—which took up two railroad cars—pointing down on us. They could see us—when we went to the latrine, they knew it, they knew what color paper we used, they knew everything," Mr. Wilson said. "They were looking right down your throat. It was like a doctor looking down your throat."

The damp cold hammered at them; they tore up blankets and wrapped them around their boots. They slept with blankets covering their faces like heavy veils hanging under their helmets, and they never stopped being cold. His mother-in-law managed to mail him fresh eggs, which arrived unbroken because she packed them so cleverly. The smell of the eggs frying drove other men wild. They lived in holes and in caves which they dug, where they made peat fires and huddled by them.

"They put in screaming-meemies. The Germans are very good at rockets—there was a bunch of rockets they had which had no directional. They would send out these six or eight rockets and it would just go into an area like the old archers used to send out bows. Or as if you took a handful of pebbles and threw them out. You never knew where they were going to go. The sound itself, when you heard them coming, was enough to kill you."

When the break-out came, when it finally came, it took them a week to get to Rome. That was June 1944. Mr. Wilson claims he got to Rome at five in the morning and that General Clark came at seven. On the way out of Anzio, men in his company captured one hundred and thirty-three Germans.

"We started in fleecing them down," Mr. Wilson said. There were one or two Germans who were older—the ages of the Americans—but the rest of the prisoners looked fourteen or fifteen years old. "When I captured a prisoner I told him 'I'm a Jew,' and I laughed at him. I'd say '*Ich bin Yid*'—I let them know I was a Jew capturing them, and if they didn't move fast enough, I'd shoot at their feet and then they got the message—*Ich bin Yid*, move, *macht schnell*.

"I had wristwatches from the prisoners; I had them all up my arm on this side and that side. And as I was walking up the street other infantry people, or officers, would come to me saying 'Hey, what kind of watches you got? How much for this one?' I'd sell. I made a fortune just like that. We couldn't just fight the war for the politicians back in the United States . . . Well, I took everything. I had an idea what's valuable. Some of my men, they wanted money. When we would capture prisoners I told them 'Okay, you guys take the money, I'll take the jewelry.'"

He said he really had a good time in Italy. The odd thing is that he does not even seem to mind the months at Anzio when the men could not even move, when it rained so much they even slept in wetness. "When it was all over, it was just one of those things," Mr. Wilson said. "When you look back at it, and you came out of it alive, you had a good time."

In Rome the 3d Division policed the city. He saw the Pope. He became much richer. He bartered candy bars and soap and everything else. And he knew how much he wanted the ring with the family crest when he saw it on the hand of the Italian. "He had nothing to say about it, I had a Baretta at his head," Mr. Wilson said. "I had nothing against the Italians, I had nothing against anybody, all I wanted was jewelry and things of— Look, the men liked me. They'd have killed for me. In this fact, this Italian with the ring almost got killed because he was a little reluctant to take it off. And my men told the guy either you take it off or you don't go anywhere in life. He took it off. Then we sold his car, he had a little Fiat, we sold that to a bunch of Australian soldiers who had a big two-and-a-half-ton truck. They pushed the little Fiat up into the back of the truck.

"I liberated a lot of things in Rome. I got sterling silver from the Grand Hotel, I liberated that. I've got sterling silver that you wouldn't believe. I had to fight the war for some reason. We were using sterling silver in this house for breakfast, dinner and supper. And I'm talking about out of the Grand Hotel in Rome! And I took good things. I hit the glasses and listened to them ring. And if they rang nice, I packed them up and sent them home.

"My mother-in-law always expected to find a dead body being shipped home because I was sending stuff home left and right. Southern France was a lot better than Italy, see, for the good times. The people there, well, you could talk to the people."

On D Day his division landed at St. Tropez; he remembers even now the sweet French cantaloupes they gorged on. "We walked sixty-one miles the first day," Mr. Wilson said. "We walked sixty-one miles the first day."

He said he landed in the long-awaited invasion of Southern France with a blanket folded and tied up, like a scarf, which held twenty cartons of cigarettes, about fifteen bars of soap and twenty Hershey bars from the PX in Italy. He did not smoke. It rained for three nights and he had no raincoat and he could not use the blanket as a cover because it held all the precious things that were wanted so much by the French.

"I want to tell you one incident that happened to me, though. One day I had a loaf of bread, I was coming out of this bakery in a village. Some refugee, a Jewish refugee, come up to me. He asked for some. I says 'Yeah.' I cut him a piece. Then he asked me for some more than what I gave him, and I said 'You goddamned Jews, I mean we're fighting this war for you and now I give you enough bread and now you want all of this. I mean listen, this don't go. We're taking care of you and that's it.' I mean, a Jew to a Jew. I mean there's some people like that in this world. You give them an arm and they'll ask—"

"He might have been starving," I said.

"If he was, all right. But how many other soldiers could he have gone up to, too? A GI is a very outgoing person. *When a GI is in a war he'll give you anything you want. He doesn't give a damn. I mean if a dog is hurt he'll stop the war and fix that dog.* He'll take care of it. *That's how a GI is.* Anyway, that was one little incident there."

He wanted to make a dollar, as Mr. Wilson puts it.

When elements of the 3d Division were sent into the Alps—he thinks they were near Grenoble—the men were in snow up to their knees. They slept on the snow and lived in it. There was talk among some enlisted men and some officers of leaving the war. "We were close enough to Switzerland that there were times we said to hell with it, let's walk that way, and we get interned in Switzerland, we were that close to Switzerland. Well, no, not deserting, just let the war take care of itself and we'll take care of ourselves." But they did not.

Not once, in the hours we talked, did he ever mention a close friend in his unit or talk about the wounded and the dead. There were those, but he skipped over them.

He was wounded in November 1944. He kept calling it "a million-dollar wound," but I argued with him. It wasn't that at all: a "million-dollar wound" is one that gets you off the line without resulting in mutilation or deformities. A million-dollar wound, the GIs used to say in Vietnam, was being hit in the rump, in the fleshy part, not in the rectum, someplace where it didn't cause too much pain or scar you up. Mr. Wilson's hand was hit by fragments of a mortar. It went through his glove, through the skin, removed the knuckle and cut the tendons. He was not unconscious. In that war there was no medic assigned to each platoon; the men all had first-aid kits and took care of each other. It happened when the company was moving near Strasbourg, on the side of a river. The platoon had walked through a marked minefield to reach a roadway when the attack mortars hit them. Mr. Wilson tried to help the men who were most badly hurt, the ones with the open wounds, then told one of his men to go back to get help. The soldier said no, he didn't want to have to cross that minefield again. So Mr. Wilson did. And all the time, holding the mashed and dripping hand, he did not worry about stepping on a mine that might not have been marked. He only thought of how he would never be able to pull a bow and arrow again. Archery was very important to him when he was that young. He reached an aid station, sent help back to the platoon, and was treated.

Born in January 1917, he was the first son of a corset maker, one of four children who grew up in Staten Island with hopeful, loving, attentive parents. His father was a Russian immigrant, his mother's parents were Russian. He moved to Texas in 1950 and has been married thirty-two years. None of the children gave him any problems, he said, they all abhor drugs. He wanted his second son, an architect, to go into the Army. But Vietnam did not seem to interest him very much. Mr. Wilson looked puzzled when I asked why, since he knew so much about war, he would want younger men to go through what he had endured.

"It makes a person out of you," Mr. Wilson said. "Because without pain you don't know what it's like, you have no way of telling." His twenty-one-year-old daughter, who wanted to study fashion, said very quietly that she disagreed with her father about Vietnam. At a junior college in Texas she saw a number of Vietnam veterans; several were paraplegics or disabled in other ways. Her father did not seem upset by such soft-spoken if firm opposition. He wasn't sure of how the other children felt because he said he had not "polled" them.

"I say this: that everybody, every man, should belong to the Army, to the armed services. They will learn discipline. No, my son didn't want to go. But in the Army when you give them an order to do something, they've got to do it and not say 'Ah, I don't want to do it,' like in a parent-son relationship. You get more people killed in automobiles than you do by war, so your chances of dying are slight.

"I'll be honest with you, if they had taken my sons into the Army, I wouldn't have cared. But if they were going to send them overseas, I was ready to go to Washington and tell those bastards that they're full of crap, that they weren't going to send my sons there until they decided to declare war. That's right. *I wanted a war to win. And that's the only way to play. You play to win, an American plays to win.* And we could have won the war, by bombing or burning the goddamned place."

I spoke of a man in Pittsburgh, a bartender, who had been wrecked by his son's death in Vietnam and who could not seem to stop grieving. He had refused to accept a posthumous decoration for his son.

"I wouldn't be destroyed because I've been in war, I know that in war there's death," he said. But he thought that his wife would have "broken up" if a son had even gone to Vietnam. His children were a different story from the people of his generation. They had never missed a meal in their lives, Mr. Wilson said. They never missed a meal in their lives, but he could remember soup made of hot water and catsup.

"Today's kids don't have patriotism and they're very selfish. They don't have anything, it's just 'I, I, I.' *They want to be either left alone as pacifists or—I don't even know if they'd even fight if somebody tried to steal something from them, some of these kids, you see?*"

He thought the antiwar movement had been disgusting. "It was atrocious and very unpatriotic," Mr. Wilson said. "And very bad for the children themselves because it's going to be a stigma against them later on down the line. As they get older, the Russians will have an idea of who they were and what they were, and as our country starts going they know that these people are weak—because they couldn't stand the gaff of the Army, that's probably what it was."

He could not understand any male who refused induction. Most of the men who had bought homes and land in his community felt the same way; they were ex-GIs.

"We know that your chances of being killed is very remote. So the kid has a little bit of a hard time living in the outdoors, but it'll make a man out of him," Mr. Wilson said. "The Army'll make a man out of you if you're a sissy or stuff like that. If these kids would turn as much energy toward fighting taxes as they did about the war, this country has a better chance of survival. You see, we're paying tax, tax, tax . . ."

I told Mr. Wilson he didn't seem like a poor man to me, despite his taxes. He said there is no poor man any more. Uncle Sam pays him.

He was sorry that he had never used the G.I. Bill of Rights. "I didn't have an education. They tell you with an education you can make five hundred thousand to a million dollars a year. I could have made more money. I have a happy life, but see, I could have been educated. I could have been a lawyer or a dentist, those are the two that I would have liked to have been. See, I've got a different background than the average guy. Before the Depression my folks had a little; after the Depression we had nothing. I bummed around New York State and worked on farms. I went to South America on a tramp steamer. I was a wanderer, I had a wanderlust, I wandered all over this world. I was in the CCC—the Civilian Conservation Corps—when I was seventeen. I learned discipline. I geared myself. Hell, there was one time I was hitch-hiking through Niagara Falls and I went to the police station and asked them to put me up for the night. 'We can't, son,' they said. 'We'll have to book you if we put you in jail.'"

He tried to find a doorway he could sleep in. He remembers falling asleep on a scale outside of Woolworth's until a policeman came and told him he would be picked up. He ended sleeping on a chair which he put inside a pit near a gasoline station.

"In the morning I got up and walked away. Now as I look back on it, it was something that helped make a man out of me," Mr. Wilson said.

When I suggested that the Depression might have scared him to death, been worse than the wound to his hand, he looked amused and denied it.

Mr. Wilson thought I made too much fuss about casualties in Vietnam. "Now, every man wants to live," he said. "But the trouble is we're all born to die. So what the hell is the difference if we die when we're eighty or if we die when we're twenty-six."

A lot of difference, I said.

"Maybe it is. Not when you see things happening and you got this trouble and all the crap on you. Maybe sometimes you wish oh Jesus, I wish I were dead. No, I don't wish that. I want to live a long life but I don't want to live long enough to see the Russians get over here. Their people will be in power. We'll have Americans, but the strings will be pulled in Russia, just like in Poland, or in Czechoslovakia."

His wife had a relative who had been an M.P. in Vietnam; the experience bored Max Wilson. "He thought the war was rough. I told him he doesn't know what rough is. And that no war is rough. It's what you make of it. But if he went over there with a chip on his shoulder, if you want to look at the bad side of things, then the time in Vietnam could be rough. I guess he was against the war, I don't know. I really never asked him. I don't even bother with him because he's so straight-laced. Goddamn, he'll arrest his own mother if she did wrong. He thinks J. Edgar Hoover was the sun and the moon and the stars, or he did when Hoover was alive."

None of the men who lived as he lived, who had been in the war, who worked as hard as he did, were for amnesty, Mr. Wilson said. "There'll always be a war, because as the population grows you gotta knock people off the earth," he said. "They're not for amnesty toward these kids. Let them suffer."

Afterward we went into the Wilson's bedroom. He kept talking about Sorrento and a jeweler he knew there who taught him how to tell good cameo from bad cameo in exchange for the bread Mr. Wilson gave him. There was one pin that the jeweler had made of marquise diamonds with his wife's initials on it. It was shaped like a dog. He wanted to show it to me. But he couldn't find it in Mrs. Wilson's top drawer or jewelry box. That bothered him. He really kept rummaging for it. But then, holding up a cameo to the light so I could see what a good piece it was, he looked happy again. He was thinking of the good times. The point is that he had risen above the war, it had not made him a loser, he had his triumphs, you could touch them.

THE PHOTOGRAPHER NAMED Denis Cameron really liked the American pilots; it didn't matter what they flew, B-52s or the little Hueys. The pilots were interested in his cameras, those lenses and filters and how he took pictures. There was no one better. During Lam Son 719, there seemed to be dozens of photographers covering the drive into Laos, some saying this was the last big push of the war, when it was not. They wore little towels around their necks like mufflers to soak up the wetness, they never wore dark glasses as the reporters did, and they hated having to photograph in that deadly, dusty glare at Khe Sanh.

Newsweek assigned Cameron to do a big spread on all the Army helicopters used in that massive operation. He took pictures of the little fat UH-1 Huey, called a slick or bird, which cost $300,000, and of the daintier OH-6 for observation which cost $100,000. He did the Cobra gunship—cost, $500,000; the CH-47 Chinook for troop and cargo transport which cost $1,500,000 and could lift 19,000 pounds of cargo or twenty-four injured men; and the Flying Crane, the $2,000,000 CH-54 which took a 20,000-pound load of equipment. It was a stupid assignment for that March in 1971—a child's primer on helicopters which had been used for more than ten years—when a lost army was lurching to its grave, when the lies in Washington and Quang Tri, Khe Sanh and Saigon were more baroque than usual, when the very word Vietnamization was not just a joke but a word for slaughter. He took all the pictures, but what he wanted to do was photograph the pilots and crews; they made him happy.

But his first picture in the *Newsweek* spread was of a dead man, face down on a stretcher, with a Huey in the background. You knew he was American by the length of him, but you could see nothing of the face or the head inside the helmet, nothing of the body concealed by a flight suit or the boots. The left arm hung over the stretcher and what showed was no more than a wrist. The photograph had been taken in that Khe Sanh glare, the light so harsh you could not see the faces of the men carrying that weight. There were so many shadows.

One woman saw *Newsweek* and knew, without question, the pilot was hers. All the mail on the photographs was sent by *Newsweek* to Denis Cameron, who was asked to identify the men. Two women thought their husbands were on the stretcher. One of them was right, for the pilot was First Lieutenant A.M. (Butch) Simpson. The wife wrote to *Newsweek*, who cabled Cameron. He cabled back yes, it was Lieutenant Simpson, whom he had known and liked. Her letter rattled us, for the picture showed nothing more than a wrist. The photographer had no idea how she knew; no one has ever explained it. He wrote the widow. Sheryl Simpson wrote him back in April:

> If you happen to have any more pictures of Butch or any other information concerning him, I'd very much like to have it and will take care of any costs involved. I'm greatly indebted for all that you did. I hope that somebody is looking after you—I know that you are in just as much danger as the troops over there.

It was not quite true. The press corps could always pull out. Unlike the troops, we were all there for a good story, to advance our careers and go on making money, war profiteers of a kind, but more useful than most.

In one of the other pictures, Cameron photographed a thin and young man with very long legs, one foot in the doorway of an observation helicopter. A man named Bennett wrote from Saufus, Maine, because the image, he said, "beared a great likeness to a very dear nephew of mine who was a helicopter pilot in Southeast Asia until his death last February." In May, Mrs. E. Schlutter wrote from Sheboygan, Wisconsin, thinking it might be a picture of her son, also a pilot, who had been killed that March. I have told the photographer to throw away the letters—it has been five years now—but he is unable to do so.

In Washington, D.C., that same March, Secretary of Defense Melvin Laird was anxious to dispel the reports in the press that Lam Son 719 was a failure. Lieutenant General John Vogt, known as one of the best briefers the Pentagon could produce, gave a news conference. The general said a vital enemy oil pipeline had been destroyed in the Laos operation, and showed a three-foot length of pipe as a bit of cheerful color. But it was not a piece of pipe that had been taken during the Laos invasion at all, only something brought back months before by South Vietnamese commandos. A correction was made by the Secretary.

SOME WOMEN HAD premonitions, and knew it was useless to deny them. Mrs. Brenda Cavanaugh Genest of Manchester, New Hampshire, became a widow at twenty-one, just as she was certain she would. She was married to Richard Genest in November 1967 in a traditional Catholic wedding; the reception was at the Manchester Country Club. Both families were proper and prosperous: the Cavanaughs sold cars; the Genests had a bakery.

"We dated steadily for two years," she said. "We couldn't understand how a war, nowadays, could go on for years."

Her husband joined the National Guard in New Hampshire to stay out of the draft, but his unit was called up in the spring of 1968. She first heard it on the radio. The uncle of a friend, a brigadier general in the National Guard, had said it would never happen unless there was an attack at the Merrimack River. The idea that Richard would be sent to Vietnam made his wife unstable. The couple went to see Senator Thomas McIntyre, when he was back in New Hampshire, but the senator said he didn't know, he couldn't tell them anything, really. She began to cry. Specialist 5 Genest was sent to Fort Bragg, but he kept coming home every weekend.

"All our bank account went down, but it was worth it," Mrs. Genest recalled. "He was such a perfect person to me." Their son was born in June 1968; two months later her husband was in Vietnam as a cook with Battery A, 3d Battalion, 197th Artillery, at Fire Support Base Thunder III, north of Saigon, near Highway 13.

Every day he was there she felt herself to be in some kind of shock. But he was only a cook, so everyone who cared for her said it's all right, cooks don't have to shoot or be shot at.

"Dick never had good luck, he always got the raw end of the deal. I knew if he went to Vietnam he was going to get killed, because there was no way he was going to survive with his luck. After his year there, when he was coming home, I thought he's going to make it, maybe. It was his last week when he was killed. The whole year I was really prepared for it."

He left the fire base in a convoy, but the driver of his truck went over on the side of Highway 13 and hit a mine; there were four of them who died.

"The night before I found out, I was sitting on the lawn of my parents' house. This little neighborhood girl said 'Dick's dead, isn't he?' I said 'No, he's not, Dick's away and he's coming home soon.' She was only four, she didn't understand what she was saying. And she goes 'Well, I know he's dead.'"

It was true. The four men came back in the light-grey metal caskets, each in a clean uniform. Senator McIntyre was at the airport, but she did not want to go near him. At Goodman's Funeral Home there were two soldiers in the room with the casket, which was covered with a flag.

"I told them 'Just leave, get out of here, you don't care, you didn't even know him, what are you doing here,'" Mrs. Genest said. She wanted them to remove the flag and to get it out of her sight.

The funeral was unusual for a conservative town like Manchester. A few people were shocked and thought she must be a dupe of the Communists. There was a harsh comment in the arch-conservative newspaper *The Manchester Union Leader*. Mrs. Genest wanted nothing military or warlike or official in St. Catherine's Church that September day. Her younger sister, Jill, sang "Where Have All the Flowers Gone" and "Abraham, Martin and John" and "Blowin' in the Wind." Two young men played guitars. Thomas, one of her brothers, read from *The Prophet*. Instead of the usual stiff floral arrangements, Mrs. Genest asked that money be sent to an antiwar group, Another Mother for Peace. A friend picked sunflowers to put in the church, and there was a little basket of spring flowers.

Afterward letters came. Some were from people who read of what she had wanted the funeral to be and sent her congratulations for her courage. General Creighton Abrams, commander of U.S. Forces in Vietnam, wrote it was his hope that she would find solace "in knowing your husband gave his life for a noble cause, the defense of liberty in the free world." And a colonel, the commanding officer, wrote that "while serving in our organization, Richard never failed to devote himself to the task at hand." But such letters could not reach her, for she knew by heart what Richard had written about the war, so she went out in the world to speak against it. During the March Against Death in Washington, D.C., the name of the dead American soldier that she carried on a sign was his.

Some letters from Richard still came, although by then he lay in the family vault. He wrote that he and the others wanted to be lifted out from Thunder III by helicopter because the highways were dangerous.

"He wrote 'As usual our last request was denied,'" she said. "That really got to me."

The last time they saw each other was January 1969, when he had R and R. They had a week in Honolulu. He looked tanned and fit, she said, he seemed himself. After his death a medic came to visit her in Manchester and mentioned that Richard had developed a nervous twitch in his face, but she saw nothing like that on the R and R.

On that last morning in the Hilton Hotel they rose at four, for he had to leave at six. It was decided she would not go to the airport. They said goodbye, he left her in that room, started down the hall, made the mistake of coming back to see her just once more, and then went away forever.

"I said to Dick if you get killed promise me that if there is any way you can communicate with me that you will," Mrs. Genest said. "But he wouldn't talk about it." She was always hoping for a signal of some kind from him but none has ever come.

Even four years later, when she was living with a decent and affectionate man from Manchester, when her son Richard seemed fine, when the couple were thinking of building their own house in the country, Mrs. Genest could not stop from crying.

SOMETIMES THE PILOTS in the small choppers were bored; one meager amusement was to try and alarm run-of-the mill civilian passengers, especially reporters. The pilots would fly very low over the trees to tickle the highest branches, or tilt the choppers. They could not see our faces, so they spoke on the radio to the door gunners, who would watch us, grinning. But I loved the flying: the dread began on the ground.

But some jokes were not as crude, were not meant to be as playful. In the summer of 1970, after a long siege, the Special Forces Camp at Dakseang, eight miles from the border of Laos, was no longer a perilous place. There were still eleven Americans there, eleven Green Berets, although the Special Forces were leaving Vietnam that year. Dakseang seemed a wretched place in the most startling blue landscape: the camp was a long grey cooked rectangle of barbed wire, bunkers, sandbags, howitzers. For years the Montagnard men had been recruited, trained and paid by the Special Forces. Their little army was called the Civilian Irregular Defense Group.

It made the Montagnards unhappy to be turned over to Vietnamese command; there was a strong distrust, and often hatred, between the two groups. The Green Berets were not pleased to see me, did not answer questions, did not want reporters there. I was a disappointment to them: perhaps too thin, too old, too serious. One officer tried to tease me, but nothing girlish or coy came back. I remember them as having huge skulls and pale eyes. One had a dog on a leash; he said if the dog ran free, the Yards would eat it. It made him chuckle. The Americans loved the Yards. On this subject they would speak. It was an old litany, and their favorite. Yards were uncorrupted by the vile cities, did not cheat or lie, were superior to the Vietnamese, they said. Yards were their kind of men. The Green Berets at Dakseang seemed to feel that the war had been taken away from them and ruined. They would say no more.

There were two hundred and sixty Montagnard families there, who lived in dark, stifling bunkers, cruel places that provided no relief from the deadening heat outside. There were two hundred and forty-seven children. The Americans had an underground medical clinic and I watched as a medic attended to a Montagnard with a stunning gash in his head. The Special Forces medics were very good, perhaps the best, and it was a pleasure to see them at work.

A Vietnamese minister and his aides arrived for a meeting at Dakseang in their own helicopter; when the group was ready to leave, there were no seats, so Luong and I sat on the floor of the aircraft. We were used to it. Two of the Green Berets who had come to the landing pad to say goodbye, suddenly leaned inside to get me. There was nothing to hold on to except the ankles of a Vietnamese in a white shirt and suit. He recoiled but did not move my hands. Luong could not help me. We had an agreement that he must never try to interfere when I was in trouble, even if I called out and looked for him, because there was nothing an ordinary Vietnamese could ever do. It was wiser for him to stay away. The Green Berets dragged me out and raised me into the small seat of the door gunner, which was outside, the most dangerous place to be if the aircraft was fired on. It was their little punishment to show a reporter who would have the last word. I kicked and I hollered; I may even have yelled "Please" for the first time. The Vietnamese sat in silence, not turning their heads. The chopper trembled and rose; in the door gunner's seat it was always cold and the wind punched. I pulled my jacket over my head and huddled next to the gunner, but he paid no attention. We did not speak. I never understood how the Green Berets could have guessed how much I hated the door gunner's seat and the machine gun. Later it hardly seemed important.

They just treated you like a new guy, a southern friend said. They would have treated a senator the same way. He thought it funny. Your trouble—this is how he usually begins the light quarreling—your trouble is that you think no one wanted to be in Vietnam, that every man felt such *reluctance*. He was in the Special Forces: sometimes when he is drunk he sees himself as he was, moving through the Ashau Valley.

"The way you see it, every man wanted to be home practicing the piano," he says. He is persuaded that I cannot understand that there were some men who came alive, who wanted the war, who miss it. But I understood it very clearly that day at Dakseang— and then again and again.

V

EXPERTS

In 1956 Saigon seemed a soft, plump, clean place of greens and yellows; for fourteen years I remembered it this way, insisting these were its colors. The greens were the tall and lush trees that darkened in the rains, held the water, cooled the air. The trees seemed to have a faint sweet smell; some had leaves which flashed silver underneath when the wind tickled or rubbed them. There were tamarind trees, flame trees, mango trees and, on some streets, rubber trees. On the Boulevard Gallieni, which linked Saigon to Cholon, the Chinese city, there were double rows of trees planted by the French, whose branches reached out to each other, touching arms high above the wide road. Behind their walls and gates, the villas were yellowy, with shuttered windows.

Saigon was a calm place then, not yelling and choking with traffic; a lame dog could stroll back and forth on rue Catinat without being troubled. It was not yet called Tu-Do Street. Some Vietnamese had bicycles, a few had motorscooters, the cars were often Citroën, Renault and Simca. The French called the tiny dented Vietnamese taxicabs "the matchboxes." The four-door black Citroëns often had slipcovers made of white muslin to cut the heat, so their interiors looked precious and dainty. Vietnamese women seemed weightless, and had an astonishing and flat beauty in their long-sleeved *ao dai* with the tight high collars. These tunics, with their slit panels, worn over satiny wide pajamas, showed nothing of them, only sketched the smallness of their arms and breasts and waists. No Vietnamese woman wore western dress; any woman who did was Chinese. The women carried parasols in the pale colors of their *ao dai*—violet and blue, white and rose—so the sun would not darken their faces or confuse their eyes.

I took a photograph once of a man over eighty who always sat under a black umbrella. Many Vietnamese thought—as he did—the sun made you ill, and they were surprised, even then, how the foreigners adored lying in it, wanting their skins to turn a tight, shiny brown. I had freckles and was pitied for it by a Vietnamese woman. I had never seen a people with such skins. They did not have the pink or the chalkiness that we had, the circles, the pimples, the pouches, the stubble, the lines that complicate and sadden western faces. Their skins were very smooth, and if a color for them must be given, it would have something to do with the palest honey. Sometimes the conical hats women wore had beautiful blue embroidery inside them and velvety ribbons under the chin. When they put their heads back, the embroidery was suddenly startling to see.

"During the day the sun's heat practically forbids walking on foot; on the other hand, it is easy to circulate by rickshaw or taxi, hired by the hour or day," the *Guide de Saigon* said. It was a small book with paper covers from A. Portail, the bookstore on rue Catinat, that long pretty ribbon of a street with its shops and restaurants, running one thousand five hundred meters from the waterfront to the huge pink-brick cathedral with twin spires which was finished in 1883. "The climate is very damp especially during the rainy season (from May to November)," the *Guide de Saigon* said. The rickshaws were not pulled by men: the drivers rode high bicycles behind the two-wheeled shaded little carriages which could only seat two people. The faster way was to take a motorized one, which made a light roaring noise.

The little book was sadly outdated in 1956—with its adver-

tisements for tailors named Wakim and Luong Nam who made
military uniforms to measure for the French; the Air Vietnam
flights to Hanoi and Haiphong, where no one could go; the big
firms which listed their branches in the north. The nine-year war
for independence against the French had been won, the colonials
who were left huddled in Saigon or went to Phnom Penh, but the
Guide de Saigon said nothing of all this. Nowhere in its pages was
there a mention of the war or the peace.

Few places were air conditioned. But the Americans had come
and were pickled by such heat, so they ordered machines which
stuck out from the windows and made it ice-cold inside. It was
better not to defy the climate, to take naps after lunch, to keep
the rooms dim and use the ceiling fans with their big blades that
could be set to *vite* or *moins vite*. At night beds turned into huge
white cribs, for the folded mosquito netting was dropped and
tucked under the mattress. The floors in the houses and apartments were tiled and made it a pity to wear shoes, to miss the
pleasure of walking with bare feet on their coolness. There were
many bats in Saigon who sometimes flew inside, but in 1956 this is
all there was to fear. In the first months of that year there were still
French soldiers in Saigon. The soldiers were short, with uniforms
that showed most of their ropy legs and pale chests. They left their
shirts unbuttoned and their pants were cut very high on their
thighs. Their little caps were always tilted. At night they sat in the
outdoor cafés, drinking LaRue beer or "33," sometimes Pernod or
calvados or pastis, laughing a lot. There was no curfew then, no
reason why people should not sit at tables on the sidewalks.

The names of the streets in Saigon were still in French. The
Guide de Saigon had a very good map showing all of them, for
they had not yet been given new Vietnamese names. There were
seven streets named for French generals, five for French admirals, two for French colonels, one for a captain and even one for a
Lieutenant Ribot whose history no one knew. There was a street

named for Rudyard Kipling, another named Champagne and one named Ypres. There was a boulevard named for Kitchener, the British field marshal, but it was misspelled in the *Guide de Saigon,* for the French do not take trouble with the names of others.

In Saigon, French was the language, as rooted as their trees, and even the cyclo drivers on their high bicycles spoke something, some words, which sounded like it. When Frenchwomen talked to each other, their voices seemed too urgent, too high and sharp. I remember: a beauty shop on rue Catinat owned by a fierce and small blond woman with short hair. She had stopped struggling to camouflage the black roots that in time looked like peculiar honorary stripes. She wore flowered dresses, sleeveless and low-cut, whose skirts were always wrinkled in the back. She complained to the customers that she could no longer get nail polish, peroxide, the hair dyes she needed from France. They knew it. Nor could she sell her business to a Vietnamese and convert all those piasters to francs and go away; no one could do that. Sometimes her face suggested she might cry, but she never did; she only lifted her shoulders in a shrug. The sight of the American men in Saigon irritated her—she did not count me as anything—and she would say to any of the customers: "They will never understand this country, they will never change the Viets, they will not be happy here." We sat under the old dryers, which snored and trembled, our faces red and glistening from the hot air. The Frenchwomen spoke of the war in Algiers, sighing and shrugging, calling out to each other on the street "Madame, Madame." I never knew any of their names; it was always just "Madame." The Vietnamese women in the beauty shop did manicures very slowly, as if they were making tiny paintings on our hands and toes, but the emery boards were soft and bent and the nail polish streaked. They seemed to hear nothing.

The French boutiques which sold Christian Dior brassieres, and blouses from Nice, and Guerlain perfumes were closing, then closed. The wines were running out, the French cigarettes, the famous French butcher named Michaud no longer had his shop. Men liked to sit on the terrace of the Hotel Continental—the old French-built hotel with the potted palms on the sidewalk—but during the day many women went to La Pagode. It was a salon de thé, a place for tea or little cakes, or café au lait in the mornings, but there were very good milkshakes. There were no windows; it was an open and pleasant place where you could see so much. Years later, when windows with grilles had gone up to protect the customers from flying glass in case of rockets or explosives, there was no longer anything special about La Pagode. The younger middle-class Vietnamese took it over in their western clothes and long hairdos.

At night the Americans often went to sit in the deep rattan chairs and have drinks outside the Hotel Majestic, run by the stout and stern-looking Corsican, Monsieur Francini, who also owned the Continental and much else. It faced the port, the great port of Indochina, where the Saigon River flowed into the Donnai and then to the China Sea. One night we watched a parade of light armored cars, jeeps and heavy weapons being taken to the docks to be shipped to the war in Algeria. It was a busy port. The *Guide de Saigon* noted that it took eighteen to thirty days to sail from Saigon to Marseilles, with stops at Port Said, Suez, Djibouti, Aden, Colombo and Singapore.

There was nothing in Cochinchine—as the French called the south of Vietnam, which had been theirs for eighty years until that spring of 1954—that told me much of the nine-year war. There were cemeteries, and watchtowers where the French and their troops waited for the Viet Minh at night, there were barracks and hospitals, there were people who spoke of something that had happened at a place called Anh Khe, of something that had happened at a place called Cao Bang in the north, but the only war name I knew then was a name I never heard the French say: it was Dien

Bien Phu. The countryside, with its shining rice fields crossed by canals and divided by dikes, was peaceful and lovely. I went everywhere: to the tea plantations at Blao, the beaches at Qui Nhon and at Nha Trang, down to the very tip of southern Vietnam called Camau, to Ban Me Thuot, to the port city called Tourane, with its long curving waterfront, which became Danang. You could drive at night or at dawn. I thought it the most beautiful country I had ever seen, and none of it looked the same.

In 1956, outside the Hotel Continental, there was a smiling Vietnamese in a clean shirt who sold books, which he carried in his arms and peddled to passers-by. Afterward the books could be bound in tiny shops which made covers of red or green leather quite cheaply, the titles tooled in gold. Once I bought a collection of letters by a soldier from the peddler, but it was not until years later that I could read French well enough to understand all of them. The letters were written by Sergeant Guy de Chaumont-Guitry. In the photograph he has a lean and assertive face and blond hair brushed straight back from his forehead, the way men did in the nineteen forties, often using water to keep it down. He arrived in Saigon in March 1947, at the age of twenty-four, and was a non-commissioned officer in intelligence. He did not work at a desk or in a base camp but, rather, moved constantly through the south, going on patrols, interrogating prisoners, training spies and agents who could identify the Viet Minh, those Vietnamese fighting the French. It was part of the "pacification" program, the word relentlessly used so much later by the Americans for their own military and civilian operations. "Pacification will be fully realized," one Frenchman wrote, "not when we will have occupied each inch of earth but when we will have conquered all the hearts and won all the minds." He was Commandant A. M. Savani, head of the Deuxième Bureau, the French intelligence apparatus; these words hung over the desk of a young New Yorker working on the American pacification of the Vietnamese.

The sergeant was in the Plain of Jars, in places called Thu Duc, Cai Lay, My Tho, Tan An, Nhi Binh, where long afterward there were Americans. He was critically wounded during a Viet Minh attack in a village named Cau Cong. He died on November 21, 1948, in a small hospital run by French nuns in Vinh Long, only a few hours after he was brought in. I have the book still; the red leather cover has protected it for twenty years. There are the typical snapshots that all soldiers take: one shows him wearing a black shirt and pajama bottoms—his garments as dark as the ones worn by peasants—standing in a rice paddy; another of him crouching in thick bushes as he might during an ambush, raising his weapon.

July 17, 1947

. . . There are times when we're so discouraged that we wish we could abandon the whole thing. The outposts always being attacked, the roads always being cut, the convoys that have to be escorted everywhere, assaults on anyone who becomes isolated (gets caught by himself), shots in all directions each evening, and for encouragement, we have the indifference of France and the help some Frenchmen are actually giving to an enemy that is building up its armaments and its organization day by day.

August 8, 1947

. . . The Vietnamese are hard workers but slow—for them, the notion of time doesn't have the same meaning it has for us. They never show any anger—that would mean losing face—and they never make extravagant gestures. You get the impression of a people laced into a strait jacket of absolute politeness.

So the merchants receive you with a great show of esteem, the "boys" serve you with alacrity, and are always hanging around to bring you whatever you want, to dust the furniture, or arrange some object. But that doesn't stop them from going out each evening to tell the Viet Minh how many men there are in the camp, the number of weapons, the deployment of defenses, or even, if that's what's required, to set fire to the outpost once an attack has started and then grab a machine gun and start shooting you, after having served you so devotedly for so many months.

. . . Obviously all this involves a mentality that is beyond our comprehension.

October 5, 1947

. . . I'm afraid we're on the way toward losing this war.

Almost everyone seems to sympathize with the Viet Minh, because for them they represent the independence they all want.

Little by little, certain elements in Vietnamese society, realizing that the Viet Minh are wrong, would gladly turn to France if they were given certain guarantees. But we make so many mistakes, that we alienate even those of the most patient good will—especially since we're clearly so unable to protect those who join with us.

On top of all this, most of the French are insensitive to the Vietnamese and wound even our best friends by the words and actions.

July 26, 1948

. . . Day after day, we nibble at Executive Committees and Assassination Committees. This morning we succeeded in catching a Viet Minh security agent with a pistol. It's the first time I've been able to capture a weapon with my agents, aside from grenades.

My financial difficulties will soon be resolved because

the village is going to form a local autonomous self-defense group. I'll enlist all of my agents, and that'll make the village elders happy because they'd never be able to recruit any men and train them. And that way, I get the community to pay for my agents.

They owe us at least that, because before we arrived nobody was collecting any taxes anyway. Yesterday, in one day, we took in two thousand piasters.

So I won't have to pay for anything from now on except my interpreter and an agent who supervises the spy network . . .

I just got an invitation to have dinner with the chief of the investigation unit, to celebrate the capture of the pistol. A great event!

October 8, 1948

. . . Only someone who's been in the Army for a long time can understand the way we work here. As a pal of mine said, if we didn't have the Americans to move us around, we'd still be somewhere in Tunisia computing transport capacities and tonnages.

Here in Indochina, we're breaking all the records. We truck one part of the battalion off to fight and leave the other half a hundred kilometers behind to bring up supplies and the women. Then the first group gets sent off to fight someplace farther off, marching until they're dead tired to some objective that won't be reached until the next month. They tell us that in January we're supposed to go back to Cambodia. In the meantime, the men are exasperated, and since their enlistments are almost up, there's a good chance they won't reenlist.

Anyway, with our system, only a half of the battalion gets resupplied and the other half becomes skeletal, and thus no good for fighting. And while one part waits to be relieved, the other part disappears somewhere and no one knows when it'll show up.

A marvelous system, which evinces deep conceptions of strategy and politics! The result:

In pacification: within a radius of eight hundred meters, everyone flees in terror when we march out of the post.

Militarily: *Our operations are like sword thrusts in water.* And this is the only place we've learned to call that success.

. . . As for the population, what good does it do for us to propagandize—it's just too fascistic. And they follow the Viet Minh anyway.

Besides, what can we expect from the people? They flee from our operations and only the Viet Minh administer them. The Viet Minh end up looking like protectors against French depravations.

Oh, it's all very well to talk about pirates and barbarians. We failed to bring them along with material prosperity, some kind of social progress. Or, if we once did, at least it's finished now . . .

In 1970 it was useful, and faster, to speak French with some of the Vietnamese generals, the older civil servants, lawyers and politicians. The higher their rank, the more comfortable they were in this language. Luong did not like the Vietnamese who were attached to France; once he pointed out that President Thieu, and some of the men in his cabinet, had fought on the side of the French in the war of independence. It repelled him, and many other Vietnamese as well.

The middle-aged Vietnamese still remembered the French rulers, and among themselves, compared them to the new ones, the Americans. In Hue an elderly official, who had served the Emperor Bao Dai during the reign of the French, said the happiest moment of his life came in March 1945 when the Japanese overthrew the French administration in the north and south of Vietnam. There was one splendid sight which the official said he had never dared hope to see: a field where Frenchmen had been forced by the Japanese to work like animals, pulling plows, as Vietnamese watched it, hardly able to believe what they saw.

It was a wonderful sight, the old man said. He wore a lady's black wool coat of a dated style which he said protected him from chills. Such talk made Luong remember too. As a child in Hanoi he had been happy that spring to see the Japanese humiliate the French, who he had always thought were untouchable, immune to injury.

Some middle-class Vietnamese in Saigon, however, preferred the French for commerce; the Americans were puzzling, abrupt or unreliable although much richer. We heard this complaint most piercingly in the Thuy Chung shop, on a side street off Boulevard Le Loi in downtown Saigon, which made plaques for American soldiers and civilians and for their wives and mothers back home. The nicknames of American military units were so strange— Jungle Eaters or Ground Pounders or Delta Death Dealers— many of the Vietnamese in the shop who engraved the chrome or brass plates hardly understood what they said. Some of the plaques which bore the Latin mottos of Army units had comments on them: "Spooking the Cong" or "To hell with Ho Chi Minh."

The owner, Mrs. Hoang Thi Dinh, said she made insignia for French soldiers during the fighting that began in 1945, and after that war her shop made nameplates for doctors and lawyers.

Occasionally, Mrs. Dinh said, she was distressed by a lack of seriousness in her American customers. "The French only ordered serious things," she said. "They never wanted dogs and bones and skulls on plaques like the Americans do. The Americans so often order plaques with strange designs on them. Really, they are crazy."

A bronze plaque in her shop, which she said many American officers choose, bore a slightly modified version of a poem by Rudyard Kipling called "Epitaph":

> *And the end of the fight is a tombstone white,*
> *With the name of the late deceased,*
> *And the epitaph drear:*
> *A Fool lies here*
> *Who tried to hustle the East.*

The poem made Luong laugh.

"I believe only educated Americans can understand it," Mrs. Dinh told us. "I have seen so many Americans stand and read it over and over without seeming to understand it at all."

WHAT I REMEMBER about them now is their purposefulness; it seemed to give off the steady, low hum of a generator. The American military wore long British shorts and knee socks. The civilians and the Foreign Service officers and various experts, who were there to fatten and shine up the government of President Ngo Dinh Diem, had very clear, terrible notions of duty which burdened them as much as iron-plated suitcases that could never be put down.

They were anxious to be pleasant, to be pals with the Vietnamese. There would be none of the French arrogance. Only one man among them was still there when I got back: an anthropologist and professor named Gerald Cannon Hickey, born in Chicago at the end of 1925, who lived in Vietnam for twelve years. In the beginning he was connected to the Michigan State University Advisory Group, but after 1962 he was a consultant to The Rand Corporation, a private research organization in Santa Monica, California, which did contract studies in Vietnam for the Department of Defense and other government agencies. Both groups—MSU and Rand—were considered despicable by elements of the anti-war movement, who said these researchers, advisors and scholars were instrumental in the imperialist policies of the United States in Indochina which caused the deaths or grievous losses of millions of Asians.

But there was no one like him. He was a gregarious and amusing man, appreciated for his wit, his scholarship and his biting, long criticisms of the policies of the board of directors of the war. He was at home in Vietnam, very fluent in the language, as few other foreigners were. The reporters, year after year, needed and wanted to know him. Most of the American journalists did a tour in Vietnam—eighteen months—had a big party to celebrate when they go out, and then were sometimes sent back again. They were not unlike a great flock of gulls skimming over the corpses and offal of the war, plunging into it, and coming up again. Dr. Hickey seemed always to be in Vietnam even when the official Americans kept changing. He outlasted everyone. He liked to tell stories; they were sardonic and chatty, long and nearly always full of names of people to whom he had said such and such: a general, a land-reform expert, a big gun in the pacification program, a CIA or a USAID man, and if you did not even know whom he meant, it hardly mattered, for that was not the point.

"You and I are ghosts," Dr. Hickey said in Saigon. I said yes. Later, when both of us had left and knew there would be no going back, he sent me a gift. It was a bound volume of old French magazines from Indochina, a collection of the illustrated monthlies from 1954 called *Indochine Sud-Est Asiatique*.

"From me—A Ghost—to Gloria—Another Ghost—a Volume of Ghost Stories" he wrote on the flyleaf.

I had seen many of the issues before, with their pictures of the French generals, the peasants being moved back and forth, the crew-cut French reporters in the press camp at Hanoi, the wounded dark-haired Vietnamese soldiers whose faces even now sometimes trick me into thinking that yes, here is the Private Moc I knew, here is Sergeant Co, Squad Leader Binh. But they are not. In the last issue of the volume there is the final piece, the last thin trumpet, called "Death of a War" by Bruno Rajan. "This war, false in its origins, uncertain in its conduct and frustrated in its objectives, brought with it a fundamental truth: it is the form of war of which the westerner is the worse prepared but it is the form of war to which he must pay most attention." In paying tribute to the French, to the Vietnamese who fought with them, to all those who chose their side, Dajan ended with these words: ". . . there is nothing else to say now but this: Forgive us for not having won this war."

But among us, in Saigon, there was not much interest in the French; the Americans learned nothing from them. All that mattered was that the French had failed, not the reasons why. In 1956 the Americans did not want to be associated with the French, and tried to make it clear to the Vietnamese that they were not greedy people seeking privilege or power. Many of them believed it: overweight men, missing winter, writing reports, making money, trying to keep their tempers when it went wrong, not colonials but anti-Communists.

"I remember the first thing I learned to say in Vietnamese was 'I am not French,'" Dr. Hickey said. "There was quite a fixation about that."

In 1959 he came back to the United States to teach undergraduates at Monteith College at Wayne State University, then he moved to New Haven to teach a graduate course at Yale University on Ethnic Groups in Southeast Asia. Vietnam was not a place anyone ever heard of, so he learned to say that he had been in Indochina. "Then people would say 'Oh, Gerry's back, he's been in India or in China,'" Dr. Hickey said, laughing.

In 1964 his book *Village in Vietnam*—the research, which he began in 1958, had been sponsored by the Michigan State group—

was published by Yale University Press, the first study of a Vietnamese village to be published in English. It was called the finest piece of American scholarship that the large-scale United States commitment in Vietnam had thus far brought about. Dr. Hickey had used the village of Khanh Hau in Long An province in the Mekong Delta, southwest of Saigon, as a microcosm for the study of the rural physical setting, the beliefs and customs of the several religions that coexisted, the kinship and family pattern, the crops and agricultural methods, the economic, administrative and legal systems, and the socio-economic structure and mobility. It was an x-ray of Vietnamese culture and how it was changing as western influences grew stronger. Few reporters in Vietnam had read it, but the book made Dr. Hickey a figure of great respect and reliability.

In the early years he traveled by train, and on a March day in Washington, twenty years later, he still remembered the trip to Nha Trang.

"You'd leave at seven-thirty in the evening and the station was always sort of chaotic, everyone was loading all sorts of cargo in the boxcars. The beds were all made up in the *couchette de luxe*, it was very clean. They had the little overhead fans to keep the cars reasonably cool, and they had those marvelous sort of shuttered windows. And the funny little dining car where they did all the cooking on braziers, so that when they'd throw a steak on the brazier the smoke would just go billowing right through the car. Of course, the windows were all open.

"It was marvelous leaving Saigon because you'd go through these quarters where people had built their houses right up to the railroad. So you'd be looking right in at the little oil lamps and people sitting on a mat having dinner, and bare-bottomed kiddies running about the place and all that. And then you'd wind your way out and finally end up in this marvelous rain forest between Bien Hoa and Phan Thiet.

"That forest! You would be going through it and the fronds would be hitting the windows, the side of the train. And they'd stop to get wood and you'd begin to see this little funny settlement with little fires burning, because the trains were all wood-burning in those days. They were marvelous engines, all polished brass, and with a funny high smokestack like the old trains had. But they were always on time."

In those days the Vietnamese did not dream of dressing as the Americans did. If the women put on western clothes, it was done for special effect. When a group of Vietnamese women, who all worked for the Michigan State group in Saigon and had studied in the United States, decided to appear on the same day in American dresses, they did it as a prank. "It was kind of a lark—they all came in giggling, wearing American clothes. They'd all been in the United States. Everybody was commenting, the coolies, the drivers, the other Vietnamese," Dr. Hickey said.

He went to the Cercle Sportif, the name of the French swimming and tennis club in Saigon, although some of the young Americans working with MAAG—Military Advisory and Assistance Group—were advised not to go to the citadel of privilege, the symbol of the white masters. But each year, of course, more Americans joined, so that by 1970 eight hundred and fifty of them—military and civilians—were members and no one remembered that early opprobrium, or cared.

"The children of the big French colonial families used to call 'Boy, boy!' at the Vietnamese waiters, screaming at them in a very arrogant manner, treating them like dirt. And the French used to complain, they were always complaining, and some of the Vietnamese who were very Frenchified said it too: that the Americans were not as cultured as the French. There was the great complaint, too, that the Americans were too nice to their servants, too nice to their chauffeurs and drivers. You know, it was true that the Americans did treat the servants better; they gave them a day off, which the French never did or the Vietnamese. People started working for the Americans because they were getting better wages, and they did get Sunday off. They were by and large quite nice to the servants. They would buy some clothes and be decent with them.

"But everybody thought he had the solution," Dr. Hickey said. "A lot of people represented a kind of missionary spirit, and there was that, it was very strong. But it was mixed with an incredible ethnocentrism that everything could be done. The solutions were American solutions. People didn't go to learn from the Vietnamese, they went there to teach the Vietnamese or to tell the Vietnamese, in some cases. Even someone like Ed Lansdale when he talked about what was good for the people, you know, getting the people to rally behind the government, his ideas were American ideas. If they would have a constitution, everybody would love the constitution and respect it. But that's a very American idea, a constitution. Well . . . I went out, not with a missionary spirit, because I was primarily interested in research on the Vietnamese. I didn't really have this notion that I was going out and save South Vietnam, that we've got to save it from communism, that our ways are best. So I didn't pay much attention to this attitude until we were doing a study for Michigan State on the Ministry of Education, the first study I got involved in right after I arrived.

"I had been working about six weeks and going around the Delta and interviewing. Because obviously, if you're going to make revisions in the Ministry of Education, I thought, you had to find out how the Ministry was structured and how things worked.

"For example, one of the problems was that when new teachers were hired, they didn't get paid for about four or five months. This was 1956. A couple of Vietnamese who were trained at the University of Chicago and I said 'Let's trace the movement of the dossiers when someone is hired and find out why it takes so long for them to receive their first pay.' This seemed like a logical thing to do.

"Well, the Michigan State offices then were right off of Cati-nat, in a dreary set of offices, and they would take a coffee break down at La Pagode, you know. So I was down having coffee one afternoon with the head of Public Administration, an American from Minnesota. And he said 'Well, I think enough work has been done, let's get the final report written on the study of the Ministry of Education.'

"I said 'We couldn't possibly, we've just gotten into it and we're beginning to find out what makes it tick, how it's working.' And he said 'No, no, that's not important, I already have the recom-mendations written. And I said 'You couldn't possibly have the recommendations written, we haven't done the research.'

"He said 'The principles of public administration as devised by the Americans are applicable anywhere in the world.' And I said 'Wally, that patently ain't so. Obviously you take these prin-ciples and take the American ideas in public administration and they've got to be adapted to a particular culture. You may write these recommendations, but the Vietnamese may not under-stand what you're talking about and it may be completely alien to them.' But we did trace the dossiers and we stalled on writing the report, much to his chagrin. The dossiers went into a thing called Fonction Publique. This was a government bureau that had to process every dossier from every ministry when a new person was hired. And we found that this was the bottleneck; it was an empire, it was someone's empire . . .

"The Americans always thought they discovered fire and they discovered the wheel in Vietnam," Dr. Hickey said. "But in 1956 Diem was really impressed by American efficiency. There was a magic involved, it was as if we had this amulet around our neck. In 1956 Diem still believed that the Michigan State group was going to work wonders, so all doors were open for us. It was a honeymoon period. When they wanted to set up an administra-tive study, we could go in and interview anybody in any ministry.

And those poor little civil servants with the dossiers piled up on their desks and their little glasses of tepid tea, usually with green plastic covers over the glasses to keep the flies out. And there they were. I'll never forget the little dossiers that were piled all over the place with little strings to hold the pack of papers together. And the offices were invariably stuffy, warm, with those overhead fans sort of barely moving. I hated doing the interviews during the afternoon because you felt so groggy having had a siesta. And by that time the heat had accumulated, you know, it was just awful."

IN 1956 HE began his research, too, on the Montagnards, the hill and mountain people of Vietnam of different racial origins. There were thirty or so different tribes—the Jarai being the largest—and their population was guessed to be eight hundred and fifty thousand. President Diem had started a land development program in the Central Highlands where the Montagnards lived: it was based on what Dr. Hickey calls "the old Bao Dai scheme to develop the Highlands and bring in the Vietnamese—in other words, to shunt the poor Montagnards aside so he could settle the poor people from the coast of central Vietnam, which were overpopulated areas, and refugees from the north." It disturbed him that some official Americans approved of this, saying that after all, the Montagnards had no land tenure system. Dr. Hickey asked Wesley Fishel, who headed the Michigan State group, to let him go to the Highlands to do a preliminary survey on land tenure in 1957.

"Not only did we include material on the land tenure, we also quoted what the Montagnards were saying about the Vietnamese and how much they disliked them because they were being badly treated. There was discrimination against them and the Montagnard civil servants were getting less money; even the Vietnamese children were arrogant with Montagnard officials and behaved like mandarins. They were cheating them in the marketplaces, they were stealing things out of the baskets that they carried their produce in to the market. And there was general discontent. The French had romanized some of their languages and taught them in schools. These were suppressed by Diem. They could no longer talk. They had to take Vietnamese names if they were in the army or the civil service. They felt their culture was being wiped out. They had to wear trousers if they went into town; they couldn't wear loincloths.

"There were certain lands that were inalienable, they belonged to the clans, and you couldn't sell them. The Rhadé particularly had a very well-defined land system tied into matrilineal clans. The women owned all the land. It wasn't all the land in the area, just certain plots. And they knew the boundaries.

"The French had to some extent honored this because in principle the plantations had only ninety-nine-year leases if they were on Montagnard claimed land. Well, Diem did away with that. So there were a lot of complaints and I wrote all of this up, putting in that the Montagnards would agree to form a commission with the Vietnamese officials to sit down and work out their claims to certain areas, and translated it into French and Diem got a copy of it.

"And he was livid, he was absolutely livid. Wolf Ladejinsky [a land-reform expert for Diem] was livid. Ladejinsky tried to get the report suppressed and he later came to the Michigan State office and said to me 'This is the worst report Michigan State has ever done. How do you expect the government to deal with these children?'

"And I said 'If you operate on the premise that they're children, you're not going to get very far.' And he said 'They look out the window and they say "I own all the land I see."' And I said 'That just demonstrates that you haven't read the report because that's exactly what they don't do.' I tried to point that out in the report, that they have well-defined claims to certain limited lands. There was a threat that Michigan State would have to let me go because everybody was against this report. But Wesley Fishel backed me, Wesley was helpful. And he didn't try to change anything in the report. I get along with Wesley. People make him out to be a dark plotter, but I don't think he was a schemer. Poor Wesley was really a bit bumbling in many ways, and his sins were sins of omission more than anything else. He backed it. I was under a terrible cloud."

But the fifties had been a fine time for him in Vietnam: his work absorbed him, and there were splashes of enormous gaiety. He always liked parties. The grandest ones were at the Cercle Sportif. He can remember the 1956 black-tie Christmas ball when the big swimming pool was partially covered over, and a *mise en scène*, a huge pagoda scene, was put over the high-dive. People came at eleven P.M., after going to dinner parties, the men in white jackets, the women in long dresses, their faces powdered and pleased, to drink champagne and dance. There was a spectacle, with Chinese dancers performing by the painted pagoda, then a ballet of little junks in the water, pushed by small French girls in bathing suits and flippers who had been trained by Maître Vatin, the swimming instructor. There was another ball, too, called the Carnival of Nice, where the guests tossed flowers at each other. Hundreds and hundreds of flowers, he said.

At the beginning of 1962 he went back to Vietnam for two months. That February he went to the opening of one of the first "strategic" hamlets, near the district capital of Cu Chi. It was an elaborate plan to contain and isolate Vietnamese communities to prevent infiltration, or contact, with the Viet Cong. Dr. Hickey was doing a report on the program, which was making the peasants in the area most unhappy. They were angry because men were being hauled off to work in Army trucks as laborers for the Saigon government, and there was no pay or even food. Furthermore, the farmers said their tobacco crops, their most important cash crop, were suffering.

That day in Cu Chi, tanks blocked Highway 1 for the elaborate, almost theatrical ceremony. There was a large reviewing stand for important Vietnamese—including President Diem's brother, Ngo Dinh Ngu—and Americans coming from Saigon. Airborne Vietnamese troops were out in such large numbers, they made up the greater part of the audience. There were, of course, some women and young people who belonged to the organizations set up by the government. They had been rounded up, but there were no villagers on hand.

"It seemed to symbolize the whole situation in Vietnam," Dr. Hickey said. "I kept saying 'Where are the people, what happened to the people?'"

Dr. Hickey went in a small shop to change the film in his camera and the Vietnamese offered him some tea, a customary politeness. He asked the Vietnamese where everybody was, where were the villagers? The shopkeepers told him the people had all been told to stay in their houses, or to throw water on a dusty little road leading to the communal temple because Ngo Dinh Ngu was expected to go there. The American colonels seemed quite elated with the goings-on. When Dr. Hickey inquired of the American military why the villagers were not at the ceremony, one officer said it was because Mr. Ngu needed protection. Dr. Hickey, who knew his sarcasm was often wasted at such times, nevertheless pointed out that the strategic hamlets were supposed to provide protection. A dark look was his answer, nothing else.

"When we wrote up our report on strategic hamlets everybody was furious. They tried to get Rand to change it. The people in Saigon said we were completely incorrect. Some of the officials in Saigon tried to talk us into changing things, and we said no. That was the only time they really did try to make me change a report. Apparently it was due to pressure brought from Washington.

"I gave General Harkins a debriefing before I left Saigon. I said the strategic hamlets aren't going to work if they impose an economic and social burden on the population. If they're relocated, they're going to have negative reactions and these haven't been properly explained. I said you've got to realize you're operating under the assumption that everybody wants protection, but the poor people in the hamlets don't need protection because they're not bothered. And if they're the ones who pay the most, then it's going to cause an adverse reaction on their part.

"Harkins said no, that can't be true, I don't agree with any of that. Well, the whole thing was hopeless. We went to Washington and gave debriefings; I had never done this before, it was an interesting experience. Over at the Pentagon, I had a real fight with General Krulak, the Marine general, that little creep. And Krulak said 'We're going to make the peasants do this, and we're going to make them do that.' I said you're not going to make the peasants do anything. You better realize it right now. They're very tough, independent people and they have ways of circumventing. You're not going to make them do anything.

"So everyone said that this report was negative. I said you simply can't build walls around every settlement, it doesn't do any good. And then we were condemned, literally. After the coup d'état the new government said the strategic hamlets plan was a failure, that it was all faked, the figures and everything."

After three years in New Haven, Dr. Hickey came back once more to Saigon in the beginning of 1964, saw that nothing was the same, would not be the same, and stayed for another nine years and three months.

"You began to see the marked changes in 1964," Dr. Hickey said in Washington, D.C. "You couldn't go out in the field and everything began to go down downhill. The next thing you knew, the trees were all dying from the defoliants—the wind carried them into the city. Also, the planes that were taking off from the airport all leaked. The first trees that went were the flame trees out at the airport, which were *very* sensitive, and the gorgeous flame trees all the way in from the airport. They cut down all the trees to widen the streets so the American jeeps and tanks could move; they cut down some of the *best* streets in Saigon to make *truck routes*. Those huge trucks with the klaxon horns—they were the *loudest* horns I've ever heard, they were *air horns!*"

But he did keep making trips, and that summer the war almost wiped him out. He was visiting a Special Forces camp in Quang Nam province when, on July 6, there was a fierce, prolonged attack by a reinforced Viet Cong battalion. Dr. Hickey thought the camp would be overrun. There were eighty stretcher cases, he said, two dead Americans, six others severely wounded, and a dead Australian, maybe the first of the war from that country. The Marines sent in helicopters, but they only circled the camp and then went away. It made him wild. Relief came the next day, when they were evacuated. He was not like most scholars who collect and analyze vast amounts of material on the war. What made him different was that he, too, had been caught inside it.

Because Dr. Hickey was asked to return in 1964 by both the Vietnamese and the Americans in Saigon, he thought he could make a difference, "I had an entrée and I knew I had to exploit it," he said. "I had to really use politics." He saw that it was not enough to do good reports with honest recommendations. The reports had to be as sharp and light as arrows and cleverly aimed. "So when I wrote one-page memos, which was the only thing they would read about relocation projects, I always had to couch the thing in terms of security. That's the only thing that cuts any ice with the Americans. Your lead line had to be a shocker. You'd say 'Security is going to tumble in Pleiku province unless . . .' Then I'd say 'Because of the following reasons . . .' And then you'd show that you did your homework.

"'These people are pro-VC, they're turning pro-VC, they have pro-VC attitudes, they're stirring up among the refugees,' you'd write. Then you had to add a little short paragraph with some positive upbeat recommendations at the end. You double-spaced the whole thing. One-page memo. We sent them to the military and they hand-carried them, all ten copies, to give to Bunker and to the science advisor, who would get them directly to Westmoreland or Abrams and not through channels. That's how I'd get things done, it was the only way to do it. And then you had to grab people at a cocktail party or somewhere and put the bee in their bonnet."

HE WAS NEVER shy or cautious about speaking his mind. He was willing to testify before Congressional committees, or talk to any high-ranking visitors who came to Saigon. He felt sickened by what was happening to the Montagnards. An American in Saigon named Don Luce remembered Dr. Hickey giving him a very long, brilliant, deadly analysis of the war, point by point. When Mr. Luce asked the anthropologist why he did not join others who were working to stop the war, he thought Dr. Hickey looked quite startled.

"He said 'I am a scholar, not an activist,'" Mr. Luce recalled.

In the spring of 1971, wanting to get out, Dr. Hickey tried to return to the anthropology department at the University of Chicago, where he had done his graduate work. It was his hope to use the research library at the university for his project on the Montagnards. The faculty members in the department refused to have him; they declined to discuss the decision. It was believed that Dr. Hickey's association with The Rand Corporation—that link with the military—was the reason for the rejection. There was some concern in the United States that a new McCarthyism, as the headline in an article in *The Wall Street Journal* asked, was arising, and that the issue of academic freedom was at stake. In Saigon he seemed saddened and upset by the rejection but he did not want to talk about it. He kept on writing reports on the pitiful plight of the Montagnards, who were being made refugees or who could no longer farm because the land had been affected by herbicides and bombing.

The ending for him was more dreadful than he had suspected it would be.

"When I left the Highlands the war was over, it was lost. It was March 1973. Kontum was a dead city. It was unbelievably depressing, this lovely, lovely, lovely little town, half of it in ruins. The shops were closed. There were ARVN soldiers wandering about aimlessly at night, eating roasted corn, which was all they could afford. The one restaurant that was open had almost inedible food.

"Then I did the last of the herbicide interviews at the old Camp Enari outside of Pleiku. I saw them build that camp, it was the headquarters for the U.S. 4th Infantry Division. And it was now filled with Montagnard refugees. The GI signs were still on the walls but they were all blackened from smoke because everyone was cooking on braziers. They said things like 'Movie at 2000,' 'Mail Call 0900.'

"And here are these poor Montagnards everywhere in what had been offices. It was filthy, filthy dirty. They were telling me such depressing stuff. They had been bombed.

"I said to an American there 'Look at this, the 4th Infantry is going to come and save them from communism and look at them sitting in the 4th Infantry camp. The 4th Infantry is gone and the people have never been worse off in their lives! The worst had happened. The Americans up there were a bunch of bums. They were the worst.' Oh, they were ghastly people. They thought of nothing but themselves, they were all shacked up with Vietnamese girls, with Montagnard girls. They were drunk. They were awful to the people. They were ex-military who had all become civilians. I think a lot of them were involved in corruption. I couldn't even talk to them. I didn't want anything to do with them. Oh, Pleiku was so dreary and dirty and the place was just so depressing. I said 'The war is over, it's lost. All the government controls are these little pinpoint towns.'

"I went down to Saigon, and Peter Glick said he was going to build a new hotel. I said 'Are you out of your mind?' And Nguyen Ngoc Lieng said he was going to start a university, and I said 'Who for, the VC?'"

When, at last, after saying for so long he wanted to leave, it was by ship. Dr. Hickey booked a cabin on the States Line ship called *Idaho*. He had lunch with friends, then people came for drinks aboard ship, then a small group went to dinner on shore at the Tour d'Argent restaurant, which always had excellent crab. The next day, at nine A.M., he sailed.

"It was strange. I wasn't sure how I'd react. I was up on deck and of course we were going through all the defoliated *rung sat*— the mangrove swamp—at the mouth of the river. It was like a desert. I just felt a sense of relief at leaving."

That day in Washington there were many statues in his apartment which I remembered from Saigon; they gave the living room a gold shimmer. One of them was of a Thai Buddhist hand, fingers together, palm upright. There was nothing there to remind you of the armies. By his desk on the floor were the charts of Montagnard genealogy on which he had worked for so long writing an ethno-history on the Montagnards.

His Montagnard assistant, Touneh Hantho, often felt depressed looking at the pictures in the old magazines from Indochina in Dr. Hickey's files. He felt so homesick for the Dan Him Valley, between Dalat and the coast.

"I tell him not to think about it too much, to think about the future," Dr. Hickey said. "I say 'Think of your family who are happy in Santa Barbara where your children are getting a nice education. The nuns out there are treating them beautifully.'"

He was occasionally irritated by the continuing work of a tiny group of the antiwar people in Washington, who he thought were acting as propagandists for North Vietnam. For years, he kept saying, a political settlement to the war and a coalition government were the only solution, but he had not much cared for any of the Vietnamese in power, in Saigon or in Hanoi. "I never thought of the North Vietnamese as God's gift, you know!" he said. "But *that gang* we had there—well, we were running a school for corruption. Everybody was out for themselves. *That gang!*"

Sometimes he glimpsed some of the young Americans who had gone to Vietnam not as experts, not as soldiers, but to work as teachers with the organization called the International Voluntary Services. Many of them had denounced the war, had become important in the antiwar movement and had put their private lives aside.

"They got caught up in a formative time in their lives. They got very caught up, somehow it became terribly meaningful, their feelings about Vietnam and the war and they threw themselves into it," he said. "The more extreme antiwar people got caught up in the revolution. But the revolution didn't pan out, it was a kind of a ripple. There was a certain impact to the whole thing but I don't think it was all that great.

"The war is over. There's a kind of funny letdown. I think they're at loose ends. It was such a high period for them in terms of commitment and meaningful behavior. Now there's a kind of low. They don't know if they can ever achieve that again or even come close to it, caring so much about anything."

Then Dr. Hickey went off to a weekend in the country with old friends in Washington, D.C., whom he had known when they worked in Vietnam for the U.S. government and who had kept in touch all those years, the way people do when they have been posted overseas together, when the friendships are fattened by pleasant memories and a shared nostalgia.

In the infancy of the war he had never imagined how it would all turn out, never dreamed that only the early memories of Vietnam would be so cheerful and endearing. There had been such grand times, like the week when the opera star Eleanor Steber came to Saigon. It was the same year, 1956, that Joseph Mankiewicz was making the film *The Quiet American* with Michael Redgrave and Audie Murphy. Dr. Hickey was hired as an extra, to play a journalist, and given a pad and a pencil for the scene. Miss Steber gave two concerts at the old Majestic Theatre, which had no air conditioning. There was a dinner for her at a fancy restaurant called Bodega, which years later became a dark, slick place with a California décor. It sold pizzas to GIs and other Americans who didn't mind paying too much. Its name was the Pizzeria.

"The old Bodega was very elegant, it was marvelous. It had this little bar and a baby grand piano. That night the fellow playing it started 'Love Is a Many-Splendored Thing.' Steber kept insisting that the song was stolen from Puccini. Then she said 'I'll show you!' She started singing 'Un Bel Di' from *Madame Butterfly*. You could have heard it all the way down Catinat. Ah, she was marvelous."

In the summer of 1976, when he was working on the contemporary history in his book on Montagnards, reviewing the years when he had been in Vietnam, Dr. Hickey had trouble. He used to say in Washington that he would not let himself brood about the war, he would not give himself over to thinking about it. It is a resolution quite commonly made by Americans who want to get on with their work and lives.

"I find it harder to block out now," he said. "I can't seem to do it any more. I'm homesick for Vietnam and Cambodia and the old days. It's with me all the time."

THERE IS THE scrapbook of that year in Vietnam, the first strange and exciting year abroad. There were always scrapbooks in my family, pushed far back on the shelves of the closet but never thrown out, and the scrapbooks of my friends, as if all of us insisted on a peculiar proof of our lives at their most deceiving. The pictures were counterfeit certificates of being alive: what they showed was almost never what counted and they were nearly always quite bad. There we were—setting forth and coming back, laughing, hugging, acting, on beaches, on boats, on the backs of camels, on foot, on rivers, in cars, up mountains and down church aisles.

The images of Vietnam in 1956 lie on the self-sticking black pages under the plastic sheets, just as I once so carefully placed them. Opening the book after so long, and dreading it, I see again the tiny children at the high raw desks in a school, the clean soldier smiling because he is being photographed for the first time in his life, the villagers washing in the river. They have not moved or disappeared.

I was in Vietnam by chance, wanting to imitate a grandmother who had once gone from Titusville, Pennsylvania, to China and because I knew a charming young man in New York named John Gates, Jr., who was being sent out there as a lieutenant in the Marine Corps although his work was for the CIA. In those days connections with the CIA were not openly spoken of but it was not considered degrading or even unhealthy work. Lots of men out of Harvard and Yale went to the agency, making little jokes when people asked them what they did.

The years before 1956 had been malignant and frightening. I can still hear the loud, crashing voice of Senator Joseph McCarthy from Wisconsin as he punched out accusation after accusation against people he claimed were Reds, traitors, dupes and saboteurs. I had a casual friend in Washington Irving High School whose parents had been Communists in the 1930s. For a while I was afraid Senator McCarthy would cite the parents, then the daughter, then her friends. There were other troubling memories: a roommate who had a friend named G. David Schine, who conducted investigations with the lawyer Roy Cohn of suspected Communist influence or infiltration for the Wisconsin senator.

All of this and the war in Korea and my own cowardice froze a crucial and questioning zone of intelligence in me that took years to thaw.

In Vietnam that first year I thought it splendid that the Americans were making a democracy in South Vietnam. It was part of our national tidying-up of the world. Eight years later I finally knew better. Fifteen years later the real punishment came when I went back to Vietnam and could not believe it was the country where I once had been.

Some of the pictures in the scrapbook are of faces I remember but do not know why. The tall, thin girl in the polo coat that was me, had my name, stands by a sign that reads: *Ligne de Demarcation Militaire Provisoire.* It was the 17th parallel. It was cold and damp, so I wore my New York coat. The 17th parallel looked like nothing. There was a wooden bridge of medium size crossing the Ben Hai River. It led to another half of the nation which I had been taught to fear. There was only a soldier standing at the other end—behind him a garrison—a flagpole and the wide plain bridge that you could run on, then turn, to pose for a photograph. The soldier did not point his gun or shout to get off. "We have decided to extirpate the Communists," a notice on a wall in Quang Tri said. It was in English, a questionable benefit, for the peasants there spoke only their own language.

In some of the photographs there is a Vietnamese interpreter named Mr. Luoc who always held his head back and looked down on the camera. When I left Vietnam that year I gave him the man's watch I wore, and years later, looking at such a huge number of soldiers, then wounded, then prisoners, I would always hope to find him again by spotting the expensive large watch. He was very keen on learning English; he said it was important for the future, but he said it in his strange, sad, astringent way. I always looked for him when I went back, everywhere. He had no address in 1956, so all I could do was keep glancing at the faces, looking at the watches. I do not know what side he chose, or if he chose at all, this complicated and angry man, or even if the watch from Switzerland kept working for him as I promised it would. There were years when I wondered what he had been trying to tell me, what kept me from hearing it.

He was an intense young man, my own age, who wanted to be in a university but had no money. Mathematics was a passion but I was of no help there, for he knew far more. He was unhappy with the government of President Ngo Dinh Diem because a male relative of his had been put in jail. Once, in Quang Tri, as we walked, he said that it would be better if President Diem was done away with. I remember my shock and how I pleaded with him not to talk like that because it was dangerous and stupid. Mr. Luoc was not convinced, said something I could not follow, and made it known that it was bad Diem came from Hue, strange people came from Hue, that he was not realistic, that he was a mystic, that what was needed was something else, that he was not admired but feared in Saigon, that Diem should be shot.

In the scrapbook there is a photograph of the President in a white suit, talking slowly, as he did for hours when I went that day to see him. It was clear even to him that his visitor could not follow the endless interlocking circles of what he was saying in French, so he wrote on a small white card, which I have kept, a précis of his remarks. It was in French. "Vietnam is conscious of representing the aspirations of non-Communist Asia. It is a grand responsibility and it is also a test for Southeast Asia . . ." He went on trips; the diplomatic corps, the American military and the experts followed him. Once we went to the Plain of Jars and to a place called Cai-San in Long Xuyen province where a huge refugee settlement for the Vietnamese from the north had been built. President Diem, wearing a hat, a dark tie and a suit, sat on a gunboat which went slowly down a canal. He was trying to smile, sitting very upright. The Americans were anxious for him to be seen by the villagers who had been lined up.

During one long stupefying ceremony that took more than two hours, a peasant in black pajamas stood before a dais, which had four microphones, and read a very long speech from a bunch of papers. He was admitting to being a Communist, regretting it, confessing his sins, saying that he had now seen the light, but the length of the speech, and its complexity, seemed to make it hard going. The self-confessions were part of a new effort called for by the Americans, which grew into the Chieu Hoi, or "Open Arms," program, meant to encourage defections. In 1970 it was hard for young Americans to believe me when I said it was such an old, old idea.

In Saigon, I lived with a group of Filipino doctors, nurses and public-health workers who were called "Operation Brotherhood." In principle, Operation Brotherhood was supported by the International Junior Chambers of Commerce; the idea was supposed to have come, like a white storm, from the Philippines, but it was actually the brainchild of Colonel Edward Lansdale, a counterinsurgency expert in the CIA who had been sent to the Philippines in 1951 to help the government crush the Hukbalahap rebellion. Later the colonel became advisor and close friend of Ramon Magsaysay, the Secretary of Defense, and helped him to become President of the Philippines in 1953.

There were more than a hundred Filipinos who lived together in a cheerful stew; the house was at 25 rue Chasseloup-Laubat, which later was renamed Hong Thap Tu. Vito, Magdalena, Buddy, Paul, Carola: They were cheerful, young, hard-working and nice. Most of them were women. They traveled in teams throughout the south, opened first-aid stations and taught some public health. The idea was that Filipinos would be more acceptable to the Vietnamese than whites, they would adjust better, it was good for an anti-Communist Catholic Asian country to be ostensibly taking the lead in helping Vietnam. But there seemed to be constant quarrels and difficulties between the Diem government and the leaders of O.B., as it was called. Some operations were done, a few clinics were set up, the nurses tried to nurse. I took notes for an article for *The Reader's Digest*.

The head of O.B. was a talented Filipino named Oscar Arellano, a friend of Colonel Lansdale. He was an architect, a gifted and inexhaustible man who chose to be a teddy bear at times, a tyrant at others. He did not much believe in sleep and kept us worried about his health. I was told, and I believed it, that during the Japanese occupation in World War II he had been without fear and taken risks that later made him a man to be honored. I did not know until I saw him in Hong Kong in 1970 quite by accident, sat with him in a restaurant, and heard in astonishment the same mush I heard so eagerly in 1956 about the wonderfulness of American intentions and the importance of O.B., that I saw him as a pitiful man or one of immense self-deceit. He suddenly seemed to choose to know very little about the war, to think nothing too nasty had happened in Indochina, that we must not dwell on the tragedy, that the ending would make all of us proud. He was a fine actor, pouring his life into that odd, unnatural role the Americans had elected him to play. The Philippines did not become an important anti-Communist force in Vietnam; the Vietnamese did not at all trust other Asians manipulated by the Americans, so there were few of them when I came back, mostly in offices, quiet people who did not count for much.

JOHN GATES, JR., who is always called by his childhood nickname Demi, was an original and romantic man of a certain impeccable eastern background, which meant St. Paul's School, Harvard, debutante parties and the New York Social Register. In the fifties I was always beguiled by men who could make me laugh—it seemed a special American talent—so his humor and bravado caught and held me for years. We were a dull generation, and a greedy one, so it was not unusual when Demi Gates said so many times how much he wanted to make money, be on the cover of *Time*. Line his pockets with the losses of lesser men, he would say, laughing. After college he had gone to Europe and settled in Spain, where he ran a small printing company in Madrid and had fun. I used to wonder if the migraine headaches, the uncertain memory and the peculiar passion for parties made him a very good man in intelligence or espionage, but it did not then matter. In 1955 and 1956 he worked for Colonel Lansdale in Vietnam, and hero-worshipped him. He had a nice way with people; the Filipinos found him charming and whimsical.

In the spring of 1975, after a fifteen-year lapse, I saw John Gates again; we met for lunch in a Brazilian restaurant near the bank on Park Avenue where he worked in investments. He married a very pretty woman from Oklahoma who rarely spoke and painted sweet murals. She was an interior decorator, they had no children but had a house in Southampton and a house in Palm Beach, which suited them both very well. That day in the Brazilian restaurant, over the black beans, he could still make me laugh, still make me see the charm, but there was nothing we could agree on.

"I love this country," he said, above the beans. "When anything gets out of whack, there is a correcting force within both the government and our society which takes care of it—something's wrong, a story comes out in *Time*, it begins to improve; things are normal again."

I said others were not so sure, that, for example, the struggle of the blacks in the civil-rights movement had not ended because of a story in *Time*. He then said something about Nixon stepping out of line and being clobbered by Congress.

His wife, Letitia, had gone to Southampton; he was alone in the apartment in the East Seventies when I came for dinner, which he cooked. The very long yellow living room had a portrait over the fireplace of Letitia holding a dog. The two tiger-skin rugs on the floor, the animal's horns coming out from the wall, all trophies of a hunting trip in East Africa, and the fancy yellow silk curtains gave the room a theatrical look, the feeling of a set waiting for the actors. It was a great room for giving parties, he said.

When the food was finished, nothing went as well. He would only say that during his two years in Vietnam he had trained the Vietnamese in a paramilitary operation. Its purpose was to make the soldiers understand how to have a good relationship with the villagers so they would be regarded as the friends of the peasants. Then, as a civilian, he worked for the Department of Defense, attached to the Military Assistance Advisory Group. He left the CIA years ago, he said not once but twice, then three times, and he had not kept up with the war. It was so long ago, he said.

"I was doing psychological warfare, civic action, political warfare," he said. "I really can't give you too much of that background."

He did not understand why I began to laugh, to tell him it need no longer be a secret, I knew more secrets now than he dreamed of, and the Pentagon Papers had been in print for four years.

"Under the Geneva Agreement, MAAG was restricted to only a certain number of military. I came home, was demobilized and went back out as a civilian, doing basically the same thing," he said.

He didn't want to talk about the war, he wanted to watch the NFL game. He said it was Monday night, the football game was the reason he was staying home and had planned to do nothing.

"I've never told anyone I was in Vietnam. No, I wasn't ashamed of it. I never mentioned it because it would always bring up an argument in which I was on one side and everybody else on the other," he said. "But I'm ashamed we got beaten so badly. What the hell, you can't really argue with people who don't know what they're talking about. And I didn't even really know what I was talking about, in retrospect."

He thought the war had been lost because of the terrain. It was too difficult for American troops, even with their air support, their superior weaponry and equipment. Jesus, that terrain, he said.

The Civic Action Program—copied from the Communists—recruited, trained and assigned cadres to live in villages and assist the villagers while persuading them of the merits of the Saigon government. It was not a success, he said. "We set it up, we pumped some money into it, we got the government to give them some help. Every time they ran out of medicine I had to run around and try to find some. We found a lot of French medicine. It was just a make-do operation; we started that thing with just nothing.

"No, I'm not ashamed of it, it's just that I just don't like to really be involved in anything that's a failure, right?"

It was he who so many years before had told me what good fighters the Viet Minh had been, what an awesome and resourceful army they were, how some of the Communist programs could be adapted by the Americans to help the Vietnamese in the south.

"I don't know . . . Look, to be perfectly frank, the Vietnamese war bores me," he said. He remembered the name of one woman whose son had been killed there, but he thought most of his friends' sons had evaded the draft, which was wrong.

He saw one antiwar demonstration, on Wall Street in 1970, when the peace marchers were attacked by construction workers. "We were all rooting for the hard hats. They weren't rough enough, in my book. The peaceniks were very irrational and impractical. They were screaming and yelling about peace and love and they were all hopped up on pot. They were freaks; they were nothing we could ever relate to. They were screaming and yelling when they came down, shouting all those crazy things. Frankly, I was all for the hard hats and I think everybody else was who was looking at it. They were literally asking to be beaten up.

"You've got to understand that I've been brought up so that when my government says go out there and fight, you go out there and fight. When I'm told by my government to do something, I do it."

But he had thought about the war, it turned out, then he had stopped paying attention around 1971. "I never talked about it. I avoided it. I used to see it on television as little as possible. When they always showed the other side of the story, I'd turn it off. They never did show anything but the other side, the antiwar side."

I thought the interview might bring on a migraine, but it didn't. He went to a couch and lay down. He felt tired.

"It was a military take-over that we were trying to fight by military means, and we lost. That's all, it's as simple as that."

Yes, he had remembered the hopes he had for the Civic Action Program, for the cadres. "Obviously they were not as dedicated as the VC cadres. It was a helpful program but it didn't work, that's all, I guess. You got them from anywhere you could. They were paid, they weren't paid enough. Remember, we only had about ten teams by the time I left."

I asked him if we had paid the cadre more, would they have believed more, been better. But by then he wanted to see the football game more than anything. He clearly did not want to hear that the Civic Action Program had lived, taken huge shape under other names and not worked either.

"Basically I still look at it as a North Vietnamese military invasion. I mean, for Christ sake, I don't really see that we're the bad boy!"

He and Letitia had taken a trip around the world in 1973—he was on leave from the New York brokerage firm where he worked and had not yet joined the bank—and it was his idea to go back to Vietnam. At lunch in the Brazilian place with the beans, he said Saigon hadn't changed much. Then he saw my face. "Well, we were only there for two days."

It was too bad that the Vietnamese didn't speak French as much in Saigon as they had when he was first there, that the Hotel Majestic wasn't what it once used to be.

"There was a lot of anti-Americanism which I didn't find distressing at all. I've always thought the minute the Koreans turned anti-American was when they wanted to fight the battle themselves. I was hoping that the South Vietnamese would say to themselves 'We can do a better job than you guys.'

"We were flying from Phnom Penh, we must have flown around some Communist areas. We came in, really, from Camau—we really flew the length of South Vietnam between Saigon and Camau. And sure, every once in a while you'd see some evidence of war. But I mean it's a hell of a big country and just how much real devastation was done, well, I question it."

He was always a kind man, sometimes squeamish, who could not bear to see people in pain. There was the summer when a young Japanese woman came to New York for more corrective surgery on her face, which had been burned at Hiroshima. He drove the two of us somewhere but he could not look at her. Seeing him again that night, I wanted to tell him that the Japanese woman's face, which had already borne so much surgery, was a pretty and functional thing compared to the faces in Vietnam without noses, eyelids, lips, chins and ears. She was only scarred, she could chew, swallow, speak, close her eyes. Napalm and white phosphorus did their work very well on human skin and bones, I said, but he turned away. What the hell, he had never listened to the voices coming at him in the sixties. He was not going to put up with the ranting now.

He spoke of the war as if it were a wild good-natured kind of poker game, as so many others have.

"They kept upping the ante until we didn't have any more cards to play with," he said. "I was hoping we'd have the same success in Vietnam we had in the Philippines. Obviously there wasn't much hope for that. I didn't think they had that kind of persistence; they showed a lot more tenacity than I thought. What am I going to believe? You think I'm going to listen to anything that the goddamned press is going to tell me about the war? It was so slanted that you didn't believe anything they said. Most people didn't believe what they said. 'The ARVN is this or that' or 'Thieu is this or that,' You no longer knew what to believe."

I knew how to answer him: the press did not plan the war or fight or vote on it. Not that many reporters had even done a good job of reporting it. The daily briefings—the meaningless recitals of the military—had been a sham, but no one refused to write them.

"Why should I feel responsible? I was sent out to do a job and I did it," he said. "It bores me, it's ancient history, I would just like to turn my back on it, I don't even like to talk about it. Well, I mean, gee whiz, Gloria, what do you want? Did you want to have the Communists walk down and just take over the whole area? I don't care how you view the Viet Cong, I think they were totally Hanoi people. I hate aggression. I'm against it. It was a bald-faced military effort by the North Vietnamese to get the rice in the south because the rice deficit in the north—"

I didn't let him finish his theory about the north wanting the rice of the south, which for years because of the war had to export large amounts of rice to feed its own people.

The quarrel began then. He went to look at the football game, muttering "I don't want to remember."

IN SAIGON, TWENTY years before, Demi Gates had been upset by a novel that was only two hundred and forty-seven pages and just being published in the United States. Its title was *The Quiet American* by Graham Greene.

In 1956 in that hot city of yellow and green, both of us read the American edition. It was a first warning for me, but I dismissed the book as brilliant but cynical, until it came back to haunt me more than I ever thought such a small, light book ever could. Demi Gates thought it was awful: a deliberate attempt to make the Americans look like meatheads and bad guys, as he put it. Actually, the novel did not make much difference then, least of all to the Vietnamese. Fowler, the narrator, is an aging British journalist covering the war between the French and the Viet Minh. The young American, Pyle, talks of democracy, quotes a book called *The Advance of Red China*, wants the Vietnamese girl Fowler has, and intends to build a third force in Vietnam which will improve the place and make it a democracy. Fowler thinks that the American, because of "his gangly legs and his crew cut and his wide campus gaze," is incapable of harm. But the Englishman cannot trust Americans like Pyle, for he knows that such "innocence is a kind of insanity."

When the two men are trapped in a watchtower at night, with two frightened Vietnamese soldiers, Fowler tells the American: *"You and your like are trying to make a war with the help of people who just aren't interested."* Pyle says—as all of us once said—they don't want communism. Fowler replies that they want enough rice, they don't want to be shot at. He goes on: *"They want one day to be much the same as another. They don't want our white skins around telling them what they want."*

"If Indo-China goes . . ." This is Pyle speaking.

"I know the record. Siam goes, Malaya goes. Indonesia goes. What does 'go' mean?"

All of us were not unlike Pyle: earnest, ignorant, friendly, hygienic, preachy. We talked the way he did. "If Vietnam goes . . ." became an obsession, a blue-eyed marching song.

The Quiet American was attacked in *The New Yorker* by A. J. Liebling, a writer and humorist who later became somewhat revered for his articles on American journalists, called "The Wayward Press." The book, which Mr. Liebling read on a transatlantic flight, made him very angry. He feared it might confuse and upset the French. In April 1956 he wrote:

> Mr. Greene's irritation at being a minor American author does not justify the main incident of the book, which is a messy explosion in downtown Saigon, during the shopping hour, put on by earnest but unimaginative Pyle in collaboration with a bandit "general" in the hope of blowing up some French officers. (The French postpone their parade, and the explosion merely tears up women and children) . . .
>
> The book begins with Pyle in the morgue. That is the big gag: A Quiet American. It then goes to the events that led up to his arrival there. . . . Near the three-eighths pole, it appears that Pyle, who is a cloak-and-dagger boy attached to the Economic side of the American Legation, is helping the bandit get plastic, which can be used in the manufacture of bombs. . . . I figured the bandit was fooling naïve young Pyle. Not at all. Pyle knew all about the bombs and the contemplated explosion. So did the whole American legation.

Mr. Liebling also referred to Mr. Greene's preface, which was a letter to friends in Saigon. The writer explained that historical events in his novel had been rearranged and none of the characters were based on originals. He had only borrowed the name Phuong from the wife of his friend because it was "simple, beautiful and easy to pronounce, which is not true of all your countrywomen's names." Mr. Liebling was vexed by the preface:

> Greene was, then, writing about a real explosion, a historical event, which had produced real casualties. And he was attributing the real explosion to a fictitious organization known as the United States State Department. . . .
>
> But whether it had or hadn't, anybody who read the book

would wonder whether the State Department was engaged in the business of murdering French colonels and, in their default, friendly civilians. . . .

He called Mr. Greene's book a "nasty little plastic bomb." "There is a difference, after all, between calling your over-successful ally a silly ass and accusing him of murder," Mr. Liebling said.

I lent the novel to a veteran who wants to write. He did not like it. His platoon had been around Dau Tieng, near the Michelin rubber plantation; like most American troops, he had never seen Saigon or any city in Vietnam. Besides, he said, all the people in the novel were old. He did not see what could still be learned from *The Quiet American* or the conversation in the watchtower between Fowler and Pyle. Almost everything, I said.

THERE WAS A "wanted" poster of Wesley Fishel. It said he was wanted for murder. He even kept one of the posters, but could not find it to show me in his office at James Madison College at Michigan State University in East Lansing. The room bulges with papers, files, bookshelves, periodicals. Dr. Fishel, a professor of political science who teaches a course to undergraduates on international politics, became a target for antiwar protests because he had for two years been a close advisor to President Ngo Dinh Diem in South Vietnam and had headed the Michigan State University Advisory Group in Vietnam from 1955 to 1958. In 1969 he was Visiting University Research Professor at Southern Illinois University at Carbondale and senior consultant to the vice-president of the university, where he had helped create a Center for Vietnamese Studies and was editor of its journal *Southeast Asia*.

His troubles in the United States started when *Ramparts*, a magazine now defunct, published an extraordinary article in the spring of 1966 on how Michigan State University had been a willing partner of the Central Intelligence Agency in South Vietnam, carrying out "counterinsurgency" tasks in support of a government denying civil liberties to its citizens.

The article was extraordinary because in 1966 there was not yet a record for the public of the secret commitments, the false official reports, the disguised escalation and what one reporter called "the contrived public relations arguments that victory was essential and turning back was unthinkable . . ."

It was the first connection made for American students on hundreds of campuses—who were not yet protesting the war or the draft in large numbers—to the link between the universities and the war machine, to the complicity between the universities and a detestable foreign policy. Furthermore, the article had an introduction by an economist named Stanley Sheinbaum who had been the campus coordinator for the Michigan State University Advisory Group in South Vietnam for three years and now deeply regretted it. Mr. Sheinbaum called the article "a specific, if shocking, documentation of the degree of corruption and abject immorality attending a university which puts its academic respectability on lend-lease to American foreign policy." He wrote of two critical failures in American education and intellectual life:

The first and more obvious is the diversion of the university away from its functions (and duties) of scholarship and teaching. The second has to do with the failure of the academic intellectual to serve as critic, conscience, ombudsman. Especially in foreign policy, which henceforth will bear heavily on our very way of life at home, is this failure serious . . . We have only the capacity to be experts and technicians to serve that policy. This is the tragedy of Michigan State professors: we were all automatic cold warriors.

Dr. Fishel provided me with an autobiography which made mention of his Vietnam connections and showed that among other organizations he had been a consultant at various times to the U.S. Department of State, that his published works included *The End of Extraterritoriality in China* and *Language Problems of the U.S. Army During Hostilities in Korea*, that he had held a Guggenheim Fellowship 1961–1962 and several other grants for research.

In *Ramparts*, Mr. Sheinbaum wrote he knew that some of the CIA agents embedded in the MSU group in Vietnam attained faculty status—some as lecturers and some as assistant professors—because he remembered signing the papers that gave them faculty rank. The first MSU professors joined Mr. Fishel in Saigon in late May of 1955; the CIA agents were ostensibly assigned to the police administrative division of the Michigan State group and worked as a self-contained unit that was not transferred to the United States Mission until 1959. The article claimed that the East Lansing School of Police Administration not only trained security forces for Diem but provided revolvers, riot guns, police ammunition, jeeps, handcuffs and radios.

Dr. Fishel denied the existence of CIA agents in the Michigan State group, and the supplying of weapons. Eight years later, he complained once more about that *Ramparts* article. "We didn't supply the police with weapons other than target pistols. What our people did was to advise the Vietnamese police services on what kinds of weapons they should be armed with, and when they got them, how to handle them. Which equipment was best and which was worst. We have here reputedly the best school of police administration in the United States. The police advisors that we sent out—only a small number of them actually came from the faculty, because the Vietnamese needs were so great that they were hired from state police forces around the country."

He did not stop going to Vietnam even when he was no longer chief of the MSU group. He had gone back on the Guggenheim Fellowship, and to write articles. In 1971 I caught sight of him in Saigon.

"I came back virtually every year after I left in 1958 for various reasons," Dr. Fishel said.

He regretted nothing he had done; it was clear, however, that he felt many other people should regret their actions. He said, for example, that Stanley Sheinbaum had been required to leave the university because he had not completed his doctorate. He added that Mr. Sheinbaum had then found a job with the Center for the Study of Democratic Institutions, "which made all of us who were his friends very happy because it tripled his salary, got him a respectable position and when he left here he was going to complete his Ph.D." Dr. Fishel said he had seen Stanley Sheinbaum's name in the papers as chief fund raiser for Dan Ellsberg during his trial in Los Angeles, but even this did not seem to convince him—for nothing could—that Mr. Sheinbaum had very deep feelings about the war. Dr. Fishel said that Mr. Sheinbaum "simply burned to get even" with Michigan State for taking him "out of academic life." Many of Mr. Sheinbaum's acquaintance find this almost humorous in its inaccuracy.

"And I was simply—as he explained to somebody else—sort of accidentally his victim," Dr. Fishel said. "He didn't really mean it against me personally, but I was the happy symbol of everything that was evil."

The Center for Vietnamese Studies at Southern Illinois University came to life in July 1969 with a one-million-dollar grant from the Agency for International Development for the purposes of "economic and social development of Vietnam and its postwar reconstructions." There were protests among the SIU faculty and other academics who feared that the Center would be used to uphold American policy in Vietnam and that AID was corrupting Vietnamese studies in the United States. Twenty of twenty-two members of the SIU Department of History signed a protest in February 1970. In October a conference was held by scholars and academics—the theme was "Scholarly Integrity and

University Complicity"—who announced an international boycott of the Center.

One of the participants was a Vietnamese, Huynh Kim Khanh,
from Ontario, who said: "I've read that the cost of killing one 'Viet
Cong' is something like three hundred fifty thousand dollars—a
real Viet Cong, that is, not just a gook or any Vietnamese. In these
terms the million dollars given to the Vietnam Center is very
cheap . . . But as the Center here is set up, it is part of a scheme to
continue the American presence in Vietnam. This is simply no
good and it is very dangerous. It is dangerous because it is part of
the pattern of the war itself. Much has been said about this war's
being a 'mistake,' as though it were correctable. It is not; it is part
of a larger pattern.

"The Center for Vietnamese Studies is an instrument of
American neo-colonialism in South Vietnam . . . After 1945 one
type of colonialism, that of small European countries with limited
resources, was replaced by a new form of domination maintained
by large countries with extensive resources, territories and pop-
ulations, operating through foreign military and economic aid
programs.

"The term aid itself reflects the fiction at the heart of these new
arrangements . . . It is only when control exercised by military and
economic means fail that the neo-colonialist powers bring troops
into their own states . . . I am looking at Czechoslovakia and at
Vietnam . . . We have to watch these superpowers, because with
them it is not a matter of ideology; it is a question of power politics."

IN 1969 WESLEY FISHEL was senior consultant to the vice-
president of Southern Illinois University at Carbondale, and a Visiting University Research Professor of Government. He, in effect,
headed the Center for Vietnamese Studies. It made him intensely
unpopular, and a symbol of the collusion between the universities

and the war, the technology and the sicknesses in the American society. At Southern Illinois, where he stayed for two years, there were demonstrations. The impetus on many of the country's campuses for reform, resistance, challenge came from chapters of Students for a Democratic Society.

"The SDS decided that I was villain number one, their most evil man," Dr. Fishel said. He spoke of Molotov cocktails being thrown through the windows of his offices on three occasions and of a May evening in 1970 when great numbers of antiwar students were "roaming the campus in bands," while the National Guard was on duty with fixed bayonets. He remembers barbed wire. Dr. Fishel worried about his extensive files on Vietnam, which included the records of the many conversations he had had with Ngo Dinh Diem from 1950 when they first met in Japan. Later the university assigned two campus police to protect him and the office.

"My phone had been bugged. We're not sure whether it was the SDS or the university. It was a sloppy job. In any event, on this particular evening there had been a crowd of about four thousand around the president's house screaming for his blood. Because of the war in Vietnam, the Center for Vietnamese Studies was a symbol of imperialism and warmongering and so on. They had banners and posters."

Dr. Fishel, who is a short man with broad shoulders and a husky body, said he was not without combat experience, which he was sure helped that night.

"I was on Iwo Jima, attached to the 3d Marine Division. I was an Army officer, commanding a detachment of interrogators. I was a first lieutenant. It was 1945 and we had the job of trying to persuade Japanese soldiers to surrender. I was under fire a good deal of the time and, I think, sort of foolish about things of this sort, or maybe I'm just normal. You don't think about the fact that you're in danger until after it's all over . . . I was trying to protect my files and my papers. I was there by myself and trying to protect the women who worked for me—four of them, three students and a full-time secretary. They were very brave, but only, I suppose, because I didn't seem to be alarmed."

He spoke about books on the war which had mentioned him unfavorably, as well as the attacks from the antiwar groups. "I feel pain, not because of the personal attacks on me. No, it's not pleasant. I was attacked in 1950 by the Beverly Hills California Republican Women's Club—for supporting Dean Acheson. There was a lot of criticism. I remember this one particular group because this was an audience of five hundred women who ended up in a screaming rage because I was defending our policy in Korea. One woman got to her feet, she said: 'When are they going to do something about those insane traitors in Washington who are selling us down the River of Rubles to Red Ruin.' I was trying to explain why the war in Korea was being fought and why the United States and the U.N. were involved." The woman, he said, believed that the United States had sold out and was not fighting the Communists in Korea.

He spoke of himself as a man who had withstood many sieges, some of them even in Saigon, and never given way. In the spring of 1958 when he had been very ill with food poisoning, there was a crisis with General "Hanging Sam" Williams and his colonels, Dr. Fishel said. The general had been urging President Diem to place the civilian police training operation run by MSU under the American military. One of the general's arguments, Dr. Fishel recalled, was that the Michigan State people were just police officers and knew nothing about fighting a war. Dr. Fishel said he rose from his sickbed, had one of his private breakfasts with President Diem in the palace, persuaded him not to turn over the police operation to the Military Advisory Assistance Group, and won. His victory made General Williams shake with rage. It pleased Dr. Fishel to remember this.

"I had a kind of rapport with Diem which they envied and which they could not duplicate," he said to me. President Diem had asked him for more MSU people to enlarge the police operation, but the university felt it was "an inappropriate project."

"It wanted really to close it out," Dr. Fishel said. "It felt that this was not an appropriate activity for the university to be involved in, however appropriate it might have seemed at the outset. It had become inappropriate. I agreed with the university's view . . ."

Dr. Fishel said, with a shrug, he had been attacked from the far left and the far right. "The ones from the far left have been more unpleasant because I consider myself a liberal. It's painful to see people who are your intellectual peers go off on a tangent—or what you consider a tangent—to be misled and to translate their interpretation of what they see into *violent emotional irrational emotional attacks*. Not just on me, but on anyone who holds a view different from theirs.

"I happen to be a very trusting, credulous person in the sense that I will take a person at face value until he or she is proved to be something other than I expected. When I see scholars who are experts in their own fields and who wouldn't stand for the slightest bit of irrationality or monkey business in their professional fields *coming into my field* and behaving like little children or like people who have just escaped from a mental institution, it shakes me. Because my image, my youthful image, of the intellectual was a kind of demigod image. Does that make sense to you? It has been with great pain over the years that I've discovered that intellectuals are even human. You don't like to see this because, as a student, you have this idealized image of the intellectual, a professor, as the great man who isn't going to be swayed by the crass kind of things."

A young instructor of Asian philosophy at Southern Illinois University seemed to have particularly offended Dr. Fishel. He was Douglas Allen, who was so outspoken and constant in his criticism of the Center, the MSU role in the war and of Dr. Fishel that he was dismissed from his job in October 1970 by the Board of Trustees at SIU. One graduate student, however, wrote that Mr. Allen was an example of "courage and dedication to many students."

"He seized on the war issue as one which he would, in effect, I guess, ride to some kind of power never clearly defined. He fancied himself a leader of the students. How deeply he believed the things he said, I'm not sure," Dr. Fishel said.

He saw such people in terms of power, wishing it for themselves. He could not understand that what they were seeking was the struggle to take power from those in command, and that what they had come to believe was that vital issues could no longer be settled by universities, presidents, statutes, decrees, politicians, generals and scholars, but in spite of them.

"He attacked me before this whole SIU field house full of people as a complete bastard, that's a quotation, and as a warmaker who must be driven from the campus. And in the recording you can hear the audience just surge with cheers and howls and applause. Okay, now, this irritated me. Didn't frighten me, it frightened some of the local police . . .

"You have to keep in mind that to almost all of these people I was nothing but a name that they had read about in *Ramparts,* thousands of copies of which were distributed free all over."

In 1967 Dr. Fishel invited Hubert Humphrey, the Vice-President, to speak about Vietnam during the last week of the term after Memorial Day. He said two thousand eight hundred students filled the auditorium. "Hubert gave a very strong, supportive speech, trying to explain what Vietnam was about. I thought it went off very well. He had a good audience and he did a beautiful job."

In 1968 *Vietnam: Anatomy of a Conflict* was published. It was a collection of essays and articles on the Vietnam war which Dr. Fishel edited and for which he wrote a long preface. In addition, each of the eight chapters—which contained articles critical of the war as well as those defending the American role—had an introduction by him. The first article in the last chapter, titled "Only Choice in Asia: Stay and Fight," was also written by him.

"I speak from a position which has been consistently misrepresented over the years. It has never been a popular position and it is a position which I suppose would be difficult for the public to understand," Dr. Fishel said. "But it was a position very similar to that of Diem in some respects—and I differed with him violently on others. Diem, as you know, violently opposed large-scale American action in Vietnam."

He agreed his career had been affected by the antiwar movement. "That doesn't bother me. It's hurt only in a salary sense. I am not one of the university's highest-paid professors, even if I am one of its best-known and perhaps respected ones. This simply reflects the fact that for a period of years I was highly unpopular and I was busy in the public arena."

Dr. Fishel said he had not given as many lectures on Vietnam in 1974 as he had previously. "Last year I probably gave a dozen, but for years I was giving anywhere from fifty to one hundred lectures a year." He thought the *Ramparts* article was inaccurate and that it had "a circulation and notoriety that far exceeded any of the expectations of the authors." In Wichita Falls, Texas, where he was giving a lecture, he was greeted by a Brigadier General Winn, whom he described as one of the highest-ranking POWs in North Vietnam.

"He told me in essence that my name was a household word in the POW camps in North Vietnam because the North Vietnamese insisted that every single POW read that article from *Ramparts* as an example of how the American establishment was imperialistic, how we had deliberately made war and so on and so forth. That sort of startled me. I had no idea I had been read about in the prison camps. And he pumped my hand and said 'I'm glad to see you in the flesh.'"

. . .

AFTER HE WAS fired by Southern Illinois University, some people suspected Douglas Allen was on a blacklist, for he could not seem to find permanent work. For three years he had one-year appointments at three different universities, until the fall of 1974 when he joined the faculty of the University of Maine. Mr. Allen, who is thirty-five, now has tenure. He teaches courses in Hindu and Buddhist philosophy.

Following his dismissal from SIU, the American Civil Liberties Union filed suit in Federal Court, the American Association of University Professors held an investigation and placed SIU on a national censure list, and the university's application for a Phi Beta Kappa chapter was rejected, he says.

None of this was as important to him as the slow, steady decline of the Center for Vietnamese Studies, which at the end of the second year of operation was moved off campus to a floor of a former dormitory building. During 1973–74 one hundred and four faculty and staff members were let go.

"There it stood: ugly and offensive, a focus for our sense of outrage, a destination for our marches and demonstrations," Mr. Allen said. "Professors housed in the same building with the Center began to sign petitions demanding its removal from campus. There was room in the struggle for the person who did scholarly research and the person who spray-painted buildings with OFF AID. The strategy was to keep constant pressure on SIU and the Center by organizing forces on many levels of opposition and by keeping the Center in a state of confusion . . ."

They did just that. The Southern Illinois Peace Committee knew exactly who were the speakers at the Vietnam Center, and leafleted them, so in time the Center stopped sponsoring public lectures. Mr. Allen, a member of the Committee of Concerned Asian Scholars, said the movement attempted to "make the life of anyone coming to Carbondale and accepting the Center's

Funds exceedingly uncomfortable." The decline of the Center was noticeable in 1970, he said, when Washington began to have doubts about the wisdom of its investment in Carbondale, for the Center was in a state of siege from January to May 1970 and the university was forced to shut down for a month.

In April 1972 fifteen Vietnamese in the antiwar movement "invaded" Carbondale. Most of them had come to the United States on AID scholarships, and they were there to persuade the seventy Vietnamese at SIU—the largest number at any American university—to hear them out. The SIU students waved Saigon flags, held high their signs, made noise, jeered and argued. They were told by Ngo Vinh Long of the role AID played in building prisons and "tiger cages," in the training and equipping of the Saigon police, in the persecution and torture of Vietnamese political prisoners. When Le Anh Tu, a Vietnamese woman married to an American medical student, spoke to the SIU Vietnamese, something surprising took place.

"She said she would not attack her Vietnamese brother. She was saddened to see that her SIU brothers and sisters had learned so well Nixon's policy of Vietnamization," Mr. Allen said. "It was an incredible sight. Most of the SIU Vietnamese, who moments before had been screaming and waving Saigon flags, were silent and shamed, their eyes cast downward. She then analyzed Nixon's policy and the situation in Vietnam, and even received some applause from the SIU Vietnamese."

It was a day he never forgot.

It was the Vietnamese themselves who finally doomed the Center by ending the war, Mr. Allen said. It now exists on a shrunken scale and a harmless one, teaching a few students Vietnamese.

"Of course, if SIU had hired one professor to teach a few students Vietnamese, there would have been little if any protest," Mr. Allen said. "But this was not what AID and SIU had in mind in 1969 when the university received an initial one million dollars and talked about future, separately funded contracts in Indochina."

He thought the crippling of those plans had been a victory for the antiwar movement, that they had played a small role in resisting Washington's policy of Vietnamization. But there was no elation, no great surge of triumph in it for him or the others.

"We shall never know how many Vietnamese were tortured or silenced because of AID police and prison training programs at Southern Illinois University and other institutions. We shall never know how many Vietnamese became 'Americanized,' became tragic victims of cultural imperialism, identified themselves with Saigon and Washington and cut themselves off from the progressive Vietnamese forces, at least partially, because of the AID educational and training programs at SIU and other institutions. But we do know, we certainly know, that the costs paid by the Vietnamese people were tremendous."

FEW OF US who were there can claim innocence. It is useless now to ask what has happened to the Vietnamese who worked for the Americans, for the reporters who required them to be what we needed for our own advancement and gain and comfort. It is not a question of their being punished now. The question is if all of us harmed them and how much. Sometimes it seemed that Luong was changing—yet not changing—and I worried about how he might be affected by working for Americans. Yet I never worried so much that I let him go. The reporting depended so much on him; he was more important than I was. If there was in this war an army which he loved, he did not reveal it. All I saw was his pity and kindness for the victims. Long ago I asked him what he thought would happen if the war ended and the other Vietnamese won.

"I would have to go to many meetings and volunteer to give up my Honda," he said. But he often spoke of breaking from us and being a simple man again, working as a farmer or in a café as a waiter. "It can be good in life to go down," he said.

On one of the rare days when he was drinking that wonderful, sharp Vietnamese beer called "33"—which made his face flush—he spoke of a small nightmare. The war was over, his family was okay, he was calm. He saw himself in a room facing a man seated at a table asking him questions. The man was his own age, thirty-five or thirty-six, a *chien si* in the National Liberation Front who had been fighting in the jungle for all the years of his youngness. Luong loses his voice before this man, he cannot answer the questions. The other man is patient and waits, only looking at him.

I think he is fine. But I wait for word and cannot send any. Some letters are getting through to the south; some are getting out. The trouble is that I have no address for him, only a map he made of his house in Gia Dinh. In the cities there were often no proper addresses for the little dwellings tucked behind the big streets or boulevards, no common names for the alleys or cul-de-sacs or roads. There is an Esso station on Luong's map which must now be gone. I did not think I would ever need an address for him, since Luong received his mail at the Saigon office of *The New York Times*. The expert reporter thought that would always be enough.

A FEW MEN were made experts in Vietnam and could not tolerate it. One of them was John Isaacs, who grew up in Silver Spring, Maryland, and in White Plains, New York, the son of a lawyer, who always wanted to be in the Foreign Service. He was accepted by the State Department and began that career in 1969. He spent thirteen months in Vietnam, but resigned in October 1971 in an unusual manner. Mr. Isaacs returned his civilian medal to William P. Rogers, who was Secretary of State, with a letter of resignation. He did not personally notify his immediate superiors in Saigon; he just packed, left a letter for the ambassador, mailed copies of it to a few senators, and went to the airport. A copy of that letter was given to a friend to hand-deliver to Ambassador Ellsworth Bunker in Saigon. Mr. Isaacs left his little apartment in good order. It was his contention that if he resigned in the normal way, it would have meant "two weeks of hassling." A very quiet and calm man, not given to arguments and futile confrontations, Mr. Isaacs is also very stubborn. "They don't like anyone resigning and so I am leaving on my terms, not on theirs," he said in Saigon. "They won't listen to my reasons anyway." He was right.

In Vietnam he was assigned to CORDS, the agency in charge of pacification, to work with refugees. He thought it was a paramilitary operation and that his work was "a perversion of the traditional duties" of a Foreign Service officer, who was expected to report what goes on in a foreign country. Instead, Mr. Isaacs felt he was actively working to support a local government, and it was so. He was first assigned to Binh Tuy province in the coastal lowlands as an advisor to a Vietnamese called a social welfare chief who was trying to resettle five thousand two hundred repatriates from Cambodia.

"I was sent into the province with no knowledge of refugees, never having seen, smelled, touched or talked to a refugee," Mr. Isaacs said. "I was supposed to advise a Vietnamese who had worked with refugees for four years." He lived in Ham Tan, the provincial capital, with a team of one hundred and twenty American men. They were mostly idle, he said, because they didn't know how to advise the Vietnamese and the Vietnamese did not want to be advised. He often wrote reports that were critical of plans to relocate Vietnamese and questioned whether the relocations were voluntary.

He was transferred to Bien Hoa, near Saigon. During those six months he realized what he could do. He began to provide a few reporters with documents, available only to CORDS personnel and usually marked *Classified*, that gave very clear examples of how the war was going. They were little case histories of deceit, greed, foolishness, corruption, malice, misunderstanding and stupidity. Some of the other young men in CORDS shared his misgivings about the war but did not try to do anything. Few Americans wanted to risk getting into trouble.

"A lot of people objected on practical grounds but they had no moral or ethical objections," Mr. Isaacs said.

He did not have many friends. He worked very hard and when he gave us documents he would sometimes summarize their contents, or underline passages, to make sure we got the point. Nothing seemed to surprise him. He thought that the pacification program, with all its long and numerous tentacles, was a fraud being perpetrated on the American people to cover up a war that had long been lost. He would write notes in a red, or sometimes a green, felt pen. He wanted to provide a record, a sort of history, of what the Americans were doing and of what was happening to the Vietnamese.

Once he gave me a very long report from an American officer who had served in III Corps and who just before he left had submitted six pages in an outburst of frustration and anger. The name of the American, the district where he worked, the names of Vietnamese and Americans mentioned in the report had all been deleted by officials in CORDS. The American was a deputy district senior advisor to a Vietnamese district chief. Each district in each of the provinces had an American advisor who often had a deputy.

The report, dated February 24, 1971, criticized the district chief for stealing from a U.S. base camp that had recently been closed down and turned over to the Vietnamese. The American officer saw materials—electrical wiring, lumber, artillery ammunition boxes, tin roofing—being carted away. "The materials being sold from this base camp represented hundreds of thousands of U.S. taxpayer dollars being taken away by one man for his personal profit," he wrote. As proof of the stealing, the American tried to take pictures of the materials being put in civilian vehicles, but he was told to desist by an armed Vietnamese who admitted such orders came from the district chief.

Another complaint in the report was that the Vietnamese in the People's Self-Defense Forces, the village militia who were required to take turns guarding their village at night and observing any suspicious behavior of other villagers at all times, were paying the district chief to be relieved of their duties. The rate was three thousand piasters for a month without duty at night.

In the report the district chief—always Vietnamese—was referred to as the DC. The man who was the district senior advisor—always an American—was called the DSA.

"The district chief and his staff had a marked tendency not to report enemy-initiated incidents or other incidents which might lower their HES rating or otherwise reflect unfavorably on the DC," the report said. HES meant Hamlet Evaluation System, the American method for grading the security of all the hamlets; it was based on reports, sent in by American advisors, which were fed into a computer in Saigon. The results were often inaccurate and optimistic. The district chief, a major, knew as well as any clever Vietnamese how obsessive the Americans were about the HES ratings, how much simpler life was if the Americans got only good news. At a meeting with local officials and police the district chief became quite nasty, warning the others to be most selective in what they let the Americans know.

"He told them specifically that if they did not personally see an incident, then it did not occur," the American officer wrote. "He then proceeded to blame the Americans for the low HES ratings in some of the villages."

The American complained in his report that the district senior advisor, a major in the U.S. Army, was an easygoing fellow who catered to the district chief and overlooked his rudeness, disrespect and dishonesty.

The Vietnamese officers at district headquarters seemed to have little regard for the lives or welfare of troops or civilians. Whenever wounded or sick troops or civilians were brought to District the Vietnamese duty officer would inevitably ask the U.S. advisors for someone to drive the casualty to the dispensary or hospital . . .

At about 1100H a young civilian girl was brought to District by a couple of women who had carried her several kilometers. The girl had a piece of shrapnel in her hip from a booby trap in a rice paddy. The Vietnamese duty officer asked us to drive her to the dispensary. I said no, that they had their own vehicles and drivers to do that. I then told the district chief, commo officer and S2 about the girl and they said they would get a vehicle to move her. When I went back to check, I met the S3 again and I asked him if he'd had the girl driven to the dispensary. He laughed and said he'd told the women to carry her there.

The report complained that the district chief had sent out local soldiers to warn villagers that they had better vote or face possible harassment to their families; one Vietnamese said he had been jailed for not voting, on the grounds that he must certainly be a VC supporter.

The American, who spoke Vietnamese, ended the report by saying that the district chief controlled the district by the "same methods the VC use, i.e., military force."

His report was upsetting to CORDS officials, who did not seem to appreciate such frankness. It was circulated in III Corps with an attached, stern reproach from Richard Funkhouser, deputy director of CORDS, who seemed most annoyed that the officer had not spoken up sooner. The deputy director did not seem to realize that the protesting American was outranked by the district senior advisor, that the Army does not like junior officers to dispute what their superiors say, and that the American had taken a rather large risk and possibly jeopardized his military career by writing the report at all. None of this impressed Ambassador Funkhouser, as he liked being called, having once served as United States ambassador in Gabon. He was not grateful to the American, only vexed that he had made it all known so crudely. The report was circulated with a stern memorandum from Ambassador Funkhouser, whose point was that the American had shown rather bad form:

> What is especially disturbing to me is the lack of information provided to this headquarters on the conditions he alleges during the period described. During the cited period visits to the district concerned by me and members of my staff revealed little information with regard to the allegations made by the deputy district senior advisor. Indeed, he noted in conversations with me that there were no problems in the district and all was going well. *His report, no matter its validity, should be a lesson to us all.* All members of CORDS must be made aware of their responsibility to pass to higher headquarters all information which might affect CORDS adversely in carrying out its advisory role.

Nothing about John Isaacs aroused suspicion. He had a quiet and diligent manner. His hair was short, he looked clean and neat, he did not complain. He was quiet and kept to himself, a man who wasted nothing. When he handed over material to us, he did not seem nervous, but we took precautions. Before he quit, he was promoted in rank in the Foreign Service.

When he returned to the United States in November 1971 Mr. Isaacs went to work for Americans for Democratic Action in Washington, D.C., as a legislative representative who also worked on the ADA monthly newsletter, analyzing Congress, bills, the budget and the voting records of the legislators. He went to anti-war demonstrations "on a nonviolent basis," as he says, and signed petitions. He did not put on blue jeans, let his hair grow, smoke marijuana, speak the language of the sixties, or dive into the music or amusements of the young. At ADA he worked hard. He never received an answer from the Secretary of State or any reference to the civilian medal he returned. A one-sentence acknowledgment from an administrative officer in the State Department said his resignation was received and accepted. He now works as a legislative aide to a New York congressman who is on the House Foreign Affairs Committee.

On the night the war ended, the last night of April in 1975, just before his thirtieth birthday, Mr. Isaacs did an unusual thing. He made two long-distance telephone calls—one to Detroit, one to New York—to speak to two reporters who had shared some of the struggle, and the strain, in Vietnam. It was an unusual thing because he prefers to write little notes. Although it is said that many Americans of his generation, who grew up in the wild, rosy days of the counterculture and tested themselves in the little furnaces of the antiwar movement, became depressed on reaching the age of thirty, it did not happen to him. In October 1974 Mr. Isaacs married a woman in the ADA office who did national political work.

He is still not a man who attracts attention or wishes it. He shows neither despair nor great hopefulness. He does not often speak of the war. He always seems overworked, a man of unusual privacy, not much changed.

"Well, I didn't go off to grow carrots in Vermont," Mr. Isaacs said. "But I regret being part of that effort in Vietnam which so hurt the country and the people. I may have counteracted that effort as best as I could. I may have taken the best course of action. I can't be sure."

PEOPLE SAID: AH, it was unbearable, a disgrace, a shame, they should all be shot or put away. They were complaining about the violence of other Americans, especially the antiwar demonstrators who used dreadful words like fuck and attacked the police and defiled public property while pretending to be so moral. You could still hear this talk long after I came home, knowing so much about murder. The violence they condemned did not mean the violence of the war in Vietnam: the twenty-one million bomb craters in the south which glistened when the rains filled them, or the thirty-nine million acres of land in Indochina infected by fragments of bombs and shells. They did not mean the violence done to the ghostly grey trees that had been poisoned. That was normal, war-normal.

In Washington, D.C., that first winter back a California boy, who had been in fourteen antiwar demonstrations, raided a draft office, been jailed three times, said yes, they had gone forth ready for violence, prepared to provoke it, sometimes needing it.

"We had to show we were not cowards," the boy said. "We had to show we weren't against the war because we were afraid of it." I said I thought I saw his point. We were sitting outside the White House, where he hung out that week, bearing a sign saying STOP ALL AID TO THIEU. He went on talking but his words made my mind wander.

The purpose of the National Commission, established by The White House in June 1968 shortly after the murder of Senator Robert Kennedy, was to examine the causes of violence and means of prevention in the United States. One of their reports on an antiwar demonstration was a careful, dry, detached document which did not even allude to the most important factor: it was the fury and helplessness felt by people persuaded their government would not see or hear them, let alone represent them.

Nothing, except this perception, seems left out of the report called *Rights in Concord*, a special staff study submitted by the Commission's Task Force on Law and Law Enforcement.

In 1969 there was a series of confrontations in Washington,

D.C., on January 18, 19 and 20, in connection with the inauguration of President Richard Nixon. The demonstrations, composed of various antiwar groups, were called by the National Mobilization Committee to End the War in Vietnam, the same organizing force that had brought together demonstrators for the March on the Pentagon on October 21, 1967, and at the August 1968 Democratic National Convention. The protesters were from a loose coalition of antiwar groups, local and national, which depended on MOBE officials to obtain the permits and make arrangements for mass demonstrations. MOBE's leaders called once again for a show of strength to protest "another four years of war, political repression, poverty and racism."

So people came back again. A vast tent went up behind the Washington Monument grounds, signs appeared—BILLIONAIRES PROFIT FROM GI BLOOD, VICTORY for the VIET CONG, REFUSE TO SERVE IN THE ARMED SERVICES, ABOLISH THE DRAFT, NIXON'S THE ONE: #1 WAR CRIMINAL. Marches formed and moved; men carried coffins with symbolic figures of Vietnamese war dead. Tiny bonfires were made of little American flags handed out by the Boy Scouts. Undercover agents from the FBI, the United States Attorney Office, the D.C. police force and the Department of Justice circulated through the crowds which gathered at the tent site. It was estimated that between five to seven thousand persons arrived for the counter-inaugural. FBI intelligence sources reported that some radicals in the tent site had bear traps and tire chains, but they were never seen. All of this is noted in *Rights in Concord*.

It was the first planned large-scale demonstration in American history to protest the inauguration of a President. Permission was granted for a counter-inaugural parade, which, symbolically, moved in the direction opposite to the inaugural parade. Men in black wore huge white sickly masks that were the faces of Richard Nixon. The morning of the huge march it rained and the grounds around the tent turned to mud, at least six inches deep in some places.

One crowd of demonstrators, which had marched from Franklin Park, stood along the inauguration parade route, held back from the street by a steel cable at the widest spot along Pennsylvania Avenue. Police from the Civil Disturbance Unit—especially trained in crowd psychology, tactical formations, use of special weapons, identification of explosive devices—stood directly in front of the demonstrators. They had thirty-inch riot batons. Units of the 82d Airborne Brigade from Fort Bragg, North Carolina, formed a line behind the police. They wore soft caps and long overcoats. The soldiers linked arms. They had no rifles. Nearly two hundred National Guardsmen, wearing battle gear and carrying rifles, lined up shoulder to shoulder next to the troops of the 82d. The effect was familiar, not startling. The street once more became a theater of war.

The report said:

> When the President's car reached the center of the crowd, a bottle and empty beer can were thrown into the street. Two cans with smoke coming from them were also hurled . . . Altogether, twelve hard objects and many wads of paper and tin foil were thrown. The President avoided embarrassment by waving at the bystanders on the other side of the street.
>
> At no time did anyone attempt to break through the police lines. No oven cleaner was used. Other than verbal abuse and the few missiles that were thrown, no commotion engulfed the crowd.

After the inaugural parade, as the demonstrators dispersed, police chased and clubbed several of them at Madison and H Streets, fearing they were on their way to the White House. At least this is what the report says they feared. There is no suggestion that the police wanted to hit, liked the hitting.

On the corner of Vermont and H Streets a young woman, clearly marked with a white armband as a medic, went to assist a youth who appeared to have been injured during a scuffle with a policeman. The policeman turned and hit her with his baton. She began bleeding at the ear.

As demonstrators moved toward 16th Street, police continued the chase, swinging and striking.

At one point a city official intercepted a policeman chasing an eleven-year-old boy. The official escorted the frightened youth to a church. An eighteen-year-old girl was chased twenty-five feet by a policeman who kept hitting her across the back with his baton.

Helicopters attempted to locate groups of demonstrators running in the streets. Multiple sightings of one group by several policemen magnified their numbers in the minds of the police. It was later believed that no more than five dozen demonstrators continued to roam the streets; many began making their way back to their homes and to bus and train stations.

The Deputy Chief of Police in charge of the CDU was notified by his Command Post that ninety arrests had been made at that time. He replied, *"Not enough. Not near enough."* Off the radio, the officer who had supplied the information said apologetically, "I'm sorry."

At 5 P.M. on January 20, 1969, the counter-inaugural was considered to be over.

The report said that the city's tolerant but firm approach to the demonstrators was responsible for avoiding large-scale violence. The report congratulated the Washington police and authorities on their handling of the counter-inaugural protest, and special credit was given to the assistant chief of the D.C. Police Department and to a MOBE attorney. There were one hundred and nineteen arrests, eighty-seven of them on that Monday, mostly during street skirmishes. Many of the arrests were for pedestrian violations. Ninety-nine males, ten females and ten juveniles were picked up. There was, of course, no praise for the demonstrators. There never was. Even now it is commonplace for men like Senator Hubert Horatio Humphrey—who once said Vietnam was our Asian adventure—to still point out how brutal and vulgar the demonstration were. He remains one of those men who did not find the draft as upsetting as people yelling "Fuck the draft."

Four years later it happened all over again. Thousands of people, some in disbelief but moved by habit and disgust, once more went to Washington for a counter-inaugural as the same man was sworn in to the same office and the same war went on. We were kept apart from the inaugural parade, apart from the happy people, the women with corsages, the bands, the floats. The policemen looked less nervous. The 82d Airborne troops were once again lined up. When a Vietnam veteran in a field jacket, who had been a medic in the infantry, reached their line and whispered "Don't do it, brothers, they'll fuck you over as they fucked us over," the soldiers did not see or hear him. They knew better. Then the veteran said it was useless being in Washington that day, we were only inconveniencing ourselves. But we already knew. It was a fiercely cold day. Our sadness and a sense of shame rose like a swamp gas that stayed fixed just above our heads, so only we could smell it.

AS A CHILD in Paris, David Sulzberger collected stamps, and this is how he first learned the names of countries in Indochina. Long afterward he could still remember their colored romantic faces.

Vietnam was in three parts: the south, called Cochin-China, was a colony of the French. North Vietnam was Tonkin, a French protectorate. Central Vietnam, called Annam, was an indirect protectorate, which meant the Vietnamese Emperor and his royal court were allowed to exist, a cherished and handsome screen which did not always conceal power exerted by the colonialist. He had stamps from Cambodia, too, showing the babyish-looking prince named Sihanouk. David's mother used to play a game with her small son: they listened to classical music on the radio and tried to guess who had composed it. When the boy was eight, in early May of 1954, a concert was interrupted to announce the fall of Dien Bien Phu. His mother cried as if she had suddenly been struck.

He is the only son of Cyrus and Marina Sulzberger, a famous couple who have lived in France since the years after World War II, famous for name and family, contacts and a newspaper. Cyrus L. Sulzberger, a columnist on foreign affairs for *The New York Times*, joined the newspaper in 1939, and after World War II was for several years chief of foreign correspondents, before he began the column. His father, Leo, was the brother of Arthur Hays Sulzberger, publisher of *The New York Times* from 1935 to 1961, when he was succeeded by his son, Arthur Ochs Sulzberger. When I was a reporter in the Paris bureau of *The New York Times*, Mr. Sulzberger was an awesome and aloof figure, not given to small talk or amusing comments. He had nothing to do with the foreign staff or the running of the newspaper.

It was a surprise when young Sulzberger left Harvard to go to Vietnam: the sons of famous men did not have to. There were always draft deferments for the privileged or for those in college.

Long after he had been in Vietnam, not as a soldier but as one of the bright young men working in the pacification program, David Sulzberger was not sorry he had gone and he knew why he had. "I was twenty years old then, with a certain amount of competitive desire to blow my father's mind," he said. "At that stage particularly, it was a way of throwing myself into a situation which couldn't be anything but interesting, which would open wide, new waves of spectra to look at. I wanted very much to get there."

WHEN I WAS a reporter in the Paris bureau Cyrus Sulzberger had two rooms in our office all his own, which none of us entered unless summoned. The walls were covered with the framed photographs of kings, heads of state, generals, sultans, prime ministers, archbishops and dictators whom he had interviewed and who had, at his request, autographed their photographs. He hung them all and took no man down even when he was deposed, dishonored or dead.

It was startling scenery. Sometimes the hundreds of solemn male faces—covering every inch of the walls in their thin black frames—had a squashing, silencing effect. There was no one of great influence or ambition whom Cyrus Sulzberger did not seem to know. It awed me that he had lunch with Malraux, could get to de Gaulle, had been damned by Mussolini. He was an indefatigable traveler, a tireless interviewer who kept meticulous notes and iron diaries of almost every conversation, every trip, every opinion, including his own, which were typed and filed and indexed by a succession of pretty girls in his office. In 1942 he married Marina Tatiana Lada, a well-born Greek woman whom he had met in Athens. During the early stages of the German occupation of Greece she was a lieutenant in the Greek Army Nursing Corps, but was able to leave to join Cyrus Sulzberger. They were married in Beirut, Lebanon. It was her husband who wrote in his memoirs about Marina Sulzberger's work in the military hospital in Athens, of how she was given the job of carrying out buckets of amputated hands and feet of wounded or frostbitten soldiers.

"My parents had interesting experiences in World War Two; there was a much more clearly defined right side and wrong side to be on. They were on the right side. They could recount all sorts of good and bad things that had happened, but basically the war for them had been a period of intense work, fascinating experience, romance, heightened consciousness and youth," David Sulzberger said.

"I was perfectly prepared to accept some of the exhilaration when the experience came along. You know, if people say to me 'Did you have a good time in Vietnam?' I'll answer 'Yes.' If people ask me what was the best thing about Vietnam, and I say the food, people will think I'm putting them on. If I close my eyes and go into a trance and think about Vietnam, it conjures up flavor, smell, light, those types of feelings. It doesn't conjure up emotion in the sense of feelings that can be practically translated into policies or books or ideas.

"Don't hold this against me. But the thing which I think I will remember about Vietnam when I am a hundred years old and will talk about it to my children is the countryside, how beautiful the women looked, and the food."

In that spring of 1975 when the provinces of Vietnam, one by one, were being taken as easily as shutters are slammed on windows, David Sulzberger remembered the impact on him of the World War II experiences of his parents, the snatches of stories he had heard, the reminiscences, the references to it, going back like fly lines. It is his small and dark mother whom he resembles, it is her slightness and dark eyes that he has, the same exuberant charm. He is an American who was born in Athens, raised in Paris, sent to an English public school named Winchester—a more intellectual school than Harrow or Eton, not as relentlessly social—then to Harvard. He worried about being drafted and thought he would rather enjoy being in the Special Forces, but people warned him there was some chance he might not make the grade or that he would have to suffer a year in the Army before going overseas.

"This would have been the summer of 1967, and for a year

before that the situation in Vietnam was becoming extremely interesting without in the least bit becoming particularly clear," he said. "Do you see what I mean? It was, from the sociologist's or politician's point of view, an interesting situation without yet being particularly controversial."

Everything pointed to a career in the State Department: it seemed the most suitable and elegant channel.

His father seemed quite pleased, his mother more so, when he set his sights on working in Vietnam. He wanted to leave, to have an Asian adventure because of a girl who had pulled away from him. In Washington, D.C., a friend steered him to AID just as CORDS was being formed. The language training program was nine months; he started in July and quit at Christmas. He did not enjoy the program. He played a hunch: if you learned good Vietnamese, you were bound to end up in the boondocks.

"On the other hand, I did speak fluent French. All the Vietnamese who were going to be interesting in terms of what I was interested in—which was finding out what the hell was going on—would probably speak French," he said. "The one thing I was least prepared for when I enrolled for Vietnam was the Americans I was going to be doing the program with.

"It sounds awfully snotty and snobbish, but it's not a question of being snotty and snobbish really so much as the fact I simply hadn't had all that much exposure. There were a lot of intelligent people in CORDS, but at the same time there was a lot of middle-mindnesses right at the beginning. There were a lot of people, for example, who were perfectly competent agrarian specialists who were learning the language with me, but I felt very isolated in terms of the group I was with."

He mentioned meeting a man named Oggie Williams at a party in Washington—a tall, pleasant man who had been in Saigon in 1956 with the CIA, I thought—who offered him the right job. It meant living in Saigon and traveling a lot all over Vietnam.

For the first year and a half he found working on the Chieu Hoi program to be interesting. The Chieu Hoi ministry was small, and unimportant in some ways, he said.

"The one thing that I could pass for was anything other than an American," David Sulzberger said. "Because of that, and because I was younger than a lot of Americans in Saigon—there were a lot of my contemporaries out in the field, but there weren't all that many wheeling and dealing in Saigon—I had access to not so much information as confidences that I think were directly related to the fact that I had no influence, or was not perceived to have influence.

"I did a thesis when I was at college on the origins of American involvement in Vietnam—on that and Franco-American relations on the subject of Vietnam from 1950–1960. I interviewed a lot of people like Jean Sainteny and General Ely, I interviewed Bernard Fall, who gave me a lot of information. I didn't know anything about it, so I had no prejudices. I also read all the French documentation. And Lacouture—he was at Harvard on a Nieman, so that was incredibly useful for me."

At Harvard there were two readers for a student's thesis. The two readers on the Sulzberger thesis were Henry Kissinger, whose history course he took, and Stanley Hoffman in the government department. "One of them gave me a magna plus and the other gave me a summa; I just can't remember which order it was in. Kissinger—I'll say one thing for him, in the few times that I've run into him since then he has had the good manners to say 'Oh, I remember you from then' sort of thing. He's usually particularly unpleasant toward former students. I think he regards himself as ill-treated by former students. I think that's it."

At first he had felt exhilarated and important and alive in Saigon. The job intrigued him. "I had never had access to an environment in which I could find out or not whether I was successful at, if you want, using my skills by being devious. By which I mean not going through regular channels. I think, instinctively, the regular channels meant the American system, and I'd never been much of a participant in that. At school I always managed to get around doing things the normal way. It didn't take me long to realize that not only was I not particularly good at going through normal channels, but that normal channels were not particularly good at providing you with any results. Here was the perfect opportunity to avoid them, and demonstrate to the people who you might be eventually responsible to that by avoiding them you could come up with useful results."

There had been two Vietnamese he was attached to and did not forget. One was a street child whom he nicknamed Public Enemy Number One, a child who sold newspapers most persistently and in a loud voice, a frowning boy who leaped at you outside the Hotel Continental. The other was a Buddhist from North Vietnam who had come south, a man who was his "counterpart" in the ministry, the word the Americans use in a futile but cheerful attempt to be tactful, since they had so much power and the Vietnamese so much less. He said this friend was a man in his fifties, a poet, who worked in the Chieu Hoi ministry, who drove an old Hillman.

In Saigon he lived in the Hotel Continental—sharing suite 19 with Kevin Buckley, a young, witty, wildly good-looking raconteur and correspondent for *Newsweek*—then he moved into a villa, a famous villa, at 47 Phan Thanh Gian, which was leased by the embassy and inhabited since the American ascendancy in 1965 by a succession of young men, out of Harvard, Yale or Princeton, who worked for CORDS. It was one way of avoiding the draft if they passed the civil service examination, for the State Department issued them an occupational deferment. They spoke Vietnamese, they wrote miles of reports, they entertained each other, they moved around the war, rarely through it, like greyhounds circling a garbage dump.

The huge villa at 47 Phan Thanh Gian was the scene of the most famous of Saigon's parties. It was given on New Year's Eve for four years; the last one, in 1970, was no less amusing and spirited than the others. The invitation to it said: "The Flower People of Saigon invite you to see 'The Light at the End of the Tunnel' Act Four." It was assumed, correctly, that the guests knew party French, so at the bottom of the invitation it read *"Cette carte sera exigée a l'entrée"* and *"pour memoire."* The invitation had something to it of the London of Evelyn Waugh in the 1930s. The names of some of the Flower People, fourth generation, listed inside the invitation included: "Angus Davidson and Ancestors," "El Gleeko," "Sir Cloudesley Shovel," "Baron de Tourane" and "The Ghost of Christmas Past J. W. Fulbright." But sometimes the real names of people—Gage McAfee, W. Stowell Doyle, M. L. Pressey, Charlie Salmon—sounded made up as well. The party had started as a huge joke, first given by people with links to the U.S. Mission, and became so famous that even more imposing people in the Mission dropped in. There was nothing else quite like that villa. Someone always made sure there were good wineglasses and tablecloths. The Cambodian silver animals looked polished. The male servant wore a white coat. There were flowers, pillows, good towels, wine. The villa had a fluffed-up feeling. Once when I went there, an American told me he had just flown to the United States for his sister's wedding, the weather for it had been fine. It seemed an astonishing thing to be able to say in Saigon. The second, and last, time I went, there was a dinner party, and a young man who worked for the head of USAID, had a stunning Vietnamese wife, spoke the language flawlessly himself, leaned across the white tablecloth and said: "We're going to stop corruption in this country." That is the way they often spoke.

David Sulzberger was much admired in Saigon for his charm, his wit, a European silkiness of speech, and the 1937 rumble-seat Citroën he bought. It was painted cream and black and caused a sensation in the streets. When he speaks of the villa, he calls it Forty-seven. "One was a whole lot less isolated there than any- where else because, you know, the one thing about Forty-seven which people picked up on was that it was the most social and most amusing with its *va-et-vien*—the coming and the going. What made it so interesting was the fact that it was a crash pad for everybody who came to Saigon unexpectedly from the field. So that you could pick up information. Vietnamese and foreign diplomats, people who would ask questions and had no ax to grind, whose promotions did not depend on whether their report sounded well or not."

He worked from February 1967 to 1970 as a reports officer for the Chieu Hoi program in CORDS.

"Within the space of three or four months, in no time at all, I was on very, very close terms with all the journalists," David Sul- zberger said. "They were enormously fun to know. I had a much more adventurous time in CORDS than other people but a much less adventurous time than a lot of journalists. So I lived to some extent vicariously off the stories and adventures of somebody else."

He traveled to forty of the forty-four provinces; he kept a map showing where he had been. His reports were largely concerned with statistics and some analysis of the trends that the statistics were supposed to indicate. He talked to Vietnamese who had "defected," but this wasn't part of his job. "The great majority were peasants from the south and really had no political—Well, as I said before, it was a population shift. Since there were so few North Vietnamese defectors, there was no set pattern as to who or what they were. There were as many officers as soldiers. Some of them had just become isolated, you know."

There were enormous masses of defectors in 1969 under the Chieu Hoi program, he said, but he had no illusions about these *hoi chanh*. It was the safest thing for a Vietnamese to do, even if you were not on one side or the other. "There was enormous abuse of the system, but I think there probably was a fairly rational and fairly acceptable reason for large numbers of people coming over at that time. It made sense. At that particular time there really was some sort of notion that maybe there would be a cease-fire and some sort of peace. And you know, defections obviously meant that you were in what was somewhat arbitrarily conceived as being on the other side. It was one way of clearing yourself, if you came from a VC-controlled area, through a fairly benign government agency and picking up some money along the way."

The program became bureaucratized, he said. In the beginning there were six Americans and six Vietnamese. By 1970 there were at least thirty people, which displeased him; it made things a little less exciting. He felt blunted.

As a propaganda device, he thought the program was certainly successful in 1969. "Nobody gave much thought to the political aspect of it, it was really a processing of the population shift," Mr. Sulzberger added. "It was one way of *not* being told you belonged to the other side and penalized for it. So you got a whole lot of people who, I think, would never belong to the other side coming in on it."

He did not think it would be an embarrassment to him to have worked for the Americans in Vietnam, that it would ever boomerang. "To be embarrassing to me, I have to be embarrassed by it, and I am not embarrassed by it. The one thing which embarrassed me, when I was there, was my detachment. I felt a bit parasitical because I felt here am I, and here I am, observing, and I really do have a front-row seat and it is fascinating. But I am not in any sense going to involve myself more deeply than that because on the one hand I see how it's unworkable and on the other side I wouldn't put myself in the hawk or dove variety. I had access to experience and information. People showed me that it was also too easy to simply say 'Let's get right out' or 'To hell with the Vietnamese.'

"I always felt particularly irked at people who loathed the Vietnamese because they weren't, let's say, as left-wing as they ought to be or as anti-Thieu as they ought to be. I mean, it's so much easier to be left-wing in somebody else's country. It seemed to me obvious that it was wrong because the elections were obviously rigged to assume that there was no political backing, no political constituency and that every single Vietnamese if given a free choice would opt for the other side.

"Certainly, going to Vietnam was good for me. It was an annealing process. It was as if you were making caramels. You drop them in cold water to have them shaped. I went to Vietnam qua Asia, rather than Vietnam qua our political problem."

AN AMERICAN BACKGROUND paper said: "The Civil Operations and Rural Development Support (CORDS), an element of the United States Military Assistance Command, Vietnam, is part and parcel of the total American effort to assist the government of Vietnam in resisting and ending Communist aggression and providing a better life for its seventeen million, two hundred and twenty-three thousand people." It made high-ranking CORDS officials very snappish when reporters wrote of the American pacification programs. No, no, they said, CORDS only advises and supports the government of Vietnam on pacification or nation-building programs that span a broad spectrum, from establishing security to initiating economic development projects. It was not true.

By May 1969 the CORDS team consisted of six thousand American advisors and technicians, twenty-five percent of them civilians like David Sulzberger. The military in CORDS were Army, Air Force, Navy and Marines. The Chieu Hoi program—in Vietnamese the words meant "open arms"—encouraged enemy soldiers, political agents and any Vietnamese supporter who gave support to VC or NVA forces to defect to the side of the Saigon government. A Vietnamese who did so was called a *hoi chanh*. If a *hoi chanh* brought in weapons or was willing to lead allied forces to an enemy arms, food or medical cache, he was rewarded with cash, the amount depending on the number and type of the weapons or the size of the cache. The numbers who did were always disappointing. The inflated figures of Vietnamese who had defected and become *hoi chanh* were held up as proof at last that the wicked had seen the error of their ways. The U.S. Mission was very keen on the Chieu Hoi program. "In terms of numbers," one document said, "one hundred thousand *hoi chanh* are the equivalent of ten enemy military divisions, or to put it another way, assuming a kill ratio of five enemy soldiers to one allied trooper would mean that for every five returnees, the life of one allied soldier would be saved."

But it did not mean that at all; often the *hoi chanh* were Vietnamese who were afraid of being punished for being in the wrong place at the wrong time, who were not combatants, who gave up for the money or the papers or the false identification the giving-up provided.

But the words *chieu hoi, chieu hoi* became famous among American soldiers who knew only three or four Vietnamese expressions. Once, in Albany, New York, after leaving an interview in a housing project too late at night, with the yelling and cries of a party or a slaughter coming from the eighteenth floor, a drunken man in a field jacket lurched into the elevator, a bottle in one hand, what looked like a knife or ice pick in the other. "*Chieu hoi*," I said, raising my arms. It made him laugh. He said that I should *Di di mau*, which meant get out of there, leave the building.

HE FINISHED HIS studies at Harvard, then went to the Harvard Business School and then to his own business, buying and selling works of Islamic art, including carpets from the Middle East. There were times when David Sulzberger missed Vietnam.

"I had a tremendously good time. I'm not embarrassed to say I had a good time. A lot of people I know had a good time. A lot of people had a terribly bad time, obviously. I would have had an appallingly bad time regardless of whether I'd been fighting and killed or not if I'd been locked up all the time in a series of A-frame green drab buildings which could have as easily been in Virginia as in Nha Trang.

"When I left Vietnam, I had an enormous awareness of the right and wrong in terms of myself, of what I liked, what I disliked, what I felt, what I didn't feel. I mean, you know, even things like food. I knew I liked carrots, and eating them in Vietnam just confirmed that. It left me very much confirmed in my western-ness. But in no sense did I come out feeling that philosophically or morally I was changed. I came back feeling very much confirmed. It's like a movie you see for the second time, several years later, and though it may seem a little dated, you remember what you liked about it and it's still good.

". . . I mean, one of the things which obviously made an impact on me was this was really my first paid job. I went to an office and after X many months I got rated and I got promoted . . .

". . . what we were trying to do was not a question of being morally right or wrong. After all, unfortunately, things that are right are things that work, very often. Things that don't work are wrong. However much there may be a moral justification—or a colonial justification or a power justification—anything that doesn't work, as soon as you are in a position to know that it isn't working, you know that it's wrong. In that sense I got a very clear picture that American policy in Vietnam was wrong. Because it didn't work and because it couldn't work and because whatever there was to gain or to lose, it was perfectly clear the longer you prolonged it the more was lost.

"America, not ever having a real colonial experience, has a superficial approach. It's not so much we have a superficial approach, but we have an innocence in all our dealings with foreign countries that allows us to think we're right and never allows us to really get in and try and understand what's going on there. We never really have a commitment that is our own. There's always this 'We're-doing-it-for-their-sake-and-if-they-can't-take-it . . .'

"It's a rather sinister thing to say right now, but I would much rather we were in there for the rubber and the manganese, because then at least we would care about whether it worked or not."

Each hour he sat in my living room that April in 1975 the Army of the Republic of South Vietnam, the army trained and equipped and supervised and pushed and paid for by the Americans, was disappearing, as if the soldiers were frenzied actors dropping through a trap door on a stage.

"I think they're doing us a great favor, really. I mean, imagine, if there were Iwo Jima flag-raising scenes, and dying to the last man, and Horatio on the burning deck right now!"

It did not astonish him in the least that so many provinces had fallen in that year and that the very last day of the war was so close. "We should have learned by now that nothing about Vietnam should surprise us. I hope to go back some day. But at the same time I know right now I'd be crucially embarrassed to go back. I mean, I've talked to you earlier about my ability to be embarrassed for other people. I used to be embarrassed for all the Germans I see going to Greece, you know, in the summer as tourists. I'm also embarrassed for the Greeks who receive them with open arms. Except the Deutsche mark is worth something.

"I would be the German in Greece. I thought last night about this. This is a sinister thing to say. I thought of how a lot of Germans must feel as innocent of that whole experience as a lot of Americans feel, will continue to feel, forever."

MARINA SULZBERGER WAS easier than her tall, stern husband, who did not give the impression that he wrote a column for a newspaper so much as the feeling that he, too, held high office and had no time to waste. He always knew her worth, for she went with him on many of his long, important trips, an asset, a calming and sweet presence. When they came back to Vietnam in February 1971—on their way to China for the first time—he was sick with the flu and some of their luggage had been lost in Calcutta, which made him furious. The brilliant young bureau chief in Saigon, Craig Whitney, stopped working to send urgent and stern messages, trying to trace the suitcase. He made telephone calls, notified other bureaus of the loss, reported daily on the progress or no progress of the search. Mr. Sulzberger, who wanted to see General Creighton Abrams and President Nguyen Van Thieu, took to his bed the first day. The bureau chief, who was bracing himself and the reporters for a Vietnamese offensive because of the collective predictions of the military, asked me to arrange an excursion for Mrs. Sulzberger. She was charming and attentive to everyone.

I HAD BEEN in Vietnam more than two years that month, had come back from the last trip in the field. It was Ben Het in the Central Highlands, where the North Vietnamese attack was supposed to start *any minute*. Ben Het was seven miles from where the borders of Vietnam, Laos and Cambodia rubbed. It had been a Special Forces camp that had come under heavy siege in 1969. There was still a sign in the Americans' quarters, a sign that had hung over the Green Berets' bar, which no one wanted to remove. "Ben Het and Loving It" the sign said. A reporter, describing the siege in 1969, had written of the Green Beret who said: "I've been hit and I ain't loving it." There were always the jokes; it was the easiest, safest language to use, sometimes the soldiers and the reporters could only speak by using jokes.

That year there were only two American advisors there. Most of the soldiers were the Montagnard tribesmen, recruited and trained by the Special Forces in earlier years; some lived there in huts with wives and children. On the main hill of Ben Het, a sprawling and lumpy base, were the South Vietnamese Rangers. The dust veiled all of it, so even the barbed wire was pale grey. The children played with nothing. They did not seem to ever speak. The covers of the sandbags, which felt like stone, had rotted and torn. Over everything was a blackness that came from the sun; the sun seemed black.

In the bunker where the Americans slept, a man had written more than once, in chalk, on the wall: "I trust in God." It was most neatly printed. He was the third advisor who was no longer there. He just went back to go to the dentist, the other Americans said, and nothing else. But in Saigon, a reporter had told me that this man had been very nervous during an interview, quite certain that Ben Het could not hold, it was a mess. The *Newsweek* man had written it all down, and thought the American was cracking up.

Luong slept with the Vietnamese at their command post; he always needed to be among his own. The second night he came to find me, saying we must get ready to E and E. He was very good with the American expressions that all the soldiers used, that curious, fast, deadly baby talk they had. E and E meant "evade and escape." An attack was expected, Luong whispered, we could not expect choppers, get water and let's go. He had heard it on the radio at the Vietnamese CP.

But the American captain—a spare man, clearly West Point, who had been seriously wounded on his first tour in 1969—said no, that couldn't be, there was a full moon, so forget it. I believed him. It was always like that: in danger, we huddled with the men whose profession I hated, expecting them to know best, to give the right orders, to defend us all. They had no choice. They had to feed and brief reporters, too, and find beds or a place where we could lie down. It was not that they always wanted the company.

I lay on the cot of the man who had written "I trust in God," who knew that Ben Het could not hold. It was too close to a North Vietnamese base camp that had been half jokingly described as

about the size of New York City. The Vietnamese Rangers did
not care; they were nearly anesthetized. A lieutenant told Luong
that the boredom was worse than anything else.

"Think of having to stay in this base all the time," the lieutenant said. "What can you do to fill such emptiness?" The lieutenant drank, he played cards, he listened to cassettes on a little
Sony player.

There was nothing to do after the nine or ten interviews, after
the morning inspecting the perimeter, so long and wiggly, with
the older American advisor who intended to be a store detective
in Pennsylvania once he got out. The sergeant looked displeased
with the trenches on the perimeter. They were paths lined with
artillery casings filled with mud and water. He denied he was
worried. At Ben Het each smell was a hundred years old.

MRS. SULZBERGER AND I went to the Air Force base at Bien
Hoa near Saigon. She wore a pretty print dress because she hated
wearing pants and refused to do it. So I wore a skirt too. An information officer led us to some pilots—their unit was nicknamed
Blue Max—who flew gunships. We stood around in an office
while she made marvelous small talk that had always worked so
well, but the men had no gift for it and did not know what was
expected of them. Mrs. Sulzberger spoke about her son, David,
who had been in Vietnam. Then one of the gunship pilots—a
man with a deceivingly simple face—asked her what her son had
done, meaning infantry or artillery or engineers or what. David
was in CORDS, Mrs. Sulzberger said, but the pilot never heard
of CORDS and it took a while for him to find that out. Mrs. Sulzberger, who did not like people to be ill-at-ease, skipped over it
and plunged on. Some of her friends had been concerned about
David's going to Vietnam but she had not listened to any of that
kind of talk.

"Every man should have his war," Mrs. Sulzberger said.

The pilot stared. He had never heard it put that way.

We were taken on a helicopter ride. A black sergeant stood by with a little ladder so that in our skirts we could gracefully climb into the aircraft. Afterward we went to Long Binh Army base and toured the offices of the chief information officer.

They had handled nice ladies before. It was the easiest thing of all. Someone arranged to have the usual out-with-the-troops photograph taken. There were two soldiers, in the fatigues and boots that everyone wore, who stood on either side of her, smiling as people cannot help doing when they see a camera. I think Mrs. Sulzberger was given a yearbook of an Army unit, and she asked the soldiers to sign their names in it. They didn't mind any of it. The clerks were always bored in those Long Binh offices and she had pretty, winning ways.

THEN CAME A demonstration so different from all the others that it surprised even those people in Washington, D.C., who had seen it all. The veterans of Vietnam massed in Washington, D.C.—only men who were veterans and could prove it—and threw back everything at the white marble Capitol, the building where Congress said yes to the war. They threw back medals for valor; they threw back stripes torn from sleeves, their campaign ribbons and sometimes parts of dress uniforms. Some Vietnamese in Saigon were a little shocked. Their own newspapers and magazines and radio made no mention of such a thing, but a few of them heard of it. An ARVN lieutenant, in from the field, was bewildered, for he had known American infantrymen for seven years and he could not imagine any of them doing this. At first the lieutenant thought the Americans wanted more money for having fought so far from home. It took some doing to persuade him this was not the reason.

"Who do they want to win the war?" the lieutenant asked me. His English was good.

"They think the war is a crime," I said. "They are ashamed of the war."

The lieutenant looked snarled: he was so sure that the Americans, above all, wanted to win the war.

Luong, who was made uneasy by such discussions, said the lieutenant had not noticed all the peace symbols the Americans wore or heard the words of their music. Although Luong could not always explain the words, he knew the music had a terrible meaning.

The five-day demonstration, organized by Vietnam Veterans Against the War, was the first time that Americans who had fought in a foreign war demanded an end to it, were not proud of being a part of it, did not think it best that their country win, and hurled back the rewards they had been given for doing their duty, for being the men their fathers and the nation wanted.

They called that five days in April 1971 Dewey Canyon III. Operation Dewey Canyon I, in February 1969, sent elements of the 3d Marine Division into Laos. Operation Dewey Canyon II was the American name given to the first seven days of the allied drive into Laos in 1971, which was then known, and for its duration, as Lam Son 719.

Dewey Canyon III took place in Washington, D.C., April 19 through April 23 in 1971. The VVAW called it "a limited incursion into the country of Congress." They started to come on a Friday, an eccentric, a strange-looking army, wearing fatigues and field jackets, helmets and their old boonie hats, the same boots they had worn in Vietnam. Some brought bedrolls and all slept outdoors on a camping site on a small quadrangle on the Mall between 3rd and 4th Streets. All came with their discharge papers so their bitterest critics could not accuse them of being imposters, although some did anyway. There were a few men who did not have two legs, a few who could not rise from wheelchairs, but they were in good spirits and among their own. Many of the people in the city who saw them were startled and saddened, for the veterans looked like men straggling back from a wilderness. It did not matter that they were long-haired or bearded, that their manner was not military, their uniforms muddled, or that they came with young women. It was impossible not to know what they had been: troops. No one laughed at them or called out that they were cowards and draft dodgers.

On one day they marched from the Lincoln Memorial Bridge to Arlington Cemetery to hold a brief ceremony honoring the war dead, which was conducted by a man who had just resigned his military chaplaincy. But they were refused entrance, which made them very angry. They also marched to the Capitol to present sixteen demands to Congress, and nearly two hundred veterans sat through hearings of the Senate Foreign Relations Committee on proposals to end the war. Groups of them spent hours talking to congressmen. Fifty veterans wanted to be arrested as war criminals, but no one would oblige them. Two hundred men and several Gold Star mothers went back to Arlington National Cemetery, where they were at last let in to lay two wreaths on a grassy knoll, apart from the graves, kneel down, pray.

There were times when they talked and sang and acted as if they knew what it was to be young, but it was not a reunion they came for. One hundred and ten of them were arrested for disturbing the peace after they marched to the steps of the Supreme Court, and sat down there, to ask why the Court had not ruled on the constitutionality of the war. None of them resisted the police: they folded their hands on their heads, as the prisoners in Vietnam used to do, and were led off. There was a candlelight march around the White House. The nicest thing that happened was the planting of a tree the veterans donated to the Mall: it was a small triumph. They cooked for themselves, they kept order, they cleaned up, and they even asked the park police for more trashcans. But the sight of the men worried some passers-by, even though the veterans did nothing that was cruel or messy or menacing.

"Son, I don't think what you're doing is good for the troops," one elderly woman said to a man handing out leaflets.

"Lady, we are the troops," he said.

A middle-aged man from Russell, Pennsylvania, wearing the fatigue jacket of his dead son, blew taps before the medals went back. Sometimes, after a man hurled a bit of a ribbon or a Bronze Star or a Purple Heart over a high wire fence the police put in front of the steps of the Capitol, he would break down and be hugged by other men. They were free at last to do it. No one was ashamed of crying or holding on to each other. Some threw in fury, others in sorrow, but nearly all made faces as they did it.

Afterward, there were men who had wept, stopped, then felt a curious, unreasonable elation. One of them, named Rusty, had been a captain with a helicopter squadron in the 1st Marine Division. He and some friends—a whole bunch, he called it—cried really hard for two hours. Then Rusty said they felt wonderful; they felt so intensely hopeful, they wouldn't have been surprised if somebody came to say that Nixon had just announced the troops were leaving Vietnam and would be back home by suppertime. They almost expected to hear it.

"We thought we'd finally done it and we'd reached everywhere," the former captain said. It was the top of the mountain, he kept saying.

Before the Senate Foreign Relations Committee, John Kerry, one of the VVAW coordinators, put the case strongly, and with an eloquence that made the older men in the room, the men in their dark suits and good shirts, pay attention. Kerry was not a mumbling, disheveled boy who used words they could not grasp.

"We are also here to ask, and we are here to ask vehemently, where are the leaders of our country? Where is the leadership?

We are here to ask where are McNamara, Rostow, Bundy, Johnson and so many others? Where are they now that we, the men whom they sent off to war, have returned?" Mr. Kerry, a former naval officer, said the men he named had deserted them; that the administration had done the veterans the ultimate dishonor by "attempting to disown us."

His address, which was quite short, ended this way:

"We wish that a merciful God could wipe away our own memories of that service as easily as this administration has wiped away their memories of us. But all that they have done and all that they can do by this denial is to make more clear than ever our last own determination to undertake one last mission—to search out and destroy the last vestige of this barbaric war, to pacify our own hearts, to conquer the hate and the fear that have driven this country these last ten years and more, so when thirty years from now our brothers go down the street without a leg, without an arm, or a face, and small boys ask why, we will be able to say 'Vietnam' and not mean a desert, not a filthy obscene memory, but mean instead the place where America finally turned and where soldiers like us helped in the turning."

A study was conducted of the veterans encamped on the Mall. Most of the men were between twenty-one and twenty-five; few had finished college, unable to capitalize on college draft deferments. A majority had enlisted. Nearly half their fathers were blue-collar workers. Most of the veterans began to change their mind about U.S. involvement in Vietnam during their first three months there.

On Friday, April 23, they broke camp. It was estimated that more than two thousand men had come from all over the country; half had camped on the Mall. There is no plaque there to show which tree is the one they planted, or how it is doing. The last American troops did not leave Vietnam for another twenty-three months; the war went on for another four years. Most of the veterans did not try again in the same way to stop the war, or to redeem themselves. They saw it was no use. One by one, they fell away.

IT TOOK A while for VVAW to die, and before it did, there was a last muster in Washington on the Fourth of July weekend in 1974, when less than a dozen men who had taken part in Dewey Canyon III came back for the protests called by Vietnam Veterans Against the War/Winter Soldier Organization. The name had been lengthened so that women and nonveterans could be included; "Winter Soldier" was derived from Thomas Paine, who in 1776 had written: "The summer soldier and the sunshine patriot will, in this crisis, shrink from the service of his country."

That summer there was hardly an organization at all. Many local chapters had disappeared; veterans had to find jobs and get on with their lives. The early VVAW leaders had been pushed out, then there were no leaders at all; funds were nonexistent, organization chaotic, informers frequent, records poor, and most important, the passion and the hope nearly spent. The few men and women who worked full time for VVAW/WSO were radicals, who did not believe, as Kerry had put it, that Vietnam would be the place where America finally turned. They did not believe there would be any turning at all, not yet, not so easily.

But, still, some came back. William C. Henschel III was there, for one, pleased to see the buttons, the banners, the campsite on the Mall. During Dewey Canyon III he had worn his dress Marine jacket with three medals pinned on his chest, the ones he tossed back. That July, Henschel was twenty-eight years old and did not seem to know many of the other men sitting on the ground. This time he was out of the wheelchair, walking on an artificial leg or using crutches. When it became too hot, or when he tired, Henschel took off the leg. It was surprisingly heavy, a shiny pink left leg which he used as a bulletin board. There were at least seven stickers on it, above the black sock and the black buckled shoe which never creases across the toes. One sticker said: The Marines Are Looking for a Few Good Men. During one march another veteran hoisted Henschel's leg and walked a long way with it over his shoulder.

It was a terrible Fourth of July; no one was there. The protesters marched everywhere: to the Veterans Administration, the Court of Military Appeals, the Justice Department, the Capitol and past the White House. Up and down the huge blank white avenues of Washington, in a long, lumpy parade, shouting their fierce slogans so that the words would pierce those miles of deadly white marble. "Fight back," shouted Henschel. "Fight back," shouted the others. The only people interested in us were police units, who ringed the campsite; some had videotape cameras and used them. There were police who looked young enough to have known Vietnam. Officer Roger Merkle, guarding the perimeter, said he had been a Marine, had been in the Ashau Valley. It was the worst thing that ever happened to him, Officer Merkle said, *the worst*. But he was not interested in talking about the war, or why he had to go to the Ashau; he did not care about the roots of the war, the reasons, the results. It was over for him.

"Wars have always been fought," Officer Merkle said. "It's always been that way." He saw no reason to speak to any of the men, their shirts off, sitting in the sun, who had been Marines too. He did not want to talk to Henschel, an ex-lance corporal in the 2d Battalion, 5th Marine Regiment. There were only a few hundred yards between them. He was not about to cross them.

Henschel was not surprised. He took such things calmly; he was used to it. He is a tall, thin man with large eyes, dark hair and a soft thin beard. His sense of humor is nice; Henschel likes the small, dry joke. He can tell his history in a few words: he was shot in the head inside the Citadel in Hue during the 1968 Tet battle. Casualties were heaped on top of tanks to be taken out. The tank that he lay on hit a mine. He was thrown off and the tank ran over him, crushing the leg and ripping off part of his buttocks. This is what he was told. He was in eleven different military hospitals, including those in Vietnam and Japan. The V.A. sends him five hundred and eighty-four dollars a month because of the head wound, which caused traumatic epilepsy leading to "seizure disorder," as the military doctors put it. He receives an additional one hundred and twenty-two dollars for the cut-off left leg. Henschel thought that his benefits were okay; he lived on the checks. That day he had run out of money but would not go off with me to eat, for he wanted to stay with the others.

"I don't have the knife in my back, like a lot of vets," he said. "I'm here more for other people than myself." His mother died before she knew how critically he was wounded, and Henschel said he was glad. His father was for the war; the two men did not see each other and Henschel said he was glad. He was living in a room in Washington, D.C., and hanging out at a YWCA that had summer programs for ghetto children. They let him help but, he said, no more than that. Maybe he would go to college, maybe. Nothing was certain.

Long after that day in the Citadel, when Henschel was home and driving a car, he picked up a hitchhiker, a young and friendly fellow, who saw something wrong about the leg. He asked about it. Henschel told. The hitchhiker was furious to be with a man who had killed in Vietnam.

"He said to me 'I wish you had died in Vietnam, fascist pig killer,'" Henschel said. "I told him I didn't want to go there, I didn't. He got out of the car. The guy even took my lighter. There was no way I could stop him either."

Each day that July weekend seemed to bring a whiter, meaner heat. On one of them, there were spasms of pushing, shoving, kicking and cracking and hollering when the police became vexed because the demonstrators did not stay on the sidewalks during a march. No one really knew how it happened; it hardly mattered. When the police came, hurling us backward, I thought of Henschel on his crutches, but he was not to be seen. Danny Friedman, who had been seriously wounded as a rifleman in Vietnam, was a massive fellow, the bravest, who ran interference for others when the police got nasty. He was cracked on the skull and had to sit down, the blood going in streamers down his hair. There were women, too, on the police line; the sight of them made me want to turn away. Their make-up was going mushy in the sun. They did not look as composed as the men. There was that instant—all of us were standing still—when a veteran said: "Jesus, I don't know, how can I hit a woman?" Someone laughed and said, "Hard."

At one point, in that baking and still city, we were gathered at the foot of the steps of the Capitol where the police were massed, booted, armed, holding their batons in front of them. It was ordinary scenery. I asked one officer—a middle-aged man with a huge, creased face who reminded me of Rod Steiger—if he was afraid of such a small crowd. His answer seemed to be one I had heard so many times before.

"No." he said. "I've been in the war."

Alfonso Riate, a former Marine and prisoner of war who had never regretted or retracted the antiwar statements he made in North Vietnam, sang for us. He had a sweet, high, haunting voice which he flung over us like a net. He sang in Vietnamese, a song called "American People Fight on with Your Music and Songs." The police nearest us looked disgusted. When Riate sang in Vietnamese, he sounded Vietnamese. Everyone felt better hearing Riate sing, listening to that song, and it did not matter at all that none of us could understand a word. It was all we had.

THEY HAD WANTED Nixon kicked out. He has long been out. The war is over. But they also wanted other things. They wanted universal, unconditional amnesty, a single-type discharge for all veterans, so that three hundred and fifty thousand men of the Vietnam era who had been given less than honorable discharges would be helped. They wanted decent veterans benefits, for the G.I. Bill was not the promising, generous program it had been after World War II. A single Vietnam veteran could not pay the average annual tuition fee at a public college on the two hundred and twenty dollars he received a month, let alone the normal costs of a private college. There is no living allowance.

Henschel thought it was all wrong. Henschel thought it was a shame. I never saw him after that weekend, but we all remember each other, and it was Henschel, after all, who said how odd it was that the only people being punished for the war were the wrong ones.

EVEN WHEN YOU are not looking for them, sometimes, but not often, you meet men who went to Vietnam and who were in Dewey Canyon III. In Durham, North Carolina, a former Marine sniper works at night behind the desk at a Ramada Inn. Chuck James said he had flung back his medals in Washington, D.C., and been glad of it. I did not quite believe him at first—he said it in such a throwaway manner—until I found a photograph. Mr. James pointed out himself in the crowd of veterans sitting on the ground, laughing, raising their fists. He was easy to spot.

"I was the only guy wearing a suit," Mr. James said. "I didn't quite know what to expect." There were four trips to Durham in 1976; I used to stay up late talking to Mr. James in the lobby when he was not busy on the adding machine or signing in other guests. There had been a few veterans in Greensboro, North Carolina, who protested the war, he said. They would do it again if anyone pulled another Vietnam on them. The day that Jimmy Carter came to Durham to campaign in the primary, and little bags of peanuts were given out, Mr. James was not impressed. He was for Mo Udall, and he knew who the southerners were who had supported the war and wanted it won, even if later they sang a different song.

There were no war stories he wanted to tell, none that I wanted to hear. Yet he was willing to show me a very long white pencil-thin scar high on his left arm, to confide that there was another scar on his back and a knee that looked so terrible he would not let his wife look at it. The young black night porter, Robby, said he regretted not joining the service, maybe he still would. There were no jobs in North Carolina, Robby said, he had been to college and was going nowhere, making nothing.

"Look at that scar," I said, wanting to change his mind. But it did not tell him anything fearful; it was only a scar and a neat one at that. Sometimes it does no good at all to show the injuries, to keep reciting the horror and the pain and the waste of the war. It makes some men more interested, even willing to prove that they are ready for risks like that.

VI

WINNERS AND LOSERS

In the last week of January in 1976, nine months after the collapse of the south and the dreadful rush of Americans and Vietnamese to get out, Graham Martin, the last United States ambassador in South Vietnam, made his first public appearance. A House Internal Relations subcommittee heard Ambassador Martin calmly state there were no failures of the Thieu regime or of his own controversial handling of U.S. policy in Vietnam and of the American evacuation.

The problem was a failure to counter "one of the best propaganda and pressure organizations the world has ever seen," Ambassador Martin told the subcommittee. He named the Indochina Resource Center, a small group set up in 1969 by former volunteer relief workers and teachers in Vietnam and Laos. One reporter described Ambassador Martin at the hearing as the "compleat diplomat, with pale-blue eyes and a complexion the hue of tallow," a man of "spectral distinction."

"The fanatic who almost had to be carried out of Saigon is almost perfectly concealed," the columnist wrote.

Two persons were cited by the ambassador, who complained of a "propaganda extravaganza" to arouse antiwar feelings. They were Don Luce and Fred Branfman, who had started the Indochina Resource Center with David Marr, a Vietnam scholar and historian. The chairman of the subcommittee, Representative Lee Hamilton, suggested to the ambassador that the government had some resources, too, like the White House, the State Department and the Defense Department.

"These individuals deserve enormous credit for a very effective operation," Ambassador Martin said. He claimed Mr. Luce and Mr. Branfman "twisted and distorted" American humanitarian concern into opposition to continuing support for the war.

"It is fashionable in some circles to blame the Congress for the final collapse of South Vietnam," Ambassador Martin told the subcommittee. "God knows there is enough blame over two decades to spare a bit for everyone, but the easy out of blaming Congress, in my opinion, just won't wash. The President and the Secretary of State were calling it absolutely right. But, in the temper of the times, this just could not be enough."

He explained that members of Congress were under so much pressure in Washington and from their home districts, it was clear why they cut the request for $1,600,000,000 in military aid to South Vietnam to $700,000,000 for the fiscal year that ended June 30, 1975.

"I have enormous respect for the abilities of Mr. Branfman and Mr. Luce," Ambassador Martin said, not kindly.

Fred Branfman, a New Yorker, was considered something of a genius in the antiwar movement, not only for digging out and compiling the statistics on the air war in Indochina, but for making it clear what the peasants of Vietnam and Laos and Cambodia were enduring. When he married a young Vietnamese woman named Nguyen Thi Ngoc Thoa, who had come to the United States with injured Vietnamese children needing advanced medical treatment, a poem was read at their wedding that the guests had never heard. It was written by a soldier in the National Liberation Front whose fiancée, also a guerrilla, had been killed in the south.

Once I loved my country because of the birds and
   butterflies
Because there were days of escaping from school.
But now I love my country because in each handful
   of soil
You are there, beloved.

Mr. Branfman, who ran Project Air War, also worked at educating members of Congress on the air war, since it seemed to be perceived by the legislators only intermittently. Nor did the public always understand what the air war was except when reports or photographs of captured pilots aroused immense waves of pity or patriotic indignation.

Mr. Branfman and his wife, called Thoa, lived in one room at the Indochina Resource Center, sleeping on a mattress on the floor because they liked it and did not care about furniture. Neither of them seemed to ever have enough sleep. Both of them worked furiously and went without privacy, the smallest luxuries, or even a few days' vacation. I remember him going up and down, down and up the long and cold halls of the Senate and House Office Buildings, trying to see members of Congress. In fact, although he was in his early thirties, he shuffled because he was tired or, being very tall, had not learned to stand up straight or his one pair of shoes did not fit, or something. People often thought he was a mild-mannered man; they did not always immediately see the passion, the fierce intelligence and the drive. Mr. Branfman rarely had any money in his pockets and often did not even realize it until he had a flight to catch or was in a taxi.

What he did not easily tolerate was the depression or sense of futility felt by people who slid in and out of the movement. He was always saying that the antiwar forces were at their most most powerful when everyone else said the movement was finished and over. Sometimes my own sadness and a lack of a sense of strategy would inspire him to tell me stories. They were always about people in North Vietnam, or political prisoners in the south, who had borne unspeakable ordeals. Yet they were even more calm, more courageous and more determined. Sometimes the stories would make me sadder. I had enough of my own memories, but he said, quite correctly, they were the wrong kind and that I would feel differently if I ever went to Hanoi. The triumph was how the Vietnamese had withstood and defeated the world's most advanced technology.

"Progress involves, even necessitates, contradictions," he would say, usually after midnight when he came to life. "Progress is not a straight even line. Adversity is a sign of progress . . ."

His wife, Thoa, so small a woman she did not even come to his shoulder, made an enormous difference in his life. He became stronger and more organized—his desk was a chaos, but what he needed was always in his head—and he trusted her above all others. She was tireless: cooking for friends, giving speeches, traveling, raising funds, confronting American officials, contacting other Vietnamese in this country. When Mr. Branfman went to California to help manage the campaign of the former radical and co-founder of SDS, Tom Hayden, for a seat in the Senate—which Mr. Hayden lost, although he received thirty-seven percent of the total vote—the separation pained Mr. and Mrs. Branfman. But they said each of us has our work to do and work came first.

In New York, when Don Luce heard he had been cited by Ambassador Martin, he thought it an honor for the Indochina Resource Center and for all the people who over the years had kept it alive. "The Vietnamese won the war," he said. "They were so angry at the Saigon regime that no amount of U.S. aid, napalm or police advisors could have won the war for America." He thought the American people were important in bringing the war to an end sooner, perhaps two or three years sooner.

"This means the peace movement saved at least two hundred

thousand lives and prevented an incredible amount of agony that could never be measured in statistical form," he said.

The Indochina Resource Center is still in the same dilapidated house on 18th Street near Dupont Circle in Washington, D.C. It has two staff members, both meagerly paid, and some volunteers. There was no other place like it in that city; I remember it as a strangely hopeful but humble place. The frailty of their finances caused a lot of problems; no one ever knew they were working for one of the best propaganda and pressure organizations in the world until Ambassador Martin said so.

IN SAIGON, DON LUCE lived in two rooms on the sixth floor of a small apartment building on rue Pasteur. There must have been furniture, for we sat on something, but the rooms seemed very uncrowded. There was a little kitchen and a bed with exhausted sheets. I had never seen an American civilian live so simply; even his toothpaste was Vietnamese. There was no American beer, whiskey, soap, shampoo, detergent, toilet paper, toilet-bowl cleaners with added enzymes, instant daiquiris, Wonder bread, instant coffee, instant pizza or chocolate cookies from the PX or commissary. There was no air conditioning, the windows were not screened.

He was then as he is now: a gentle and austere man, born without a temper, almost unable to return anger. He grew up on a small dairy farm in East Calais, Vermont. It was a beginning that could be guessed by his face and his manner. At twenty-two he had a master's degree in farm management from Cornell University, the author of "Cost and Returns of Pig Production in Western New York"—Agricultural Bulletin No. 31. As an undergraduate at Cornell he knew some Malay students, liked to hear them speak of their countryside and thought of going to Asia. He went as an expert on sweet potatoes, the subject of his doctoral thesis, which was never finished. In Vietnam he was assigned to Banmethuot, as an agricultural volunteer running an experimental agricultural station for the International Voluntary Services to help the Rhade Montagnards grow a better variety of sweet potato. He talked with farm people—where to dam the tiny stream to get irrigation water to their vegetable plots, how to get better varieties of fruit trees in the area, whether rubber or coffee would be a better cash crop. The door of the experiment station was never locked; no one stole. It was 1958. He was very happy there. There was nothing he needed for himself or missed.

In front of the tiny bathroom in his Saigon apartment there was a door that led out to a balcony. You could climb over it onto another building that faced Pasteur and Le Thanh Ton streets, go inside, take an elevator and reach the street. Vietnamese students often came to the apartment to be with him; the balcony was the escape route if the police raided the apartment. It was a most important balcony.

He had a press card that year, but he was not like the other reporters, stuck in the tar of useless briefings, press releases, daily war stories, endless operations, endless assessments. He knew better. He lived apart, he did not go out on the Army choppers or mingle with the American troops, or interview official Americans. He did not seem to be pulled into the depressions that every so often flattened and mashed the rest of us, making reporters do peculiar things to be consoled and calmed. His life was austere. His was a Vietnamese world; so well did he speak and write their language, he could make jokes in it. His Vietnamese friends were not people he hired. Some came to him, as they came to no other American, with information. He kept careful clear notes on everything. He saved documents other reporters did not read. Yet the little apartment on rue Pasteur was oddly peaceful. You could see nothing but the Saigon sky. He did not want to move, but his Vietnamese landlady became nervous when the special police came around asking questions, wanting to know who came to see him, and their names, how often there were visitors. The balcony was no longer enough.

The trouble began after he led two congressmen and an aide to the cells known as the "tiger cages" on Con Son Island in July 1970. They flew there on a clear morning, uncertain if they could succeed in what needed to be done.

They had an escort, an American named Frank Walton, who headed the Public Safety Directorate, an advisory program under the wing of CORDS.

No journalists had visited the tiger cages since French rule. The Americans in Saigon said, to all inquiries, that the tiger cages were a thing of the past, yet some Vietnamese gave Mr. Luce proof that they were still in use. At 10:23 A.M., in the office of the Vietnamese warden on Con Son, the aide, Thomas Harkin, broke off the polite conversation, over little cups of café filtre, about the weather and the beauty of the island. He said to Colonel Nguyen Van Ve that he had a list of specific prisoners the group wanted to see. There were six names. It was, of course, Mr. Luce who compiled the names. Colonel Ve, who spoke English beautifully, looked sorrowful. He said permission would have to come from the Ministry of Interior in Saigon. The group said please do this. The colonel handed a telegram to a clerk, speaking in Vietnamese. "Whether they answer or not is not important," he said. Colonel Ve was unaware that Mr. Luce understood every word.

Mr. Walton scolded the visitors for their request to see six of the prisoners. He suggested the congressmen go to the little shop that sold articles made by the prisoners and buy souvenirs. Finally the delegation was allowed to tour the place and Luce was able to speak to some of the prisoners when the guards were not close by. He heard wretched things from them. Randolph Berkeley, chief of the Corrections and Detention Division of the Public Safety Directorate, said in a jovial voice that Colonel Nguyen Van Ve even played soccer with the prisoners and was well liked. The visitors were taken to another part of the prison but they insisted on going back to Camp Four, where Luce had been told there was an entrance to the tiger cages. It was described as a narrow path between two walls, with some vegetables along the side. They saw a very small door, and in their desperation, shook and hammered it.

It was a tiny door. Colonel Ve protested: the door was always locked, was not interesting, led nowhere. But then a guard opened the door to find out what was going on, why so much noise. The congressmen, the aide and Mr. Luce plunged in. The tiger cages were small stone compartments which seemed not quite five feet across and about nine feet long. There were three prisoners in each cage. The men walked up a stairway and looked down at the prisoners below bars. The prisoners stared up. Not one could rise to his feet. Mr. Luce told the Vietnamese who they were, why they had come. He did not understand, in those first seconds, what had happened to them. They told. The prisoners were usually bolted to the floor, handcuffed to a bar or rod, or put in leg irons with the chain around a bar or rod. It did not take very long to ruin the legs, to bring partial or complete paralysis. The prisoners were occasionally released but always put back in the shackles. Always, they said, always. Above each cell was a wooden bucket of lime. Colonel Ve, following them, said the lime was to whitewash the cells, but the prisoners, shouting and talking together, told the foreigners it was used on them. They said they could not breathe, blood came up when the lime was thrown on them. Mr. Luce saw the floors of some cages were covered with lime.

"They crawled over on their hands because they couldn't stand up," Mr. Luce said. He kept translating for the congressmen as quickly as he could.

"The congressmen reacted very differently. Congressman Hawkins was very, very angry. You could see the anger. Congressman Anderson was sadder—he was more sad than angry. He was apologetic about asking me to translate, and one time he said 'I'm going to stop this, I'm going to stop this.'

"My first, my deepest reaction, was so painful, is still painful. I kept thinking I can't have been a part of this. Tom Harkin had given me a candy bar that he'd gotten from the commissary, I had that in my pocket, I wanted to toss it down between the bars to someone who looked starving . . ."

The prisoners chanted in thin voices of thirst, hunger, beatings. There was sand and pebbles in the rice, a man said. Another yelled that he had been shackled for months; still another said he had been a Buddhist monk who spoke out for an end to the war in 1966. The men told them there were women prisoners. They knew because they could hear higher voices rising into screams. The congressmen, the aide and Mr. Luce went down the stairs into an adjacent building. Each cage they saw held five women. Mr. Luce thought the women must have ranged in age from fifteen years to one woman who was seventy. Some lay without moving, while others tried to fan them with odd bits of filthy cloth. Many pleaded for water, but Mr. Luce had no water. Nearly all had sores on their faces and bodies. Their eyes looked strange, full of pus or a very deep pink.

When the group went outside, Frank Walton was waiting. His agitation was immense. "You have no right to interfere with Vietnamese affairs," he said. "You have come here trying to stir up trouble. You are guests of Colonel Ve here. You aren't supposed to go poking your nose into doors that aren't your business."

Congressman Hawkins said it was their business because of United States aid. Ninety percent of the funds used by the Saigon government came from the United States that year. The congressman said that he hoped the Americans who were prisoners in North Vietnam were being treated in a more humane way. Mr. Walton said in a louder voice that they were judging an entire prison of ten thousand inmates on how four or five hundred were being treated. "This prison is equal to the standards of many of the prisons in our own country," he said.

"These are very bad people," Colonel Ve said. "They will not salute the flag. They will not even salute the American flag."

One of the male prisoners had a tremendous scar on his head, as though the skull was a potato that had been split by a cleaver. Mr. Luce could not bring himself to ask the man how it happened. Another prisoner had three fingers missing; others said the fingers had been cut off as punishment. One of the women pulled herself up to the side of the cage and called up to them how cruel were the guards. She was very short of breath but she kept on. There was one guard, she said, who urinated on them. The man came over then, in a fury, yelling at her in front of Mr. Luce and the others. The guard said the woman had refused to salute the flag when she came to Con Son. She said she never would do it, never salute it. All the time Mr. Luce kept translating for the others. Mr. Harkin took photographs.

In Saigon, before the delegation left, Congressman Anderson asked Mr. Luce to give something to the Vietnamese who had described the location of the tiger cages. The gifts were a letter opener and a key chain with the Congressional seal—the fierce eagle—on them. The Vietnamese was very correct when Mr. Luce next saw him. He looked at the letter opener and the key chain with their handsome seals. The congressman is very kind, the Vietnamese said, I accept his kindness, but I have no need for such things.

Mr. Luce was embarrassed. "He symbolically took them and then of course he gave them back," he said.

After the congressmen left, Mr. Luce sent word to come to his apartment. It was the first time we had ever met. He told me about the tiger cages. I questioned him and looked at his notes for two hours. He wanted to give the story to *The New York Times* and to Morley Safer of CBS. I took unusual pains to make the report very clear, very certain. The story ran on page three of *The New York Times*, above a brief confirmation by one of the congressmen, who was planning to reveal more at a news conference. A denial by American authorities appeared on page one of *The New York Times* the same week. The editors were still cautious about giving credence to anyone like Don Luce in the antiwar movement. It made them nervous.

The U.S. Embassy was embarrassed and upset by the furor. Mr. Walton was forbidden to say anything. Reforms were promised. A spokesman for the United States Embassy said it would all be cleared up. There was no official comment. That month more than five hundred inmates of the prison were flown to Saigon, where they were to be released.

In the An Quang pagoda in Saigon, Mr. Luce took me to meet one of the prisoners, who was resting there. He was twenty-eight; I thought him to be over forty. Mr. Luce translated, going very slowly. The Vietnamese, who called himself by a family nickname, Anh Ba, said he had been in one of the airless, putrid tiger cages from 1965 to 1966. There were two to five men in each cell. He thought it was a little more than three feet wide, about six and a half feet long and almost six feet high. His calves were withered, no larger than my wrists, with deep rings around the ankles as if the skin had been sliced away. The scars were from the shackles, Anh Ba said. He did not wince or jerk when hot ash from my cigarette dropped on his left leg. I rubbed the skin, which felt like bark, but he could feel nothing. It surprised him very much to see me rubbing that light, dead leg.

He had been flown in a C-130 with an American pilot to Saigon, held in a local prison until his papers were in order, put in a truck and let out, with five other men, on a street corner in Saigon, where he knew no one. None had money. The others took turns carrying him piggyback to the pagoda, and he felt a little safe but his nervousness was very great, making his arms and hands jump.

Once I was a tailor, Anh Ba said. So many Vietnamese spoke of themselves this way. *Once I was*, they said. *Once I was* . . . He was from a village near Tay Ninh; on a July night in 1965 a clash broke out between the Viet Cong and South Vietnamese soldiers. When it was over, some national policemen came for him, saying he was an agent of the Viet Cong.

"But I said no, no, I was just sewing in my house. They did not believe me."

He was taken to Tay Ninh, where things were done to him no matter how much he cried out and said no. The questions poured over him like gravel.

In the pagoda, he spoke very clearly, always looking around to see who might be listening. He sat on a cot. He could sit up and he could lie down, not more. The legs would not move unless they were lifted and tucked in. His face was the color of a man who had just died.

"Did I have liaison with the Viet Cong? I said no. Had I given money to Viet Cong? I told them no, no I did not. Had I given rice to Viet Cong? I told them I had not, I had not even seen the Viet Cong."

The trial in Saigon was an astonishing thing. No one from the village was permitted to come, no one could watch, let alone speak for him. There was no lawyer. It was very rapid. He was sentenced to five years. At Con Son he began by being stubborn, not knowing any better. He refused to do hard labor, telling all who would listen that his sentence specified a term without hard labor. After he had spent a year in the tiger cages, he had to be carried to different prison quarters. He had forgotten what it was to walk. When he was released that July he had been at Con Son longer than five years; no one there was ever sure when they would be freed. Anh Ba said he hoped the right food and medicines would make it possible for him to walk again. We said nothing. I fed him cigarettes; money was given to him for the bus home, for food, for any medicines he had in mind. It was his hopefulness that I remember. He said he would crawl to his house if he had to.

I knew the name of the village but have never told it, because he was so fearful of being arrested again. Much later Luong and I went there to see how he was. But first we made ourselves known and did not start off asking where he lived. It was not difficult because there was a third, perhaps fourth, cousin of Luong's who had a sister-in-law living in the same village. She knew we were not spies, were not working for the Americans or the police. But Anh Ba was not there; the people thought he was still in jail or had perished. The bus from Saigon always came, but Anh Ba was never on it. Something happened to him. They took such risks, these Vietnamese, when all I could promise was no more than a story in an unheard-of foreign newspaper, such a small, pale record of what they had borne, what they had said. We never found him.

THE HARASSMENT BEGAN slowly that year, after the tiger cages became one of the most widely printed stories of the war. He wrote about them himself; two Vietnamese newspapers in Saigon, *Cong Luan* and *Tin Sang*, printed his account, but the police confiscated copies. In September, Peter E. Galuppo, of the embassy, questioned three American acquaintances of Mr. Luce to see if he was collaborating with the Viet Cong. In October he was told by the Vietnamese head of the National Press Center, Nguyen Ngoc Huyen, that he would not have his press card renewed. It was then taken away. He was accredited to the Ecumenical Press Service of the World Council of Churches in Geneva and could show dozens of clippings of stories. Many other reporters, who were free-lance, had press cards but were not required to show proof of any of their work because it did not much matter. In October he was told the reason was the trip to Con Son. Then a plainclothesman began following him very closely, so closely that at times the policeman could have touched him. He was informed by an American captain that he could no longer receive or send mail through the APO system, a convenience granted to all Americans in the press and to those working for volunteer agencies. It upset him because the captain would not even hand over mail that had already arrived. "I have my orders," the captain said.

It was all made worse when, in February, Mr. Luce disclosed that the construction consortium of Raymond, Morrison, Knudson-Brown, Root and Jones had a contract with the U.S. Department of Navy to build new "isolation" cells at Con Son to replace the tiger cages. The new cells were to be two square feet smaller. Mr. Luce persisted in writing that the increased budget for the Saigon police and for Vietnamese prisons was coming from American tax dollars. In May 1971 it was all over. His visa to stay in Vietnam was not to be renewed. Mr. Luce was told to leave.

In that spring of 1971 he thought he might be killed by the Saigon government. So did I. A Vietnamese friend in one of the ministries had warned him to be quite careful. I thought he might be run over by a truck late at night, but Luong said no, that was too simple, then everyone would know the government had done it. Mr. Luce did not know the details of such a plan. All he could do was talk to another Vietnamese, who he suspected worked in police intelligence, saying that in the event of his death a letter, which had been taken to Hong Kong, would be published. It was the only precaution he could take.

Mr. Luce was very calm. The night before he left, in May, his apartment was robbed. The door was kicked open, his papers and files scattered, some were removed. It did not matter because he had made copies. For the first time in twelve years in Vietnam he felt ghastly. Luong was sure he had been poisoned, but the sickness was the early stage of hepatitis. Luong said a man who had lived so simply, who had eaten Vietnamese food for so long from the streets and lived in the villages would not get such a disease. Nonsense, I said. We used to argue about it. The last night, Mr. Luce was given a party by some Vietnamese who had themselves been in prison, or had relatives in prison, and had formed a committee for reform. He promised not to forget them, not to stop speaking about them in his own country, never to stop telling Americans about the war. It was a happy evening although he could hardly eat or move easily. On May 11 he went. It was three days before the expulsion date, but he wanted to testify before the Senate Foreign Relations Committee headed by Senator William Fulbright. He left a letter, in Vietnamese, for all his friends, saying it was time for him and all foreigners to leave, but that he would come back when there was peace.

HE HAD ALWAYS caused trouble; perhaps the surprise was that Don Luce had not been expelled earlier. In 1961, three years after he arrived, Mr. Luce became director of International Voluntary Services in Vietnam. Six years later he resigned, but not quietly, to protest the war. There were fifty of them, all civilian volunteer workers fluent in Vietnamese, who signed a letter to President Lyndon B. Johnson opposing the American policies of free-fire zones, the continued creation of refugees, defoliation, bombing of the north and south. The IVS volunteers were already a problem to the embassy; one of them had written a letter protesting defoliation which had been used by the antiwar movement. Mr. Luce went to the embassy to ask if the letter to President Johnson could be sent through the pouch. Colonel George Jacobson tried to dissuade him, then said he certainly could not see Ambassador Bunker, who was far too busy.

"We said if they would stop making refugees, stop the bombing, stop the defoliation, then we wouldn't send the later," Mr. Luce said. Colonel Jacobson said Mr. Luce and the others were trying to bribe the United States. He was suddenly sent in to see Ambassador Bunker, who was polite and cool. The Vietnamese always called him *Ong Lanh*, Mr. Refrigerator.

"He said it was impolite to send the letter, he said you are guests in this country, you should not send the letter because it would be upsetting to the Vietnamese government. *And later he said if I sent the letter I would not be able to get a job with the United States government.* I said I understood that but I did not plan on applying for such a job."

Mr. Luce left Vietnam and spent a year as a research associate in the Center for International Studies at Cornell University, and speaking against the war. At the end of 1968 he went back, and a year later was working for the World Council of Churches.

In December 1970 a letter was sent to President Nixon and the Secretary General of the United Nations, signed by him and forty-eight others who were mostly Americans in Vietnam with voluntary agencies working on social welfare and development projects. The letter said that the United States actions in Indochina violated the Geneva Convention and other international treaties on the conduct of the war and the treatment of prisoners. The charges were very precise. The letter was five pages long. The signers were teachers, social workers, doctors, nurses, therapists, missionary teachers, agriculturists. But that year such a letter did not cause great excitement. It said: "Mr. President . . . we do not see peace any closer in Indochina today than it was when you took office in January 1969. We urge you . . . We urge you . . ."

There was no reply.

HE KEPT THE promise. Every day he kept it, he still keeps it. In July 1971 Mr. Luce started the Indochina Mobile Education Project. Its office was in a room on the top floor of the house in Washington on 18th Street. Project Air War was on the floor below. Both groups were part of the Indochina Resource Center, which served as an independent clearinghouse for information on contemporary Indochina. It had nine general sponsors from the academic community and sixteen academic associates to help provide information on the social, economic, political and historical realities of Vietnam, Cambodia and Laos. The Center put out a newsletter called "Indochina Chronicle." It also contacted and worked with legislators, set up briefings and seminars, and developed a series of audio-visual programs on Indochina to be loaned out across the country. There were always posters on the walls of the house, which seemed to burst with files, cabinets and people.

The mobile education project on Indochina consisted of photographs, drawings, slides, movies, artwork and crafts. The art was mounted on forty panels of large screens, which were set up in shopping centers, empty stores, schools or churches, auditoriums in small or medium-sized cities for a period of one to three days. During this time local groups—often those that were not connected with any position on the war—organized television, radio and newspaper coverage for Mr. Luce, who gave interviews, made speeches and met with local people to discuss America's role in Indochina. Sometimes, on a single day, he had as many as sixteen meetings.

He traveled all the time, driving the little bus at night or sleeping while another person drove—there were usually two or three in one team—so that he looked far more tired and drained in his own country than he did in Vietnam. It was very odd how his face changed: the color grew a little greyish and his eyes looked duller, as if the food were wrong or the air not good for him. He went everywhere in the truck, sometimes sleeping in people's houses, always talking about the war, getting the screens up. The curious thing about him is that he was always very patient, very tolerant, very unruffled. He never accused people of doing wrong; he said it was being done in their name.

Between July 1971 and October 1972 he went to twenty-one states. Mr. Luce, and the others with him, never knew in advance when it was going to get ugly.

It seemed quite routine the time they went to Missouri. The South County Shopping Mall in St. Louis had put out a big sign saying "Indochina Exhibit"; the panels were displayed in an arcade connecting the different shops. Someone wrote "nuke the gook" on one of the sketches done by a Lao refugee of the American plane bombing his village. Another person wrote bad things on a sketch made from memory by a South Vietnamese officer of Lam Son 719—the drive into Laos—which showed a soldier unable to hold on any longer to the runners of a helicopter. There were obscenities on other pictures too. Mr. Luce always carried the white correction fluid used by typists so he could paint clouds over the writing. He even had a competition with whoever accompanied him to see who could paint the fattest, nicest clouds.

"One of the things we found out was that if someone puts writing and graffiti on one picture and you leave the graffiti, within a matter of hours there will be more graffiti on the others," he said.

At five o'clock, the first afternoon, the manager of the shopping mall asked them to move out because of a steady stream of protesting telephone calls coming in all day. But traveling in other parts of Missouri was calm and pleasant. Mr. Luce thought the most hostile state was Indiana, because so many people were indifferent or impervious.

He spoke at Indiana University in Bloomington; eight people showed up. In Columbus, Indiana, there was a debate, sponsored by the Columbus Peace Education Council. John Rutherford, the news editor of *The Republic*, appeared on the panel, opposing Mr. Luce and a Vietnamese named Doan Hong Hai, twenty-five, who was traveling with the exhibit. In Mr. Rutherford's column on March 22, 1972—it is called "Hi Neighbor!"—he wrote of Mr. Luce:

He, in fact, did present a very convincing picture of the horrors of war and of the political repression in South Vietnam. Yet he failed to convince me that America was, and is, to blame.

. . . What I do not understand is how it is that so many Americans can come to know so much about other countries and yet know so little about their own country and what it stands—and fights—for.

The only time Mr. Luce was assaulted was in Augusta, Georgia. The exhibit was near the Dart Pharmacy, under a large awning on the street.

"One of the managers came out and was looking at a picture of a woman sitting in front of her house—it was only a culvert—with her boy, about four years old, standing by her. The caption explained that this woman asked me to take the picture to send to her husband, who was in the army. And this guy got very, very upset at this picture of a smiling Vietnamese. He said 'You're a foreigner!' And I said 'I'm not a foreigner, I'm an American.'"

The man yelled that if he was really an American, he'd be showing pictures of Americans, not pictures of "gooks."

"He grabbed me by the throat and said he was going to kill me. I leaned up against a car; people gathered to watch. The man said 'You're a coward.' He said he had been in the war—it must have been World War II. He was about five feet ten, slightly taller than I am, and wearing a suit . . . He wasn't squeezing my throat very hard at that point and I said if I were a coward I wouldn't have spent twelve years in Vietnam. 'Well, I'm not a coward,' the man said. 'I've been in the war and I've got a scar across my gut to prove it.'

Jacquelyn Chagnon, a pretty, sturdy young woman with very long dark-brown hair, came over to the man attacking her friend and said he must leave Don Luce alone. The man told her to shut up or that night the women in his family would find her and yank every hair out of her head.

It was a Saturday morning; quite a lot of people were out. The crowd around the two men grew thicker and more curious.

"'I'm not a foreigner,' I said, 'I am from Vermont.' The man said 'I told you you were a foreigner' and walked off."

The car he was pushed against seemed an old and trembly thing. When Mr. Luce finally stood up, an elderly black couple claimed it. The man shook his hand and said: "I wish you good luck. Thank you." The couple was very relieved that nothing had happened to their car.

They had to move the exhibit because the supermarket next to Dart Pharmacy began to receive threatening telephone calls. One of the anonymous callers wanted to shoot Mr. Luce.

He only remembers all this because it was so peculiar.

The question that most people asked him was if he was ever in danger in Vietnam; it was the question that he most hoped would not be asked. "It was very frustrating because one of the things that people try to do is make you a hero, and I kept pointing out that what I was talking about was happening to the Vietnamese," he said. "Sometimes in grade schools the children would ask a lot more. They wanted to know if I had seen anyone die."

In Logan, Ohio, a small town with less than ten thousand people, it was decided on the day he arrived with the exhibit that the high school students could not come to see it, or hear him, until the teachers came first that night. But the special-education class was allowed to come on the first day. These were the children considered slower than the others. He thought perhaps their teachers felt the exhibit couldn't do the slow learners any harm. There were about twenty. They looked at each of the panels very carefully. After school was over, all of them came back to see it again on their own time. A photograph showing a Montagnard crossbow was of interest to some boys who did not know whether you could shoot rabbits with it. One youngster, perhaps sixteen, kept looking at one photograph for at least five minutes. It showed two Vietnamese boys on a water buffalo, with heavy clouds in the sky. Mr. Luce watched the youngster leave the picture, come back to it, walk away, and come back to look at it again.

"Finally I asked him 'Do you like this picture?'" Mr. Luce said. The boy said yes, it was a good picture, but it sure looked as if it was going to rain, didn't it.

Some photographs showed injured small Vietnamese. These puzzled the children.

"Jacqui and I were both there at the time, talking to them, and they kept asking, well, why would anyone hurt a little child? They asked several times whether the children who looked hurt were in car accidents, and we said no, it was the war. Then they said but these are little children. They seemed to think that war only touched grown-up men . . ."

He always wanted Americans to see the Vietnamese not just as victims but a people who loved their land, their trees, their poetry, their music, their language, their food. He thought the antiwar movement might have made a mistake in showing only the people in pain.

He wanted to show their strength, not just their suffering.

"We found we got as much reaction to happy Vietnamese as to atrocities—sometimes as much adverse reaction, too. The hawkish people, who wanted us to win the war, would be upset by happy Vietnamese. My own analysis is that underneath what they were saying is a tremendous frustration that, with all of our bombs, all of our technology, we have not been able to destroy human spirit. That really bothered people, as it did the man in Augusta."

IN SMALL, RURAL places he felt himself at home. The people would ask questions about the Vietnamese. What do they eat and how do they live. Very often people would say to him that the Vietnamese put a low value on life, that a Vietnamese family didn't feel the way Americans felt if a son was killed, that they didn't mind being made to move because their houses weren't worth very much. If we stopped bombing in Vietnam, people would say, then they would kill each other because they don't value life. They would talk of the Japanese kamikaze pilots and how Buddhist monks in Vietnam burned themselves to death.

"One time I was talking to a minister—I can't even remember what city this was—who said something about the Buddhists burning themselves, how the Vietnamese didn't care about life. I said but would you argue that Christ put a low value on life because he allowed himself to be crucified? He got very, very angry. He wanted to know if I was a Christian, because a Christian would not say things like that."

They had a small plan to involve people, to teach them something about Vietnam, so they invited them to help prepare a Vietnamese meal, which was cooked by Jacquelyn Chagnon. She always carried a *wok* for cooking the vegetables; a Vietnamese salad was served. The chicken, Thit ga Nuong, was prepared and roasted as the Vietnamese do it. When people came together to chop vegetables—which took some time—Jacquelyn would talk about Vietnam, a country of farmers and the effect of herbicides on their crops and forests. She spoke very plainly and did not accuse them of anything. They played cassettes of Vietnamese music. In Iowa City nearly one hundred people came to a Vietnamese dinner given in a church.

"Even the sheriff of Iowa City came," said Mr. Luce. "People were moving toward the food when, unannounced, a local guerrilla theater group, white-faced, wearing black, burst in. Five adults and two children. They sang a song, did a skit, then they shot the children. They had BB guns. They screamed a lot. Everyone was nervous because no one knew what they were going to do. No one knew what to do themselves. It was sort of sad . . . Everyone just stood there. People were going through the line picking up their chicken, you know, and people didn't know— well, we all thought should we eat our chicken?"

He thanked the guerrilla theater group on their way out. The people thought the food tasted fine. The sheriff said he was glad he had come, it was an example of the community doing the kind of thing that the students at the University of Iowa were *always* telling them they should be doing.

THEY HAD POSTCARDS made of photographs of Vietnamese— happy-looking people and children—to sell. They collected translations of Vietnamese poems in a book called *We Promise One Another*. In 1973 Mr. Luce went on a long speaking tour for the American Friends Service Committee while others took over the Indochina Mobile Education Project. In May 1973 he was in San Diego at the University of California. A woman in her early fifties admired some photographs he was showing. The one she liked was taken in a rice-growing village sixteen miles outside of Hanoi. She was not pleased to hear it. "They're Communists," the woman said. "They're despicable Communists."

Toward the end of his speech, the dark-haired woman sat in the front row, saying over and over, in a low voice, "Traitor, traitor, traitor." Sometimes only her mouth would move: Traitor, traitor, traitor. He spoke for twenty minutes, leaving an hour for discussion. There were not more than fifty people in the auditorium. Because he had mentioned the tiger cages, the woman asked Mr. Luce if the people kept in them were Communists.

"I said I don't know. Some of them may have been Communists but they were not gun-carrying Communists. She said they're all the same and they should be killed."

There was a Vietnamese student studying physics who wanted

to speak. The woman asked him if he was from North Vietnam or South Vietnam.

"Vietnam is only one country," the student said. "I am from Vietnam." The woman said: "You are a Communist if you think Vietnam is just one country."

But Mr. Luce never spoke harshly, never insulted, never gave up with the people who despised him.

"I've been to thirty cities or towns in the last three months," Mr. Luce said. "I have just been in Champaign-Urbana, which are twin cities. Before that, Springfield, McComb, Davenport, Iowa; a day in Chicago; three days in Windsor, Canada. Then I was in Kalamazoo, Lansing, Ann Arbor, Detroit, Omaha, Lincoln, Central City, Grand Island—that's Nebraska—Fort Collins, Colorado Springs, Boulder in the Denver area. Before that, Phoenix, Albuquerque, San Diego, Los Angeles, the San Fernando Valley, Santa Barbara, San Francisco, Ashland and Medford in Oregon . . ."

People asked him why he was doing it. The question was often "How much money do you make?" He told them his salary per month was one hundred and twenty-five dollars. People sometimes found it hard to believe, he said. They shook their heads and could not quite conceal their suspicion.

Sometimes it was not enough to talk about the Vietnamese, or even the American, deaths. He talked about money.

"I find that probably the strongest antiwar statement that I've been able to make in the last few months is that the United States is paying for twenty-five thousand barrels of fuel for the war each day," he said in 1974. "Each barrel has forty-two gallons, which means a million gallons a day, three hundred and sixty-five million gallons a year. And if you go to get ten miles to the gallon, that's three thousand, six hundred and fifty billion miles. That seems to be a stronger statement than in the first year of 'peace' in Vietnam in 1973 there were one hundred and twenty-five thousand casualties on both sides."

He was often asked how many people in the United States saw Vietnam as much more than a well-intentioned mistake, saw it as a war of crime, and were sickened by it. A reporter suggested to Mr. Luce that maybe ten percent of the population had this view. "Ten percent is too high," he said. "Less." He never fooled himself about that. Three times he went to North Vietnam. On one trip, in 1973, he was led into the south and taken on a tour of Quang Tri province. The visitors went to the site of the former U.S. Army base known as Camp Carroll. The Viet Cong were raising chickens in the bunkers built and inhabited by Americans. The chickens pleased him. In the summer of 1974 he became co-director of Clergy and Laity Concerned, a group originally formed to protest the war in Vietnam in 1965, and moved from Washington, D.C., to CALC headquarters in New York. That same year he led an American delegation of two bishops and two reverends to North Vietnam.

Now, so much later, he is still making speeches, still winding his way through the country, talking to people about sending aid to Vietnam through a group called Friendshipment, a coalition of organizations raising money for the medicines and supplies and clothing so desperately needed. He is still talking about Vietnam, the need for unconditional amnesty, the high defense budget, the B-1 bomber, and political prisoners in other countries—South Korea, Indonesia, Iran, Chile and Uruguay, whose governments, he says, receive so much support from the United States.

He is now paid ninety-six dollars a week and shares a railroad apartment with two other people on Second Avenue and 10th Street. His bunk bed is over the john. He likes the neighborhood—considered run-down, if not menacing, by many people—because it is the closest thing in the city to a village in Vermont, or in Vietnam.

He does not think in terms of being happy or unhappy; the words mean nothing to him. In six years he has never complained about his life, never asked for a vacation, never said he was tired or that he needed a change now that he is forty-one years old. Yet there was one day that was wonderful, a day that renewed and restored him. It was not even a day, perhaps no more than fifteen or twenty minutes. He was in a village called Hai Duong, between Haiphong and Hanoi, in early December of 1974. He was talking to the villagers, then to one family. "Then we sat for a while," Mr. Luce said. "I sat outside with three Vietnamese leaning up against the family house. None of us said anything. We just sat. And I felt . . ."

But he could not quite say what he felt, only that he needed it: the silence, the ground, the Vietnamese, the sky.

AMBASSADOR GRAHAM MARTIN, testifying on that January day, made a curious plea. He spoke of a dog named Nit Noy who had lived in Saigon, too, and made the perilous escape.

"The fact is that it was not my dog, but my daughter's. The fact is that I did not intend to bring it out but had arranged for Nit Noy to seek asylum with the ambassador of France. However, a correspondent of the *Los Angeles Times*, a journal not noted for its uncritical support of American policy in Vietnam, decided otherwise. He put the dog under his coat and took it out, leaving his typewriter behind as more than compensating weight. To leave his typewriter behind certainly qualifies George McArthur as a qualified dog lover.

"I shall always be eternally grateful to him because my wife was devoted to that dog, and in my family, my wife suffered most in the evacuation of Vietnam. Her contribution to stability was an enormous one in those last days. Had we begun to pack our household items, the signal would have been all over Saigon.

"So all our small collection of things that were of great sentimental importance to us remained untouched. On the last day the Marine log shows that I returned to the residence at 11:03 and departed at 11:14. My wife had eleven minutes to pack one bag and walk away from all those things we had found comfortable to live with in the places we had served our country. I have been told our residence is now occupied by a very senior North Vietnamese official. *One hopes the next time a senior American official visits Saigon, it might be gently indicated that the return of some of her things, particularly her granddaughter's portraits, would be favorably regarded.*"

These particular remarks upset no one. No man hearing the ambassador even laughed. The ambassador, who cared so much for that dog, who made it clear that the gentlemanly thing for the Vietnamese to do was to return every one of his wife's possessions, did not seem embarrassed to bring up such matters. Indeed, he spoke as if he did not remember, had never known or thought about, the losses of the Vietnamese.

Civilian war casualties in South Vietnam, killed or wounded, 1965–1973	1,435,000
Civilian war casualties in South Vietnam, 1973–1975	339,882
Refugees generated in South Vietnam, 1965–1973	10,270,000

Among the Vietnamese disabled, it is reckoned that amputees number 83,000; paraplegics, 8,000; blind, 30,000; deaf, 10,000; and in other categories, 50,000.

Ambassador Martin also told the committee that when the "totally uninformed" criticisms of the evacuation began to appear, it made his wife furious. She told him that he had served his country for over one-fifth of its life and two-thirds of his own, that the record was clear and that historians would treat him kindly. Ambassador Martin ended his testimony by saying he thought his wife, even if prejudiced, might be right about the historians.

It is quite possible, of course, that the ambassador never knew that South Vietnam was a land of widespread malaria, bubonic plague, leprosy, tuberculosis and venereal disease. Studies done after the war by the World Health Organization revealed that four out of every five soldiers had venereal disease, the incidence of tuberculosis was one of the highest in the world, malaria was increasing, and that South Vietnam might be one of the few places on earth where leprosy was spreading and bubonic plague still taking lives. A two-day meeting in Manila in March 1976, organized by the World Health Organization regional committee for the Western Pacific, was an effort to help Vietnam and the Vietnamese. The Vice Minister of Health, Dr. Hoang Dinh Cau of Hanoi, gave some statistics. He told delegates that 7,600,000 tons of bombs—more than three times the total amount dropped during World War II—fell on towns and cities of North Vietnam during the war. Over half a million tons of toxic chemicals and 7,000 tons of toxic gas were also dropped in these areas between 1964–1969, Dr. Hoang said. The United States did not attend the WHO meeting, saying it was not American policy to give aid to the regimes in Saigon or Hanoi.

WHEN AT LAST, after his polite yet urgent letters, we had a reunion in California, I thought at first he was in disguise. He looked so peculiar in those California clothes: a zippered baby-blue jacket, in a clammy material that could be wiped clean, and plaid trousers. In Saigon he always looked fine in his old short-sleeved shirts, which often had ink on their pockets, and the same pair of dark and baggy trousers that were too old to even hold a shine.

Inside the new house he went barefoot although he kept on

the baby-blue jacket, which made him look sallow and old. As many Vietnamese did, he found California in February to be a trifle cool. It was a Sunday, so he did not choose to get into shoes and socks. The entire family—all ten of them—kept their sandals outside on the front steps; this is how I knew it was their house. His wife spoke not a word of English, she could not manage hello or goodbye. But she smiled to see me again; she smiled at any American who came inside.

Please don't give my real name, he said, seeing my notebook. We made up a new one, Mr. Bao. He was nervous about getting into trouble, or losing the pension paid by the U.S. government, which had employed him for nearly twenty-four years. We had not seen each other in four years. He seemed deflated and even more vague, as if he could not find his glasses or something which he had just put down. Mr. Bao said he missed his books in Saigon. The idea of losing his little library made him feel very mixed up.

We did not meet again that Sunday, in a flat little town three hours from Los Angeles, because in Saigon we had been friends. It was nothing of the sort. We both wanted something from each other, and we got it. Mr. Bao wanted me to bring him certain books. I wanted to know what had happened to one Vietnamese family who were among the 140,000 people evacuated in April 1975 and brought to this country. He had written me for the books. The number-one request was for an English translation of *The Tale of Kieu*, the literary masterpiece of the Vietnamese. Mr. Bao knew there were no copies of any book in Vietnamese, but the children were swallowing new English words each day. Bring *Tale of Kieu* for them, he wrote, and *Fire in the Lake* for me, plus . . . In Saigon he was always asking me for books, usually obscure volumes of poetry. I provided what I could and later learned that he had never opened or read the much-wanted books. He only needed to own them.

His wife gave us a Vietnamese soup for lunch, rice and vegetables, at a table in the kitchen. The children had beautiful manners and ate without fuss or chatter. They range from a sixteen-year-old girl and a fifteen-year-old boy to a fourteen-month-old baby who is greatly admired by the others. Mr. Bao looked into his soup; it depressed him to trace the last year of his life.

"We never believed we should leave Vietnam, not until the last moment. Everybody goes, we go. And I, I was considered 'high risk.' Yes, 'high risk.' It was a kind of frantic moment, so when we are given a chance to go, we just go." In Saigon he read that any Vietnamese who worked for the U.S. government or the police was in danger. The American chief of the Reports Section in the Defense Attaché Office where he worked told him to get ready to leave, to pack lightly, to tell only the members of his immediate family. The family went to the airport in two sedans and Mr. Bao insisted that all of them had to lie down in the cars so people in the street would not see them, and spread panic.

After I left Saigon in 1972 Mr. Bao found a new job working for the Americans in the DAO in the big building at Tan Son Nhut airport, jokingly called "Pentagon East." The work was tiring and difficult, he said. His job was to check the transcripts of intelligence reports from the field which had been translated from Vietnamese.

"The Americans send in these reports. I don't know, sometimes they used the code G2 or G3—the man responsible was always an American field officer. Yes, yes, the American military was supposed to have gone away, but these were officers in civilian clothes. I had to make the reports readable in English, that's all."

Although the house could barely accommodate all of them, Mr. Bao had a place of his own, a little room the Americans call a den which had a deadening fake wood paneling on the walls. He had a few dozen newly acquired books on shelves.

"Will you always be a Vietnamese?" I said. It was a stupid

question, even a cruel one, but he kept repeating that he and his family were immigrants. He knew they were not just refugees with a chance of going back. His English was always good, so he knew the difference.

"Yes. My spirit is. This"—he touched his clothes and looked around the room—"has nothing to do with my spirit. You gave me some books but I don't have anything special for you except this poem. I just glorify Vietnam in my poems. I'm not for the left or the right. I believe in the history of Vietnam. Someday the south will liberate the north."

But he did not explain why or how. The truth is that he was not interested in politics or historical analysis. He always said of himself that he was a poet and a mystic, a Confucian Buddhist. His poems always seemed unusually bad to me: flat and stale things derived from the French, full of perpetual clouds, lakes and Doomed Man. When we met in Saigon he was a forty-six-year-old Vietnamese who worked in the library of the American Cultural Center and who had already been married for twelve years to a strong and handsome woman from the Delta who each year seemed to be carrying another child. He was fond of his family. But Mr. Bao needed peace and distance for his reading and poetry. In 1970 he was clearly wretched in his job but he could not pull himself away after so many years in the employ of the Americans. There was nowhere to go.

"There were several times I want to resign, you know, but somehow I did not want to lose my seniority, so I keep holding on. Maybe because I had done studying in the United States, and I know so many Americans, so I want simply to stick to the Americans. I keep holding on, hoping that after I retire I will do free-lance writing and be on my own, no longer having anything connected to the Americans."

He had been sent to the United States on a government scholarship to study at Michigan State University in 1954. It was his ruin, for that year was such a triumph, the voyage so long, the new friends and the journalism courses so exciting, that he felt honored. But years later in Saigon, when he was paid about five hundred dollars a month by the Americans, he acted as if some unspoken promise made to him had not been kept. When a small delegation wanted to complain about their wages, he went with them to make a call on Edward J. Nickel, director of the Joint United States Public Affairs Office, but nothing came of it.

"You know how he treated us? He put his shoes on the desk," Mr. Bao said, meaning the American put his feet up. "We really resented that. Well, he was the boss. We were not well paid at all. If I had worked for *The New York Times*, I'd have been better paid."

It was a reproach which I ignored. I had tried using Mr. Bao as a translator before finding Nguyen Ngoc Luong, and knew in the first five minutes it was hopeless. He could not concentrate during an interview. My questions bored or puzzled him, perhaps it was embarrassing for him. Although someone spoke for twenty-five minutes, his translation came out like a tiny coded telegram. Besides, I did not trust Mr. Bao. Saigon was a city that demanded constant suspicion, which grew like a ferocious fungus in a damp cellar covering everything. Spying was encouraged, if not required, by the Vietnamese and the Americans. Some people were paid, others did it because they had no choice.

But there was one interview Mr. Bao and I did early in 1970 with the head of a middle-class family in Saigon. He was a sixty-two-year-old retired civil servant named Nguyen Van Ba, an angelic-looking old man who grumbled that he worked like a "nursemaid" when any of his twelve grandchildren were underfoot. The traffic in Saigon, the noise and the poisonous fumes, discouraged him from leaving his six-room house. At night Mr. Ba turned on a Japanese-made television set and turned to the station of the Armed Forces network to watch *The Fugitives* and

Bonanza. He found both programs most entertaining while never quite catching on to the plot or the dialogue. Afterward the television set was carefully put back into a large carton to protect it from dust or damage. Mr. Ba had three sons—none in combat, all in the army—and a rose garden. He and his wife, who kept talking about high prices, both knew a little of the My Lai massacre although their government ignored the accounts published in the American press. The Thieu government did not want the massacre discussed or reported. It embarrassed the Americans. Besides, it was of no consequence, a cabinet minister had said.

"It may be true and yet it may not be true," Mr. Ba said. "For reports of such things are often exaggerated." He saw no reason to reach an opinion about it. Mr. Ba and his wife had also heard about the large numbers of Americans protesting the war but they thought these must be worried mothers.

There were many middle-class Vietnamese, some rich, others not, who did not know much about the war beyond the inflation and the draft and the presence of so many foreigners. They could not imagine what was happening in the villages, what had been done. One reason, of course, was that ordinary Vietnamese could not clamber aboard Army helicopters to go watch the war for a day, as reporters did, or go on operations.

Mr. Bao kept his distance from the war. "We just stayed in Saigon and did not see how the war was going—except through American magazines, *Time* and *Newsweek*," he said that Sunday in Southern California. He did not see the irony of it.

"Why did you ever work for the Americans?" I asked. For his career with them went back to 1951 when he was hired by the United States Information Service in Saigon.

"Because I don't have any degree from any Vietnamese school, from any Vietnamese university. So I had to find a job to support myself. I passed a test and I was admitted as a junior translator. I kept thinking it was a way to improve my English." It was.

• • •

THEY WENT FROM Saigon to Clark Field in the Philippines, then to Guam for a week, then on to Camp Pendelton in California for a month before an American sponsor was found. At Camp Pendleton, which became a Vietnamese village, it was cold and uncomfortable for them living in a tent with two other families. It made him feel like a prisoner, he said. A Vietnamese friend advised him to try for a sponsor from a church, any church, and to convert if that is what it took. He did.

An American who had been a missionary in Vietnam took the Vietnamese family to a ranch in California where they were housed, fed, clothed and put to work. The chores came as a slight shock to Mr. Bao. "We had to work hard, we become farmers. We cleared the land and planted seeds. All my children have helped. My wife must have planted twenty sunflowers!"

Through the church they found a couple in the small town willing to help them resettle, find housing, get him a job, make dentist and doctor appointments, find church funds for such expenses, get the children into school, and begin to show Mr. Bao and his wife the hang of things. He was given a job as a teacher's aide in an elementary school. The salary was minuscule but he had a pension from the U.S. government for his years of employment. His wife and the older children do go to church. When we were having lunch, the sponsors came in: a young American couple who were serious and energetic. They often dropped in, as Mr. Bao did not have a telephone or a car. I spoke to the man, who was in his thirties and thought we could have won the war in Vietnam if we had not lost our will. He was disgusted that Lieutenant Calley was tried. It was his opinion that Calley should have wiped out all the Vietnamese at My Lai, yes sir. Mr. Bao paid no attention. He was eating his soup and trying to remember how many books he had left behind in Saigon.

"I am very confused," Mr. Bao said later. "Even when I sleep I think about returning to Vietnam, but I have no other dreams. Sometimes I dream of returning even for a visit. My wife—well, she wants to lead a simple life with parents and relatives in the Delta. She is from Rach Gia, you know. Even the children say something about missing Saigon."

But it was too late. There was not much hope at all that the Vietnamese now in this country could get back, I said. Perhaps in twenty years. Be patient. You cannot blame the new leaders for not trusting you.

"We sacrifice everything for the children, my wife and I," Mr. Bao said, as parents are apt to do. "So that they can decide their own future. We thought that if we stay in Vietnam, the authorities would tell them what to do. At least here they have a chance to do what they want."

He did not sound convinced of anything. Later he sent me a copy of the letter he wrote to "The Head Librarian, Library of Congress" explaining who he was and what he had lost and asking them to advise him where he could order the works on Tibetan Lamaism and mysticism, particularly those by his favorite writers. ". . . The books I desperately need for my studies," Mr. Bao wrote.

Before I left I handed over a suitcase of clothes to his wife, thinking the children could use them. But in the walk-in closet there were already so many piles of sweaters, shirts, pants, blouses, pajamas that the shelves were jammed. The older girls were very excited about the walk-in closet. They had never seen so many clothes, in such colors. They did not know of course that the clothes did not do them justice and took away much of their grace and delicacy.

Saying goodbye to Mr. Bao, I warned him that I did not think I could really find a copy for him of the *Tibetan Book of the Dead*. I wished him well but I felt no pity for him, no real interest, no pleasure at the reunion. He was as he had always been.

One thing more: I was having coffee on Third Avenue with a young man who had worked for *Newsweek* in Vietnam and had not much liked it. He was telling me about his very last trip to Saigon, after the American troops had left in February 1973 and when the press corps became so much smaller. The city was quiet and full of ghosts for him. We talked, as all of us always do, about the Vietnamese, when he asked a question that I had never heard before, and I did not know how to give him the answer he wanted.

"Do they miss us?" he said.

THEIR ELDEST SON, Robert C. Ransom, Jr., died shortly before Mother's Day in May 1968 in a surgical hospital in Chu Lai eight days after he stepped on a mine in Quang Ngai province. He was a twenty-three-year-old second lieutenant leading a platoon. In such a war, there was nothing unusual about his terrible injuries. The boy, who was always called Mike, was born when his father was in the European Theater of Operations during World War II, a first lieutenant with the OSS attached to the Ninth Army. A telegram was sent to him announcing the birth of his child and namesake on October 2, 1944, which he received in Maastricht, Holland. The Americans in G-2 were working in military head-quarters set up in a high school. By coincidence the telegram was delivered to him by a signal officer whom he remembered from Deerfield Academy. He knew of the birth of his son because his wife, Louise, had immediately written him, but his own father, William Ransom, a former president of the American Bar Association and partner in a New York law firm, had pulled strings to have the telegram sent because he thought mail might take forever, and no one in his family was quite sure where the lieutenant was.

Mr. Ransom remembers that telegram, how the words were pasted in little strips on a piece of paper so it looked like a commercial telegram. This one was signed Dwight D. Eisenhower. The language of the message was in the peculiar stilted voice of all Army messages and told him to acknowledge. When he did not, another telegram came asking when acknowledgement from Lieutenant Robert Charlie Ransom could be expected. His middle name is Crawford not Charlie: it was the word used in the military alphabet to designate the letter C. It rather amused the lieutenant to be Robert Charlie. The baby was no more than ten days old when the Eisenhower telegram reached him. When the child was eight months old, the lieutenant was able to come home suddenly on leave, surprising his wife, who was asleep, and seeing the baby at last. Something of the joy of that morning still moves across his face when he speaks of it.

Eight months is such a wonderful age for babies, he said. Mrs. Ransom's father, a dignified lawyer, felt the celebration so deeply that morning that when they at last sat down for breakfast he poured a little bourbon in their orange juice.

Robert Ransom and his wife were married in September 1942, the day after he graduated from Officers Candidate School. After the war he finished up at Yale Law School, and they had five other sons, naming them Lawrence, Mark, John, Matthew and Daniel.

Mrs. Ransom remembers not just the huge grief caused by the death of Mike, but the anger she and her husband felt, which was not diminished by the reaction of others they knew. "People would come up to say 'Isn't it satisfying that he died for his country?'" she said. But they did not believe their son had.

That June the couple went to Dorset, Vermont, where they have a house, to attend the wedding of the daughter of close friends. The minister was the Reverend William Sloane Coffin, Jr., who for some time had been active in the antiwar movement and was encouraging resistance to the draft. She listened to him when he said how much he wished the mothers in America would object to the war, and risk arrest. "He opened a path," Mrs. Ransom said.

On July 3, 1968, she began: chaining herself to a draft resister at an antiwar demonstration at the Whitehall Street Induction Center in New York, taking the risks just as Reverend Coffin hoped she would. At night, on weekends, and whenever he could, her husband started draft counseling to hundreds of young men in Westchester County.

She went to Washington, D.C., to give back the two medals posthumously awarded to her son by the government of South Vietnam. She left them with a letter to Ambassador Bui Diem at the South Vietnamese Embassy, saying it was a tragic irony that her son died to "help perpetuate a regime that has devoted itself to destroying . . . freedom . . .

"We will accept nothing from such a government."

The couple replied to all the official letters of condolence. Mr. Ransom answered a letter from President Johnson: "Why can it now not stop? Why is it that we ourselves do not have the courage to confess the past errors?" To Congressman Richard Ottinger, he wrote: "It is just not possible for us to believe that our son died in a 'just cause' . . . Though we are Republicans, we have voted twice for you and will continue to do so in the belief that you will do everything in your power to oppose the efforts of the Administration to prolong this senseless war."

When they were first informed that their son was wounded, Mr. Ransom, a high-ranking lawyer for IBM, called everyone who he thought could give them additional information or advice. What he did not know, could not even imagine, was that in those eight days he could have reached the hospital in Chu Lai by taking a commercial flight to Saigon and then Army transport to the 2d Surgical. In World War II, fuel and places on aircraft were not given to civilians seeking their sons; there were no jeeps or helicopters for such a purpose. It did not occur to Mr. Ransom that he could have gone there until long after the death, and then it occurred to him many times. An Army nurse, Captain Connie Schlosser, wrote them that she had cared for their son daily during the last eight days of his life. "I have never written a letter like this before, but then in my six years of nursing I have never met so courageous an individual as your son," she wrote. Her letter, which reassured them that no mistake in identity had been made, saved the parents from having to open the closed casket. The nurse spent a weekend visiting them in Bronxville.

In April 1973 Louise Ransom and Carl Rogers, a Vietnam veteran who had been in the antiwar movement for many years, joined with others to form a group called Americans for Amnesty. Mr. Ransom backed his wife, as he always had, taking her to places where she was a speaker, writing letters himself, speaking out on the war even when it was not welcomed. They lost some friends—"those on the other side," Mr. Ransom calls it—and made new ones. In the antiwar movement they were an unusual couple, not because of their age but because of their background and connections, and their assurance.

An energetic and good-natured woman, Louise Ransom graduated from Vassar, class of 1942, an English major who liked creative writing. She has an open, cheerful face with the large blue eyes of a child. But when she speaks about the war and for unconditional amnesty—not for a pardon, which implies guilt—then something happens to the well-dressed and high-spirited woman from Bronxville and an urgent, different person calls out.

They neglected their five children; both admit it and worried, but their sons understood and bear them no ill-will. In January 1974 Mr. Ransom went to South Vietnam with a small group of Americans opposed to the war. It was a short visit, but he took one day for himself in Quang Ngai province and went to the area, described by his son in his letters, to see where the boy had been so hurt. He says he found the place; he knew he did.

"I feel my son's life was utterly wasted," Mr. Ransom said on more than one occasion. But neither he nor his wife could bear to think of it as wasted, so this pushed them harder to work more. Mrs. Ransom directs Americans for Amnesty in a tiny, cluttered office where funds are always a problem. It is one of twenty-four national organizations affiliated with the National Council for Universal and Unconditional Amnesty. Over her desk is a sign saying *Densister*.

THE LETTERS OF Lieutenant Robert C. Ransom, Jr.—United States Army, Company A, 4th Battalion, 3d Infantry, 11th Infantry Brigade—and two citations for the Bronze Star and the Bronze Star with First Oak Leaf Cluster were privately printed by friends of the parents. In his last letter, May 2, 1968, he wrote how much he liked Sergeant Richard Western, who was twenty-one and from Larchmont, New York. The lieutenant had recommended the sergeant for a Silver Star because he had grabbed and thrown back a grenade tossed by an enemy soldier. The lieutenant jokingly suggested that the two mothers meet to talk about their faraway sons. Sergeant Western was killed in action nine days after Lieutenant Ransom died. Mr. Ransom went to that funeral, but his wife could not.

Their other sons were not safe as each year the war grew greedier and needed more men. Their second son, Lawrence, failed his Army physical, to their relief. The third son, Mark, applied for conscientious objector status, was turned down by the draft board without a correct hearing, appealed their decision but was not classified as a C.O. until a year later. Still another son had to register. It was not until the fall of 1971 that the two younger boys were exempted from military service when Congress amended the draft law to provide that the brothers of a combat casualty could not be conscripted.

In August of 1975 the couple went to Montreal for a convention of the American Bar Association's three-hundred-forty-member house of delegates which determines policy. There was a very brief, heated flare-up on amnesty among the ABA members, who presented two resolutions. Mr. Ransom was denied permission to speak when he failed to get unanimous approval, usually a formality, from the delegates. Another lawyer said it was the first time in his twenty-five years of meetings that he had seen anyone denied the right to talk. When the question of allowing Mr. Ransom to speak was put to a voice vote, half a dozen delegates shouted: "Objection!" The reason was their impatience to cut off the debate on amnesty, not to let it go on. It was not an issue of compelling interest to most of the lawyers.

"They spent a good two hours allowing everyone to talk on resolutions dealing with obscure criminal statutes, but on an issue that's crucial to all Americans, debate was limited to two minutes," Mr. Ransom said later.

His wife was furious. She has always been good at writing pointed, clear letters; this one was sent to *The Montreal Star.*

To the Editor:

I read with interest your coverage of the final session of the House of Delegates of the American Bar Association at which my husband was denied the privilege of speaking in favor of unconditional amnesty for American war resisters.

There is an interesting irony to the juxtaposition of that story with the announcement of the awarding of the ABA's most prestigious award to Watergate prosecutor Leon Jaworski. Over thirty years ago my father-in-law received that same award for his contribution to the "search for true and universal justice."

A further irony is that part of Mr. Jaworski's citation honored him for his role as prosecutor in the Nuremberg war criminal trials following World War II. Those who created American war policy in Vietnam have received their

de facto *amnesty, surprisingly without even any reference
to the possible application of the Nuremberg principles that
Mr. Jaworski helped to formulate. Sad indeed that the leading organization of attorneys and judges in our country will
not now even permit debate on the question of amnesty
for those who refused to implement those war policies.*

*My husband would have liked to inform the bar that
universal and unconditional amnesty would honor our oldest
son, killed in Vietnam in 1968. We are far better qualified to
make that judgment than they are.*

*As we return to New York, we would like to express our
appreciation to all those Canadians who have provided the
haven for our many American sons that they are denied
at home.*

The letter was printed without the last paragraph.

The last time I saw her speak, on the stage of the auditorium of
Washington Irving High School, she said that the best memorial
for the Americans who died would be unconditional and universal amnesty; a memorial for the Vietnamese who died would be
the reconstruction of their beautiful country. Amnesty, reconstruction, reconciliation. Then she called out a deserter from the
Marine Corps named Austin Hodge who had been on the run for
eight years until he gave himself up in February 1976.

"I want all of you to know that my own son did not die in
Vietnam because Austin deserted, he died because of the policy of
his own government, and it is important that you understand this,
that you see us here together tonight."

She kissed Austin Hodge on the cheek, then again. People
cheered and clapped.

The memorials still do not exist. Sometimes, although not
often, she finds it hard to keep up the practiced cheerfulness, the
necessary optimism. She has become fond of many of the young

people in the movement, the deserters and the draft evaders whom she has known. But they all worry her, too, at times, even the most outgoing and stable among them.

"How can a generation continue to struggle, with no victories?" Louise Ransom said. "They've known nothing but losing."

THE LETTER CAME as a surprise; I read it twice, then again. It came from Bruce Payne, a thirty-four-year-old political scientist at Duke University. He had been kind the night of a party at Duke, for I had lost my temper when a professor said his own wife had made a better movie about our involvement in Vietnam than the film *Hearts and Minds*, which had not affected him very much. The wife—a pale and handsome lady—looked pleased by such puffery, although later I found out her film, shown on television years before, was not brilliant. It hardly mattered. I considered sliding the salad on my plate over the head of the professor, but instead, went to sit in the kitchen. One of the hired cook-dishwashers had just joined the Marine Corps, intended to stay in for life and knew it would work out fine. It was Mr. Payne who finally persuaded me to leave the kitchen when the party was over and the guests had gone. He was a modest man who, when pressed, would tell a few stories about the years in the South in the civil-rights movement, the years in the North in the antiwar movement. The early stories—even his memory of the day he was pulled out of a car by two other white men and beaten—seemed more cheerful than the later ones, for they had a beginning and an end, and even little victories.

"Your friend who thinks Vietnam gave you direction has misunderstood quite a lot," he wrote, for I had complained to him about the remarks of someone who thought the war had made me a better writer than I might have been. "Vietnam was a dead end for most of our best hopes and purposes, and many of those who worked against the war are casualties. We need to free ourselves of the bitterness, and heal what we can of the hurt—not to forget, but so that we can remember and use the memories and the learning to save lives and strengthen what decency we can find. The aftermath of the war has been like a long and terrible grieving for someone we loved, a crippling kind of grief that is hard to get beyond . . ."

This summer there is no anger, no accusations, no ridicule. Once again the face of Senator Hubert Humphrey is on television and in the newspapers, the eyes nearly always wet, as he whacks out the old and frozen speeches that thaw fast enough. There is no rank smell to him now. He is not the villainous creature he was at the 1968 Democratic National Convention in Chicago, where he found the protesters more of a problem than the war. He is speaking now at another convention of Democrats, spraying the air with his Fourth of July promises: I expect a ghostly yell, an echo, perhaps, of "Dump the Hump"—the terrible shout from Chicago—or some reminder that he was a disgraced man, but no one calls out anything and no one even sees him as a joke. They clap.

"But there has to be forgiveness," the veteran said. It was a telephone conversation three years ago. The veteran was Bob Mueller. The other person was complaining that the consequences of the war were not being felt by McNamara, by the Bundy brothers, by any of the men on the board of directors.

"Why?"

"Otherwise we'd all go crazy, right?" Mr. Mueller said. It was interesting advice coming from a paraplegic who had been in the Marines, in Vietnam, in demonstrations, in all of it.

A FORMER NAVY pilot in Holt, Georgia, who bombed North and South Vietnam, is not proud of what he did. "It'll take a pretty good cause to convince me to send my three sons off to the next war, and I'm sure other veterans feel the same way." Many do not. In Dothan, Alabama, an ex-infantryman does not think the war was worthless. Vietnam is not worming inside him. In a small town in Tennessee, a man who was driver for his battalion's commanding officer says he wouldn't have missed being in Vietnam for the world.

"Sure it was a funny war," he said. "You got all sorts of people that's come and gone from it. Some of them give their life for the United States in fighting. Some would fight because they believed in it and some wouldn't spit across the street." There wasn't much else to say, he thought.

A woman living in Contra Costa County who wanted to be a revolutionary, who began in the Free Speech Movement in 1964 at the University of California at Berkeley, now grows organic vegetables for herself and is learning to weave. She feels worthwhile making her own spaghetti and bread. In New York a thirty-two-year-old receptionist remembers being in a demonstration against the war at "some fort in New Jersey" but now she feels it was the wrong way to change anything.

"Not with a bayonet at my nose," she said. "That isn't me, or my kind of thing. I'm coming from a stronger place now. Revolution is in your head. I don't believe in that kind of confrontation; you take on some of the characteristics of the aggressor." A psychologist, all smile and water, says TM helps bad dreams, as if dreams were unnecessary, an impediment to life. Sometimes Luong comes into my dreams; I am always glad to see him there.

A man from Richmond, Virginia, who was too young to have had to worry about the draft, said he was concentrating on his consciousness and how to lift it. "As far as Vietnam is concerned, I went to all the demonstrations, all the peace marches, but I never knew what any of it meant. I kept trying to translate the rhetoric into human terms. I am realizing now that so much of that rhetoric, even on 'our side,' is part of the oppressor's language. It doesn't translate; you have to look behind it and look somewhere else."

A draft evader from Ohio who spent six years in exile, and wrote constantly about the war and men and women who defied it, has moved to a small town in Colorado, where he finds it hard going to be a journalist. What he writes is not so useful now. A deserter who gave himself up, after seven years in Sweden and Canada, served a short sentence in prison and now works in a hospital in the Bronx as an orderly. He likes it. Some men feel guilty for avoiding the draft and some are proud because they did not. In Illinois a man with a doctorate in physics said he did not evade military service because he could not bring himself to accept what he saw as the advantage of being middle-class.

"There was also another factor for me: I decided that I could only refuse on moral grounds to perform specific immoral acts, as opposed to the generality of military service, which presumably was not a priori unethical (not being a Quaker). At any rate, my two years in the Army were not unpleasant. I made no terrible sacrifices. I saw no combat. Nevertheless, I have always been proud of what I did. I have also been very reticent about discussing the matter, perhaps because I expect people to think I am a liar or a fool."

In Washington, D.C., yet another man who might have legitimately avoided the Army went in and for fifteen months worked on *Armor Magazine* (The Magazine of Mobile Warfare). He feels that the men who avoided the draft "disrupted their lives more significantly than those of us who could not honorably resist and thereby joined.

"Many of those who stayed out continued on in school so long that it has permanently affected their ability to function in society. They are not so much transformed by the Vietnamese experience . . . as stymied, forever unsure of their role in society. In some respects they are true victims of the war."

I did not see them as victims that strange jellied year I stayed at Harvard, hating it. It was never easy to talk to the students. Many of them were so bright, so curious, so ferociously informed, they knew everything about the war except how it felt to be in it. Nothing could have come as a surprise to them. One day I tried to speak of the war with a few students whom I liked. I did not tell them of the woman hung by her hair to a tree or a burned boy in Saigon, for they were too important. I spoke only of the day, on Highway 13, when Luong and I had tried to get directions to a village from a half dozen Vietnamese resting by the road. He spoke, and then there was silence. He spoke again, still nothing. They would not move their eyes or lift their faces. We were not there. They heard and saw nothing. That was their answer. But the soft little story was an anticlimax to the students who knew of so many cruel things and it made them uncertain about what I was trying to say.

A radical from the sixties insists that huge and fine changes came from the antiwar forces, for he says that now, in 1976, everyone sees Vietnam as a mistake, when ten or eleven years ago such an idea was unthinkable. No one bothers to argue that many people feel the war was lost because the United States did not want to win, but occasionally a voice goes up. In Kentucky a retired admiral, once the chief of chaplains for the Navy and Marine Corps during the war, is now a minister for two tiny rural Baptist churches. The sixty-two-year-old minister would like to see a monument go up in Washington, D.C., with a frieze of grieving or tormented figures and an inscription that reads: "When you send us to war, make sure you give us everything we need to win. Or, don't send us." It is the minister's feeling that the Congress and the President didn't have the will to win the war or the guts to call it off. It was all for nothing, he said. The one thing the radical and the minister have in common, although they do not know it, is that neither of them believes there will not be another war. Everybody expects one.

• • •

FOR A WHILE there was a name for the rage and guilt felt by Vietnam veterans who had been in combat. It was Post-Vietnam Syndrome, or PVS, a label for an incapacitating guilt and anger that the survivors experienced. But in Kansas City a large and affable fellow who still wore his GI boots with the shrapnel hole in one heel didn't think the PVS stuff was that special. He insisted on calling it Post-Vietnam Struggle, not Syndrome. His name was Randy, he had been a medic with the Wolfhounds, a unit of the 25th Infantry Division. He had gone to Vietnam—not wanting to—because prison seemed much worse.

"I was in Mississippi in 1964 working with SNCC and I had the same situation. When I came back I'd say 'Wow, wow, man, the dogs jumped on these people and the sheriff's patrol beat us and blah-blah' and pretty soon people would say 'I went to a party last night,'" he said. "You could have the Post-Black Mississippi Struggle or the Post-East Harlem Struggle or the Post-Prison Struggle. It's being put in a situation you don't understand and that nobody else you like or relate to can understand either. You say 'I saw this brain laying there in the dirt and somebody put a cigarette package inside the skull to take a picture' and people answer 'I have a date tomorrow' or 'I got laid last night . . .'"

He was nonviolent, Randy kept saying. He had not wanted to carry a weapon in Vietnam, but that was a hassle, so he did.

"The first firefight I shot up all the ammunition I had in about three or four minutes. Somebody had to come down and tell me to quit shooting. It's pretty hard to be Gandhian unless you've had a lifetime of training. I fired all the time, I fired at anything."

He thought he had been a good medic, he always tried his best. Sometimes things went very wrong. Once when the unit called in artillery because they wanted white phosphorus to hit some enemy bunkers, the shells felt short—he said the company that made them probably saved millions of dollars by shorting the powder, an ounce to every shell—and the Willy Peter, as they called it, came in about two hundred yards from their own position.

"One guy caught a great gob of it in the chest and he fell down screaming. I ran over, but I didn't know whether to shoot him with morphine and let him die happy or try and dig it out with a knife real fast. But it was burning through his chest cavity *so fast* that with one hand I was trying to scrape it off and with the other hand I was shooting him full of morphine. He kept screaming. The morphine took effect in twenty minutes and he lived about forty minutes."

In Kansas he was able to get a job with the Head Start program working in different areas with Indians, then migrants, then on career development programs. He worked with the local antiwar groups, he gave speeches and he showed his slides from Vietnam, but there were never any of the American dying. He was always too busy to stop and take pictures when there were American casualties. Or he didn't feel like it. After a while it became so ordinary to see their own dead that the soldiers stopped seeing them at all and were even able to eat their C-rations not far from corpses, for they had to eat somewhere. One morning in the war he had been out with men minesweeping a road when they discovered some Americans who had been ambushed. The faces of these men had been deformed, although he did not know whether it was done by a machete or an entrenching tool, the military name for a shovel. It was a precaution taken by the VC, he thought. None of the living felt sick or swore revenge.

"Maybe they did it that way to save ammunition; we used to go around and do it with a rifle, making sure everyone was dead," he said. "We had no reaction. After the first two or three you didn't pay any attention, unless, of course, it was a friend."

The dead man he remembered was a Vietnamese who was beginning to stiffen a little. A GI stamped on his hand to open it and then wrapped the fingers around a beer can and raised the dead man, an arm around him, to pose for a photograph. A colonel had seen it, been furious, and said leave that body alone you sadistic son of a bitch.

"But those colonels, they were as much a cause of it as anyone else. They didn't give you a pass unless you killed so many people—then they came out and gave you hell for doing stuff like that," he said.

On a trip to Washington, D.C., he had gone to see Congressman Richard Bolling, a powerful Democrat from Kansas City, first elected to the House in 1948, a World War II veteran who for years had been active in national veterans' groups. The congressman was unmoved by the encounter. "He wasn't really curt with me, but what he was saying was that I didn't represent the large majority of veterans. He didn't want to hear me out. And as far as me having any strength to do anything about the war, I could just go back to Kansas City and forget about it. I guess he was right."

He was thirty-four years old when he told all this: none of the veterans are young men any more, although it is hard to picture them as old men with wide waists and empty eyes. There had been discouragements, Randy said, the huge changes had seemed close, then not come closer at all, but even the people in the war-against-the-war could not have forgotten all that they learned.

"Look at me, yes, look at me. There is no way I'll buy the American dream again. I've seen what we've done to people. I see what we do to people in prisons, I've seen it in Vietnam, I've seen it in the civil-rights movement. I mean you're never going to sell me that shit again. That's all there is to it. There were a lot of people clubbed in Chicago who said the system is all screwed up and who are now driving Cadillacs and working as IBM salesmen. But they had experience, they got some foresight into the system. That's never going to be purged; it has a carry-over that is never going to be taken away from them."

WINNERS AND LOSERS | 513

Others are not so sure. Again and again there is someone to say we have always been people who dropped the past and then could not remember where it had been put.

AS EACH YEAR goes, the war fades as surely as one of the huge harsh chalk murals on a city wall begins to smudge and lift, so the great lines of it are there only for those who get up very close to look. "What is napalm?" the young man named Gregory asks me. He is a twenty-three-year-old assistant in a publishing house, two years out of Williams, a gentle and well-mannered man. I explain its chemical composition, how it spreads so quickly, how deeply it eats the skin. He listens solemnly. "It certainly sounds like a satanic invention," he says, looking sad. I report the conversation to a twenty-seven-year-old editor, who says goodness, someone not knowing about napalm makes him suddenly feel quite old.

But the editorial assistant is not so young. It is only the blanks inside him that give him the blameless air of a small boy. He is older than many of the lieutenants in Vietnam, certainly not younger than the demonstrators in Chicago that August week in 1968 who were so easily cut down by the police. The beatings were not just for them, of course; others had their share: some report-ers, the campaign workers for Senator Eugene McCarthy from Minnesota, even the people who were standing quietly behind the police barriers in front of the Conrad Hilton Hotel watch-ing the protesters across the street in Grant Park. They were the ones pushed through the plate-glass window. The police had tear gas, Mace, clubs, plexiglass face shields and an old-fashioned fury that made them attack like the ideal troops that generals always hope to have. There was also the National Guard, some tanks, two-and-a-half-ton Army trucks and jeeps with thick rectangles of barbed wire in front. The young called them Daley's Dozers in honor of the Mayor of Chicago who loathed them.

A month after Senator McCarthy lost the nomination to Vice-President Hubert Humphrey—as even his supporters thought he would—he and his wife went to the French Riviera to rest. With them were Howard Stein, finance manager for the campaign and head of Dreyfus Mutual Funds, Mrs. Stein, Mrs. Don Edwards, wife of the California representative, and a song-writer named Bart Howard. The senator was in hiding, but the editors in New York wanted a story *soonest*, their cables said. I flew to Nice, then went by taxi to a famous French hotel. It was an interview I dreaded, expecting to find all of them saddened and unwilling to speak of the horrors of Chicago. No such thing; they were sitting on a sun deck of a cabana, changing color. The sena-tor was composed, witty, grateful for the sun and briefly interested in a blister on his heel that came from playing tennis.

"The gift of tears is pretty much gone in religion—you see more of it in politicians these days," he said. "There are the pol-iticians who cry straight. Others just well up but the tears never really come. It's a great gift, that welling up."

For a while they joked about what he might have done if he had been elected President. The senator lay on a mat and mum-bled, so that unless I bent over, or sat on his legs, it was impossible to hear. He knew it, and said he mumbled so I wouldn't hear him. I had been afraid that day that he might be so sorrowful I would sink myself, but instead he made all of us laugh. That summer it was the best of gifts.

"It's been pointed out that we are the first great nation whose military establishment is called the Department of Defense—and if you thought of yourself as always being on the defensive, there was no limit to what you can do. I would have a Department of Offense to keep the Department of Defense busy," he said, look-ing for the suntan oil.

That throw-away manner of speaking, the refusal to ever gal-lop and jump, the ironic epigrams, the elegance of his speech, made some people furious or distraught. They found it almost indecent. He's not serious, they said. They still do say it.

The police had burst into the rooms of the McCarthy headquarters on the fifteenth floor of the Hilton on August 30. He remembered that some of the kids had been playing bridge; one girl told him later she held a twenty-one-point hand when the attack came, which the senator said was much like the shooting up of a saloon when you had a straight flush. None of this made Mrs. McCarthy smile, as he, perhaps, hoped it would.

His campaign organization was not much but the people in it were great, the senator said. "There were many personal acts of heroism. Just people standing up to"—he groped for a word to describe the police—"those things. There were no riots—there were only the police charges. No one charged the police."

Sometimes I see him in New York, maybe once or twice a year, and am glad of it. Someone who worked in his campaign said the senator had paid a very high price for opposing the war: a lost career and a divorce. Others are not so sure. He would probably not care for such an assessment himself. One year he worked for a publishing house in New York but did not do much in the way of roping in moneymaking writers. Well, too many books were being published anyway, the senator said, he had done his bit to keep a few more from emerging. Then, at lunch at a good restaurant in the Fifties, he seemed deeply angry at how many old people on Social Security could not manage enough to eat, but he put the anger away and did not speak again of it. The next year, because I had filled in for him at a lecture on women's rights—I spoke of Cambodia, not the Equal Rights Amendment, to the annoyance of some in the audience—he took me to dinner. First we had drinks, in a huge soft beige living room that had a startling view of the East River, with a woman writer who knew him much better and an Irish poet. We were talking about Libya or California or poetry when he mumbled something. I caught it, for by then I had learned how. He was speaking to no one in particular.

"We should never have gone to Chicago, not with the National Guard there," he said. "Not when there were those 'people detainers.'" That was the official name for the jeeps with the barbed-wire plows, the Daley's Dozers.

I had no idea what suddenly on a winter night reminded him of that week in August six years ago, but perhaps almost everything does.

HE CAME TO Saigon in 1971, on one of many trips, and it was a relief, although at first I hardly knew who he was. The senator from South Dakota was not pompous or confused, not seduced by the military and the helicopter rides, as were so many of the legislators who came whizzing through, wanting to know it all in a day and have a little taste of war. It was a long time before George McGovern spoke of a son-in-law who had been a Marine fighting in the Ia Drang valley in the fall of 1965 and who said it was a war we might not ever win. He is not the sort of man to unroll everything all at once. The week he was in Saigon it was not calm. A terrible explosion blew up a nightclub on Tu-Do Street, just down the block from the Hotel Caravelle, and it occurred to me that the palace would not have been too sad if the senator had been inside it that night. His views on the war were well-known to the South Vietnamese government. When a most secret meeting was arranged in a room in a church for Senator McGovern to meet a few Vietnamese who opposed the Thieu government and wanted an end to the war, too many of them came. It was hardly a surprise when the Saigon police plunged in, caused panic, made some arrests and broke the meeting up. The police chief later said the senator had been meeting with the Viet Cong—which was untrue—and the senator demanded an apology, which of course never came. I was glad to see him go before he was hurt. To be that suspicious was a sign of health, not madness, in that city that year.

Afterward, when it seemed like ten years but was not more than two, Senator McGovern talked about losing the election to Richard Nixon. It puzzled him why so many intelligent people still said that Richard Nixon was good in foreign affairs.

"I don't consider it a great foreign policy record," the senator said. "You know, it's like a deathbed confession by a gangster. You don't say this man had a marvelous life of purity when at the last hour he gets right."

He thought the next three and a half years under President Nixon were going to be unhappy ones; he was never a man to overstate.

"I was asking the people to recognize the war as a mistake and to learn the lesson so that we wouldn't repeat it. President Nixon wanted it interpreted as a glorious venture which we were justified in undertaking and that we therefore must not end on any terms except victory or glory. That required no humiliation."

He had waited until the spring of 1965 to speak to the new President, Lyndon B. Johnson, about the bombing of North Vietnam, and the conversation was so bizarre he remembered it word for word. The senator said he began respectfully by asking the President if he did not see the dangers in the bombing. Senator McGovern put his case firmly but in his courtly, pleasant way.

"I said 'If the bombing is pressed to a certain point, one or two things could happen. First, you'd get major land movements from the North Vietnamese. Since they don't have air power, they may respond on the ground. My understanding is that they have only a handful of troops in the south, but if we start bombing, they have an army of three or four hundred thousand men and they may commit a major part of it to the fighting in the south. Or the Chinese may enter the war.'

"The President said 'I'm watching that very closely. I'm going up her leg an inch at a time . . . I'll get to the snatch before they know what's happening, you see.' I said 'Well, Mr. President, sometimes when you start that kind of thing you get slapped.' He said 'I'm aware of that.'"

The last time Senator McGovern saw him was during his own presidential campaign when he went to the LBJ ranch near Austin, Texas, to confer with President Johnson, who had been out of office for four years. The meeting shocked many of his supporters, who saw President Johnson as a warmonger.

"He said 'I thought you were as crazy as hell in your opposition to our efforts in Vietnam and I still do. I suppose you haven't changed either, so there's no point in getting into that.' So we never discussed the war at all. I was there for four hours. He spent most of the time giving us political advice. He said he had heard I didn't like to use the telephone but, he said, 'nevertheless, you should discipline yourself to do that.' He said he had done it for John Kennedy when he was his running mate in 1960 and it was a great help in the campaign. He also urged me to talk about my love for America, he didn't think it was coming across as well as it should in public statements . . . I really do love this country and that didn't require any act on my part, that's one of the reasons I hated this war because I love this country."

He was able to conceal his sadness that summer; for a few months the clarity of his defeat—being crushed in the 1972 election, as everyone put it—had made him a weary and brooding man. He recovered.

"What do you regret most in your political career?"

He did not mention the disastrous choice of Senator Thomas Eagleton as Vice-President, whose concealed history of treatment for mental illness became public and required his being dropped from the ticket. He did not mention losing anything for himself.

"I regret voting for the Tonkin Gulf Resolution. It angers me that it was used as justification for accelerating the war. No one would have voted for it if we had been told that is what it was for."

There was heavy mail long after his defeat, as if people had no one else to whom they could turn. "My heart aches for you because you lost the election and that crumb Nixon is still in power," Mr. Michael J.P. Gorman of Clarksburg, Massachusetts, wrote.

I'm a Vietnam veteran. I got shot in that miserable war making Viet Nam safe from Viet Namese. How the hell can those creeps in the White House want to cut my pension after they were so damn willing to send me there. Mr. McGovern I can't work because I can't walk. I'm not very educated and I need my pension to survive. Please don't let the Nixon lackies take the bread off my table. Jesus don't I rate something for my sacrifice? A sacrifice I didn't give willingly. I was drafted, I didn't say "send me to Nam and get me shot."

I'm in bad shape, but friends of mine like Bill Decotean, he's got brain damage and a left hand like a lobster's claw, he can't sleep nights cause he sees the dead he killed haunting him. That's his gift from Viet Nam. Russ Roulier has an arm like a pendulem. It just hangs on his shoulder. How can he work? We're just people without college degrees, sons of factory workers, we fought that crumby war and got shot up in it. Don't let them cut our pensions. They've already cut our dreams and hopes.

In Clarksburg, Mr. Gorman said he was no great writer but he had always liked English lit. His life after high school had been so strange. He had gone to vocational school to stay out of the draft; he worked part time as a welder and went to school, then he transferred to North Adams State to major in English but the math and science courses bored him and he quit before he failed.

For eight weeks he stuffed feathers into sleeping bags and then the Army had him. He was trained as a single turbine utility helicopter mechanic, then because his eyesight was so good he had a second Military Occupational Speciality as a door gunner.

"When I was young I could always run further and run faster and swim longer than other people," Mr. Gorman said. He wasn't tall, he said, he had only been five foot six, so that meant he couldn't go in for basketball of course. In the wheelchair he looked no special size. Sometimes muscle spasms made him have to shift his weight for relief.

"I don't blame the North Vietnamese, I blame the United States government. I like the North Vietnamese better that the South Vietnamese. And that's the honest-to-God truth. We were afraid of the North Vietnamese, we respected them. They would never run away from you. Boy, they were brave. The VC were good at laying ambushes, and that was about it."

He saw the face of the man who shot him. That day the AK-47 bullets hitting the helicopter sounded like bees coming at him. He was in the left side of the ship, firing, when he saw the soldier in the pith helmet crouching down in the clearing, firing right at him.

"We were only about forty to fifty feet off the ground, what we used to call 'low and slow,' no better than forty or fifty knots, when the major said 'Gorman, there's a spot of gooks down there.' I saw them before he did. I started shooting and they moved. Except for this one guy who just crouched in the middle of the clearing. I was trying to hit him, he was trying to hit me. We were almost on top of each other. And then my gun, the M-60, jammed, because it was double-springed, I know that's the reason. I bent over to cock it, then I could see the twinkle of his rifle, the muzzle flash."

In the hospitals in Vietnam he had been bothered a lot by some of the other patients. One man next to him had been shot in his vocal cords; all he could do was make a small, squeaking sound.

He couldn't be comfortable lying down or sitting up. He made those little squeaks all the time, Mr. Gorman said, he must have felt like he was suffocating all the time.

Much later, in a V.A. hospital, he had an unforgettable friend in the bed next to him, a man he loved whose name he never knew how to spell. He was a young psychiatrist who was dying of encephalitis. It was the only psychiatrist he ever talked to; no such treatment was provided.

"Ah, he was such a nice guy," Mr. Gorman said. "Doc Melofski, what an intelligent man. When the people in the wards used to get on my back—they'd say you're not doing enough—he had a saying for me—and was it true. The people in the wards were just people hired off the streets; they didn't have any training. They were always on you, they used to keep at you, telling you what you could do if you *really* felt like it. In other words, they were saying you were malingering. Doc Melofski would say, 'Everybody knows how to be a paraplegic, don't they.'"

The young asked him questions because they were curious, Mr. Gorman said, and it was okay, he said he had been shot. Sometimes older people wanted to know his story, but then they didn't let it go, sometimes they began acting very chummy, which he said he hated, it drove him nuts. People will always be kind, I said. He smiled and knew exactly what that meant.

NOTES

Page

9 In her book on rape, *Against Our Will* (Simon & Schuster), Susan Brown-miller wrote that by 1971 "the feminist movement and the antiwar move-ment had gone their separate and distinct ways, each absorbed with its own issues to the exclusion of the other." Miss Brownmiller wrote that when asked to bring out other women in the feminist movement to show solidarity with the peace movement, her response was that if the antiwar movement "cared to raise the issue of race and prostitution in Vietnam, I would certainly join in." It is clear that she did not, however, although both rape and prostitution were often mentioned, as were the defoliation of the land, the use of napalm, the heavy bombings, the use of torture, the policy of creating refugees.

13 N.W. Ayer, the advertising agency that does Army recruiting advertise-ment, began its "The Army wants to join you" campaign about the time of the trial of Lieutenant William Calley, Jr., according to Jerry J. Siano, director of creative services (*The New York Times*, July 7, 1975) In a story by Philip S. Dougherty, Theodore M. Regan, Jr., associate director at the agency, said the advertising worked, although, he said, "it was like run-ning airline advertising after a crash." The Army account had its difficult moments, Mr. Regan said, some suppliers wouldn't handle the work and there was "some client or potential client resentment." Things are better now, the article said.

No precise estimates exist of how many troops served a combat role in South Vietnam, and how many more performed service and logistic duties. In Vol. II, *War Without Shadows* by Robert B. Asprey (Doubleday), the author writes: "Such was the appetite of conventionally organized

523

American units that a division (15,800 men) required a logistics 'tail' of over forty thousand troops. Put another way, of every hundred thousand troops committed in South Vietnam, perhaps twenty thousand would serve in a combat role, and of the twenty thousand, a significant percentage would be performing service and logistic duties."

In *Newsweek* (July 5, 1971), Colonel David Hackworth, an Army officer with considerable experience in Vietnam with the infantry, said although American forces there had numbered 546,000 "... you never had more than 43,000 out in the boonies at one time."

How to Talk with Practically Anybody on Practically Anything by Barbara Walters (Doubleday).

20 "Celebrations of the war's end, like the one in Central Park a few Sundays ago, had the wanness of a class reunion, its participants moist-eyed and nostalgic for the sixties' gallant hopes, communal ardors and risks antic and real," Susan Sontag wrote in *The New York Review of Books*, June 12, 1975. "The Vietnamese won politically; the antiwar movement lost ... The Movement was never sufficiently political; its understanding was primarily moral; and it took considerable moral vanity to expect that one could defeat the *Realpolitik* mainly by appealing to considerations of 'right' and 'justice' (See Thucydides, Book V, the Melian Dialogue)," she wrote.

The question of unconditional, universal amnesty—not the same as a pardon, which implies guilt—which was mentioned often by speakers at The War Is Over Rally is not a new one in this country's history.

From 1795 through 1952, fourteen presidents, as well as Congress, have issued a total of thirty-seven proclamations pardoning insurrectionists, deserters, political prisoners, and draft evaders. Amnesties specifically covering deserters and draft evaders were passed in the wake of the War of 1812, the Civil War, World War I, and World War II. For a detailed summary of amnesties in American history, see *Editorial Research Reports*, Vol. II, No. 6, August 9, 1972, p. 611, "Amnesty Question" by Helen B. Shaffer. *Editorial Research Reports* is a publication by Congressional Quarterly.

28 The prayer by Dr. Gordon Livingston originally appeared in an article by him in *Saturday Review*, September 20, 1969. It was seen by others in the Washington, D.C., newsletter put out by Concerned Officers Movement in July 1970, in which he wrote: "In my experience, Patton was neither the best nor the worst of the military there. He was simply the product of the misbegotten and misguided idea that single-minded dedication to destruction is to be highly rewarded." After handing out his prayer at the ceremony, Dr. Livingston was relieved of duties. He was not court-martialed, but given a letter of reprimand; his request to complete his Vietnam tour at the 93d Evacuation Hospital was denied. On his

return to the United States he resigned from the Army and was given a general discharge in July 1969. He was a member of Concerned Officers Movement, an antiwar group.

31 The author was present at the Gainesville Eight trial in August 1973, where she observed the judge's reactions. The account of the defendant's request to observe sixty seconds of silence, and the judge's denial and irritation, was an AP story, August 14, 1973.

35 The "Bell Telephone Hour," which Albert Lee Reynolds heard about in Saigon, was a form of torture used by American interrogators. It involved the use of field telephones with electrodes which were attached to the genitals or other sensitive parts of Vietnamese to cause acute pain and which left no marks.

40 "The biggest white elephant of them all is the World Trade Center," said an article in *Fortune*, February 1975. "Despite various tax breaks the complex is losing money—nearly $10 million annually, according to the center—and would still be in the red even if fully occupied."

In an interview with Joe McGinniss, *Harper's*, April 1975, General William Westmoreland said he missed flying helicopters. The general, who was then the chairman of the Governor's Task Force in Economic Growth in South Carolina, also told Mr. McGinniss: "I guess basically I'm kind of a do-gooder. Kind of a crusader."

Secretary of Defense James Schlesinger made his remarks about the outcome of losing part of Southeast Asia in a copyrighted article in the *Philadelphia Sunday Bulletin*. Quotes by him were excerpted by the AP and appeared in the *New York Post*, March 24, 1975.

"A golden opportunity . . ." came from an article written by Howard Callaway, then Secretary of the Army, Op-Ed page, *The New York Times*, July 17, 1964.

"All wars are the glory and agony . . ." was in a speech by President Ford to the VFW convention August 19, 1975, on amnesty.

46 UPI in Washington, D.C., on January 31, 1975, reported on the Census Bureau's findings on the widening gap between America's rich and poor in 1974. The Census Bureau reported that the 12 percent inflation rate of 1974—the worst since World War II—eroded wage and salary gains made in the previous four years but hurt the richest least.

UPI also reported on the findings of the Catholic Church's antipoverty agency, which said there were forty million poor people in the United States. In an 80-page report, "Poverty Profile 1975," the Catholic Church's Campaign for Human Development said: "The government's yardsticks for measuring the number of poor Americans is radically unfair, given any of the variables listed—real cost of living, provision of adequate diet and habitable housing, decent participation as a member of society."

"The top 20 percent of our population receives 41 percent of all income," Bill Moyers wrote on June 16, 1975, in his column for *Newsweek*.

47 In his letter of February 18, 1975, President Brewster also wrote: "I happen to share your views about the Vietnam war, and of course, Mr. Bundy, among other Yale men, was in part responsible. However, there were others such as Mr. Harriman and Mr. Vance at the official level who tried to halt it. And there were still others, like Coffin and Spock, who sparked the opinion which finally turned the tide . . . Finally I have learned that the failures of a man in some of his life do not disqualify him for all time or all purposes; nor does a lapse in one area of judgment tarnish his other thoughts or accomplishments. McGeorge was a most accomplished, skillful and wise Dean of the Faculty of Arts and Sciences at 'that other place.' So his views on elderly educational institutions seem pertinent."

49 An English translation of the article by Nguyen Tu for the *Chinh Luan* newspaper in Saigon was carried by UPI on March 18, 1975.

52 The letter of Maurice Braddell appeared in *The New York Times*, February 20, 1973. Mr. Braddell also wrote: "It [the United States] ought to go out of its way to make reparations, not to the brutal government of Hanoi, but to the wretched, charming people of Vietnam, whom it has so badly hurt."

54 The interviews with Mr. Berkowitz and Mr. Gollan for their reactions to the Vietnam cease-fire were in *The New York Times*, January 25, 1973, in an article by Israel Shenker.

57 The description of the Yale Club of Saigon meeting came from Thomas C. Fox, who was a graduate student at Yale, and at the time, a journalist in Saigon. He took notes.

59 The remarks about the precision of the American bombing of North Vietnam were made by Dennis Doolin before the House Armed Services Committee and appeared in *The New York Times* March 1, 1973.

The preliminary survey made by the North Vietnamese, and quoted by Hanoi Radio, on the damages and casualties of the American bombing, is from a dispatch in *The New York Times*, January 5, 1973.

The AP account of the Christmas tree mailed to Nixon was in *The New York Times*, December 25, 1973.

61 Flora Lewis of *The New York Times* Paris bureau, January 28, 1975, in her account of the signing of the cease-fire agreements described "an eerie silence, without a word or gesture . . ."

The results of a Gallup Poll (*The New York Times*, January 30, 1973.) conducted by telephone among 577 persons, eighteen years of age and older, showed that 58 percent agreed with President Nixon's claim that the United States had achieved "peace with honor" in Vietnam. In addition, the poll found that 57 percent believed the recent heavy bombing of North Vietnam had helped bring about the Paris Peace Agreement.

73 Daniel Ellsberg and Anthony J. Russo, Jr., were charged with fifteen counts of espionage, theft and conspiracy in the Pentagon Papers case. The documents, which the men said they had copied, were a secret Pentagon study of American involvement in Vietnam from the early 1940s to March 1968. In his testimony Dr. Ellsberg said the documents contained 1,000 pages depicting American war crimes and illegal actions, not by troops but by high government officials. Both men said they wanted the American people to have full access to the history of U.S. involvement in Vietnam and that their 89-day trial served the purpose of "telling the truth, the very painful truth" to the American people. The case against them was dismissed in May 1973 by a U.S. District Court judge because of government misconduct.

Dr. Ellsberg was a strategic analyst at The Rand Corporation and a consultant to the Department of Defense, which he joined in 1964. In 1965 he went to Vietnam for the State Department as a member of the team of General Edward Lansdale. He worked on Secretary Robert McNamara's study of U.S. decision-making in Vietnam, called the Pentagon Papers.

76 In an editorial, July 8, 1946, the *Washington Post* urged the government to show concern over the rights of 2,500-odd conscientious objectors who "remain conscripted in Civilian Public Service camps." It said although church groups administered most Civilian Public Service camps, the entire conscientious-objector program remained under essentially military control and was subject to the whims of Selective Service. "High Selective Service officials throughout the war reflected the attitude that objectors were criminals," the editorial said. "They took it upon themselves in a mandate never intended by Congress in openly regarding the Civilian Public Service program as punishment."

82 The Department of Defense supplied the statistics on injuries and deaths, hostile and non-hostile, and ages of the casualties.

83 General Westmoreland's remarks at the Associated Press Managing Editors Convention were from a story in the *Richmond-Times Dispatch* by Ron Sauder, October 10, 1975.

II. FAMILIES: TOGETHER AND NOT TOGETHER

90 The interview with Michael "Cyclops" Garrod in Vietnam was written by Kevin Buckley of *Newsweek* in January 1970. It was never published in *Newsweek*. The author showed the story to Mr. Garrod, who said it was correct and that the remarks attributed to him were accurate.

115 President Johnson's criticism of the name MASHER is in the Pentagon Papers as published by *The New York Times*, Quadrangle Books.

118 The fighting in Bong Son was described in an AP story, January 14, 1975.

The former medic with the 173d Airborne who wrote about the end of the war was John Hamill, in *The Village Voice*, April 7, 1975.

136 In answer to my letter to the publishers Scott, Foresman and Company in Glenview, Illinois, asking how many schools were using *Sidewalks, Gunboats and Ballyhoo* as a textbook, the director of market research replied: "Sales history, by necessity, is confidential and cannot be released." However, the series called *Promise of America* had been sold in all states in both the eleventh and eighth grade social studies markets. "The sales to date have been above our original expectations," he said.

141 The three men also wrote, in their critical analysis of textbook material on the Vietnam war:

There is a consistent use of prejudicial language to describe NLF-DRV actions and motives, while U.S. premises and tactics are presented either in benevolent or technical-military terminology. Thus the "Viet Cong" and the "Reds" used "terror" upon the people to gain their support (although it is admitted in liberal-dove texts that they had some support among the people because of the excesses of the Diem regime), while U.S. actions are framed in terms such as "massive firepower," etc. It is not suggested that U.S. tactics, including defoliation, search and destroy missions, and civilian bombing raids were inherently terroristic and genocidal, clearly war crimes as defined by the Nuremberg Tribunal ... There is no real appreciation of the fact that the Vietnamese who fought against the U.S. were in fact principled and dedicated patriots, as opposed to the officially supported parade of businessmen, clergy, generals, landlords and pimps. There is simply no recognition of Carl Oglesby's insight; that we might be "the enemies of men who are just, smart, honest, courageous and *correct* . . ." The existing framework avoids even a cursory examination of this possibility.

Twenty-eight textbooks examined the most profound and divisive conflict in recent American history without calling into question a single fundamental premise surrounding the event. The limited margin of debate and dissent was maintained, safe from "partisan" and "passionate" attacks upon the honor and integrity of our leaders or the nation itself. The textbook analysis is even secure from the impact of the Pentagon Papers. These documents, which revealed once and for all the utter bankruptcy of the liberal-dove position, are avoided.

142 The Swedish poll was reported by UPI, *Washington Star*, August 23, 1975.

152 Ngo Cong Duc was mentioned in a story from Bangkok by David Andel-

man, *The New York Times*, August 30, 1975, as "one of the former members of the so-called Third Force opposition in South Vietnam [that] have quietly begun appearing in the governing bodies being set up by the Communist government . . ." While most of the Vietnamese were "relatively unknown members of what was the non-Communist opposition to President Nguyen Van Thieu," Mr. Duc was cited as as a National Assembly deputy and former newspaper publisher.

152 The interview with Nguyen Khac Vien appeared in *Jeune Afrique*, No. 631, February 10, 1973, under the title of "Vietnam: Un Combattant Explique." The interview and essays by Dr. Vien appear in "Tradition and Revolution in Vietnam," printed by the Indochina Resource Center, Washington, D.C., which considers these essays "the first serious political analysis by a Vietnamese writer to a general English-language audience."

155 The remarks of James Ealy Johnson, January 24, 1973, in Johnson City, Texas, were in an interview by B. Drummond Ayres, Jr., *The New York Times*, January 25, 1973.

Jimmy Carter's speech was quoted by Tom Wicker in *The New York Times*, April 25, 1976.

"An American Woman's Bicentennial Prayer" by Marjorie Holmes appeared in *Ladies' Home Journal*, May 1976.

"Bomb-bomb-bomb. Yatta-yatta-yatta . . ." is from an interview with Janis Ian, by Cliff Jahr, *The Village Voice*, December 15, 1975.

177 Richard Perrin is one of the deserters interviewed in *The New Exiles*, Chapter V, by Roger Williams (Liveright), who was a draft evader himself and spent five years in Canada.

183 The four members of President Ford's Clemency Board, in a minority report submitted to the White House, complained that the chairman, Charles Goodell, and his staff appeared to have "misinterpreted, circumvented and violated at least the spirit" of the presidential order establishing an amnesty program. They were: Lewis W. Walt, a retired Marine Corps general; Ralph Adams, president of Troy State University in Alabama; James B. Dougnovito, instructor at Michigan Technical University; and Barry C. Riggs. The core of their complaints, according to an AP story, *The New York Times*, September 20, 1975, was that Senator Goodell had too lenient, or liberal, an outlook on who deserved amnesty.

The criticism of the amnesty program from the ACLU in New York was published March 31, 1975, by the Project on Amnesty, directed by Henry Schwarzchild, which issued a fact sheet #2. It also said:

> Unconvicted draft violators, or alleged draft violators, fall under the clemency jurisdiction of the Department of Justice. The final list of those in jeopardy of draft prosecution now comprises about

4,400 names, to which must be added those who failed to register for the draft in the first instance. The 4,400 number is down about 1,500 from the October 1974 list because of dismissals by the Justice Department of indictments even the federal prosecutors did not think worth pressing. Only 13% of the 4,400 (or 550) have asked for clemency, even with 5 years in the penitentiary staring them in the face. The draft refusers knew a bad war when the government offered them one, and they know a bad clemency.

In addition, the ACLU said:

The Defense Department claims there were about 12,500 military deserters eligible for the Presidential Clemency Program. Independent specialists think the number of military absentees who are underground or in exile to be far greater. But taking the Defense Department's figures, fewer than half (or about 5,300, i.e., less than 45%) have accepted clemency. Even at the low rate, it is the highest proportion of any part of the program, because the military clemency does not in fact require the performance of alternate service. (The alternate-service pledge for military clemency applicants is virtually unenforceable, as the Defense Department openly admits.)

185 Deputy Attorney General Silberman was quoted in the *Wall Street Journal*, September 17, 1974.

The story of the ACLU making public a copy of the final report of the Presidential Clemency Board, and criticizing its contents, appeared in *The New York Times*, January 7, 1976.

Warren Hoover made this statement in a UPI story, *Richmond News Leader*, September 15, 1975. He also said: "Less than 20 percent of the people eligible applied and many of them have since dropped out."

III: SMALL PLACES

192 The legal case against sending a National Guard unit to Vietnam, which involved Specialist 4 Ronald E. Simpson—the only plaintiff among the casualties in Bardstown, Kentucky—was based on the contention that it was unconstitutional to send any National Guardsmen overseas. In *The New York Times*, July 5, 1969, Anthony Ripley wrote: "A key issue in the case is whether, as the plaintiffs contend, guardsmen cannot be sent overseas because Article I, Section 8, of the Constitution specifies only the militia can be called up to 'execute the laws of the Union, suppress insurrections and repel invasions.'"

200 Colonel Hal Moore, of Bardstown, Kentucky, who was given a Vietnam Day party, is described in *The Face of South Vietnam*, text by Dean Brelis

and photographs by Jill Krementz (Houghton Mifflin). Colonel Moore, who had been to the Armed Forces Staff College, the U.S. Naval War College, the Command General Staff College, was commander of elements of the 1st Battalion, 7th Cavalry, 1st Air Cavalry Division which made a combat assault into the Ia Drang valley. The Americans came under intensive fire after crossing the valley and reaching the foot of Chu Phong mountain. Colonel Moore called for air strikes and artillery as he ordered his men to hold their position. Mr. Brelis, who arrived at the end of a 72-hour period of fighting, wrote:

> I marched over to where Colonel Hal Moore was hunched over his map. He was young-looking and he described some of the fighting, and his voice was choked and tears were in his eyes. "I don't know what they're saying in Berkeley or any other place back home, but I just want to tell you that these are the bravest men any country ever had . . . This was man-to-man fighting, a free-for-all like they can never describe in the textbooks. You know I had a platoon out there, B Company, and they were surrounded. They ran out of everything—dexedrine, morphine, bandages and they were running down to their last rounds of ammunition—and all the time they were talking to me, and they never once said anything about quitting . . ."

211 ". . . it looks as if a stream of brilliant candy apples . . ." was said by Sergeant Robert Lessels, U.S. Air Force, and quoted in *Air Force Magazine*, November 1971. His remark also appeared in *Air War*, a handbook prepared by Project Air War and Indochina Resource Center, March 1972.

Lieutenant General Julian J. Ewell's statement appeared in an interview in *The Hurricane*, April 1970, a publication of II Field Force Vietnam, published monthly by the 16th Public Information Detachment and the Information Office. General Ewell also said: "I think the bulk of criticism in the last few years has not been so much of the Army per se, but of the Vietnamese war, and I think some of the more vocal and less thoughtful members of U.S. society would criticize motherhood if they thought they could attack the Vietnamese war by so doing."

212 General Tran Va Tra was quoted in *The New York Times*, March 16, 1972. He is believed to be the architect of the Communist offensive, Tet, 1968. The general also said of Saigon: "The trees are gone and the city has somehow lost its Vietnamese character." He headed the Saigon military government, installed after the Communists won the south on April 30, 1975, until it was replaced in January 1976 by a civilian administration known as the People's Revolutionary Committee.

222 The statistics on unaccounted-for and missing Americans were given in *The New York Times*, September 7, 1976.

223 In Jon Stallworthy's biography of Wilfred Owen (Oxford University Press/ Chatto and Windus, London), he writes that the English officer and poet took German lessons while recuperating in a military hospital for nervous disorders in Scotland: "There were three or four of these lessons, and after the last of them, talking in a café of the Germans and their language, Owen spoke as he rarely did of the horrors of the Front." The tutor's name was Frank Nicholson.

"He told Nicholson of photographs of the dead and mutilated that he carried in his wallet and his hand moved toward his breast pocket, only to stop short as he realized, with characteristic delicacy, that his friend had no need of that particular lesson in reality."

The comment that Americans had only one happy war was made by Governor Roger Branigin in the *Indianapolis Star*, April 26, 1968, when he had entered the 1968 Indiana presidential primary race as a stand-in for President Lyndon B. Johnson. The governor also said: ". . . There is no such thing as instant happiness. There is no such thing as instant peace, nor are there instant answers." A Democrat, considered one of Indiana's most popular governors and a staunch supporter of President Johnson's Vietnam war policy, Mr. Branigin died in November 1975.

224 The Department of Defense cannot provide the number of men blinded in the Vietnam war. In the hearings before a Senate subcommittee on Veterans Affairs, on the oversight of medical care of veterans wounded in Vietnam, in December 1969, Irvin P. Schloss, a former national president of Blinded Veterans Association, told the committee: "As is the case with other types of severe disability, service-connected blindness during the Vietnam era is occurring at three times the rate in World War II. There are now about four hundred Vietnam blinded veterans; and based on the experiences of veterans of other wars, we can expect this number to triple over the years. It appears there is a higher incidence of severe additional disabilities such as amputations, than was the case among blinded veterans of World War II and Korea."

SENATOR ALAN CRANSTON: "Could you explain what there is about the nature of the fighting in Vietnam that accounted for the threefold increase in blindness?"

MR. SCHLOSS: "I would suspect that it is the quick evacuation and medical treatment of head wounds in particular. I have no doubt that many of those during World War II and Korea who sustained similar wounds died."

SENATOR CRANSTON: "Basically, it is a matter of survival due to the instant treatment?"

MR. SCHLOSS: "Yes, sir, I believe that is the reason. In fact, there is a much higher incidence among Vietnam-era blinded veterans of additional severe disabilities such as multiple amputations and severe brain damage than there was during World War II or Korea."

235 William L. Males, the deserter from Cheyenne, Oklahoma, was interviewed by Thomas Linden in *Yale Alumni Magazine*, February 1971. In January 1975 Mr. Males wrote from Sweden to the *Elk City Daily News* explaining why the "vast majority of dissenters" refused to have anything to do with President Ford's amnesty program, which he termed "a thinly veiled punishment coupled with a presupposition that all we who resisted the war are traitors."

The publisher of the paper, Larry R. Wade, wrote in an Editor's Note: "Because we so much respect this young man's father, we discussed with him this letter before publishing it. He would have preferred it not be written, but with the courage and fortitude for which he is known, could not ask us not to publish it."

Mr. Males wrote: "I deserted because I thought the war was wrong. The U.S. government still doesn't accept that the war was wrong. They want to put me on the spot. I want to put the war on trial."

236 "Look into that free-fire zone business . . ." Senator Russell said to Harry McPherson, Special Counsel to President Johnson, 1964 to 1969, Deputy Under Secretary of the Army for International Affairs in 1963. In his book *A Political Education* (Houghton Mifflin), Mr. McPherson describes an incident during his visit to Vietnam in the spring of 1967:

> Coming back to Saigon one afternoon, we were followed by a rescue helicopter. Corpsmen lifted out a young soldier, about twenty-three, and with an almost womanly gentleness, carried him towards a waiting ambulance . . . Two big packs, soaked in red, lay on his belly . . . The soldier's boots and britches were wet from the paddy where he had lain until they reached him. Driving to my quarters a wave of grief came over me. What if all we had tried to do was wrong. What if the stakes were not worth this suffering and waste, this effort to build a line of defense in a bog. God Almighty. I did not want to think about that.

On his return to Washington, D.C., he wrote to LBJ: "We are simply there, and we should be."

254 It was Ellen J. Hammer, in *Vietnam: Yesterday and Today* (Holt, Rinehart and Winston), who said that as of 1887 Vietnam had ceased to exist for all practical purposes.

255 "I have never talked or corresponded with a person knowledgeable in Indochinese affairs who did not agree that had elections been held . . . possibly 80 percent of the population would have voted for the Communist Ho Chi

Minh," President Eisenhower wrote in *The Mandate of Change*, Vol. I of his memoirs *The White House Years* (Doubleday).

256 The Phoenix Program was directed by William Colby, later director of the Central Intelligence Agency, who said in an interview with Philip Nobile, columnist for Universal Press Syndicate, *Richmond Times Dispatch*, May 30, 1976:

> The object of the Phoenix Program was to identify, capture or seek the defection of Communist terrorists. We recorded the fact that 20,000 in the Viet Cong apparatus were killed. Yet 85 to 95 percent died in military battles. Were some Vietnamese wrongly killed? Yes, but a very, very small number . . . The Phoenix Program, as opposed to the Communists, actually implied moral rules that substantially improved the behavior of the South Vietnamese. For example, I issued an American directive against assassination in the program and took steps to see that it was carried out.

IV. ODD THINGS NOT YET FORGOTTEN

263 The Americans' fear of the dark is described in Vol. II of *War in the Shadows* by Robert Asprey (Doubleday).

267 "What Combat Does to Our Men" was a survey commissioned by the *Reader's Digest:* the article on Mr. Gallup's findings was written with Blake Clark in the June 1968 issue.

The study on college and noncollege youths appears in Daniel Yankelovich's book *The New Morality, A Profile of American Youth in the Seventies* (McGraw-Hill).

The remarks of the Reverend Billy Graham, evangelist, were made in an interview with Edward Fiske, *The New York Times*, January 21, 1973.

The interview with former President Richard Nixon was held in May 1975 and was the first he granted since leaving office at noon, August 9, 1974; it was conducted by William M. Fine for his article "Sunday with Richard Nixon."

268 The death totals by home state of record do not include the period October 1 to December 31, 1975. During this three-month period fifty-one names were added. Deaths due to nonhostile causes in Thailand, where there were U.S. Air Force bases, were not included in the Department of Defense official totals of casualties in Indochina. But according to the Department's information, given early 1976, there were 677 deaths in Thailand, January 1, 1961, through December 31, 1975.

280 The Emma Goldman Brigade was named in honor of the Russian-born American anarchist, 1869–1940, who was co-publisher with Alexander

Berkman of the paper *Mother Earth*. Imprisoned in 1916 for publicly advocating birth control, deported in 1919, she took an active role with the anti-Franco forces in the Spanish Civil War.

285 The interview with Claire and Steve Cleghorn was in *The Daily Rag*, May 4–18, 1973.

286 Ralph Blumenthal's story on military chaplains appeared in *The New York Times*, June 22, 1971.

304 The Associated Press carried the story on the findings of the coroner's jury on the death of Sergeant Kavanaugh, *The New York Times*, September 12, 1973. A later AP story in the *New York Post*, June 27, 1974, said his widow had decided not to file a damage suit against the Pentagon for negligence or wrongful death. Mrs. Kavanaugh had become a Jehovah's Witness. "I'm a whole new person and my views have changed on everything," she said in the AP story. "We don't look to the U.S. government as our government. It will be destroyed."

333 An account of the supplies sent to Vietnam from Pulaski County appeared in the *Nashville Tennessean*, November 15, 1956.

　　The Vietnamese poem was written by Hoang Son and was published in the 1974 poetry anthology *Of Quiet Courage*, compiled and edited by Jacqui Chagnon and Don Luce of the Indochina Mobile Education Project.

338 Participants in the conference at the Naval War College, November 16 and 17, 1972, agreed to keep their remarks off the record. However, the Navy Public Affairs Monthly *Direction*, in the February 1973 issue, published an account of the proceedings which made such an agreement invalid.

351 The statistics on draftees in Vietnam are from *The Discarded Army: Veterans After Vietnam* (Charterhouse Books). It was written by Paul Starr with James Henry and Raymond Bonner. During 1971 and 1972 Mr. Starr was project director of a task force on Vietnam, veterans and the Veterans Administration, at Ralph Nader's Center for the Study of of Responsive Law in Washington, D.C.

364 The March 15, 1971, issue of *Newsweek* carried the photographs by Denis Cameron, including the one of the dead pilot. In the same issue was an account of General Vogt's briefing during which he produced the "vital enemy pipeline."

V. EXPERTS

376 The letters of Sergeant Guy de Chaumont Guitry are in *Lettres d'Indochine* (Editions Alsatia, Paris). The translations were done by Iver Peterson.

387 In the interview with Dr. Gerald Hickey, mention is made of Edward Lansdale, who was a colonel in Saigon in 1956. He had been sent to Vietnam in

June 1954 as a chief of a Saigon military mission, with orders to "beat the Geneva timetable of Communist take-over in the north," according to the historian Frances FitzGerald in her book *Fire in the Lake* (Atlantic-Little, Brown). "By August, during the period of negotiated truce, Lansdale's teams were scattered from Hanoi to the Camau peninsula conducting sabotage operations and what can only be called agitprop work in direct violation of the U.S. government's promise at Geneva to 'refrain from the threat or use of force,'" she wrote. In her assessment of Lansdale, Miss FitzGerald said: "With all his expertise in black propaganda and every other form of unconventional warfare, Lansdale had an artless sincerity. No theorist, he was rather an enthusiast, a man who believed that Communism in Asia would crumble before men of good will with concern for the 'little guy' and the proper counter-insurgency skills."

The reputation of Lansdale in 1956 in Saigon was remarkable. He was a romantic figure to many young men and respected by most Americans for his role in the Philippines—where he was on special assignment to the Filipino government—during the rise of the Hukbalahaps, the local Communist insurgency movement. Lansdale's star rose, dimmed and went out during various years of American ascendancy in South Vietnam. Sent out to Vietnam in 1965, once more at the behest of the CIA, Lansdale was not kindly regarded by the more orthodox, entrenched members of the U.S. Mission because he did not approve of the large-scale American presence.

Miss FitzGerald wrote: ". . . the bureaucrats narrowed his 'area of responsibility' to the point where they had effectively cut him off from the mission command and from all work except that of a symbolic nature."

(See further references to Lansdale on pages 293 and 294.)

395 The front-page article in *The Wall Street Journal*, November 18, 1971, on Gerald Hickey had a headline NEW McCARTHYISM? *Blackball of Scholars for Links to the War Stirs Heated Debate.* It was by Everett Martin, a former Vietnam correspondent.

404 In the Pentagon Papers, as published by *The New York Times*, Quadrangle Books, there are excerpts from a memorandum from Brigadier General Edward Lansdale to General Maxwell D. Taylor, President Kennedy's military adviser, on "Resources for Unconventional Warfare, S.E. Asia," undated but apparently from July 1961. The information General Lansdale noted was compiled by Defense and CIA. There is a reference to Operation Brotherhood, which by then no longer existed in South Vietnam but in Laos. The same memorandum said: "There is another private Filipino public-service organization, capable of considerable expansion in socio-economic-medical operations to support counter-guerilla action. It is

now operating teams in Laos, under ICA auspices. It has a measure of CIA control." The same can be assumed of OB when it operated in Vietnam.

413 A.J. Liebling's review of *The Quiet American*, from *The New Yorker*, April 7, 1956.

414 The April 1966 article in *Ramparts* magazine, called "The University on the Make," with an introduction by Stanley Sheinbaum, was by Warren Hinckle, the editor of the magazine, in conjunction with research editor Sol Stern and foreign editor Robert Scheer. Material on Michigan State University's role in Vietnam originated in Mr. Scheer's pamphlet "How the United States Got Involved." The *Ramparts* article, which caused a furor, ended: "The essential query, which *must* be asked before the discussion of Michigan State's behavior can be put in any rational perspective, is this: what the hell is a university doing buying guns, anyway?" Mr. Hinckle, editor of *Ramparts* from 1964 to 1969 until its bankruptcy, wrote in his autobiography *If You Have a Lemon, Make Lemonade* (Putnam) of the types of MSU men who went to Vietnam: "Gary Wills called them the 'Bogart Professors'—academics who, tiring of the humdrum of college routine, discovered the wonderful world of exciting government contracts."

422 The returned prisoner of war who greeted Dr. Fishel was Brigadier General David D. Winn of Edina, Minnesota, who held the rank of colonel during his four and a half years in prison in North Vietnam. In an AP story, *Huron (S.D.) Daily Plainsman*, April 1, 1973, the ex-POW said he was subjected to torture three times "but they didn't have enough muscle to hurt me." He was captured in August of 1969 when his F-105 fighter was shot down.

424 The chronology of events, letter, documents, articles and speeches made against the existence of the Center for Vietnamese Studies at Carbondale, Illinois, was published in a special February 1971 issue of the *Bulletin of Concerned Asian Scholars*. Articles on the Center were by C. Harvey Gardiner, Robert G. Layer, Douglas Allen, David Marr, Nina Adams, Ngo Vinh Long, Huynh Kim Khanh and Gabriel Kolko. Articles on AID by Ngo Vinh Long, Earl Martin and Al McCoy were included, as were articles on "The University" by Stanley Sheinbaum, Eqbal Ahmad, Arthur Waskow and Douglas Dowd.

425 The sixth annual report for the fiscal year 1975 to the Agency for International Development in Washington, D.C., from Southern Illinois University—dated March 15, 1976, title: 211 (d) Grant, AID/ csd 2514: A Grant to Strengthen Southern Illinois University's Competence in Vietnamese and Contiguous Area Studies—said:

A. Statistical Summary:

Period of Grant: 30 June 1969 to 29 June 1975

Amount of Grant: $1,000,000.00

Expenditures for Report Year: $53,506.62
Accumulated Expenditures: $1,000,000.00
Anticipated for Next Year: -0-
*As amended by Grant Amendment #3 approved April 26, 1974.

I. GENERAL BACKGROUND AND PURPOSE OF THE GRANT:

From 1961–1970 Southern Illinois University acquired considerable experience on Vietnam while serving there as the contracting institution for three different technical assistance programs. These technical service contracts with USAID provided for the establishment of four Normal Schools and a Demonstration School for elementary school teachers, advisory assistance to the Phu Tho Polytechnic Institute, and program development for the Saigon National In-Service Elementary Teacher Training Center. During this period many SIU faculty and staff became intimately acquainted with the vital humanitarian needs of Vietnam and Indochina and through either their actions as advisors in the field or as researchers at home became both knowledgeable and concerned with Vietnam.

Through these combined efforts and interests, much expertise was developed at SIU. Many of these individuals became increasingly sought as consultants on the educational, social, and economic problems of Vietnam. Therefore in order to better organize these talents, to more effectively respond to these requests, and to fill a growing need for a center of academic research and training on Vietnam in the U.S., a Center for Vietnamese Studies and Programs was proposed by the University and adopted by the Illinois Board of Higher Education on June 3, 1969.

No other U.S. university was known at that time either to have or to be planning to establish a Center for Vietnamese Studies. The Center was designed to provide an intellectual climate and a physical location in which scholarly knowledge about Vietnam in particular, and Indochina in general, could be developed.

But permanent establishment of such a Center would require "seed monies" of such a quantity that no state institution could expect to have easily approved. While SIU was devoting what resources it could to institutionalize its interests and expertise, it was apparent that only through secure, long-term assistance sought externally could SIU ever hope to realize its desires for a Center for Vietnamese Studies.

A request therefore went out to the Agency for International

Development for a 211 (d) assistance grant for the development of the Center. In response to this request, AID approved Grant number csd-2514 on June 29, 1969.

This Grant was to strengthen the existing competence of the Southern Illinois University Center for Vietnamese Studies in the four general areas: professional staff development, fellowship awards to students, library/research capacities, and travel as it related to the first three categories. It was anticipated that the Center for Vietnamese Studies would become a center of expertise and activity concerning Vietnam within the American academic community. The Grant was based on the University's "commitment to the continued growth and development of the Center" with the first five years (1969–1974) being regarded as the basic development period.

USAID, for its part, was interested in awarding this Grant for the purpose of "strengthening within Southern Illinois University competency in Vietnamese studies and programs related to the economic and social development of Vietnam and its post-war reconstruction." . . . It was only later when peace for Vietnam was less certain with the war in Indochina raging violently and the American people becoming more restless with the social and economic consequences of that conflict—that a much modified purpose for the Grant had to be postulated. Thus, on September 15, 1971, Amendment #2 to the Agreement altered the original purpose of the Grant to read, "to strengthen Southern Illinois University's competency in Vietnamese and contiguous area studies." It is only now, with the 211 (d) funds exhausted, that attention could again be focused on the post-war economic and social rehabilitation of Vietnam. For it is only now that anything resembling a post-war period is developing in Indochina.

The report also said:

. . . Reviewing these objectives it is readily perceived that some accomplishments have occurred in all the areas mentioned. While virtually all higher educational institutions in the U.S. are beginning to face serious budgetary restrictions and the necessity to adapt their curricula to the more pressing and very real needs of the contemporary world, SIU has maintained the Center for Vietnamese Studies (CVS) and the Asian Studies Program (ASP) in respectably good order. The overall objective still remains to free these two programs from all outside support. If prestige and the competence of these programs can be further established, then they will survive and prosper beyond these troubled times.

During the 1974–75 report period, the activities of the two campus programs were a continuation of the programs of previous grant years. While the Center for Vietnamese Studies (CVS) at Carbondale and the Asian Studies Program (ASP) at Edwardsville remained separate programs, the overall objectives and resultant activities continued to reflect a consensus of purpose. The CVS program focused on Indochina and Vietnam while the ASP concentrated on the international affairs and relations of those nations. Together these two programs, with the generous assistance of the 211 (d) Grant, have fostered further understanding and study of the problems and conditions of Vietnam and Asia.

427 The documents that John Isaacs gave to a few correspondents in Saigon were usually classified on a low level. For example, the report quoted—written by an American Deputy District Senior Adviser, revealing how wretchedly things were going in his area despite the good reports going to CORDS in Saigon—was marked *Confidential*. It was stamped "Group 4. Downgraded at 3 year intervals; declassified after 12 years." Since the circulated version of the American's critical report contained none of the names of the Americans, contained no information useful to the "enemy," or information they did not already have on the misbehavior of local Vietnamese officials, it hardly deserved to be marked *Confidential* except to save CORDS from any more embarrassment.

433 *Rights in Concord,* The Response to The Counter-Inaugural Protest Activities in Washington, D.C., was a special staff report, not a report of the Commission on the Causes and Prevention of Violence.

438 In *A Long Row of Candles, Memoirs and Diaries 1934–1954* (Macmillan), Cyrus Sulzberger told of his wife's work in an Athens military hospital during World War II. Mr. Sulzberger, who was a foreign correspondent for *The New York Times* until October 1954, when he became the foreign affairs columnist, wrote of his years in the Balkans:

> In my day I came to know their Kings and Communists, to argue with their priests and politicians, to love their princesses and dancing girls. I learned to speak three of their languages, badly but fluently, accompanied four of their armies, was expelled from two countries and fled two others before advancing Nazi hordes. In the Balkans, I was bombed, bullied, coddled, arrested and enticed . . .
> In the Balkans, I left part of my soul and found my wife.

456 Information on the VVAW "incursion into the country called Congress" came from interviews with ten veterans who had participated and stories from the *Washington Post* and the *Evening Star* April 20, 21, 22, 23 and 24, plus material later provided by VVAW.

458 The study on the veterans was done by Hamid Mowlana and Paul H. Geffert as an appendix to *The New Soldier*, by John Kerry and Vietnam Veterans Against the War, edited by David Thorne and George Butler (Collier Books).

464 A single-type discharge has long been a grievance raised for years, and is still unresolved. In a handbook called *Facts on OTHER-THAN HONORABLE DISCHARGES* And What Can Be Done About Them, researched, written and published by the American Veterans Committee, it says:

Discharge certificates are issued to servicemen separating from military service under the statutory authority of Title to U.S. Code 3811.

Following are the kinds of discharges issued by the military departments:

TYPE OF DISCHARGE	CHARACTER OF DISCHARGE OR SEPARATION	GIVEN BY
Honorable	Honorable	Administrative action
General	Under honorable conditions	Administrative action
Undesirable	Under conditions other than honorable	Administrative action
Bad Conduct	Under conditions other than honorable	Sentence of special or general court-martial
Dishonorable	Dishonorable	Sentence of general court-martial

Robert L. Hill, national director of the Veterans Education and Training Service (VETS), a project of the National League of Cities and United States Conference of Mayors, in an Op-Ed piece for *The New York Times*, March 3, 1975, wrote: "Some 350,000 Vietnam-era veterans left the service with less-than-honorable discharges. Of, this number, most have been black, brown, poor and undereducated. And less than honorable discharges and a veteran's opportunity for employment are directly related. With a less-than-honorable discharge, a veteran's chances for employment are minuscule."

Of the five types of discharges issued by the Armed Forces, honorable, general, undesirable, bad-conduct and dishonorable, the last three are less-than-honorable and the last two are conferred by sentences of special and general courts-martial. "In many cases, the veteran with a less than honorable discharge will find as he re-enters civilian life that he is ineligible for the benefits of the GI Bill, such as educational assistance, medical care, Veterans Administration loans, employment assistance, unemployment benefit and civil service point preferences," Mr. Hill wrote. He added that because of the lengthy and complicated procedures involved, as well as the expenses the veteran must pay, only one out of every five veterans who receives a bad discharge ever appeals, only about 3 percent have had their discharges upgraded.

The photograph of Vietnam veterans demonstrating against the war, showing the ex-Marine sniper Chuck James in their midst, the only man wearing a suit, is in *The New Soldier* (see note for page 458).

VI. WINNERS AND LOSERS

465 The remark by Ambassador Martin, testifying before the House subcommittee, was quoted in the *Washington Post*, January 28, 1976. The article by Don Oberdorfer also quoted Christina Macy, a former associate of the Indochina Resource Center, as saying the Center had eight staff members and an annual budget of between $50,000 and $65,000 at the height of its activity in 1974–75. The reporter who described Ambassador Martin was Mary McGrory in her syndicated column in the *New York Post*, January 31, 1976. Henry Bradsher's story's in the *Washington Star*, January 28, 1976, also quoted Ambassador Martin as saying the overriding factor in the fall of South Vietnam was the reduction of aid to the Communists.

"Martin's assertions met with some disbelief from the House International Relations Committee's investigations subcommittee," Bradsher wrote. "Surely there were reasons for the reversal other than the U.S. economic cuts,' said Pierre S. duPont IV, R-Del.'" The ambassador declared that he could not "in good conscience say" that anything in the fabric of South Vietnam's war effort was responsible for the defeat.

466 Fred Branfman worked as a teacher of English in Laos, where he first learned what the air war was doing to the country and its inhabitants. He later compiled *Voices from the Plain of Jars*, Life under an Air War (Harper & Row), in which he said: "In September 1969, after a recorded history of seven hundred years, the Plain of Jars disappeared." The book is a collection of essays by Laotian peasants who once lived in the area, with sketches done by them of the destruction and death that came from U.S. aircraft.

489 In January 1976 the *Report*, a newsletter from Clergy and Laity Concerned, said in an article by Deborah Huntington:

A class action suit against the CIA, the National Security Agency and select corporations was filed in Washington by the ACLU on behalf of Don Luce, CALC, and seventeen other organizations and individuals. The plaintiffs in the suit represent a group of at least 7200 persons and 1000 organizations who were subjects of CIA surveillance under "Operation CHAOS." Among the defendants listed in the ACLU brief are former directors of the CIA Richard Helms and William Colby, and James Schlesinger, former Secretary of Defense, and Director of the CIA from February through July, 1973 (as well as fourteen other individuals who served in an official capacity during the period of Operation CHAOS); Western Union Telegraph Company, RCA Global Communications, Inc., American Cable and Radio Corporation and ITT World Communications, Inc.

During and after August 1967, the CIA, with direction from Helms, Colby, Schlesinger and others, established within the CIA a Special Operations Group known as Operation CHAOS. CHAOS' purpose was to collect, coordinate, evaluate, file and report information on "foreign contacts" of American citizens who were involved in expressing opposition to the war and other government policies. Information from other governmental organizations such as the FBI was assembled as well. As Congressional investigation recently noted, there were no significant connections between the antiwar groups and foreign political groups. However, Operation CHAOS continued until 1974.

CHAOS recruited approximately forty undercover agents to infiltrate the domestic organizations, and to disrupt or discredit such groups when desirable. "Personality" files on over 7000 individuals and "subject" files on over 1000 organizations were maintained concerning the associational and political activities of the plaintiffs, and this information was conveyed to the White House, the FBI, and other governmental agencies.

Sometime after September 1969, CHAOS supplied a "watchlist" of US citizens (including the plaintiffs) to another CIA unit, which resulted in the opening of these citizens' first class mail without judicial warrant. Copies of their letters were put into CHAOS files. The CIA also supplied a "watchlist" to agents and employees of the National Security Agency which included the names of the plaintiffs.

For an unknown period of time the NSA monitored and intercepted international communications, including telephone and telegraph cables, with the assistance and cooperation of Western Union, RCA, American Cable and Radio Corporation, and ITT. In November 1974, NSA supplied CHAOS with approximately 1000 pages of summarized communications concerning activities and travels of the plaintiffs, which is presently in the CHAOS files, intact with the other CHAOS material.

The individuals of both the CIA, NSA and the corporations involved acted in full knowledge that their activities violated the constitutional rights of the plaintiffs in their freedom of speech, assembly, and association.

The demands of the plaintiffs are that such actions be declared illegal, that the court issue an injunction enjoining the defendants from such conduct, and ordering that the CIA deliver to the plaintiffs the complete contents of the CHAOS files. Also being demanded is the sum of $100 per day per defendant as liquidated damages, as well as $50,000 punitive damages and lawyers' fees.

490 The remarks by Ambassador Martin before the House subcommittee were from a transcript of his prepared statement, which he read for fifty minutes to open the hearing on January 27, 1976. It was his first appearance before the subcommittee, which had been, according to the *Washington Post*, "demanding testimony from Martin since last June."

491 The figures on civilian war casualties in South Vietnam were prepared by Le Anh Tu, National Action/Research on the Military Industrial Complex (NARMIC), a project of the American Friends Service Committee. The figures on the disabled were based on estimates of the U.S. Senate Refugee Subcommittee of the Committee on the Judiciary, and used by NARMIC.

The ambassador's remarks are from the transcript of his statement to the House subcommittee.

491 Reports on the medical problems and needs in Vietnam, north and south, at a two-day "Aid to Vietnam" meeting in Manila of a World Health Organization committee were filed by the Los-Angeles Times/Washington Post News Service (*Richmond News-Leader*, March 30, 1976) and Associated Press (*The New York Times*, March 21, 1976).

512 "When you send us to war . . ." was said by James W. Kelly, who was interviewed by Gary Robertson, *Richmond Times-Dispatch*, June 28, 1976.

515 Napalm, which was dropped in thin containers, from a low altitude for accuracy, is gasoline jellied by mixing it with a special soap powder. In *The Air War in Indochina*, edited by Raphael Littauer and Norman Uphoff, Air War Study Group, Cornell University (Beacon Press) it says: "A later type . . . consists of 50 percent polystyrene, 25 percent gasoline and 25 percent benzene, yielding a longer burning fire and greater stickiness . . . Napalm is sticky and cannot be readily removed from surfaces against which it has been splattered; attempts to brush it off result in further spreading."

521 Senator George McGovern is not alone in saying he regretted voting for the Tonkin Gulf Resolution. On August 2, 1964, the destroyer *USS Maddox* was reportedly attacked in the Gulf of Tonkin by patrol boats of North Vietnam. On August 4 both the *Maddox* and *C. Turner Joy* were said to have been attacked. President Lyndon Johnson authorized "reprisal" air strikes against the north. At the time of the attacks the President briefed leaders of Congress and had a resolution of support for his policy. On August 7, 1964, the resolution—which was used by the President as a mandate for war—passed with near-unanimity in both Houses. Later, LBJ complained that Senator William Fulbright's attacks on his constitutional right to commit U.S. troops to Vietnam puzzled him because the Tonkin Gulf Resolution permitted him "to take all necessary steps to assist any member or protocol state of the Southeast Asia Collective Defense Treaty requesting assistance in defense of its freedom."

INDEX